Meta-Heuristic Algorithms for Advanced Distributed Systems

Meta-Heuristic Algorithms for Advanced Distributed Systems

Edited by

Rohit Anand
Department of Electronics and Communication Engineering
G.B. Pant DSEU Okhla-1 Campus
(formerly G.B.Pant Engineering College)
Government of NCT of Delhi
New Delhi, India

Abhinav Juneja
KIET Group of Institutions
Ghaziabad, India

Digvijay Pandey
Department of Technical Education,
Government of Uttar Pradesh,
Kanpur, India

Sapna Juneja
Department of CSE (AI)
KIET Group of Institutions
Ghaziabad, India

Nidhi Sindhwani
Amity Institute of Information Technology
Amity University
Noida, India

WILEY

Published by John Wiley & Sons, Inc., Hoboken, New Jersey.
Published simultaneously in Canada.

For general information on our other products and services or for technical support, please contact our Customer Care Department within the United States at (800) 762-2974, outside the United States at (317) 572-3993 or fax (317) 572-4002.

Wiley also publishes its books in a variety of electronic formats. Some content that appears in print may not be available in electronic formats. For more information about Wiley products, visit our web site at www.wiley.com.

Library of Congress Cataloging-in-Publication Data applied for:

Hardback ISBN: 9781394188062

Cover design: Wiley
Cover image: © zf L/Getty Images

Set in 9.5/12.5pt STIXTwoText by Straive, Chennai, India

SKY10068516_022824

Contents

About the Book

The main aim of using a distributed system is to simplify the problem of computation by sharing a common objective and distribute the complex problem into many simpler problems. The failure of each component is independent of the failure of the other components, and hence a distributed system is very reliable. Further, a distributed system may be scaled as per requirements. But a distributed system suffers from overhead more than a basic centralized system, and there is an issue of security and troubleshooting due to the distributed computing in the system.

Meta-heuristic techniques have a huge scope in optimization, and hence they may be applied to increase the efficiency of the distributed system and also to minimize cost and time. These intelligent techniques are based on global and local search and are very simple to apply. Various kinds of meta-heuristic techniques are derived from nature, and hence a lot of development is going on in this field.

This book will focus on the existing/modified/innovative meta-heuristic techniques for optimization purposes in various kinds of distributed systems.

About the Editors

Dr. Rohit Anand is currently working as an assistant professor in the Department of Electronics and Communication Engineering at G.B. Pant DSEU Okhla-1 Campus (formerly G.B.Pant Engineering College), Government of NCT of Delhi, New Delhi, India. He was awarded his PhD in the field of microwave and optimization. He has more than 19 years of teaching experience, including teaching undergraduate and graduate courses. He is a life member of the Indian Society for Technical Education (ISTE). He has published 6 book chapters, 12 papers in Scopus/SCI-indexed journals, more than 20 papers in international conferences, and 4 patents. He has chaired a session in fourteen international conferences. His research areas include electromagnetic field theory, antenna theory and design, optimization, wireless communication, image processing, optical fiber communication, IoT.

Dr. Abhinav Juneja is currently working as a professor at KIET Group of Institutions, Ghaziabad, India. He has also worked as an associate director and professor at BMIET, Sonepat. He has more than 19 years of teaching experience teaching postgraduate and undergraduate engineering students. He completed his doctorate in computer science and engineering from M.D. University, Rohtak, in 2018 and has a master's degree in information technology from GGSIPU, Delhi. He has research interests in the fields on software reliability, IoT, machine learning, and soft computing. He has published several papers in reputed national and international journals. He has been the organizer of several national and international conferences. He has been a resource person for faculty development programs on recent issues related to cybersecurity. He is the reviewer of several international journals of repute. He has been the mentor of several postgraduate and undergraduate research-oriented projects.

Dr. Digvijay Pandey is currently working as an acting head of department in the Department of Technical Education, Kanpur, Government of Uttar Pradesh, India. Before this, he joined TCS in 2012 as an IT analyst and worked on various US/UK/

Canada projects until 2016. He is also a faculty member at IERT Allahabad. He has teaching and industry experience of more than 11 years. He works as an editor for a peer-reviewed international journal. He has over 11 years of experience in the field industry as well as teaching. He has written 16 book chapters and 70 papers that have been published in Science Direct (Elsevier)/SCI/UGC/Scopus-indexed journals and also acts as an editor for a peer-reviewed international journal. He has presented several research papers at national and international conferences. He has chaired sessions at IEEE International Conference on Advance Trends in Multidisciplinary Research and Innovation (ICATMRI-2020). He has four patents that have been published in The Patent Office Journal and two that are currently being processed in the Australian Patent Office Journal. He serves as a reviewer for a number of prestigious journals, including Scientific Reports (nature Publication). Clinical and Translational Imaging (Springer), ijlter (Scopus indexed), and a slew of others. His research interests include medical image processing, image processing, text extraction, information security, and other related fields.

https://scholar.google.com/citations?user=uie7AAYAAAAJ&hl=en
https://orcid.org/
0000-0003-0353-174X.

Dr. Sapna Juneja is working as Professor in Department of CSE(AI) at KIET Group of Institutions, Ghaziabad, India. She has more than 16 years of teaching experience. She completed her doctorate and Master's in Computer Science and Engineering from M. D. University, Rohtak in 2018 and 2010 respectively. Her topic of research is Software Reliability of Embedded System. Her areas of Interest are Software Engineering, Computer Networks, Operating Systems, Database Management Systems, Artificial Intelligence etc. She has guided several research thesis of UG and PG students in Computer Science and Engineering. She is the reviewer of several international journals of repute. She has published several patents. She has published various research papers in the renowned National and International Journals.

Dr. Nidhi Sindhwani is currently working as an assistant professor at Amity Institute of Information Technology, Amity University, Noida, India. She has her PhD (ECE) from Punjabi University, Patiala, Punjab, India. She has teaching experience of more than 17 years. She is a life member of the Indian Society for Technical Education (ISTE) and a member of IEEE. She has published 13 book chapters, 10 papers in Scopus/SCIE-indexed journals, and 4 patents. She has presented various research papers in national and international conferences. She has chaired a session at twelve international conferences. Her research areas include wireless communication, image processing, optimization, machine learning, and IoT.

List of Contributors

V. Abhinav
Koneru Lakshmaiah Education Foundation
Vaddeswaram, Andhra Pradesh
India

Sunil Adhav
Faculty of Management (PG)
Dr. Vishwanath Karad
MIT World Peace University
Pune, Maharashtra
India

Frakruddin A. Ahmed
School of Management
Presidency University
Bangalore
Karnataka
India

Tanweer Alam
Islamic University of Madinah
Department of Computer Science
Faculty of Computer and Information Systems
Madinah
Saudi Arabia

Shaik Altaf
Koneru Lakshmaiah Education Foundation
Vaddeswaram, Andhra Pradesh
India

Rohit Anand
Department of ECE
G.B. Pant DSEU Okhla-1 Campus
(formerly GBPEC)
New Delhi
India
and
Department of Electronics and Communication Engineering
G.B. Pant Engineering College
(Government of NCT of Delhi)
New Delhi
India

M. Anirudh
Koneru Lakshmaiah Education Foundation
Vaddeswaram, Andhra Pradesh
India

Sri R.R. Annapureddy
Koneru Lakshmaiah Education Foundation
Vaddeswaram, Andhra Pradesh
India

Ashima Arya
Department of Computer Science and Information Technology
KIET Group of Institutions
Ghaziabad, Uttar Pradesh
India

Rashika Bangroo
Department of Computer Science and Information Technology
KIET Group of Institutions
Ghaziabad, Uttar Pradesh
India

Manish Bhardwaj
KIET Group of Institutions
Ghaziabad, Uttar Pradesh
India

K. Bhavana Raj
Department of Management Studies
Institute of Public Enterprise
Hyderabad
India

Bhawna
KIET Group of Institutions
Ghaziabad, Uttar Pradesh
India

Luigi P.L. Cavaliere
Department of Economics
University of Foggia
Foggia
Italy

Chunduru R. Chandan
Koneru Lakshmaiah Education Foundation
Vaddeswaram, Andhra Pradesh
India

Radha R. Chandan
School of Management Sciences (SMS)
Department of Computer Science
Varanasi, Uttar Pradesh
India

Aarti Dawra
Manav Rachna International Institute of Research and Studies
Faridabad, Haryana
India

M.K. Dharani
Department of Artificial Intelligence
Kongu Engineering College
Erode, Tamil Nadu
India

Satish M. Dhoke
Moreshwar Arts Science and Commerce College
Department of Commerce
Jalna, Maharashtra
India

Venkata Harshavardhan Reddy Dornadula
Startups and IIC
Chairman Office
Sree Venkateswara College of Engineering
Nellore, Andhra Pradesh
India

Lavanya Durga
Koneru Lakshmaiah Education Foundation
KL University
Guntur, Andhra Pradesh
India

S. Durga
Koneru Lakshmaiah Education Foundation
Vaddeswaram, Andhra Pradesh
India

Syed M. Faisal
Department of Management
Jazan University
Kabul
Saudi Arabia

Ernesto N.T. Figueroa
Universidad Nacional del Altiplano de Puno
Academic Department of Computer and Statistics Engineering
Puno
Peru

Umakant B. Gohatre
Department of Electronics and Telecommunications Engineering
Smt. Indira Gandhi College of Engineering
Navi Mumbai, Maharashtra
India

José L.A. Gonzáles
Department of Business
Pontifical Catholic University of Peru
Lima
Peru

Brijesh Goswami
Institute of Business Management
GLA University
Mathura, Uttar Pradesh
India

Sushmita Goswami
Institute of Business Management
GLA University
Mathura, Uttar Pradesh
India

Jitendra Gowrabhathini
K L Business School
Koneru Lakshmaiah Education Foundation
K L University
Vijayawada, Andhra Pradesh
India

Shouvik K. Guha
The West Bengal National University of Juridical Sciences
Kolkata, West Bengal
India

Amit K. Gupta
KIET Group of Institutions
Ghaziabad, Uttar Pradesh
India

Deena N. Gupta
CDAC
Mumbai, Maharashtra
India

Priti Gupta
P.G. Department of Economics
Bhupendra Narayan Mandal University (West Campus) P.G. Centre
Saharsa
India

T.V.N.J.L Haritha
Koneru Lakshmaiah Education Foundation
Vaddeswaram, Andhra Pradesh
India

Nayana Harshitha
Koneru Lakshmaiah Education Foundation
Vaddeswaram, Andhra Pradesh
India

Yu-Chen Hu
Department of Computer Science and Information Management
Providence University
Taichung City
Taiwan

Julio C.L. Huanca
Academic Department of Basic Sciences
Universidad Nacional de Juliaca
Puno
Peru

Sujay M. Jayadeva
Department of Health System Management Studies
JSS Academy of Higher Education & Research
Mysuru, Karnataka
India

K. Jayalakshmamma
Government RC College of Commerce and Management
Bengaluru, Karnataka
India

Kapil Joshi
Uttaranchal Institute of Technology
Uttaranchal University
India

Abhinav Juneja
KIET Group of Institutions
Ghaziabad
India

Sapna Juneja
Department of CSE(AI), KIET Group of Institutions, Ghaziabad, India
IITM Group of Institutions
Murthal
India

Latika Kharb
Jagan Institute of Management Studies
Rohini
Sector-5
Delhi
India

Nitin Kulshrestha
Christ (Deemed to be University)
Bengaluru, Karnataka
India

Cheedella A.S. Lakshmi
Koneru Lakshmaiah Education Foundation
Vaddeswaram, Andhra Pradesh
India

S. Mahabub Basha
Department of Commerce
International Institute of Business Studies Bangalore
India

Gangu N. Mandala
Department of Business Administration
Central Tribal University of Andhra Pradesh
Konda Karakam, Andhra Pradesh
India

Geetha Manoharan
School of Business
SR University
Hyderabad, Telangana
India

S.S.C. Mary
Loyola Institute of Business Administration
Business Analytics
India

Haider Mehraj
Department of Electronics and Communication Engineering
Baba Ghulam Shah Badshah University
Rajouri, Jammu and Kashmir
India

Kamakshi Mehta
TAPMI School of Business
Manipal University
Jaipur, Rajasthan
India

Charles I. Mendoza-Mollocondo
Universidad Nacional del Altiplano de Puno
Academic Department of Computer and Statistics Engineering
Puno
Peru

Kali Charan Modak
IPS Academy
Institute of Business Management and Research
Indore, Madhya Pradesh
India

Debasis Mohanty
Department of Commerce and Management
Kalinga University
Raipur, Chhattisgarh
India

Vinay K. Nassa
Rajarambapu Institute of Technology
Walwa, Maharashtra
India

Samad Noeiaghdam
Industrial Mathematics Laboratory
Baikal School of BRICS
Irkutsk National Research Technical University
Irkutsk
Russia

M.Z.M. Nomani
Faculty of Law
Aligarh Muslim University
Aligarh
India

Digvijay Pandey
Department of Technical Education
IET
Dr. A.P.J. Abdul Kalam Technical University
Lucknow, Uttar Pradesh
India

Veena Parihar
KIET Group of Institutions
Ghaziabad, Uttar Pradesh
India

T. Pavan Reddy
Koneru Lakshmaiah Education Foundation
KL University
Guntur, Andhra Pradesh
India

Venkateswararao Podile
K. L. Business School
Koneru Lakshmaiah Education Foundation
Vaddeswaram, Andhra Pradesh
India

B. Rachanasree
Koneru Lakshmaiah Education Foundation
KL University
Guntur, Andhra Pradesh
India

T.S. Rajeswari
Koneru Lakshmaiah Education Foundation
Department of English
Vaddeswaram, Andhra Pradesh
India

K.K. Ramachandran
Management/Commerce/International Business
DR. G R D College of Science
Coimbatore, Tamil Nadu
India

J.V.N. Ramesh
Department of Computer Science and Engineering
Koneru Lakshmaiah Education Foundation
Vaddeswaram
Guntur, Andhra Pradesh
India

P.S. Ranjit
Department of Mechanical Engineering
Aditya Engineering College
Surampalem
Kakinada, Andhra Pradesh
India

A.S.K. Reddy
Department of CS and AI
SR University
Warangal, Telangana
India

Dhyana S. Ross
Loyola Institute of Business Administration (LIBA)
India

Kanamarlapudi P.S. Sabareesh
Koneru Lakshmaiah Education Foundation
Vaddeswaram, Andhra Pradesh
India

K.V.D. Sagar
Koneru Lakshmaiah Education Foundation
KL University
Guntur, Andhra Pradesh
India

Devati B. Sambasiva Rao
Koneru Lakshmaiah Education Foundation
Vaddeswaram, Andhra Pradesh
India

Abdullah Samdani
School of Law
University of Petroleum & Energy Studies
Dehradun
India

Saurabh
KIET Group of Institutions
Ghaziabad, Uttar Pradesh
India

Franklin J. Selvaraj
Vignana Jyothi Institute of Management
Department of Marketing
Hyderabad
India

Asif I. Shah
Xavier Law School
St. Xavier's University
Kolkata
India

Kunjan Shah
Unitedworld School of Computational Intelligence
Karnavati University
Gandhinagar, Gujarat
India

Arti Sharma
KIET Group of Institutions
Ghaziabad, Uttar Pradesh
India

Dilip K. Sharma
Department of Mathematics
Jaypee University of Engineering and Technology
Guna Madhya Pradesh
India

Himanshu Sharma
United World School of Business
Karnavati University
Gandhinagar, Gujarat
India

M.K. Sharma
Department of Mathematics
Chaudhary Charan Singh University
Meerut, Uttar Pradesh
India

Sanjiv Sharma
KIET Group of Institutions
Ghaziabad, Uttar Pradesh
India

P. Shreya Sarojini
Koneru Lakshmaiah Education Foundation
KL University
Guntur, Andhra Pradesh
India

Ajay Kumar Shrivastava
KIET Group of Institutions
Ghaziabad, Uttar Pradesh
India

Someshwar Siddi
St. Martin's Engineering College
Secunderabad, Telangana
India

Veer B.P. Singh
School of CSIT
Department of Cyber Security
Symbiosis Skills
and Professional University
Kiwale, Pune
India

Yashasvi Singh
KIET Group of Institutions
Ghaziabad, Uttar Pradesh
India

Swasti Singhal
Department of Computer Science and Information Technology
KIET Group of Institutions
Ghaziabad, Uttar Pradesh
India

S. Silas Sargunam
Department of Management Studies
Anna University Regional Campus
Tirunelveli, Tamilnadu
India

Nidhi Sindhwani
Amity Institute of Information Technology (AIIT)
Amity University
Noida, Uttar Pradesh
India
and
Amity School of Engineering and Technology Delhi
Amity University
Noida
India

Pratibha Singh
Department of CSE
Guru Ghasidas Vishwavidyalaya
Bilaspur, Chhattisgarh
India

Dharini R. Sisodia
Army Institute of Management & Technology
Department of Management
Greater Noida, Uttar Pradesh
India

Katakam V. Siva Praneeth
Koneru Lakshmaiah Education Foundation
Vaddeswaram, Andhra Pradesh
India

K. Suresh Kumar
MBA Department
Panimalar Engineering College
Chennai, Tamil Nadu
India

Ayush Thakur
Amity Institute of Information Technology (AIIT)
Amity University
Noida, Uttar Pradesh
India

Mohit Tiwari
Department of Computer Science and Engineering
Bharati Vidyapeeth's College of Engineering
Delhi
India

Abhinav Tripathi
KIET Group of Institutions
Ghaziabad, Uttar Pradesh
India

Mano A. Tripathi
Motilal Nehru National Institute of Technology
Department of Humanities and Social Sciences
Allahabad
India

Fred Torres-Cruz
Academic Department of Statistics and Computer Engineering
Universidad Nacional del Altiplano de Puno
Puno
Peru

Shyamasundar Tripathy
KL Business School
Koneru Lakshmaiah Education Foundation
Guntur, Andhra Pradesh
India

Makarand Upadhyaya
University of Bahrain
College of Business
Bahrain

Rashmi Vashisth
Amity Institute of Information Technology (AIIT)
Amity University
Noida, Uttar Pradesh
India

Veena P. Vemuri
NKES College of Arts
Commerce
and Science
Mumbai
India

Y. Venkata Ramana
KL Business School
Koneru Lakshmaiah Education Foundation
Guntur, Andhra Pradesh
India

Suruchi Verma
Amity Institute of Information Technology (AIIT)
Amity University
Noida, Uttar Pradesh
India

G.H.A. Vethamanikam
Department of Business Administration
Ayya Nadar Janaki Ammal College
Sivakasi, Tamil Nadu
India

Nadanakumar Vinayagam
Department of Automobile Engineering
Hindustan Institute of Technology and Science
Chennai, Tamil Nadu
India

W. Vinu
Department of Physical Education and Sports
Pondicherry University
Pondicherry
India

Elena Y. Zegarra
Academic Department of Accounting Sciences
Universidad Nacional del Altiplano de Puno
Puno
Peru

Preface

1. The Future of Business Management with the Power of Distributed Systems and Computing

Distributed systems and computing increase operations, decision-making, and customer experience and will shape firm management in this chapter. Distributed systems and computing improve corporate management scalability, flexibility, availability, efficiency, and affordability. Inventory, supply chain, customer relationship, finance, accounting, data analytics, decision-making, collaboration, and communication use distributed systems and computing. Edge computing, blockchain, and AI in distributed systems and computing may affect business management. We also cover distributed systems and computing research and innovation prospects, such as developing new algorithms and protocols, exploring new applications, and evaluating their social and ethical impacts. Distributed systems and computing enable digital-age firms to operate better and compete. Distributed systems and computing pose several challenges and threats. Distributed systems and computing and their difficulties can help businesses prosper in the digital age.

2. Applications of Optimized Distributed Systems in Healthcare

This chapter discusses healthcare applications of optimized distributed systems. Distributed systems, their architecture, and their uses in many industries are introduced in the chapter. Telemedicine and big data analytics were developed to address healthcare practitioners' communication and service issues. Optimized distributed systems with unrestricted parallel data processing, fault tolerance, and higher availability were developed after these methods failed. These systems improve patient care and lower healthcare costs, as described in the chapter.

3. The Impact of Distributed Computing on Data Analytics and Business Insights

Distributed computing affects data analytics and business insights. We define distributed computing and its significance in data analytics, emphasizing its benefits for large-scale data processing. We also examine business insights and how data analytics affects business operations. We then discuss how distributed computing facilitates data analytics, highlighting the benefits of numerous popular systems. We emphasize distributed computing for large-scale data processing, real-time data analytics, and machine learning. Distributed computing for data analytics and business insights has pros and cons. Scalability, latency, integration, and maintenance might affect distributed computing for data analytics and business insights. Distributed computing provides important insights into operations and a competitive edge in their marketplaces, outweighing the hurdles.

4. Machine Learning and Its Application in Educational Area

Machine learning (ML) is utilized to develop several sectors, including education, which will profoundly revolutionize learning and teaching. Educational institutions collect a lot of student data, which can be used to narrow down the changes that will improve student success. Machine learning can help instructors enhance student retention, grading, etc. Machine learning creates new insights. This chapter addresses how machine learning can be used in education to solve student and teacher issues and inform future research.

5. Approaches and Methodologies for Distributed Systems: Threats, Challenges, and Future Directions

Distributed systems are widely used, raising security concerns. With more internet-connected devices, security breaches are a huge concern. This chapter covers distributed system security threats such as hacking, malware, and denial-of-service assaults. We will also review distributed system security standards and protocols, including industry and government proposals. We will also address distributed system security, including wireless communication and network integration. The chapter will also discuss distributed system access control mechanisms like RBAC, DAC, and MAC. Finally, we will review the main distributed system security issues and outline future study and development.

6. Efficient-Driven Approaches Related to Metaheuristic Algorithms Using Machine Learning Techniques

Recent research on using machine learning (ML) to find effective, profitable, and adaptive metaheuristics has grown. Many stochastic and metaheuristic algorithms have delivered high-quality results and are cutting-edge optimization strategies. This study lacks a comprehensive survey and classification, despite many methods. This study examines numerous machine learning-metaheuristics combinations. It applies synergy to the many ways to achieve this goal. Search component-specific taxonomies are supplied. This taxonomy covers the optimization problem, minimal metaheuristics, and raised components. We also want optimization scholars to use machine learning techniques in metaheuristics. This chapter highlights unresolved scientific questions that require further study.

7. Security and Privacy Issues in Distributed Healthcare Systems – A Survey

Recent research on using machine learning (ML) to find effective, profitable, and adaptive metaheuristics has grown. Many stochastic and metaheuristic algorithms have delivered high-quality results and are cutting-edge optimization strategies. This study lacks a comprehensive survey and classification despite many methods. This study examines numerous machine learning-metaheuristics combinations. It applies synergy to the many ways to achieve this goal. Search component-specific taxonomies are supplied. This taxonomy covers the optimization problem, minimal metaheuristics, and raised components. We also want optimization scholars to use machine learning techniques in metaheuristics. This chapter highlights unresolved scientific questions that require further study.

8. Implementation and Analysis of the Proposed Model in a Distributed e-Healthcare System

Designing complex, distributed services like e-healthcare is difficult. Service-oriented design supports modular design, application integration and interoperation, and software reuse, enabling such systems. Open standards like XML, SOAP, WSDL, and UDDI enable interoperability between services on different platforms and applications in different programming languages under a service-oriented architecture. This chapter describes designing, deploying, invoking, and managing a decentralized electronic healthcare system using the service-oriented architecture. Our e-healthcare solution helps patients, medical staff, and patient monitoring devices. Because it supports text, graphics, and speech, the technology is more client-friendly than current e-healthcare systems.

9. Leveraging Distributed Systems for Improved Educational Planning and Resource Allocation

This chapter reviews distributed systems' educational planning and resource allocation benefits and drawbacks. Distributed systems that optimize resource consumption and provide personalized learning might help educational institutions plan and allocate resources. The research examines distributed system architectures and emphasizes infrastructure requirements for successful education implementation. Distributed system data management and analysis are also mentioned. Distributed education systems face security and privacy issues, according to the research. Distributed systems' benefits outweigh their drawbacks, and with effective planning and administration, educational institutions may overcome them to improve student outcomes. Distributed systems can improve academic achievements, personalize and collaborate on learning, and increase access to education, according to the chapter. Educational institutions could consider distributed system adoption to improve collaboration and communication, resource allocation, and digital education access.

10. Advances in Education Policy Through the Integration of Distributed Computing Approaches

Distributed computing advances education policy, according to this chapter. The chapter introduces technology's role in education policy and how distributed computing may solve many of the education sector's problems. The second section defines distributed computing and gives education policy examples. Distributed computing improves access, personalized learning, and data-driven decision-making in education policy, as discussed in the third section of this chapter. Distributed computing in education policy presents privacy and technological issues, which is discussed in the fourth section. Distributed computing benefits must be realized without sacrificing student and instructor privacy and security. These technologies may improve distributed computing in education policy as they grow. Distributed computing could transform education policy and student results.

11. Revolutionizing Data Management and Security with the Power of Blockchain and Distributed System

Modern organizations must secure and manage sensitive data. However, conventional centralized systems lack security and transparency. Blockchain technology (BT) and distribution systems (DS) may solve these problems. BT and DS may improve data management and security, as explored in this chapter. It begins by highlighting the necessity of data management and security in modern organizations. Additionally, it examines blockchain technology's scalability, interoperability, data management, and security difficulties. We examine the benefits and drawbacks of blockchain technology and distribution systems for data management and security. The chapter concludes with future research topics and the possible influence of these technologies on data management and security. Researchers, practitioners, and decision-makers interested in data management and security might use this chapter. We should expect more transparency, security, and efficiency in managing sensitive data with this new method.

12. Enhancing Business Development, Ethics, and Governance with the Adoption of Distributed Systems

Distributed systems could transform business operations, ethics, and governance. Decentralization, transparency, and security enable new business models, cut costs, and increase efficiency in distributed systems. Ethical and governance practices can help organizations use distributed systems responsibly and sustainably. This chapter summarizes distributed system concepts and applications in business development, ethics, and governance. It explains distributed systems, describes their properties, and explores their business growth benefits. The research also studies how distributed systems promote ethics in corporate development and governance. The study also defines governance in distributed systems and analyzes its importance, benefits, and possible solutions. The review study also discusses distributed systems' constraints in commercial development, ethics, and governance. Technical complexity, scalability, interoperability, regulatory issues, and governance issues must be handled. By understanding these challenges, organizations may employ distributed systems to improve governance, ethics, and growth. Distributed systems can significantly change how firms are founded, run, and regulated while encouraging moral behavior and participant confidence.

13. Leveraging Distribution Systems for Advanced Fraud Detection and Prevention in Finance

Fraud in the financial sector is rising due to the prevalence of financial crimes worldwide. Fraud detection (FD) and prevention are crucial to financial integrity and protecting organizations and individuals from financial losses. Distributed systems' (DSs) ability to analyze enormous amounts of data and perform real-time analysis makes them an attractive FD and prevention solution. DSs, a computer network, collaborate to complete a task. Scalability, fault tolerance, and high performance are their benefits. DSs can overcome the disadvantages of rule-based and machine learning-based FD methods. In this chapter, rule-based, machine learning-based, and hybrid FD and preventative techniques and their pros and cons are discussed. Then, it investigates how DSs can be used for FD and prevention in rule-based and mixed systems. The chapter concludes by discussing FD and preventive DS implementation issues and potential prospects. DSs for FD and prevention can increase these systems' accuracy and efficiency, improving financial security and reducing financial losses. However, DS implementation brings various problems, including data privacy concerns, security hazards, and the requirement for specialized skills and resources. Overcoming these obstacles and improving DSs for FD and prevention will be the focus of future research.

14. Advances in E-commerce Through the Integration of Distributed Computing Approaches

Distributed computing in e-commerce has improved digital enterprises. This chapter describes distributed computing approaches, their benefits, problems, and e-commerce integration issues. The concept of Distributed Computing improves scalability, flexibility, performance, efficiency, security, privacy, cost savings, operational complexity, and customer experience. The chapter also explores cloud computing, big data, and artificial intelligence trends in e-commerce distributed computing. Distributed computing is helpful for e-commerce enterprises, but they must consider hazards and take precautions. This chapter discusses the pros, cons, and future of distributed computing in e-commerce. This chapter can help firms comprehend this integration and use its benefits to stay competitive in the digital age.

15. The Impact of Distributed Computing on Online Shopping and Consumer Experience

Distributed computing affects online purchasing and consumer experience. Distributed computing lets online shopping platforms analyze and store vast volumes of data, speed up websites, and improve security. Thus, people demand smooth, personalized online shopping experiences that fit their needs. Distributed computing technology and online purchasing platforms are introduced in the chapter. Distributed computing affects website speed, personalization, and security; can increase expenses and technology dependence, as discussed in this chapter; and has transformed online shopping expectations by making it faster and more personalized. Websites must now load quickly, offer appropriate recommendations, and protect personal data. Retailers that fail to match these standards risk losing customers to competitors with a better online buying experience. While overusing this technology may have problems, it benefits shops and consumers. Distributed computing may shape the future of internet shopping as technology advances.

16. Wireless Sensor-Based IoT System with Distributed Optimization for Healthcare

WSNs are geographically distributed, purpose-built sensors that monitor and record environmental parameters and wirelessly communicate data to a central server connected to the internet in the IoT. IoT devices can assist hospitals beyond patient monitoring. IoT sensors can track wheelchairs, defibrillators, nebulizers, oxygen pumps, and other medical devices in real time. Healthcare requires scattered optimization. Healthcare IoT is hard for WSNs. Thus, WSN-based IoT and healthcare consider traditional research methodologies.

17. Optimizing Financial Transactions and Processes Through the Power of Distributed Systems

Distributed systems (DSs) improve FT efficiency, according to this chapter. like supply chains and blockchain technology can increase FT, process, security, transparency, and cost. This chapter defines, challenges, and solves FT and processes and uses DSs for payment processing, digital identity verification, supply chain financing, and insurance. These systems have scalability, interoperability, legal compliance, security, and user acceptance challenges. This chapter discusses BT and SC definitions, properties, benefits, and finance application cases, as well as DSs' financial potential and challenges. The chapter improves DS and processes for researchers, programmers, and practitioners. To maximize system utilization, the chapter discusses removing various barriers.

18. Leveraging Distributed Systems for Improved Market Intelligence and Customer Segmentation

DS increases market intelligence and client segmentation. Market intelligence, customer segmentation, and DS research follow. It provides advantages and disadvantages of DS for market intelligence. DS's real-time customer behavior research and customized marketing methods boost client segmentation. This chapter examines R&D challenges and directions. It recommends market intelligence and customer segmentation research using artificial intelligence, machine learning, blockchain technology, data visualization, ethics, and governance in DS. It shows various systems' pros and cons.

19. The Future of Financial Crime Prevention and Cybersecurity with Distributed Systems and Computing Approaches

Technology has enabled new financial crime prevention and cybersecurity methods. Distributed systems and computing can improve financial transaction security and efficiency. This chapter reviews blockchain technology and distributed ledgers for financial crime prevention and cybersecurity. It also tackles regulatory and compliance difficulties, interoperability and standardization issues, and system and infrastructure integration. These technologies improve transparency, minimize fraud, and other financial crimes, and boost financial industry innovation, yet they also have drawbacks. By tackling the issues holistically, these technologies can be used to their full potential while minimizing their drawbacks. Financial professionals and cybersecurity enthusiasts will benefit from this chapter.

20. Innovations in Distributed Computing for Enhanced Risk Management in Finance

Distributed computing may improve financial risk management. Comparing traditional risk management systems to distributed computing-based ones sets the chapter's goals. Finance risk management and distributed computing theory are covered in this chapter. Innovative strategies and trends in financial risk management include distributed computing architectures and frameworks. Distributed computing for finance risk management has technical challenges. Finally, finance risk management and distributed computing best practices are provided. This chapter suggests adopting and implementing a distributed computing solution for finance risk management and discusses distributed computing technologies in finance risk management, including pros, cons, and best practices.

21. Leveraging Blockchain and Distributed Systems for Improved Supply Chain Traceability and Transparency

In this chapter, distributed systems (DS) and blockchain improve supply chain (SC) traceability and transparency. As systems become more complicated and global, stakeholders lose visibility and accountability. SC data is protected by blockchain and DS. Food safety, traceability, counterfeiting, efficiency, and transparency are improved by SC blockchain and DS. The chapter then explores SC blockchain and DS applications including tracking commodities and raw materials and product validity. DS, AI, IoT, blockchain, and SC smart contracts. Finally, these technologies' effects on SC stakeholders and society, including the need for standardization, regulation, efficiency, transparency, and accountability, are examined. SC traceability and transparency may be enhanced with blockchain and DS. These technologies can improve SC for businesses and customers, despite their limitations. SC should use blockchain and DS.

22. Advances in Resource Management Through the Integration of Distributed Computing Approaches

This chapter discusses resource management for grid, cloud, and EC. These technologies lack flexibility, scalability, data analysis and processing, resource scheduling, administration, monitoring, data protection, and management. Researchers are creating distributed computing resource allocation algorithms. Distributed computing resource management changes organizational computer infrastructure. Networks and systems process data, increase computer infrastructure, and save money. These technologies are necessary for future research, despite their shortcomings.

1

The Future of Business Management with the Power of Distributed Systems and Computing

Venkateswararao Podile[1], Nitin Kulshrestha[2], Sushmita Goswami[3], Lavanya Durga[4], B. Rachanasree[4], T. Pavan Reddy[4], and P. Shreya Sarojini[4]

[1] *K. L. Business School, Koneru Lakshmaiah Education Foundation, Vaddeswaram, Andhra Pradesh, India*
[2] *Christ (Deemed to be University), Bengaluru, Karnataka, India*
[3] *Institute of Business Management, GLA University, Mathura, Uttar Pradesh, India*
[4] *Koneru Lakshmaiah Education Foundation, KL University, Guntur, Andhra Pradesh, India*

1.1 Introduction

Distributed systems and computing have become increasingly prevalent in the business world, transforming the way organizations manage their operations, data, and communications. The benefits of these technologies are clear, including improved efficiency, agility, and cost savings, which have led to their widespread adoption. This chapter aims to explore the potential of distributed systems and computing in shaping the future of business management. The fundamental concepts of distributed systems and computing find their applications in various areas of business management, including inventory management, customer relationship management (CRM), financial management, data analytics, and collaboration. We will also examine the challenges and risks associated with these technologies and explore real-world examples of their successful implementation. As the field of distributed systems and computing continues to evolve, there is great potential for further advancements and opportunities for innovation. Therefore, we will discuss emerging trends and technologies in this field and their potential implications for the future of business management. A comprehensive

Meta-Heuristic Algorithms for Advanced Distributed Systems, First Edition. Edited by Rohit Anand, Abhinav Juneja, Digvijay Pandey, Sapna Juneja, and Nidhi Sindhwani.

understanding of the power of distributed systems and computing in business management and its potential to transform the way organizations operate in the future [1–3].

1.1.1 Distributed Systems in Business Management

Due to their capacity to increase the effectiveness and efficiency of various business operations, distributed systems and computing have grown in significance in the field of business management. Through the use of these technologies, businesses are able to distribute their computing resources among various platforms, such as cloud platforms, edge devices, and peer-to-peer networks, processing and storing massive amounts of data in real time. The ability to optimize supply chain and inventory management processes is one of the main benefits of distributed systems and computing in business management. Due to the real-time tracking of inventory levels and shipments made possible by these technologies, businesses are better able to adapt to demand changes and better manage their resources. Customers should be treated with more personal attention, and businesses should offer them services that are more pertinent to their needs. This makes financial reporting, forecasting, and analysis more effective. Distributed systems and computing can also facilitate data analytics and decision-making by giving organizations access to real-time data and cutting-edge analytical tools. This enhances an organization's capacity to respond to changes in the business environment by enabling quick and effective decision-making. Distributed systems and computing can facilitate easier information and resource sharing among teams, enhancing collaboration and communication both within and between organizations. As a result, the organization may experience increased productivity and innovation. The value of distributed systems and computing lies in their capacity to increase the accuracy, agility, and efficiency of various business operations, giving organizations a competitive edge in the market [4, 5].

1.2 Understanding Distributed Systems and Computing

Distributed systems and computing are a type of computing model that involves multiple computer systems working together to achieve a shared goal. In this model, tasks are divided into smaller, more manageable pieces and distributed across different systems that are connected by a network. This allows the systems to collaborate and work together more efficiently, which can improve the overall performance of computing tasks. In cloud computing, for example, a shared pool of computing resources, including servers, applications, and storage, is accessed on-demand through the Internet. Edge computing, on the other hand, involves processing data and running applications closer to the source of the data, which can reduce latency and improve efficiency. Peer-to-peer networks allow devices to share resources and computing power, which can improve the resilience and efficiency of the system. However, distributed systems and computing also present challenges and risks, such as security vulnerabilities, data privacy concerns, and interoperability issues. Therefore, businesses need to carefully evaluate and plan for the adoption of distributed systems and computing to ensure its successful implementation and long-term sustainability [6–8].

Let's understand this with an imaginary example

Suppose a clothing retailer is experiencing stockouts and overstock issues in its supply chain, resulting in lost sales and increased inventory costs. The retailer decides to implement a distributed system to better manage its inventory and improve its supply chain. The distributed system utilizes a network of sensors placed throughout the supply chain, which collects and transmits data on inventory levels, sales trends, and production schedules. This data is then processed and analyzed in real time using advanced data analytics algorithms, allowing the retailer to make more accurate and timely decisions regarding inventory management and production scheduling.

As a result, the retailer is able to reduce its inventory costs by 20%, increase its sales by 15%, and improve its on-time delivery rate by 10%. The implementation of the distributed system also results in a more efficient and streamlined supply chain, reducing lead times and improving overall customer satisfaction. This example highlights how distributed systems and computing can be applied to improve business management by providing real-time insights and enabling more efficient and effective decision-making. The retailer was able to achieve these improvements by utilizing a distributed system that allowed for real-time monitoring of inventory levels at each store. With this information, the retailer was able to optimize its inventory levels and reduce the amount of excess inventory, which in turn reduced inventory carrying costs. In addition to better inventory management, the retailer also used the distributed system to improve its supply chain management. By monitoring the supply chain in real time, the retailer was able to identify bottlenecks and other issues that were causing delays in the delivery of products. By addressing these issues, the retailer was able to improve its on-time delivery rate by 10%. Finally, the retailer was able to increase its sales by 15% by leveraging the data provided by the distributed system.

Table 1.1 and Figure 1.1 show the sales volume of three products across two sales channels: online and in-store. For example, Product 1 had sales of 500 units online and 300 units in-store, for a total of 800 units sold. Similarly, Product 2 had sales of 750 units online and 400 units in-store, for a total of 1150 units sold. These sales figures could be used to inform decisions about how to allocate inventory,

Table 1.1 Sales volume of three products across two sales channels: online and in-store.

Product	Sales channel	Sales volume
Product 1	Online	500
	In-store	300
Product 2	Online	750
	In-store	400
Product 3	Online	1000
	In-store	800

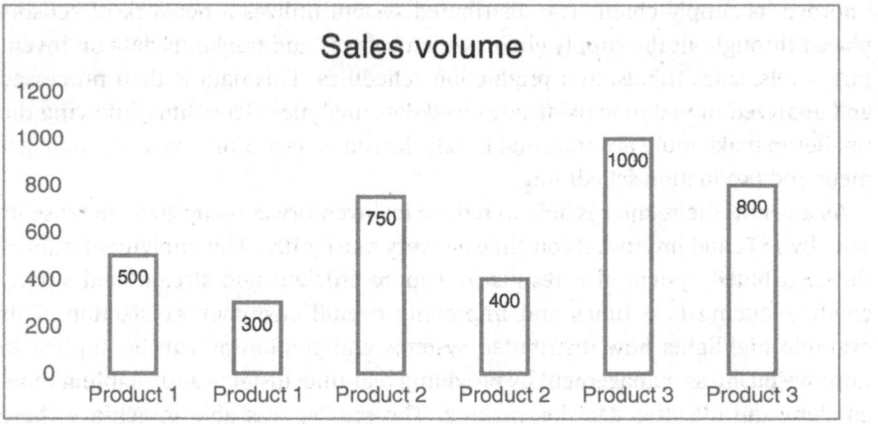

Figure 1.1 Sales volumes.

allocate marketing budgets, or make other business decisions related to product sales.

In the aforementioned illustration, distributed systems are essential for effective inventory management and supply chain optimization. The manufacturer can gather and analyze production and transportation data by utilizing distributed systems and computing to get a better understanding of their inventory levels and supply chain performance. Real-time data can be gathered from numerous sources using the distributed system, which then allows for quick processing and analysis using cutting-edge analytics software to produce insights and forecasts. This enables the manufacturer to make data-driven decisions about inventory levels, production plans, and transportation routes in real time, which can aid in supply chain optimization and cost savings. Additionally, utilizing distributed systems can improve coordination and communication throughout the entire supply chain. Increased trust and cooperation among supply chain participants may result from this, which may further boost efficiency and cut costs. In general, distributed systems and computing have the potential to revolutionize supply chain optimization and inventory management in the manufacturing sector, assisting companies in cutting costs, boosting productivity, and maintaining their competitiveness in a market that is changing quickly.

1.2.1 Definition of Distributed Systems and Computing

Distributed systems and computing are a type of computing model that involves multiple computer systems working together to achieve a shared goal. The systems are connected through a network and can be physically located in different geographic locations. In a distributed computing system, tasks are broken down into smaller pieces and distributed across different systems, allowing the workload to be spread out and completed more efficiently. In client–server architectures, one or more central servers provide services to multiple clients, while in peer-to-peer networks, all nodes in the network are connected and can share resources with one another. Cloud computing involves accessing shared resources, including computing power, applications, and storage, on demand through the Internet. It has also become more accessible due to advancements in technology, such as improvements in networking and cloud computing platforms. The adoption of distributed systems and computing has led to improvements in efficiency, scalability, and cost savings for businesses. However, it also presents challenges, such as the need for specialized expertise and potential security and privacy concerns [9, 10].

1.2.2 Advantages for Business Management

1) *Scalability:* Distributed systems and computing can easily scale to handle increasing workloads, as new computing nodes can be added to the network as needed. This allows businesses to handle larger volumes of data and requests without being limited by their infrastructure.
2) *Fault tolerance:* Distributed systems and computing are designed to be fault tolerant, meaning that if one node fails or experiences issues, the other nodes can continue to function and provide services. This improves reliability and ensures that the business can continue to operate even in the event of system failures.
3) *Flexibility:* Distributed systems and computing offer greater flexibility in terms of resource allocation, as computing resources can be allocated dynamically

based on the current workload. This allows businesses to optimize resource usage and minimize waste, which can result in cost savings.

4) *Cost savings:* By utilizing shared resources, businesses can reduce their infrastructure costs and only pay for the computing resources they need at any given time. This can result in significant cost savings over traditional computing models.

1.2.3 Characteristics of Distributed Systems and Computing for Business Management

1) *Decentralization:* Distributed systems and computing are designed to be decentralized, with no central authority or control. Instead, each node in the network is responsible for its own processing and decision-making.
2) *Resource sharing:* Distributed systems and computing rely on resource sharing, where different computing nodes can share processing power, storage, and other resources to achieve a shared goal.
3) *Communication:* Distributed systems and computing rely on communication between nodes in the network, which is facilitated through messaging protocols and other communication mechanisms.
4) *Autonomy:* Each node in a distributed system is autonomous, with its own processing power and resources. This allows the system to be more fault tolerant and resilient.
5) *Heterogeneity:* Distributed systems and computing can include different types of hardware and software, making it possible to utilize a wide range of resources and capabilities in the network.

1.3 Applications of Distributed Systems and Computing in Business Management

Distributed systems and computing have numerous applications in business management. Here are some examples [11–14]:

1) *Big data analytics:* Large data volumes can be processed quickly and effectively by businesses using distributed systems and computing for big data analytics. Businesses can gain insights that can guide decision-making, enhance customer experiences, and boost operational efficiency by analyzing data from various sources.
2) *Cloud computing:* A type of distributed computing known as "cloud computing" enables companies to pay-as-you-go access computing resources via the Internet. Businesses may benefit from the adaptability, scalability, and

affordability that cloud computing can provide for managing their computing requirements.

3) *Decentralized collaboration:* Distributed systems and computing can facilitate decentralized collaboration among team members who are geographically dispersed. This can be particularly useful for businesses with remote workers, as it can help maintain productivity and collaboration while reducing costs associated with travel and in-person meetings.
4) *Blockchain:* Blockchain is a distributed ledger technology that can be used to create secure, decentralized business applications. By using a distributed network of nodes to verify transactions, blockchain can provide greater security and transparency compared to traditional centralized systems.
5) *Content delivery networks (CDNs):* CDNs are a form of distributed computing that can help businesses deliver digital content, such as videos, images, and other files, to end users quickly and efficiently. By caching content in multiple locations around the world, CDNs can reduce latency and improve user experiences.

1.3.1 Inventory Management and Supply Chain Optimization

Inventory management and supply chain optimization are critical aspects of business management that can benefit from distributed systems and computing. Here is a more detailed explanation of how distributed systems and computing can help businesses in these areas:

- *Inventory management*: Distributed systems and computing can be used to optimize inventory management by enabling real-time inventory tracking, forecasting, and demand planning. For example, warehouses and transportation systems monitor inventory levels, track shipment locations, and optimize inventory replenishment.
- *Supply chain optimization*: Distributed systems and computing can help businesses optimize improving communication and collaboration among suppliers and partners, and optimizing logistics and transportation. For example, businesses can use distributed systems and computing to track the movement of goods from suppliers to customers, optimize shipping routes to reduce costs, and improve coordination among partners.
- *Smart contracts*: In self-executing contracts known as smart contracts, the terms of the agreement between the buyer and seller are directly written into lines of code. Supply chain management can automate and enforce contract terms with smart contracts, which lowers transaction costs and boosts efficiency. Businesses can lessen the risk of fraud and mistakes in the supply chain by executing and verifying smart contracts using a distributed network.

- *Real-time collaboration*: Real-time collaboration can be facilitated using distributed systems and computing, enabling suppliers, partners, and customers to work together in real time. Optimize supply chain operations and improve the quality of their products and services for example, businesses can use distributed systems and computing to enable real-time collaboration on design and production, reducing time to market and improving product quality.

1.3.2 Customer Relationship Management

Distributed systems and computing can also be used to enhance CRM in business management. CRM can be understood in Figure 1.2. Here are some ways in which distributed systems and computing can help businesses improve their CRM [15–17]:

1) *Data collection and analysis:* Distributed systems and computing can help businesses collect and analyze customer data in real time. This can help businesses better understand their customers' needs, preferences, and behaviors and tailor their products and services accordingly. For example, businesses can use distributed systems and computing to collect data from social media platforms, websites, and customer interactions and analyze it to gain insights into customer behavior.
2) *Personalization:* Distributed systems and computing can be used to personalize the customer experience, enabling businesses to deliver customized products, services, and promotions to individual customers. For example, businesses can

Figure 1.2 Customer relationship management.

use distributed systems and computing to track customers' purchase history, preferences, and behavior and deliver personalized product recommendations, offers, and discounts.

3) *Multichannel customer service:* Distributed systems and computing can help businesses provide multichannel customer service, allowing customers to interact with businesses through various channels such as social media, email, phone, and chat. This can help businesses improve customer satisfaction, response times, and customer loyalty. For example, businesses can use distributed systems and computing to integrate various communication channels, enabling customers to switch between channels seamlessly and providing a consistent experience across all channels.
4) *Customer segmentation:* Distributed systems and computing can help businesses segment their customers into different groups based on various criteria such as demographics, behavior, and purchase history. This can help businesses develop targeted marketing campaigns and improve the effectiveness of their sales and marketing efforts. For example, businesses can use distributed systems and computing to segment customers based on their preferences and behavior and develop personalized marketing campaigns that are more likely to resonate with different customer groups.
5) *Automated customer service:* Distributed systems and computing can also be used to automate various aspects of customer service, such as chatbots, virtual assistants, and automated responses. This can help businesses reduce response times, improve customer satisfaction, and reduce costs. For example, businesses can use distributed systems and computing to develop chatbots that can answer common customer questions and resolve issues without human intervention.

1.3.3 Financial Management and Accounting

Distributed computing and systems can also be used to improve accounting and financial management in business management. Here are a few ways that distributed systems and computing can assist businesses in strengthening their financial and accounting practices. Distributed computing and systems can aid in automating accounting and financial management tasks, making it simpler for businesses to manage their finances and increasing accuracy. The use of cloud-based accounting software is one method for utilizing distributed systems and computing for financial management and accounting. Using any device with an Internet connection and access from anywhere, this kind of software enables businesses to manage their financial data in real time. By doing this, businesses can stay informed about their financial situation and make wiser financial decisions. Utilizing blockchain technology is another way that distributed systems and computing can be used for accounting and financial management. With the help of blockchain technology, businesses can track their financial data and stop fraud by creating a secure and open ledger of financial transactions.

Planning and forecasting for the financial sector can benefit from distributed systems and computing. Distributed systems and computing, for instance, can be used by businesses to pinpoint the most lucrative goods or services, project future earnings and costs, and make any necessary alterations to their financial plans. Distributed computing and systems can also be used to enhance financial reporting and compliance. Businesses can save time and lower the risk of errors that could result in regulatory noncompliance by automating financial reporting processes. In order to comply with financial rules, businesses can do this and stay out of trouble with the law and fines. Businesses can greatly benefit from distributed systems and computing when it comes to financial management and accounting, including improved accuracy, efficiency, transparency, and compliance [18, 19].

1.3.4 Data Analytics and Decision-Making

Data analytics and decision-making in business management can also be enhanced by distributed systems and computing [20]. Listed below are a few ways distributed systems and computing can assist businesses in enhancing their data analytics and decision-making. Predictive analytics can also be made more accurate by using distributed systems and computing. Making predictions about the future using historical data is a process known as predictive analytics. Businesses can process massive amounts of historical data faster and more accurately by using distributed systems and computing, which enables them to predict future events with greater accuracy.

Distributed computing and systems can also be used to enhance decision-making. Businesses can find trends and patterns in their data that can be used to make better decisions by using data analytics and machine learning (ML) algorithms. Businesses can use distributed systems and computing, for instance, to determine the most profitable goods or services, project future earnings and costs, and make necessary changes to their business strategies. When it comes to data analytics and decision-making, distributed systems and computing can offer businesses many benefits, such as faster, more accurate, and more insightful results [21, 22]. Businesses can improve operations, make better decisions, and gain a competitive edge in their markets by utilizing the power of distributed systems and computing.

1.3.5 Collaboration and Communication Within and Across Organizations

Distributed systems and computing can also improve collaboration and communication within and across organizations. Here are some ways in which distributed systems and computing can help businesses improve collaboration and communication.

One way that distributed systems and computing can improve collaboration is by enabling remote work [23]. Distributed systems and computing allow employees to work from anywhere, which can be especially useful in situations where employees are unable to be physically present in the office, such as during a pandemic. By using distributed systems and computing, employees can access the tools and resources they need to collaborate with their colleagues and complete their work, regardless of their location. Distributed systems and computing can also improve communication within and across organizations. In addition, distributed systems and computing can improve collaboration and communication by enabling the sharing of data and resources. By using cloud-based platforms, employees can share documents, files, and other resources with their colleagues in real time, regardless of their location. This can help streamline collaboration and ensure that all employees have access to the information they need to complete their work. Finally, distributed systems and computing can improve collaboration and communication by enabling real-time collaboration on projects [24–26]. By using tools such as Google Docs, employees can work on documents in real time, making changes and suggestions as needed. This can help to streamline the collaboration process and ensure that all employees are on the same page when it comes to project goals and deadlines. Distributed systems and computing can provide businesses with many advantages when it comes to collaboration and communication, including increased flexibility, efficiency, and productivity. By leveraging the power of distributed systems and computing, businesses can improve collaboration and communication within and across organizations and gain a competitive edge in their industries [27, 28].

1.4 Limitations of Distributed Systems in Business Management

While distributed systems and computing offer many benefits to business management, there are also several challenges and risks associated with their use. Here are some of the challenges and risks that businesses may face when implementing distributed systems and computing:

1) *Security risks:* Distributed systems and computing often rely on cloud-based technologies and the Internet, which can expose businesses to security risks such as data breaches and cyberattacks [29–32]. These security risks can be particularly concerning for businesses that handle sensitive or confidential information.

2) *Network connectivity issues:* Distributed systems and computing depend on reliable network connectivity in order to function properly. However, network connectivity issues such as downtime, latency, and slow speeds can negatively impact business operations and productivity.
3) *Integration challenges:* Integrating different systems and technologies can be a complex and challenging process, especially if the systems and technologies are developed by different vendors or use different protocols. This can lead to compatibility issues, which can negatively impact business operations and efficiency.
4) *Cost:* Implementing distributed systems and computing can be expensive, requiring businesses to invest in new hardware, software, and network infrastructure. Additionally, ongoing maintenance and support costs can add up over time, making it difficult for some businesses to justify the investment.
5) *Complexity:* Distributed systems and computing can be complex and difficult to manage, requiring specialized skills and expertise. This can be a challenge for businesses that do not have the resources or expertise to manage these systems effectively.

Businesses that are considering implementing distributed systems and computing should be aware of these challenges and risks and take steps to mitigate them. This may include investing in robust security measures, ensuring reliable network connectivity, working with vendors to ensure compatibility, and carefully evaluating the costs and benefits of implementing these systems. By doing so, businesses can reap the many benefits of distributed systems and computing while minimizing their risks and challenges.

1.4.1 Security and Privacy Concerns

Security and privacy are two major concerns when it comes to distributed systems and computing in business management. Here are some of the specific security and privacy concerns that businesses may face:

1) *Data breaches:* Distributed systems and computing often rely on cloud-based technologies, which can be vulnerable to data breaches. These breaches can expose sensitive business and customer data, leading to reputational damage and legal consequences.
2) *Insider threats:* Businesses must also be mindful of insider threats, such as employees intentionally or unintentionally accessing and disclosing confidential information.
3) *Cyberattacks:* Cyberattacks such as denial-of-service attacks and malware attacks can disrupt business operations and compromise data security.

4) *Lack of control:* With distributed systems and computing, businesses often rely on third-party vendors to provide the underlying infrastructure and services. This can make it difficult for businesses to have full control over their data and systems.

To address these concerns, businesses should take a proactive approach to security and privacy. Additionally, businesses should carefully evaluate third-party vendors and ensure that they have strong security and privacy policies in place. Finally, businesses should stay up-to-date on relevant regulations and standards and work to ensure that their distributed systems and computing are fully compliant. By taking these steps, businesses can mitigate security and privacy risks and ensure that their distributed systems and computing are secure and compliant.

1.4.2 Technical Issues and Maintenance

In addition to security and privacy concerns, there are also technical issues and maintenance challenges associated with distributed systems and computing in business management. Here are some of the specific technical issues and maintenance challenges that businesses may face:

- *Compatibility issues*: With distributed systems and computing, businesses may also face compatibility issues with different hardware and software platforms. These compatibility issues can cause system failures and downtime.
- *Maintenance*: Maintaining distributed systems and computing can be complex and require specialized technical skills. Businesses must ensure that they have the necessary technical resources to maintain their distributed systems and computing.
- *Reliability*: Distributed systems and computing must be highly reliable to ensure that business operations are not disrupted. Ensuring high reliability can be challenging, as it requires a comprehensive understanding of the underlying technology and infrastructure.

To address these technical issues and maintenance challenges, businesses should work with experienced technical professionals who can design and implement distributed systems and computing that are reliable, scalable, and maintainable. Additionally, businesses should have clear processes in place for maintaining their distributed systems and computing, including regular system backups, testing, and updates. By taking a proactive approach to technical issues and maintenance challenges, businesses can ensure that their distributed systems and computing are reliable and can support their business operations effectively.

1.4.3 Organizational and Cultural Challenges

In addition to technical issues and maintenance challenges, businesses may also face organizational and cultural challenges when implementing distributed systems and computing. These challenges may include resistance to change, lack of expertise, and communication breakdowns.

One of the main challenges is resistance to change. When introducing new technology or new ways of working, employees may be resistant to change, which can lead to delays and difficulties in implementation. This can be due to various reasons, such as fear of job loss, lack of understanding of the new system, or simply being comfortable with the old way of doing things.

Another challenge is the lack of expertise within the organization. Implementing distributed systems and computing may require specialized technical skills that the organization may not have in-house. In such cases, the organization may need to invest in training or hire new employees with the necessary expertise. This can be costly and time-consuming, which can lead to delays in implementation.

Communication breakdowns can also be a significant challenge. Distributed systems and computing rely heavily on communication and collaboration between different parts of the organization. When there is a breakdown in communication, this can lead to delays, misunderstandings, and even errors. This is particularly true when the organization has a geographically dispersed workforce, which can make communication more challenging. To address these challenges, businesses must be willing to invest in change management strategies that focus on training, communication, and collaboration. It is essential to have open and transparent communication channels to ensure that employees are on board with the changes and understand their roles and responsibilities. By addressing these organizational and cultural challenges, businesses can successfully implement distributed systems and computing and reap the benefits they offer [33, 34].

1.4.4 Legal and Regulatory Compliance

Distributed systems and computing also bring forth challenges in terms of legal and regulatory compliance. This is due to the fact that businesses are bound to follow specific legal and regulatory frameworks when it comes to their operations, and distributed systems may pose some obstacles to compliance. One such challenge is related to data protection and privacy laws. With data being distributed across different systems and locations, it becomes difficult to ensure that these data are being processed and stored in compliance with the relevant laws and regulations. This may include requirements around data encryption, access controls, and data breach notification, among others. Failure to comply with these requirements may result in legal penalties and reputational damage. Another challenge is related to the jurisdiction of the data. As data may be stored and processed across different countries and regions, it becomes important to consider the regulatory frameworks of these different locations. This may include issues around data sovereignty and international data transfer, which can be complex and require specialized legal expertise to navigate.

Additionally, distributed systems may also pose challenges related to audit and compliance monitoring. With data being distributed across multiple systems, it can be difficult to track and audit data flows and ensure that compliance requirements are being met. This may require specialized tools and processes for compliance monitoring and additional efforts to ensure that distributed systems are auditable and transparent. In order to address these challenges, businesses may need to adopt specialized legal and compliance frameworks that are tailored to the unique challenges of distributed systems and computing. This may require collaboration with legal and regulatory experts, as well as the adoption of specialized compliance monitoring and reporting tools. Overall, legal and regulatory compliance is an important consideration for businesses that are looking to adopt distributed systems and computing in their operations [35, 36].

1.5 Future Developments and Opportunities

The use of distributed systems and computing in business management is expected to grow rapidly in the coming years, driven by advances in technology and the increasing availability of high-speed Internet connections. One key area of development is the expansion of the Internet of Things (IoT), which will allow for even more interconnected devices and systems. The development of blockchain technology is also likely to have a significant impact on the use of distributed systems in business management, particularly with respect to supply chain management and financial transactions.

Another area of growth is the use of ML and artificial intelligence (AI) in distributed systems and computing. These technologies have the potential to revolutionize data analysis and decision-making and could be used to automate many business processes, freeing up human resources for other tasks.

As distributed systems and computing become more widely adopted, there will be increasing opportunities for businesses to collaborate and share resources across different organizations. For example, companies could share computing resources and infrastructure to reduce costs or collaborate on research and development projects to drive innovation.

However, there are also challenges to be addressed as these technologies continue to evolve. Particularly as more sensitive data is shared across networks. Another challenge is the need for standardization and interoperability, as different systems and platforms may use different protocols and formats. Finally, there is a need for ongoing maintenance and support to ensure that these complex systems remain functional and secure over time. Addressing these challenges will be critical to the continued growth and success of distributed systems and computing in business management.

1.5.1 Potential Future Developments and their Implications for Business Management

There are numerous potential future developments that could have significant ramifications for business management as distributed systems and computing continue to advance. Utilizing AI and ML more frequently in distributed systems is one of the most notable trends. Supply chain optimization, risk management, and decision-making could all be completely transformed as a result of this. AI and ML can enable businesses to make more precise and informed decisions while also spotting trends and patterns that might otherwise go unnoticed, thanks to their capacity to process and analyze enormous amounts of data in real time.

The increased use of blockchain technology is another potential development. Supply chain management, payment processing, and contract management are just a few of the areas of business management that this decentralized technology has the potential to revolutionize. Blockchain could help lower fraud, mistakes, and disputes by supplying a transparent and secure way to record and track transactions. Furthermore, the application of blockchain technology could aid companies in achieving higher levels of effectiveness, transparency, and cross-departmental collaboration. Increased productivity, quicker decision-making, and more dependable performance in industries like manufacturing, logistics, and customer service are possible outcomes for businesses.

In addition, it is anticipated that the IoT will continue to expand and have a big impact on how businesses are managed. Businesses will have access to enormous amounts of data that can be used to enhance customer experiences, optimize supply chains, and improve processes as more and more devices become connected. Businesses will need to invest in new technologies and procedures in order to manage, examine, and secure this data, though. Overall, it is likely that future developments in computing and distributed systems will have a big impact on business management. In order for businesses to stay competitive and adaptable in a market that is constantly changing, it will be crucial to stay current with these developments and make the necessary adjustments to new technologies and trends as they appear.

1.5.2 Opportunities for Research and Innovation in the Field

The continued development of distributed systems and computing offers numerous opportunities for research and innovation in the field of business management.

As organizations increasingly rely on these technologies to improve their operations, there is a growing need for innovative solutions to address the challenges and capitalize on the advantages.

One area of potential research and innovation is the development of more efficient and effective distributed systems and computing architectures. As the complexity and scale of distributed systems continue to grow, there is a need for new models and approaches to designing and managing these systems. Another area of opportunity is in the development of new applications and tools for distributed systems and computing in business management. As businesses continue to adopt these technologies, there is a need for new software and tools to manage and analyze data, optimize operations, and facilitate communication and collaboration within and across organizations. In addition, there is a need for research to address the challenges and risks associated with distributed systems and computing in business management. As these technologies become more pervasive, there is a need to address security and privacy concerns, as well as technical issues and maintenance. Research in this area could explore topics such as cybersecurity, data privacy, and system maintenance to develop new solutions to address these challenges. The field of distributed systems and computing offers a wide range of opportunities for research and innovation in business management. By addressing the challenges and capitalizing on the advantages of these technologies, researchers and innovators can help businesses improve their operations, increase efficiency, and drive growth in the future.

1.6 Conclusion

In conclusion, computing and distributed systems have revolutionized how businesses run, and their significance will only grow in the future. Among the developments and trends that will continue to influence the business landscape are the adoption of cloud computing, the growth of the IoT, and the emergence of blockchain technology. Increased productivity, better decision-making, and improved customer engagement are just a few of the advantages that these technological developments offer businesses. In order for businesses to fully utilize the potential of distributed systems and computing, they must be aware of these difficulties and develop plans to address them. To address the difficulties and possibilities that distributed systems and computing present, there is also a need for ongoing research and innovation in the area. Researchers and creative thinkers can examine the potential of cutting-edge technologies and look into fresh approaches to incorporating these systems into operational procedures. The capabilities of distributed systems and computing have profound implications for business management in the future. Distributed systems and computing will be crucial in determining the business landscape in the years to come as businesses continue to face ever-increasing demands for innovation and efficiency.

References

1 Beckman, P., Dongarra, J., Ferrier, N. et al. (2020). Harnessing the computing continuum for programming our world. In: *Fog Computing* (ed. A. Zomaya, A. Abbas, and S. Khan), 215–230. Hoboken, NJ, USA: Wiley.

2 Morichetta, A., Casamayor Pujol, V., and Dustdar, S. (2021). A roadmap on learning and reasoning for distributed computing continuum ecosystems. In: *Proceedings of the IEEE International Conference on Edge Computing (EDGE)*, Chicago, IL, USA, 5–10 September 2021, 25–31. New York, NY, USA: Institute of Electrical and Electronics Engineers.

3 Costa, B., Bachiega, J., de Carvalho, L.R., and Araujo, A.P. (2022). Orchestration in fog computing: a comprehensive survey. *ACM Comput. Surv.* 55: 1–34.

4 Dustdar, S., Casamayor Pujol, V., and Donta, P.K. (2023). On distributed computing continuum systems. *IEEE Trans. Knowl. Data Eng.* 35: 4092–4105.

5 Yu, S., Chen, X., Zhou, Z. et al. (2021). When deep reinforcement learning meets federated learning: intelligent multitimescale resource management for multiaccess edge computing in 5G ultradense network. *IEEE Internet Things J.* 8: 2238–2251.

6 Xia, X., Chen, F., He, Q. et al. (2021). Cost-effective app data distribution in edge computing. *IEEE Trans. Parallel Distrib. Syst.* 32: 31–44.

7 Ullah, A., Dagdeviren, H., Ariyattu, R.C. et al. (2021). MiCADO-edge: towards an application-level orchestrator for the cloud-to-edge computing continuum. *J. Grid Comput.* 19: 47.

8 Hastbacka, D., Halme, J., Barna, L. et al. (2022). Dynamic edge and cloud service integration for industrial IoT and production monitoring applications of industrial cyber-physical systems. *IEEE Trans. Ind. Inform.* 18: 498–508.

9 Pusztai, T., Nastic, S., Morichetta, A. et al. (2021). A novel middleware for efficiently implementing complex cloud-native SLOs. In: *Proceedings of the 2021 IEEE 14th International Conference on Cloud Computing (CLOUD)*, Chicago, IL, USA, 5–10 September 2021, 410–420. IEEE.

10 Gheibi, O. and Weyns, D. (2022). Lifelong self-adaptation: self-adaptation meets lifelong machine learning. In: *Proceedings of the SEAMS'22—17th Symposium on Software Engineering for Adaptive and Self-Managing Systems*, Pittsburgh, PA, USA, 22–24 May 2022, 1–12. New York, NY, USA: Association for Computing Machinery.

11 Kirchhoff, M., Parr, T., Palacios, E. et al. (2018). The Markov blankets of life: autonomy, active inference and the free energy principle. *J. R. Soc. Interface* 15: 20170792.

12 Pearl, J. (1988). *Probabilistic Reasoning in Intelligent Systems: Networks of Plausible Inference*. San Francisco, CA, USA: Morgan Kaufmann Publishers Inc.

13 Forti, S., Bisicchia, G., and Brogi, A. (2022). Declarative continuous reasoning in the cloud-IoT continuum. *J. Log. Comput.* 32: 206–232.

14 Rihan, M., Elwekeil, M., Yang, Y. et al. (2021). Deep-VFog: when artificial intelligence meets fog computing in V2X. *IEEE Syst. J.* 15: 3492–3505.

15 Esfahani, N. and Malek, S. (2013). Uncertainty in self-adaptive software systems. In: *Lecture Notes in Computer Science* (including subseries Lecture Notes in Artificial Intelligence and Lecture Notes in Bioinformatics), vol. 7475, 214–238. Berlin/Heidelberg, Germany: Springer. ISBN 978-3-642-35812-8.

16 Chang, C. (2000). *Performance Guarantees in Communication Networks*, Telecommunication Networks and Computer Systems. London, UK: Springer; Chapter 7.

17 Saltzer, J., Reed, D., and Clark, D. (1984). End-to-end arguments in system design. *ACM Trans. Comput. Syst.* 2.

18 Davies, N., Holyer, J., and Thompson, P. (1999). An operational model to control loss and delay of traffic at a network switch. In: *The Management and Design of ATM Networks*, vol. 5. London, UK: Queen Mary and Westfield College pp. 20/1–20/14.

19 Gupta, A., Srivastava, A., Anand, R., and Tomažič, T. (2020). Business application analytics and the internet of things: the connecting link. In: *New Age Analytics*, 249–273. Apple Academic Press.

20 Gupta, A., Srivastava, A., and Anand, R. (2019). Cost-effective smart home automation using internet of things. *J. Commun. Eng. Sys.* 9 (2): 1–6.

21 Anand, R., Singh, B., and Sindhwani, N. (2009). Speech perception & analysis of fluent digits' strings using level-by-level time alignment. *Int. J. Inf. Technol. Knowl. Manage.* 2 (1): 65–68.

22 Anand, R., Sindhwani, N., and Juneja, S. (2022). Cognitive internet of things, its applications, and its challenges: a survey. In: *Harnessing the Internet of Things (IoT) for a Hyper-Connected Smart World*, 91–113. Apple Academic Press.

23 Anand, R., Singh, J., Pandey, D. et al. (2022). Modern technique for interactive communication in LEACH-based ad hoc wireless sensor network. In: *Software Defined Networking for Ad Hoc Networks*, 55–73. Cham: Springer International Publishing.

24 Sindhwani, N., Anand, R., Niranjanamurthy, M. et al. (ed.) (2022). *IoT Based Smart Applications*. Springer Nature.

25 Badotra, S., Tanwar, S., Rana, A. et al. (ed.) *Handbook of Augmented and Virtual Reality*. De Gruyter.

26 Kaura, C., Sindhwani, N., and Chaudhary, A. (2022). Analysing the impact of cyber-threat to ICS and SCADA systems. In: *2022 International Mobile and Embedded Technology Conference (MECON)*, 466–470. IEEE.

27 Byers, J., Luby, M., Mitzenmacher, M., and Rege, A. (1998). A digital fountain approach to reliable distribution of bulk data. In: *Proceedings of the ACM SIGCOMM '98 Conference on Applications, Technologies, Architectures, and Protocols for Computer Communication*. New York, NY, USA: Association for Computing Machinery.

28 Kelly, F. (1997). Charging and accounting for bursty connections. In: *Internet Economics* (ed. L.W. McKnight and J.P. Bailey), 253–278. Cambridge, MA, USA: MIT Press.

29 Pandey, B.K., Pandey, D., Wariya, S. et al. (2021). Deep learning and particle swarm optimisation-based techniques for visually impaired humans' text recognition and identification. *Augment. Hum. Res.* 6: 1–14.

30 Pandey, B.K., Pandey, D., Gupta, A. et al. (2023). Secret data transmission using advanced morphological component analysis and steganography. In: *Role of Data-Intensive Distributed Computing Systems in Designing Data Solutions*, 21–44. Cham: Springer International Publishing.

31 Kumar Pandey, B., Pandey, D., Nassa, V.K. et al. (2022). Encryption and steganography-based text extraction in IoT using the EWCTS optimizer. *Imaging Sci. J.* 1–19.

32 Pandey, D., Pandey, B.K., and Wariya, S. (2020). An approach to text extraction from complex degraded scene. *IJCBS* 1 (2): 4–10.

33 Perros, H.G. and Elsayed, K.M. (1996). Call admission control schemes: a review. *IEEE Commun. Mag.* 34: 82–91.

34 Watson, R.W. (1989). The delta-t transport protocol: features and experience. In *Proceedings of the 14th Conference on Local Computer Networks*, Mineapolis, MN, USA (10–12 October 1989), pp. 399–407. IEEE Computer Society.

35 Clegg, R.G., Di Cairano-Gilfedder, C., and Zhou, S. (2010). A critical look at power law modelling of the Internet. *Comput. Commun.* 33: 259–268.

36 Anand, R., Daniel, A.V., Fred, A.L. et al. Building integrated systems for healthcare considering mobile computing and IoT. In: *Integration of IoT with Cloud Computing for Smart Applications*, 203–225. Chapman and Hall/CRC.

2

Applications of Optimized Distributed Systems in Healthcare

Ayush Thakur, Suruchi Verma, Nidhi Sindhwani, and Rashmi Vashisth*

Amity Institute of Information Technology (AIIT), Amity University, Noida, Uttar Pradesh, India

2.1 Introduction

Talking about distributed systems, what first comes to mind is a system that is distributed or divided into several parts, or, in this case, devices. That is exactly what a distributed system is in layman's terms. Consider a number of autonomous parts that are spread across several machines. These machines have a communication network that is used to accomplish shared objectives. And, all of this is hidden from the end user, who sees it just as a single interface or computer even though the machines are at different, often remote, locations [1]. Figure 2.1 shows the distributed system architecture.

The remote location is a necessity to improve connectivity at isolated places. So users, anywhere around the world, can access the system's services. Furthermore, it ensures the availability of those services even after one or more components of the system malfunction. This means that the system, as a whole, would maximize resource usage and information while preventing breakdowns [1]. Users can put in as many service requests to be fulfilled without fail.

Distributed systems have their feet in technologies like sensor networks, cloud computing, the Internet of Things, service-oriented architectures, and the Internet as well (as shown in Figure 2.2). It impacts practically every part of the everyday lives of people, from delivering the news read to the applications used to order things to the infrastructure that drives business application environments and even sensors, networks, and controllers. Distributed computing is thus a critical

*Corresponding author Nidhi Sindhwani (nidhiece15@gmail.com)

Meta-Heuristic Algorithms for Advanced Distributed Systems, First Edition. Edited by Rohit Anand, Abhinav Juneja, Digvijay Pandey, Sapna Juneja, and Nidhi Sindhwani.

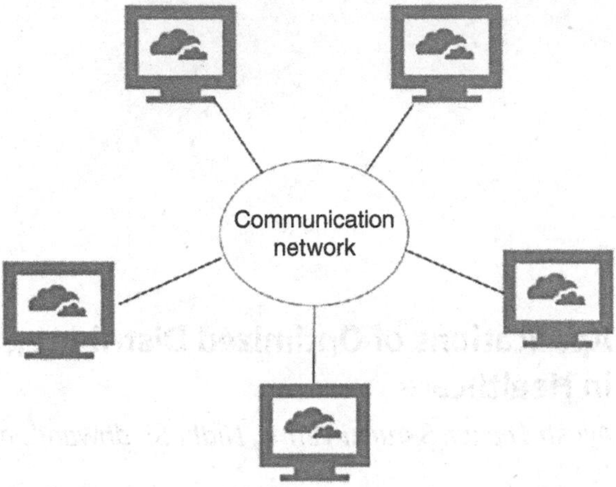

Figure 2.1 Distributed system architecture.

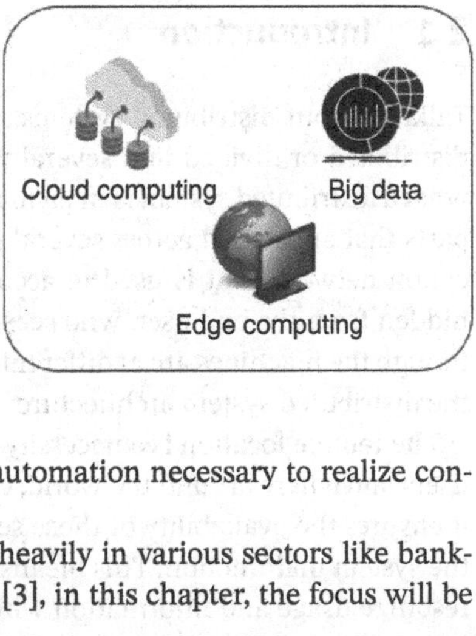

Figure 2.2 Technologies using distributed architecture.

technology for enabling the high degree of automation necessary to realize concepts such as Industry 4.0 [2].

While distributed systems are being used heavily in various sectors like banking, airlines, and supply chain management [3], in this chapter, the focus will be on its usage in the healthcare sector.

The question would come, why would a so complex technology be required by medical practitioners? The primary health centers that are set up all over the country have poor communication and the services there are inadequate. The workers have to handle administrative work, alongside, which slows down the whole process and prevents patients from becoming the first priority of the doctors. Not just the presence of extra work but their focus on the patients and medicine prescription is also limited to insufficient data. Results of any tests required for the diagnosis will take a lot of time to reach the doctors at the centers and thus, treatment would be delayed [4].

This situation has been curbed by the use of distribution systems. They consider each center as a client system and this application has been successfully renamed as "Telemedicine" [5].

Telemedicine is the use of telecommunications and other technologies to offer medical expertise in areas unable to get proper access. It has led to reduced costs and greater help. Professionals can offer their services without having to visit the location and patients can reach out instantly. Telemedicine has highly ameliorated the delivery of healthcare in rural areas [5]. Health centers have also begun using the benefits of big data analytics to acquire more insightful information, control expenses, and provide patients with better care alternatives. Information may refer to research in various fields by doctors and monitoring reports of patients by nurses. This can lead to advantages like improved clinical decision assistance, fewer administrative expenses, better fraud detection, and simplified data-sharing formats [4].

However, the era of distributed systems saw issues in communications, allocating tasks and, at times, the inability to maintain consistency. Industries, especially healthcare, demand a system with unrestricted parallel data processing with a provision for storage of billions and trillions of unstructured datasets; one that offers fault tolerance alongside easier and greater availability [4]; thus, creating a need for an optimized version of the distributed systems. Here, optimized distributed systems are discussed followed by their applications in healthcare.

2.2 Literature Survey

Distributed systems are becoming a crucial component of many sectors, including healthcare. Poor communication and a lack of services provide problems for healthcare professionals, which led to the development of telemedicine and big data analytics. These techniques run into problems, which result in the development of distributed systems that are optimized and offer unrestricted parallel data processing, fault tolerance, and higher availability.

Medical professionals may now provide their knowledge in places with poor access to quality treatment thanks to telemedicine. Reduced expenses and more assistance have resulted from the use of telecommunications and other technologies. Rural healthcare delivery has greatly improved, and patients may now contact professionals right away. In order to gather more insightful data, manage costs, and provide patients with better care options, health facilities have started adopting big data analytics. Information utilization by healthcare professionals can result in better clinical decision support, lower administrative costs, greater fraud detection, and more straightforward data exchange formats.

Unfortunately, these techniques have issues with consistency, task distribution, and communication. Due to these problems, distributed systems must be improved to provide limitless parallel data processing, fault tolerance, easier and higher availability, and the capacity to store billions and trillions of unstructured datasets. A more effective method of handling datasets is provided by an optimized distributed system, which results in quicker diagnosis and treatment, better patient care, and cheaper costs.

2.2.1 Need for Optimization of Distributed Systems

The need for the optimization of distributed systems can be understood with the help of Figure 2.3.

- Improved Data Security
  A distributed system that has been optimized can help healthcare professionals guarantee the security of critical patient data. The highest levels of privacy and secrecy may be ensured by implementing advanced authentication mechanisms [6]. To further safeguard the data and guard it against unauthorized access or loss, data storage and transfer technologies can be used. Several actions may be taken by healthcare organizations to guarantee the confidentiality and protection of their patient information.
- Improved Data Insights
  Healthcare providers are now able to access the most current data and insights, allow them to make informed diagnoses, provide exact treatments, and monitor patient health conditions quickly and accurately. This real-time information helps doctors make the most effective decisions for their patients – resulting in better health outcomes and increased satisfaction [7].
- Improved Patient Outcomes
  An optimized distributed system allows for seamless data flow among healthcare providers, which enables better collaboration and communication. With access to all necessary data, healthcare providers can make better decisions about patient care, ultimately leading to improved patient outcomes.

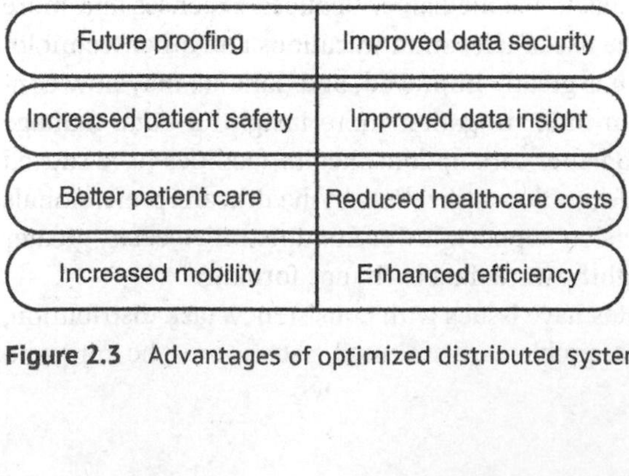

Figure 2.3 Advantages of optimized distributed systems.

- Reduced Healthcare Costs
  An optimized distributed system can help reduce healthcare costs by avoiding duplicate testing and unnecessary procedures. Additionally, it can help identify potential health problems early, leading to more cost-effective treatment options.
- Enhanced Efficiency
  With data accessible to all necessary parties, an optimized distributed system can help healthcare providers streamline their workflows and reduce the time it takes to make informed decisions [8]. It can also help prioritize patient care and ensure that patients receive the necessary care as soon as possible.
- Future Proofing
  As the volume of healthcare data continues to grow, an optimized distributed system will become even more important to ensure that healthcare providers have access to all the necessary information to make informed decisions [9]. With ever-increasing technological advancements, an optimized distributed system will undoubtedly play a critical role in the future of healthcare.
- Increased Patient Safety
  An optimized distributed system can help reduce errors by providing healthcare providers with access to the most up-to-date information. It can help ensure that patient data are secure and that only authorized personnel have access to it. This can ultimately help increase patient safety and reduce the risk of medical errors.
- Better Patient Care
  An optimized distributed system allows for seamless communication between healthcare providers and patients, leading to better patient care. Increased transparency and access to medical records promote a better understanding of care plans and more personalized care [10]. As a result, patients benefit from a greater sense of autonomy and control over their healthcare, providing them with the best possible health outcomes.
- Increased Mobility
  An optimized distributed system allows healthcare providers to access and share data in real time from any location. This ensures that patient care is not delayed or disrupted due to geographical limitations, providing patients with faster and more comprehensive care. Additionally, it allows healthcare providers to quickly respond to urgent medical needs and offers greater flexibility in case of travel or relocation.

2.2.2 Performance Optimization of Distributed Systems

Once the need for optimization was established, parameters needed to be set. These would define what all aspects required improvement and what all needed to be added. The following parameters [11] were majorly kept in mind while optimization took place (as shown in Figure 2.4):

- *Multithreading:* If the information that is asked for is not immediately available, the server will go into waiting while this query is serviced. This delay needed to be resolved. It is solved by the addition of a multithreading feature which essentially distributes other queries in a queue to other threads.
- *Reply Cache:* There may be a difference in the pace of the client system and the system that handles requests. It is not possible to synchronize the systems since clients can send any number of requests at any time and the processor will take a fixed amount of time to handle each. So, to ensure each query is resolved efficiently, a reply cache is required which stores results of previous queries and sends them to the user.
- *Remote Procedure Call (RPC) Protocol:* The amount as well as the rate of data transferred over the network needed to be reduced. So the protocol specifications for procedure calls need to be defined with adjustments.
- *Light Remote Procedure Call (LRPC) Protocol:* This facility is used in operating systems where the calling and called procedures are on the same system. It would be beneficial if this protocol was used in distributed systems.
- *Multiple processors with shared memory:* Several processors with shared memory are utilized to achieve great performance in terms of high call throughput and low call latency. This is also achieved using LRPC. By eliminating pointless lock contention and using fewer shared data structures, throughput may be

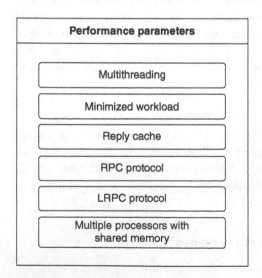

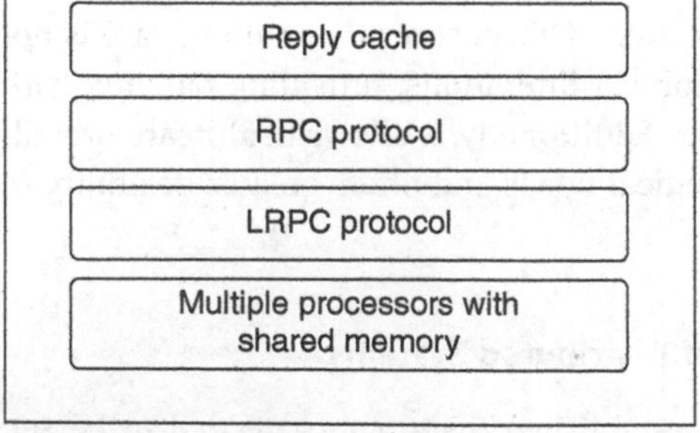

Figure 2.4 Parameters for optimization.

raised, and latency can be decreased by minimizing the burden of context switching.

- *Minimized workload:* Performance always depends on the kind of queries, which means that if the request is brief, the servicing will be more efficient. Thus, a minimum workload for each server needed to be ensured.

2.2.3 Characteristics of Optimized Distributed Systems in Healthcare

Distributed systems are becoming more important in the healthcare industry, and it's critical that they must be optimized to deliver the best outcomes. Scalability, fault tolerance, data integrity and security, interoperability, and performance (see Figure 2.5) must all be considered in order to accomplish this. Healthcare organizations may ensure that their distributed systems are stable, safe, and efficient by enhancing these aspects.

- *Scalability:* A system's capacity to scale refers to how quickly and easily it may be modified to meet increasing demand or to include additional services and devices. Healthcare businesses' technology has to be scalable to keep up with growth and change. This can entail growing to accept more people with different levels of access or scaling up to accommodate more data [12].
- *Fault tolerance:* Fault tolerance is the potential of a system to function regardless of if a component fails or is interrupted [13]. To ensure that essential services are always available, even in the event that a single data center or component fails, a system must be created and managed with redundancy. Data loss and major outages are less likely as a result.
- *Data integrity and security:* Data security and integrity are essential in dispersed healthcare systems. The system must be designed with many levels of encryption and authentication to protect the data's security and privacy. Additionally, utilizing both local and cloud-based systems, all data must be continuously backed up. As a result, there is a guarantee that any erased data may be found and restored [14].
- *Interoperability:* Interoperability is the ability of various systems and devices to communicate and share data. Since several systems and equipment are being created by multiple vendors, this is crucial for dispersed healthcare systems [15].

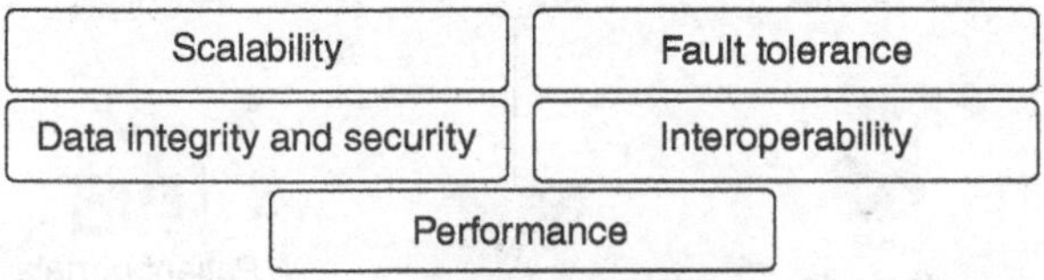

Figure 2.5 Characteristics of optimized distributed systems.

By creating an interoperable platform, healthcare companies can ensure that all of their devices and systems can connect and work together.

- *Performance:* When considering distributed systems in healthcare, it is a major issue. For the system to function effectively and efficiently, good performance is necessary. This comprises the system's dependability, capacity for handling huge data demands, and speed at which data may be accessed. Also, the system has to be planned such that resources are used effectively and there are no bottlenecks.

2.2.4 Applications of Optimized Distributed Systems in Healthcare

- Electronic health records (EHR) System
  An electronic health records (EHR) is a patient chart system. It enables visibility of all information regarding the patient, including a patient's medical history, treatment schedules, diagnoses, allergies, radiological pictures, prescriptions, dates of vaccinations, and results of lab and test work, to nurses and doctors tending to the patient. It is instant and secure. This is based on the distributed technology since it can be accessed by other healthcare providers and organizations – such as laboratories, pharmacies, emergency facilities, specialists, medical imaging facilities, and school and workplace clinics – so anybody involved in a patient's treatment has accessibility to the records at any point in time, anywhere [16].
  Distribution of EHR Systems is shown in Figure 2.6.

A wider perspective of the patient's treatment can be included in an EHR system. They are designed to encompass more than typical clinical data gathered in

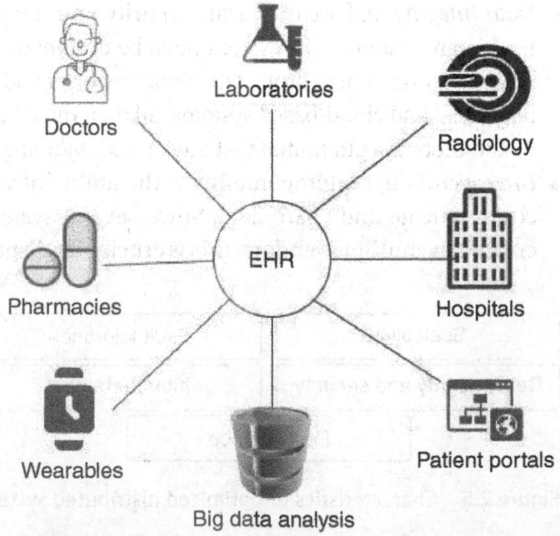

Figure 2.6 Distribution of electronic health records systems.

a provider's office. But this is not all they are limited to. They provide clinicians access to evidence-based tools they may use to decide how to treat a patient. It also simplifies and expedites the workflow of providers.

- Health information exchange system
  It enhances the efficiency, safety, effectiveness, and affordability of patient care by enabling physicians, pharmacists, nurses, other healthcare professionals, and patients to appropriately access and securely communicate a patient's critical medical information electronically.

The immediate exchange of critical patient data (as shown in Figure 2.7) may aid physicians in making more informed choices while providing treatment and prevent readmissions, medication mistakes, incorrect diagnoses, and unnecessary testing. This can integrate with EHR for ameliorated healthcare.

- Telemedicine and telehealth
  Telehealth (as shown in Figure 2.8) is the use of digital technologies by patients, the medical community, and other stakeholders to enhance human health. It includes medical training, virtual clinical meetings, and health check-ups through apps [17, 18]. Checking blood pressure or cholesterol levels using a mobile app, viewing lab reports, making appointments, and ordering prescriptions come under this.

Doctors provide medical treatments remotely in case of telemedicine. Telemedicine offers services that patients may obtain through typical in-person sessions with their doctors. Sharing test results remotely and consulting a doctor on calls or video calls comes under this. The following benefits are gained from this technology:

- Patients can have doctor consultations anytime, anyplace.
- Doctors can remotely monitor patients' vitals using wearable technologies like smartbands.

Figure 2.7 Exchange of patient data.

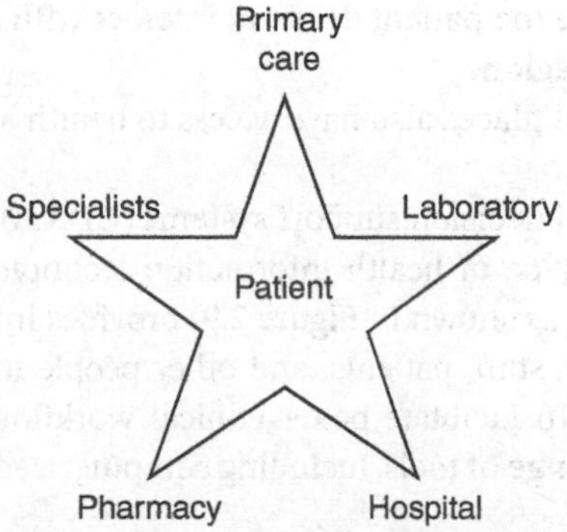

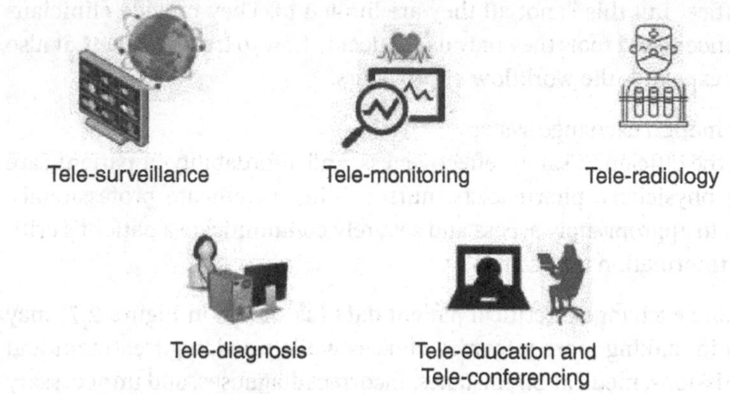

Figure 2.8 Telehealth constituents.

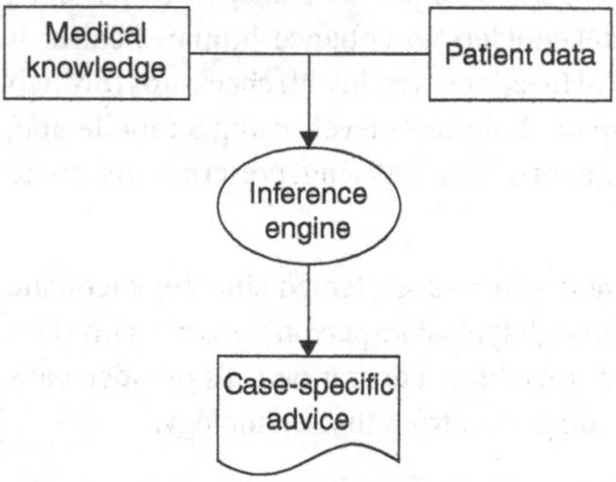

Figure 2.9 Clinical decision support system.

- Costs are reduced at both ends. Patients do not need to travel to clinics and hospitals can save infrastructural as well as maintenance costs.
- Since the patient does not interact with anyone in real life, there is no risk of contagion.
- Rural places also have access to health services.

- Clinical decision support systems (CDSSs)
  It is a type of health information technology. Clinical decision support system (CDSS, as shown in Figure 2.9) provides information and patient-specific data to doctors, staff, patients, and other people to help with health and medical treatment. To facilitate better clinical workflow decision-making, CDSS includes a wide range of tools, including computerized alerts and reminders for patients and

healthcare professionals, clinical recommendations, condition-specific order sets, concentrated patient data reports and summaries, documentation templates, diagnostic support, and contextually relevant reference material. Using various patient data elements, it is an active knowledge system that creates suggestions for medical care [19, 20]. It leads to reduced clinical mistakes.

2.2.5 Technologies Being Used in Healthcare

It has been mentioned that distributed systems contribute not just to industries but also to other technologies like cloud computing, edge computing, big data analytics, and data warehousing [21-25]. Some of these technologies being used in healthcare integrate with optimized distributed systems to give much better outcomes [26-28].

2.2.5.1 Spark

A large-scale data processing software by Adobe. Adobe Spark is a data processing program designed for large-scale data processing developed by Adobe. It is being used in the healthcare industry as:

- *Precision medicine:* A strategy to prevent and treat diseases that take into account a patient's unique variance in genes, lifestyle, and environment is known as precision medicine [4].
- *Genomics algorithm:* Researchers, trying to make the best of distributed systems, are transitioning genomics algorithms to Spark since it speaks their language and offers infrastructural advantages.
- *Computational neuroscience:* Researchers are developing libraries of analytical tools based on Spark and Python API for scientific computing and visualization. Summary statistics, regression, and clustering computations are being parallelized.

2.2.5.2 Hadoop

This is a technology used to handle big data. The usage of Hadoop in healthcare has allowed medical data to be stored in its native form no matter how large [4]. Data is stored securely. This method is also cost-effective and improves the quality and affordability of the data. Big Data in Healthcare is shown in Figure 2.10. Its usages include:

- The life sciences sector has been quick to adopt Hadoop, focusing mostly on next-generation sequencing and straightforward read mapping since developers found that a lot of bioinformatics issues translated well to Hadoop, especially at scale.
- Medical specialists are able to examine high-velocity data in real time from a variety of sources, including financial data, payroll data, and EHRs [29, 30].

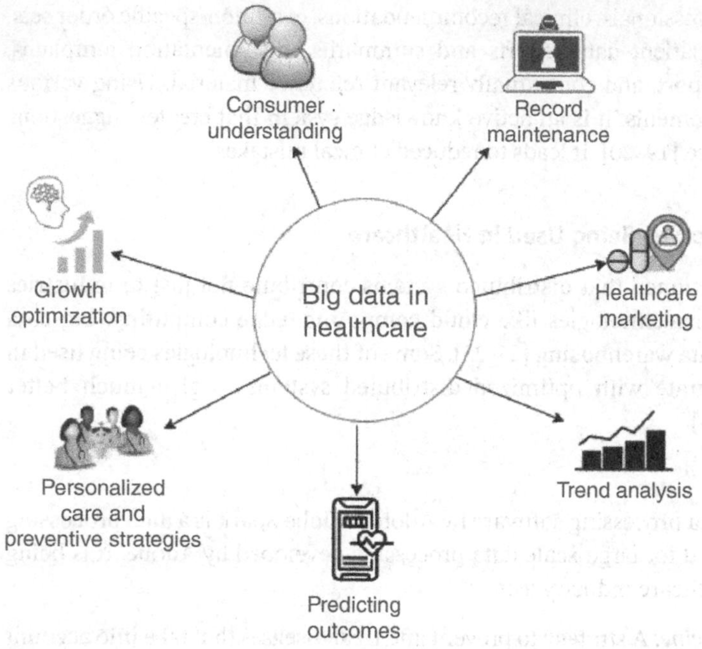

Figure 2.10 Big Data in healthcare.

- The development of healthcare intelligence applications using Hadoop technology has helped hospitals, payers, and healthcare organizations improve their competitiveness by coming up with clever business strategies.
- The utilization of past and real-time data from call center notes, salaries, weather, voice recordings, demographics, and medical claim data has helped insurance firms successfully construct predictive models to detect fraud.

2.3 Real Cases

- Sorted merging of massive VCF files
  Modern genetics and genomics research has created vast volumes of data that need to be processed using very advanced methods [31-33]. Large variant call format (VCF) file-sorted merging is one of the crucial challenges in this sector. Because merging VCF files is a computationally demanding procedure that needs a lot of computing power, standard ways might not be successful enough to accomplish this task [34]. Researchers have created unique schemas for Hadoop (MapReduce), HBase, and Spark to support the sorted merging of several VCF files in order to solve this problem. These schemas divide the merging

effort into successive phases using the divide-and-conquer strategy, which greatly enhances scalability and efficiency. These unique schemas were compared to well-known single/parallel multiway-merge techniques, the popular VCF tools, and an MPI (message passing interface)-based high-performance computing implementation in the study.

The findings of this study show that in terms of scalability and efficiency, bespoke schemas for Hadoop, HBase, and Spark greatly exceed traditional methods. These schemas provide a generalized method for doing sorted merging of genetics and genomics data using distributed platforms. These schemas allow for the faster and more accurate processing of huge VCF data, facilitating the identification of novel insights, and enabling more accurate genetic disease diagnosis and treatment.

Ultimately, the creation of these unique schemas represents a significant advance in the study of genetics and genomics since it offers a workable method for managing the massive amounts of data produced in this area. These schemas have the potential to completely change how we comprehend and treat genetic disorders by making it feasible to handle and analyze enormous volumes of genetic data quickly and effectively.

- Howard Hughes Brain Institute

One of the most intricate and mysterious systems in existence is the human brain. It is a massive network made up of billions of neurons that exchange complex electrochemical signals with one another. For us to better understand human behavior, cognitive function, and neurological illnesses, we must comprehend how this system operates.

Ground-breaking research to decode the activity of vast networks of neurons in the brain during behavior has been launched by the Howard Hughes Brain Institute [4]. Researchers may gather enormous volumes of data using cutting-edge brain imaging technologies; for a single mouse brain, one imaging session can produce up to 50–100 terabytes of data.

The researchers used the strength of big data analytics and machine learning to take on the enormous challenge of analyzing this data. They utilized the Python API and preexisting modules for scientific computing and visualization to build Thunder, a collection of analytical tools built on the Spark platform. Researchers may use Thunder to transform complicated neurological data into resilent distributed dataset (RDD) processes, which gives them the ability to use MapReduce to parallelize a variety of calculations, including regression, grouping, and summary statistics.

In the field of neurology, Thunder is a game changer because it gives researchers the resources they need to process, analyze, and visualize large volumes of data fast and effectively. Using Thunder, scientists may learn more about how the brain functions, opening the door to ground-breaking discoveries and therapies for neurological illnesses. This study marks a crucial turning point in neuroscience, and its effects will last for many years.

- Data Distribution Service

  The demand for dependable and effective middleware has increased more than ever in the modern world where real-time data processing has become the standard. Data Distribution Service (DDS) is useful in this situation [35]. As a middleware option for real-time systems, DDS has experienced tremendous growth. It was built on top of the Real-Time Publish-Subscribe protocol, which the Object Management Group standardized. From tiny business systems to massive sensor and actuator systems, DDS provides a real-time information exchange service that is appropriate for a variety of systems. Because of its adaptability and flexibility, it is an ideal solution for sectors like healthcare where real-time data processing is crucial.

  The Quality of Service (QoS) guidelines provided by DDS are many and improve the dependability and effectiveness of healthcare systems. The QoS guidelines also contain a transport priority, history, latency budget, and time-based filter. These characteristics allow healthcare systems to analyze data effectively and efficiently, improving patient outcomes and enabling more accurate diagnoses. Healthcare practitioners can depend on real-time data processing using DDS to give their patients fast and accurate care [36-38]. DDS has revolutionized real-time data processing by offering a dependable and effective solution for sectors like healthcare. As more and more organizations choose it as their preferred middleware option for real-time systems, its influence is being seen across sectors [39, 40].

2.4 Conclusion

The importance of distributed systems in healthcare and their possible effects on the sector have been examined in this study. We have talked about various distributed system types, including cloud computing, edge computing, and big data analytics, as well as how they are used in the medical field. Better patient outcomes, increased efficiency, and cost savings are all advantages of these systems. We have also looked at some of the particular technologies utilized in the healthcare industry, such as Hadoop and Spark. By enabling healthcare professionals to store and analyze massive volumes of data more effectively, these technologies have enhanced patient care and yielded greater insights. Healthcare-related distributed systems have proven successful in real-world scenarios like the sorted merging of enormous VCF files, the Howard Hughes Brain Institute, and the DDS. These examples demonstrate how distributed systems may be utilized in healthcare for a variety of purposes, including precision medicine and genomics algorithms. Therefore, it is evident that distributed systems will play an important part in healthcare in the future [41]. The demand for more effective and efficient ways to store, handle, and analyze that data will only increase as the volume of data created by the sector rises. Healthcare providers may enhance patient care, cut costs, and ultimately save lives by utilizing the potential of distributed systems [42-45].

With the above writing, one can come to the conclusion that distributed systems have been helping make lives better in a lot of ways, especially in the healthcare system. Without it, even basic amenities have limits to which they can reach remote locations. Optimization in this technology will not only lead to improvement in the working of systems but also ameliorate the solution that this system has been offering over the years.

References

1 Wu, J. (1999). *Distributed System Design*, 1e. Boca Raton, FL: CRC Press https://doi.org/10.1201/9781315141411.

2 Pérez, F., Irisarri, E., Orive, D. et al. (2015). A CPPS architecture approach for industry 4.0. *2015 IEEE 20th Conference on Emerging Technologies & Factory Automation (ETFA)*, Luxembourg (8–11 September 2015). IEEE. ieeexplore.ieee.org/abstract/document/7301606.

3 Hussain, M., Khan, M., and Al-Aomar, R. (2016). A framework for supply chain sustainability in service industry with Confirmatory Factor Analysis. *Renew. Sustain. Energy Rev.* 55: 1301–1312. https://doi.org/10.1016/j.rser.2015.07.097.

4 Sarkar, B.K. and Sana, S.S. (2018). A conceptual distributed framework for improved and secured healthcare system. *Int. J. Healthc. Manag.* 13: 74–87. https://doi.org/10.1080/20479700.2017.1422338.

5 Saini, A. and Yadav, P.K. (2015). Distributed system and its role in health care system. *Int. J. Comput. Sci. Mobile Comput.* 4 (4): 302–308. https://ijcsmc.com/docs/papers/April2015/V4I4201575.pdf.

6 Xu, W., Zeng, Z., Xu, Z. et al. (2020). Public health benefits of optimizing urban industrial land layout – The case of Changsha, China. *Environ. Pollut.* 263: 114388.

7 Seixas, A.A., Olaye, I.M., Wall, S.P., and Dunn, P. (2021). Optimizing healthcare through digital health and wellness solutions to meet the needs of patients with chronic disease during the COVID-19 era. *Front. Public Health* 9: 667654.

8 Mubashar, A., Asghar, K., Javed, A.R. et al. (2022). Storage and proximity management for centralized personal health records using an IPFS-based optimization algorithm. *J. Circuits, Syst. Comput.* 31 (01): 2250010.

9 Fo, A.R.A.V. and Mota, I. (2012). Optimization models in the location of healthcare facilities: a real case in Brazil. *J. Appl. Oper. Res.* 4 (1): 37–50.

10 Lucidi, S., Maurici, M., Paulon, L. et al. (2016). A simulation-based multiobjective optimization approach for health care service management. *IEEE Trans. Autom. Sci. Eng.* 13 (4): 1480–1491.

11 Yan, F., Ruwase, O., He, Y., and Chilimbi, T. (2015). Performance modeling and scalability optimization of distributed deep learning systems. *KDD '15: Proceedings of the 21th ACM SIGKDD International Conference on Knowledge Discovery and Data Mining* (August 2015). pp. 1355–1364. https://doi.org/10.1145/2783258.2783270.

12 Qiu, Y., Song, J., and Liu, Z. (2016). A simulation optimisation on the hierarchical health care delivery system patient flow based on multi-fidelity models. *Int. J. Prod. Res.* 54 (21): 6478–6493.

13 Buschiazzo, M., Mula, J., and Campuzano-Bolarin, F. (2020). Simulation optimization for the inventory management of healthcare supplies. *Int. J. Simul. Model.* 19 (2): 255–266.

14 Luo, Y., Liu, Y., Yang, W. et al. (2023). Distributed filtering algorithm based on local outlier factor under data integrity attacks. *J. Franklin Inst.*

15 Zhang, D.J., He, F.Z., Han, S.H., and Li, X.X. (2016). Quantitative optimization of interoperability during feature-based data exchange. *Integr. Comput. Aided Eng.* 23 (1): 31–50.

16 Cowie, M.R., Blomster, J.I., Curtis, L.H. et al. (2017). Electronic health records to facilitate clinical research. *Clin. Res. Cardiol.* **106**: 1–9. https://doi.org/10.1007/s00392-016-1025-6.

17 Dixon, B.E. (ed.) (2016). Chapter 1 - What is health information exchange? In: *Health Information Exchange*, Navigating and Managing a Network of Health Information Systems, 3–20. Elsevier. https://doi.org/10.1016/B978-0-12-803135-3.00001-3.

18 Stowe, S. and Harding, S. (2010). Telecare, telehealth and telemedicine. *Eur. Geriatr. Med.* 1 (3): 193–197.

19 Shen, Y.-T., Chen, L., Yue, W.-W., and Xu, H.-X. (2021). Digital technology-based telemedicine for the COVID-19 pandemic. *Front. Med.* 8: https://doi.org/10.3389/fmed.2021.646506.

20 Beeler, P.E., Bates, D.W., and Hug, B.L. (2014). Clinical decision support systems. *Biomed. Intell.* 144 (5152). https://doi.org/10.4414/smw.2014.14073.

21 Pandey, B.K., Pandey, D., Anand, R. et al. (2022). The impact of digital change on student learning and mental anguish in the COVID era. In: *An Interdisciplinary Approach in the Post-COVID-19 Pandemic Era*, 197–206.

22 Pandey, D., Pandey, B.K., Sindhwani, N. et al. (2022). An interdisciplinary approach in the post-COVID-19 pandemic era. In: *An Interdisciplinary Approach in the Post-COVID-19 Pandemic Era*, 1–290.

23 Saxena, H., Joshi, D., Singh, H., and Anand, R. (2022). Comparison of classification algorithms for Alzheimer's disease prediction. In: *2022 Seventh*

International Conference on Parallel, Distributed and Grid Computing (PDGC), 687–692. IEEE.

24 Sharma, S., Rattan, R., Goyal, B. et al. (2022). Microscopic and ultrasonic super-resolution for accurate diagnosis and treatment planning. In: *Communication, Software and Networks: Proceedings of INDIA 2022*, 601–611. Singapore: Springer Nature Singapore.

25 Bommareddy, S., Khan, J.A., and Anand, R. (2022). A review on healthcare data privacy and security. In: *Networking Technologies in Smart Healthcare*, 165–187. CRC Group.

26 Singh, H., Pandey, B.K., George, S. et al. (2022). Effective overview of different ML models used for prediction of COVID-19 patients. In: *Artificial Intelligence on Medical Data: Proceedings of International Symposium, ISCMM 2021*, 185–192. Singapore: Springer Nature Singapore.

27 Gupta, A., Anand, R., Pandey, D. et al. (2021). Prediction of breast cancer using extremely randomized clustering forests (ERCF) technique: prediction of breast cancer. *Int. J. Distrib. Syst. Technol.* 12 (4): 1–15.

28 Sindhwani, N., Anand, R., Vashisth, R. et al. (2022). Thingspeak-based environmental monitoring system using IoT. In: *2022 Seventh International Conference on Parallel, Distributed and Grid Computing (PDGC)*, 675–680. IEEE.

29 Meslie, Y., Enbeyle, W., Pandey, B.K. et al. (2021). Machine intelligence-based trend analysis of COVID-19 for total daily confirmed cases in Asia and Africa. In: *Methodologies and Applications of Computational Statistics for Machine Intelligence*, 164–185. IGI Global.

30 Lelisho, M.E., Pandey, D., Alemu, B.D. et al. (2022). The negative impact of social media during COVID-19 pandemic. *Trends Psychol.* 1–20.

31 Sim, I., Gorman, P., Greenes, R.A. et al. (2001). Clinical decision support systems for the practice of evidence-based medicine. *J. Am. Med. Inform. Assoc.* 8 (6): 527–534. https://doi.org/10.1136/jamia.2001.0080527.

32 Rashid, Z.N., Zeebaree, S.R.M., and Shengul, A. (2019). Design and analysis of proposed remote controlling distributed parallel computing system over the cloud. *2019 International Conference on Advanced Science and Engineering (ICOASE)*, Zakho - Duhok, Iraq. pp. 118–123. https://doi.org/10.1109/ICOASE.2019.8723695.

33 Lee, J., Kao, H.-A., and Yang, S. (2014). Service innovation and smart analytics for industry 4.0 and big data environment. *Proc. CIRP* 16: 3–8.

34 Sun, X., Gao, J., Jin, P. et al. (2018). Optimized distributed systems achieve significant performance improvement on sorted merging of massive VCF files. *GigaScience* 7 (6): https://doi.org/10.1093/gigascience/giy052.

35 Almadani, B., Saeed, B., and Alroubaiy, A. (2016). Healthcare Systems Integration using real time publish subscribe (RTPS) middleware. *Comput. Electr. Eng.* 50: 67–78. https://doi.org/10.1016/j.compeleceng.2015.12.009.

36 Anushka, M.V., Bhardwaj, S., and Vashisth, R. (2021). Design and development of SMART CART system using artificial intelligence. In: *2021 6th International Conference on Signal Processing, Computing and Control (ISPCC)*, 127–130. IEEE https://doi.org/10.1109/ispcc53510.2021.9609507.

37 Manhas, M., Sanduja, D., Aggarwal, N., and Vashisth, R. (2021, IEEE). Design and implementation of Artificial Intelligence (AI) based Home Automation. In: *2021 6th International Conference on Signal Processing, Computing and Control (ISPCC)*, 122–126. https://doi.org/10.1109/ispcc53510.2021.9609482.

38 Manhas, M., Sanduja, D., Vashisth, R., and Aggarwal, N. (2022). Automated gate control system using face mask detection. In: *2022 International Mobile and Embedded Technology Conference (MECON)*, 184–188. IEEE https://doi.org/10.1109/mecon53876.2022.9752417.

39 Kundra, P., Vashisth, R., and Dubey, A.K. (2022). Designing of fuzzy controller for adaptive chair and desk system. *Smart City Infrastruct.* 163–183. https://doi.org/10.1002/9781119785569.ch6.

40 Vashisth, R., Tripathi, S., Goel, H., and Srivastava, P. (2022, IEEE). Visualization of covid-19 pandemic data: an analysis. In: *2022 3rd International Conference on Computation, Automation and Knowledge Management (ICCAKM)*, 1–6. https://doi.org/10.1109/iccakm54721.2022.9990151.

41 Meena, R.S., Talukdar, R., Kannadasan, B. et al. (2023). PID control and estimation of the attitude model applied to geostationary satellites. In: *Advances in Signal Processing, Embedded Systems and IoT: Proceedings of Seventh ICMEET-2022*, 631–642. Singapore: Springer Nature Singapore.

42 Babu, S.Z.D., Pandey, D., Naidu, G.T. et al. (2022). Analysation of big data in smart healthcare. In: *Artificial Intelligence on Medical Data: Proceedings of International Symposium, ISCMM 2021*, 243–251. Singapore: Springer Nature Singapore.

43 Sindhwani, N., Rana, A., and Chaudhary, A. (2021). Breast cancer detection using machine learning algorithms. In: *2021 9th International Conference on Reliability, Infocom Technologies and Optimization (Trends and Future Directions) (ICRITO)*, 1–5. IEEE.

44 Ahuja, A., Patheja, S., and Sindhwani, N. (2022). Impact of COVID-19 on various sectors. *Infect. Dis. Microbiol.* 33.

45 Khongsai, L., Anal, T.S.C., AS, R. et al. (2021). Combating the spread of COVID-19 through community participation. *Global Social Welfare 8*: 127–132.

3

The Impact of Distributed Computing on Data Analytics and Business Insights

Haider Mehraj[1], Vinay K. Nassa[2], A.S.K. Reddy[3], K.V.D. Sagar[4], Dilip K. Sharma[5], Shyamasundar Tripathy[6], and Franklin J. Selvaraj[7]

[1] *Department of Electronics and Communication Engineering, Baba Ghulam Shah Badshah University, Rajouri, Jammu and Kashmir, India*
[2] *Rajarambapu Institute of Technology, Walwa, Maharashtra, India*
[3] *Department of CS and AI, SR University, Warangal, Telangana, India*
[4] *Koneru Lakshmaiah Education Foundation, KL University, Guntur, Andhra Pradesh, India*
[5] *Department of Mathematics, Jaypee University of Engineering and Technology, Guna, Madhya Pradesh, India*
[6] *KL Business School, Koneru Lakshmaiah Education Foundation, Guntur, Andhra Pradesh, India*
[7] *Vignana Jyothi Institute of Management, Department of Marketing, Hyderabad, India*

3.1 Introduction

For businesses of all sizes, data analytics has emerged as a critical component of corporate strategy. Due to this, distributed computing has emerged, providing a scalable and effective method for handling huge data collections. The ability to analyze vast volumes of data and derive insightful conclusions is essential for organizational success in today's data-driven business environment. Traditional data analysis techniques have grown increasingly inadequate due to the exponential expansion of data from numerous sources [1–5]. This method provides a scalable and economical means of handling huge datasets. Distributed computing enables faster data processing and analysis by splitting data into smaller pieces and processing them in parallel. Distributed computing has had a huge impact on business insights and data analytics, allowing firms to make data-driven choices immediately. Because data quantities are continuing to increase exponentially and are becoming more difficult to analyze, distributed computing is now a must

Meta-Heuristic Algorithms for Advanced Distributed Systems, First Edition. Edited by Rohit Anand, Abhinav Juneja, Digvijay Pandey, Sapna Juneja, and Nidhi Sindhwani.

for data analytics. Distributed computing has also produced useful business insights that can aid firms in making wise decisions. The practice of leveraging data to find patterns, trends, and opportunities that might give firms a competitive advantage is known as business insights. Distributed computing enables businesses to produce these insights more quickly and precisely, enabling them to make better decisions. This chapter aims to provide a thorough understanding of how distributed computing affects data analytics and business insights, as well as to assist businesses and organizations in making defensible judgments regarding their data analysis plans. To sum up, distributed computing has significantly impacted data analytics and business insights, allowing firms to handle massive amounts of data more quickly and produce insightful data that fosters corporate growth. The usage of distributed computing is anticipated to become even more important for enterprises as the volume of data continues to rise [6, 7].

3.1.1 Role of Distributed Computing in Data Analytics

Distributed computing refers to the use of multiple computers or nodes working together to perform a task. Traditional data analysis methods and tools can become slow and inefficient when dealing with large datasets, resulting in delays and errors in data processing. Distributed computing, on the other hand, allows for the parallel processing of data, breaking it into smaller parts and processing each part simultaneously. This approach results in faster data processing, allowing for real-time data analysis and insights. Data analytics relies heavily on distributed computing to help businesses gain important insights from their data. Large volumes of data can be processed and analyzed more quickly, which is necessary for making decisions in real time. Businesses can use the data analytics insights produced by distributed computing to find patterns, trends, and opportunities that can help them make strategic decisions and expand their operations. Moreover, distributed computing allows for cost-effective data processing and analysis, as it reduces the need for expensive hardware and software, making it accessible to organizations of all sizes. It also facilitates scalability, as additional nodes can be added as data volumes increase, ensuring that organizations can handle growing datasets without sacrificing performance. Distributed computing plays a crucial role in data analytics enabling businesses [8, 9].

3.1.2 Importance of Business Insights in Decision-Making

Business insights are important facts discovered through data analysis that support firms in making wise choices. These perceptions give a greater comprehension of corporate operations, consumer behavior, market trends, and other important elements that affect the performance of organizations. The capacity to derive actionable insights from data is crucial for maintaining competitiveness and achieving business growth in the highly competitive business climate of today.

Instead of depending entirely on intuition or conjecture, business insights allow firms to make data-driven decisions. Businesses can find patterns, trends, and opportunities by analyzing data that may not be immediately obvious. Marketing is a case study illustrating the value of business knowledge. Businesses can more successfully target their marketing efforts by understanding consumer behavior and preferences through the analysis of consumer data. Higher conversion rates, more revenue, and better client retention may result from this strategy. Supply chain management is yet another case in point. Businesses can spot bottlenecks, inefficiencies, and chances for optimization by analyzing supply chain data. This strategy can assist businesses in cutting expenses, speeding up delivery, and improving customer satisfaction. In the highly competitive corporate world of today, business insights are essential for decision-making. Organizations can obtain deeper insights into their operations and gain a competitive advantage because of the capabilities of distributed computing and the expanding availability of data [10, 11].

3.1.3 Overview of Distributed Computing and Data Analytics

Distributed computing is a method of processing and storing data using a network of computers working together. It involves breaking up a large dataset into smaller parts and processing each part simultaneously on different computers, which can result in faster processing times and increased efficiency. Data analytics is the process of examining large sets of data to extract insights and information. It involves using a variety of statistical and analytical tools to explore, understand, and analyze data. Data analytics can produce insights that can help decision-makers and promote business growth. Data analytics benefit greatly from distributed computing because it enables organizations to process and analyze enormous volumes of data more quickly and effectively. Data processing can be done in parallel when it is dispersed across several computers, thanks to distributed computing. Thus, businesses trying to maintain their competitiveness and obtain a market advantage. This strategy can assist firms in gaining insights more quickly and making better decisions. Businesses can grow their data processing capabilities via distributed computing, which enables them to manage higher volumes of data.

3.2 Distributed Computing and Data Analytics

Distributed computing and data analytics are two fields that are increasingly intertwined in the modern business environment by breaking up data into smaller parts and processing each part simultaneously on different computers. On the other hand, data analytics involves the examination of large datasets to gain insights and inform decision-making. Data analytics is an essential tool for businesses seeking to gain a competitive edge. As a result, organizations looking to stay competitive and gain an edge in the marketplace. The insights generated through data analytics can inform strategic decisions, optimize operations, and drive business growth. However, the processing and analysis of large datasets can be time-consuming and resource intensive. This is where distributed computing comes in. By using a network of computers working together, distributed computing enables businesses to process and analyze large volumes of data more efficiently. Businesses can acquire insights and make wise decisions in real time, thanks to this method's quicker processing times and higher efficiency. Distributed computing also gives companies the ability to expand their data processing capacities. More nodes can be added to the network as data volumes grow, enabling more effective data processing. Using this method, less expensive technology and software are not required, making data analytics available to companies of all sizes. Data analytics and distributed computing have a lot of potential to completely change how firms run. Distributed computing and data analytics are therefore crucial tools for firms looking to improve operational understanding and spur growth [12–14]. Distributed computing and data analytics are depicted in Figure 3.1.

3.2.1 Distributed Computing

A computational problem can be solved by a group of computers working together in a distributed computing environment. The calculation task is broken down into smaller tasks in distributed computing, and each task is assigned to a separate machine in the network or node. When all of the jobs have been finished, the

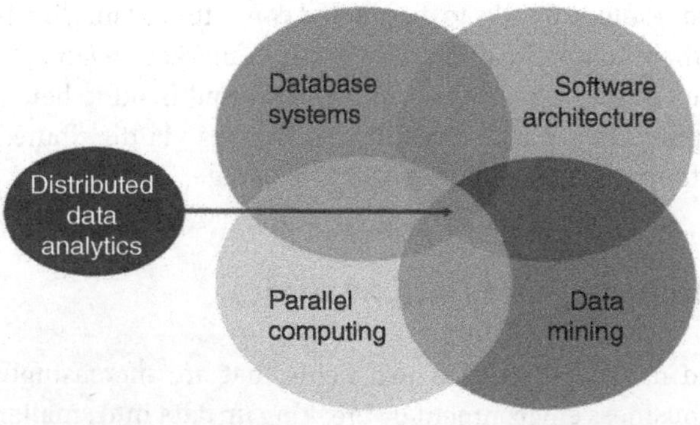

Figure 3.1 Distributed computing and data analytics.

output is merged to create the final product. These nodes handle the computational problem simultaneously. Large-scale, sophisticated computations that can't be handled by one computer are frequently handled through distributed computing. By using a network of computers, distributed computing can achieve much higher processing power than a single computer. This approach allows organizations to process large volumes of data faster and more efficiently, leading to improved productivity and reduced costs. There are different types of distributed computing systems, such as client–server systems and peer-to-peer systems. Scientific research, financial modeling, weather forecasting, and machine learning are just a few of the many uses for distributed computing. Distributed computing, for instance, can be used to train models on massive datasets in the field of machine learning, increasing accuracy and speeding up training. Distributed computing is a potent computing technique that enables businesses to process massive amounts of data more quickly and effectively. Distributed computing is quickly becoming a crucial tool for companies looking to acquire a competitive edge as a result of the growing availability of data and the demand for quicker processing speeds [15, 16].

3.2.2 Overview of Data Analytics

The practise of analyzing massive databases to find trends, patterns, and insights that might guide business decisions is known as data analytics. Data analysis encompasses a range of tools and methods, including statistical analysis, machine learning, and data visualization. There are numerous uses for data analytics in various industries. Data analytics can be used in marketing to comprehend consumer behavior and preferences, allowing businesses to create tailored marketing efforts. Data analytics can be utilized in the financial industry for risk management and fraud detection. Data analytics can be utilized in the healthcare industry to analyze patient data and create individualized therapies. Data analytics can also be utilized to improve performance and operational effectiveness. Businesses can find operational inefficiencies and improve processes for greater performance by analyzing data. Predictive analytics can also be applied to data analytics, giving firms the ability to anticipate future trends and make wise decisions. Business intelligence is another area where data analytics is used. Businesses can learn more about their performance and market trends by analyzing data. Growth can be fueled by using this knowledge to guide strategic decisions. Python, R, SQL, Tableau, and Microsoft Excel are a few of the often-used tools in data analytics. Data analytics also frequently employs machine learning methods including decision trees, random forests, and neural networks. Data analytics is more crucial than ever because of the rise in data availability and the demand for real-time decision-making [17].

3.2.3 Distributed Computing in Data Analytics

Distributed computing plays a critical role in supporting data analytics. With the explosion of big data in recent years, traditional computing resources have become insufficient to handle the massive amounts of data generated by businesses. With distributed computing, it is possible to add more computational resources to the network as needed, enabling businesses to scale up their data processing capabilities to meet growing demand. This is particularly important for businesses that are dealing with large and complex datasets that require significant processing power to analyze. Distributed computing also offers improved fault tolerance in data analytics. In traditional computing, if a single computer fails, the entire computation can be disrupted. In distributed computing, however, the workload is distributed across multiple computers, so if one computer fails, the other computers can continue to process the data. This enables businesses to perform data analytics with greater reliability and availability. Another benefit of distributed computing in data analytics is faster processing times. This enables businesses to perform real-time analytics, which is critical in many industries where timely decision-making is essential. Finally, distributed computing enables businesses to reduce costs in data analytics. By leveraging multiple computers, businesses can reduce the need for expensive high-performance computing resources, which can be cost-prohibitive for many organizations. This enables businesses to process large datasets more efficiently and cost-effectively, making data analytics accessible to a wider range of organizations. Distributed computing is a powerful tool that supports data analytics by providing scalability, improved fault tolerance, faster processing times, and reduced costs. By leveraging the power of distributed computing, businesses can gain insights into their operations and customers, inform strategic decision-making, and drive growth. Table 3.1 shows the benefits of distributed computing for data analytics [18, 19].

Table 3.1 summarizes the key advantages of using distributed computing to support data analytics. The first benefit, scalability, refers to the ability to add more computational resources to the network as needed. This enables businesses to scale up their data processing capabilities to meet growing demand.

The second benefit, fault tolerance, refers to the ability of distributed computing to continue processing data even if a single computer fails. In traditional computing, a single failure could disrupt the entire computation, resulting in lost time and resources. Distributed computing, on the other hand, distributes the workload across multiple computers, allowing the remaining computers to continue processing the data in the event of a failure. This improves the reliability and availability of data analytics, reducing the risk of data loss and disruption to the computation.

The third benefit, faster processing times, refers to the ability of distributed computing to process large datasets in a fraction of the time it would take a single computer to perform the same task. By harnessing the power of multiple computers working in

Table 3.1 Benefits of distributed computing for data analytics.

Benefit	Explanation
Scalability	Distributed computing allows businesses to add more computational resources to the network as needed, enabling them to scale up their data processing capabilities to meet growing demand.
Fault tolerance	In distributed computing, if a single computer fails, the other computers in the network can continue to process the data, reducing the risk of data loss or disruption to the computation.
Faster processing times	By harnessing the power of multiple computers, distributed computing can process large datasets in a fraction of the time it would take a single computer to perform the same task, enabling businesses to perform real-time analytics.
Reduced costs	Distributed computing can reduce the need for expensive high-performance computing resources, making data analytics more accessible and cost-effective for a wider range of organizations.

parallel, distributed computing can analyze data more quickly, enabling businesses to perform real-time analytics.

The final benefit, reduced costs, refers to the ability of distributed computing to lower the cost of data analytics. By leveraging multiple computers, businesses can reduce the need for expensive high-performance computing resources, which can be cost-prohibitive for many organizations. This makes data analytics more accessible and cost-effective for a wider range of businesses, informs strategic decision-making, and drives growth.

The table highlights how distributed computing can support data analytics by providing scalability, fault tolerance, faster processing times, and reduced costs. These benefits enable businesses to analyze large datasets more efficiently and effectively, improving their decision-making and driving growth.

3.3 Business Insights and Decision-Making

Business insights refer to the information and knowledge that businesses gain from analyzing their data. Effective decision-making is essential to the success of any business. It involves analyzing available data, weighing different options, and selecting the course of action that is most likely to achieve the desired outcome. Businesses may make more strategic and informed decisions, lowering the risk of expensive errors and raising the likelihood of success, by employing data analytics to acquire insights into their operations and consumers. Marketing, finance, operations, and customer service are just a few of the many corporate functions that might benefit from applying business insights. For instance, understanding customer behavior can influence product development and marketing strategies, while understanding internal operations can help organizations find cost-saving opportunities and areas for improvement. Businesses can streamline processes, increase profitability, and gain a competitive edge in the market by using data analytics to uncover these insights. However, it is important to note that business insights are only valuable if they are acted upon. Businesses must be willing to act based on the insights gained from their data analytics, whether that involves changing a product offering, adjusting a marketing strategy, or optimizing internal operations. By doing so, businesses can turn their data into a strategic asset, driving growth and success in today's data-driven marketplace [20–22].

3.3.1 Definition of Business Insights

Business insights refer to the information and knowledge that businesses gain from analyzing their data. Business insights can be used to optimize operations, improve the bottom line, and gain a competitive advantage in the marketplace [23].

3.3.2 Importance of Business Insights in Decision-Making

Business insights are essential in decision-making because they provide valuable information that helps businesses make informed and strategic decisions. In today's data-driven business environment, companies that leverage business insights to inform decision-making have a significant advantage over their competitors. Businesses can make more informed decisions, reduce the risk of costly mistakes, and drive growth. Business insights can also help businesses identify new opportunities for growth and innovation. For example, insights gained from customer data can inform new product development or help businesses identify unmet customer needs that can be addressed with new products or services. Insights gained from operational data can help businesses optimize their processes and identify cost savings, improving their bottom line and enabling them to invest in growth initiatives. Moreover, by leveraging business insights, businesses can stay ahead of changing market trends and consumer preferences, helping them adapt and stay relevant in a constantly evolving business landscape. This adaptability and agility are essential for long-term success and growth. Business insights are essential for decision-making because they provide businesses with the information and knowledge, they need to make informed, strategic decisions. By leveraging data analytics to gain these insights, businesses can optimize operations, identify new opportunities for growth and innovation, and stay ahead of changing market trends, driving success and growth in today's data-driven business environment [24–26].

3.3.3 Applications of Business Insights and their Impact

There are many examples of business insights and their impact on decision-making and business performance. Here are a few:

1) *Customer segmentation:* This can inform marketing strategies and product development, helping businesses tailor their offerings to different customer groups. For example, a clothing retailer may identify a segment of customers that prefers sustainable and eco-friendly products and develop a new product line to cater to that segment. This can lead to increased sales and customer loyalty.
2) *Operational efficiency:* A retailer may analyze data on their inventory management system and identify ways to optimize the system to reduce overstocking and out-of-stock situations. This can improve the customer experience and reduce costs associated with excess inventory.
3) *Fraud detection:* By analyzing transaction data, businesses can identify potentially fraudulent activity and take action to prevent losses. For example, a financial institution may analyze data on customer transactions and identify patterns of suspicious activity that indicate potential fraud. This can help the institution prevent losses and maintain customer trust.
4) *Predictive maintenance:* This can reduce downtime and increase equipment lifespan, leading to cost savings and improved productivity. The business insights on decision-making and business performance can be significant, driving growth, reducing costs, and improving competitiveness in the marketplace.

3.4 Challenges and Limitations

- *Data movement:* One of the key challenges of distributed computing is moving data between nodes, particularly if the data is very large. This can be time-consuming and can slow down the overall processing speed of your analytics.
- *Latency:* Depending on the size and complexity of your data, distributed computing can introduce latency or delays in processing time. This can be particularly challenging if you are working with real-time data, where latency can impact the accuracy and usefulness of your analytics.
- *Integration:* Integrating distributed computing with existing systems and processes can also present challenges. It can be difficult to ensure that your distributed computing platform works seamlessly with your other systems and tools and that your data is being moved and processed correctly.
- *Maintenance:* Distributed computing platforms require ongoing maintenance and optimization to ensure that they are functioning correctly and efficiently. This can be time-consuming and require a significant amount of technical expertise.

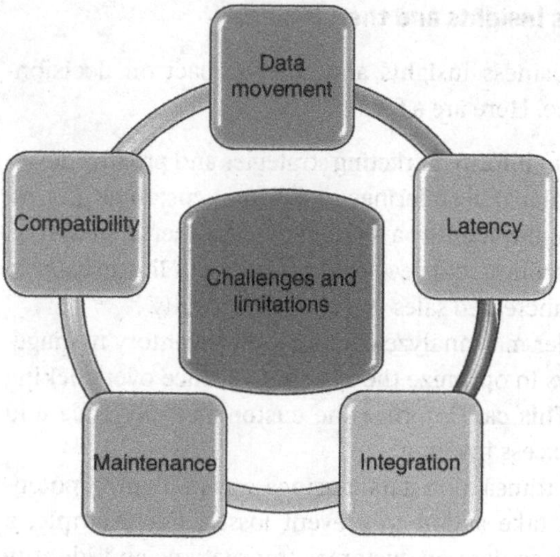

Figure 3.2 Challenges and limitations.

- *Compatibility:* Depending on the specific distributed computing platform you are using, there may be compatibility issues with certain types of data or tools. It is important to carefully evaluate the compatibility of any distributed computing platform before implementing it in your data analytics process.

These challenges and limitations shown in Figure 3.2 are important to consider when deciding whether to use distributed computing in your data analytics. However, for many businesses, the benefits of distributed computing far outweigh the drawbacks, particularly as the amount of data that businesses need to process and analyze continues to grow.

3.5 The Impact of Distributed Computing on Data Analytics

Traditionally, analyzing massive amounts of data would require significant computing power, making it expensive and time-consuming. However, with distributed computing, businesses can break down large datasets into smaller pieces and distribute them across multiple computers, which can work in parallel to process the data. This results in much faster processing times and more efficient use of computing resources. Because of distributed computing, organizations may now analyze data in real time or nearly real time, allowing them to make quicker choices and seize opportunities as they present themselves. Another game changer has been distributed computing's scalability, which makes it simple for organizations to add or subtract computing resources as needed for data processing. This has helped businesses to handle large datasets and peaks in demand without having to invest in expensive infrastructure. In addition to faster processing times and improved scalability, distributed computing has also been cost-effective for businesses. By using distributed computing, businesses can use computing resources only when needed, leading to cost savings compared to traditional on-premise computing solutions. This has made data analytics more accessible to businesses of all sizes, enabling them to compete with larger organizations that have more resources.

Businesses may now use advanced analytics techniques like machine learning and artificial intelligence, thanks to distributed computing. These more sophisticated analytics tools can find insights and patterns in data that are hard or impossible to find with conventional computing techniques. Because of this, there are now more opportunities for firms to innovate and expand, giving them a competitive advantage. Distributed computing has had a huge impact on data analytics, allowing firms to process and analyze enormous amounts of data fast and effectively. This has produced better decision-making, cost reductions, and fresh chances for development and innovation. The usage of distributed computing is anticipated to become even more crucial in the future as organizations continue to generate and collect vast volumes of data, enabling them to remain competitive and develop [27, 28].

3.5.1 Distributed Computing in Improvising Data Analytics

Distributed computing has improved data analytics in several ways. First, it has enabled businesses to process and analyze large and complex datasets in a fraction of the time that it would take with traditional computing methods. By breaking down data into smaller pieces and distributing it across multiple computers, businesses can process data in parallel, significantly reducing processing times. This has enabled businesses to get insights faster and make better-informed decisions based on data.

Second, distributed computing has made data analytics more scalable. Businesses can easily add or remove computing resources as needed, allowing them to handle large datasets and spikes in demand without having to invest in expensive infrastructure.

It has made data analytics more cost-effective. By using computing resources only when needed, businesses can reduce their costs compared to traditional on-premise computing solutions.

This enabled businesses to perform advanced analytics, such as machine learning and artificial intelligence [29–33]. These more advanced analytics techniques can uncover insights and patterns in data that would be difficult or impossible to detect with traditional computing methods. This has opened up new possibilities for businesses to innovate and grow, creating new opportunities for business development and competitive advantage. Finally, distributed computing has enabled businesses to perform real-time analytics. This means that businesses can analyze data as it is generated, allowing them to react quickly to changes in the market and take advantage of opportunities as they arise. This has enabled businesses to make better-informed decisions and stay ahead of the competition. Overall, distributed computing has improved data analytics by making it faster, more scalable, more cost-effective, and more accessible to businesses of all sizes. It has also enabled businesses to perform more advanced analytics and real-time analytics, creating new opportunities for growth and innovation [34, 35].

3.6 Conclusion

In conclusion, the impact of distributed computing on data analytics and business insights has been significant, providing a wide range of benefits and opportunities for organizations across various industries. With the ability to process large and complex datasets in a scalable and efficient manner, distributed computing has revolutionized data analytics and provided new insights into business operations and customer behavior. Through this chapter, we have examined the definition of distributed computing, its role in data analytics, and the benefits of using distributed computing for data analytics and business insights. We have also explored several examples of distributed computing platforms and their impact on organizations. However, it is important to note that the use of distributed computing is not without its challenges and limitations, including scalability, latency, integration, and maintenance. Organizations must navigate these obstacles to maximize the effectiveness of their data analytics and business insights. Despite these challenges, the benefits of using distributed computing for data analytics and business insights far outweigh the risks. By leveraging the power of distributed computing, organizations can gain valuable insights into their operations, improve decision-making, and gain a competitive edge in their respective markets. As such, we expect to see continued growth and adoption of distributed computing technologies in the field of data analytics and business insights.

References

1 Pandey, B.K., Pandey, D., Anand, R. et al. (2022). The impact of digital change on student learning and mental anguish in the COVID era. In: *An Interdisciplinary Approach in the Post-COVID-19 Pandemic Era*, 197–206.

2 Pandey, D., Pandey, B.K., Sindhwani, N. et al. (2022). An interdisciplinary approach in the post-COVID-19 pandemic era. In: *An Interdisciplinary Approach in the Post-COVID-19 Pandemic Era*, 1–290.

3 Saxena, H., Joshi, D., Singh, H., and Anand, R. (2022). Comparison of classification algorithms for Alzheimer's disease prediction. In: *2022 Seventh International Conference on Parallel, Distributed and Grid Computing (PDGC)*, 687–692. IEEE.
4 Sharma, S., Rattan, R., Goyal, B. et al. (2022). Microscopic and ultrasonic super-resolution for accurate diagnosis and treatment planning. In: *Communication, Software and Networks: Proceedings of INDIA 2022*, 601–611. Singapore: Springer Nature Singapore.
5 Bommareddy, S., Khan, J.A., and Anand, R. (2022). A review on healthcare data privacy and security. In: *Networking Technologies in Smart Healthcare*, 165–187.
6 Laney, D. (2001). *3D Data Management: Controlling Data Volume, Velocity and Variety*, Application Delivery Strategy, vol. 949. Stamford, CT, USA: META Group.
7 McAfee, A. and Brynjolfsson, E. **(2012)**. Big data: the management revolution. *Harv. Bus. Rev. 90*: 60–68.
8 Fosso Wamba, S., Akter, S., Edwards, A. et al. **(2015)**. How 'big data' can make big impact: findings from a systematic review and a longitudinal case study. *Int. J. Prod. Econ. 165*: 234–246.
9 Wang, Y., Kung, L., Wang, W.Y.C., and Cegielski, C.G. **(2018)**. An integrated big data analytics-enabled transformation model: application to health care. *Inf. Manag. 55*: 64–79.
10 White, M. **(2012)**. Digital workplaces: vision and reality. *Bus. Inf. Rev. 209*: 205–214.
11 Kambatla, K., Kollias, G., Kumar, V., and Grama, A. **(2014)**. Trends in big data analytics. *J. Parallel Distrib. Comput. 74*: 2561–2573.
12 Addo-Tenkorang, R. and Helo, P.T. **(2016)**. Big data applications in operations/supply-chain management: a literature review. *Comput. Ind. Eng. 101*: 528–543.
13 Richey, R.G., Morgan, T.R., Lindsey-Hall, K., and Adams, F.G. **(2016)**. A global exploration of big data in the supply chain. *Int. J. Phys. Distrib. Logist. Manag. 46*: 710–739.
14 Yu, W., Chavez, R., Jacobs, M.A., and Feng, M. **(2018)**. Data-driven supply chain capabilities and performance: a resource-based view. *Transp. Res. E Logist. 114*: 371–385.
15 Roßmann, B., Canzaniello, A., Von der Gracht, H., and Hartmann, E. **(2018)**. The future and social impact of big data analytics in supply chain management: results from a Delphi study. *Technol. Forecasting Social Change 130*: 135–149.
16 Russom, P. (2011). Big Data Analytics. TDWI Best Practices Report, Fourth Quarter. tdwi.org (accessed 12 July 2018).
17 LaValle, S., Lesser, E., Shockley, R. et al. **(2013)**. Big data, analytics and the path from insights to value. *MIT Sloan Manag. Rev. 52*: 21–31.
18 Loshin, D. (2013). *Big Data Analytics: From Strategic Planning to Enterprise Integration with Tools, Techniques, NoSQL, and Graph*. Waltham, MA, USA: Elsevier.
19 Tiwari, S., Wee, H.M., and Daryanto, Y. Big data analytics in supply chain management between 2010 and 2016: insights to industries. *Comput. Ind. Eng.* **2018** (115): 319–330.

20 Gilad, B. and Herring, J.P. (1996). *The Art and Science of Business Intelligence Analysis*. Greenwich, UK: JAI Press Ltd.
21 Davenport, T. and Prusak, L. (1998). *Working Knowledge*. Boston, MA, USA: HBS Press.
22 Berson, A., Smith, S., and Thearling, K. (2000). *Building Data Mining Application for CRM*. New York, NY, USA: McGraw-Hill.
23 Simon, A. and Shaffer, S. (2001). *Data Warehousing and Business Intelligence for E-Commerce*. San Francisco, CA, USA: Morgan Kaufmann Publishers.
24 Solomon, N. **(2004)**. Business intelligence. *Commun. Assoc. Inf. Syst. 13*: 177–195.
25 Fan, S., Raymond, Y.K., Lau, J., and Zhaob, L. **(2015)**. Demystifying big data analytics for business intelligence through the lens of marketing mix. *Big Data Res. 2*: 28–32.
26 Manyika, J., Chui, M., Brown, B. et al. (2011). *Big Data: The Next Frontier for Innovation, Competition, and Productivity*. Washington, DC, USA: McKinsey Global Institute.
27 Kang, M., Kim, S., and Park, S. **(2012)**. Analysis and utilization of big data. *J. Inf. Sci. Soc. 30*: 25–32.
28 Liang, T. and Liu, Y. **(2018)**. Research landscape of business intelligence and big data analytics: a bibliometrics study. *Expert Syst. Appl. 111*: 2–10.
29 Singh, H., Pandey, B.K., George, S. et al. (2022). Effective overview of different ML models used for prediction of COVID-19 patients. In: *Artificial Intelligence on Medical Data: Proceedings of International Symposium, ISCMM 2021*, 185–192. Singapore: Springer Nature Singapore.
30 Gupta, A., Anand, R., Pandey, D. et al. (2021). Prediction of breast cancer using extremely randomized clustering forests (ERCF) technique: prediction of breast cancer. *Int. J. Distrib. Syst. Technol. 12* (4): 1–15.
31 Sindhwani, N., Anand, R., Vashisth, R. et al. (2022). Thingspeak-based environmental monitoring system using IoT. In: *2022 Seventh International Conference on Parallel, Distributed and Grid Computing (PDGC)*, 675–680. IEEE.
32 Lelisho, M.E., Pandey, D., Alemu, B.D. et al. (2022). The negative impact of social media during COVID-19 pandemic. *Trends Psychol.* 1–20.
33 Anand, R., Nirmal, V., Chauhan, Y., and Sharma, T. (2023). An image-based deep learning approach for personalized outfit selection. In: *2023 10th International Conference on Computing for Sustainable Global Development (INDIACom)*, 1050–1054. IEEE.
34 Tankard, C. **(2012)**. Big data security. *Netw. Secur. 7*: 5–8.
35 Ram, J., Zhang, C., and Koronios, A. **(2016)**. The implications of big data analytics on business intelligence: a qualitative study in China. *Procedia Comput. Sci. 87*: 221–226.

4

Machine Learning and Its Application in Educational Area

Abhinav Tripathi, Yashasvi Singh, Arti Sharma, Ajay Kumar Shrivastava, and Saurabh Sharma

KIET Group of Institutions, Ghaziabad, Uttar Pradesh, India

4.1 Introduction

In this era of technology, every sector is affected directly or indirectly by the new advancement in technology. Machine learning (ML) is a subset of artificial intelligence that is implemented on various provided datasets which are further used for the prediction of output that can be more exact after various steps of regressions. We can make use of ML to solve real-life problems or prediction of new output data that can be used to solve further problem or make process efficient.

Due to modernization, the mode of education has evolved over time chalkboards have been updated to whiteboards and smart boards. Notebooks and textbooks have been replaced with laptops and iPad. As mode of education is not confined to the traditional classroom, where teacher can effectively watch how much a student has assimilated from his/her session. Therefore, to cross hurdles of modern way of education, we need ML to predict student's performance , test students, virtual help to students, effective grading of students, and analysis of content delivered.

To track the use of ML in education, we must classify it on the basis of:

- categorization of research papers in the implementation of ML in educational domain
- how the trends in ML in educational domain are changing day by day.

Meta-Heuristic Algorithms for Advanced Distributed Systems, First Edition. Edited by Rohit Anand, Abhinav Juneja, Digvijay Pandey, Sapna Juneja, and Nidhi Sindhwani.

The literature review used in this study is Systematic Literature Review (SLR; in this first, we find the type of research paper which critically gives solution or a review to the existing problem statement that has been addressed, and we select those content for formulation) for collection of primary data for purpose of research. The results of classification are divided mainly into five categories:

- Grading student
- Improvement of retention of students [1]
- Predicting student performance [2]
- Various parameters for testing students [3]
- Student dropout prediction [4]

4.2 Previous Work

To answer these questions, we performed a literature study from which we came to know that big educational institutes are using ML algorithm for intentional student advisory system.

In this chapter, we are going to use,

- SLR method to collect relevant primary study data (electronic search).
- Various database are: IEEE Xplore Digital Library (IEEE), Scopus database, and Google Scholar.
- Commonly used terms for the search were "machine learning and education," "machine learning in educational domain," and "machine learning in academic advancement" [5, 6].

4.3 Technique

These are various methods that are being turned into account for full and proper use of ML algorithms for enhancing the current scenario of ML.

4.3.1 Machine Learning

- Algorithm of normal task can be designed very easily by programmer but for complicated task that requires real-time upgradation of algorithm [7–9]. We need ML so that we can update the algorithm of problem through the process of solving each step. ML focuses on making predictions using datasets. It can automatically improve through earlier data and experiences [10].
- ML is used in education system for learning analytics (as shown in Figure 4.1). It can have noteworthy influence on student performance. It can perform various operations without being explicitly programmed to do so [11].

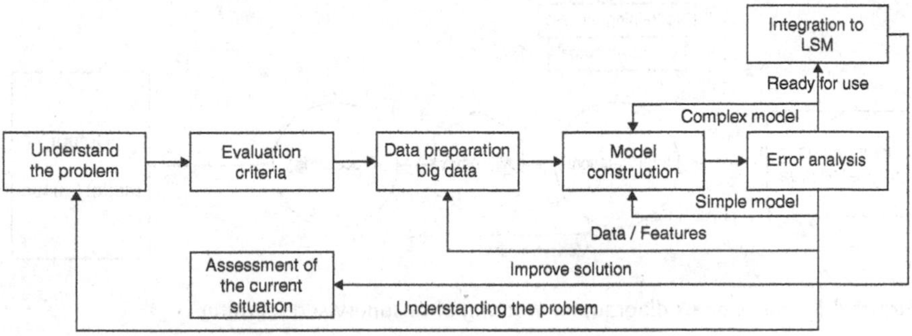

Figure 4.1 Block diagram for phases of machine learning in education system.

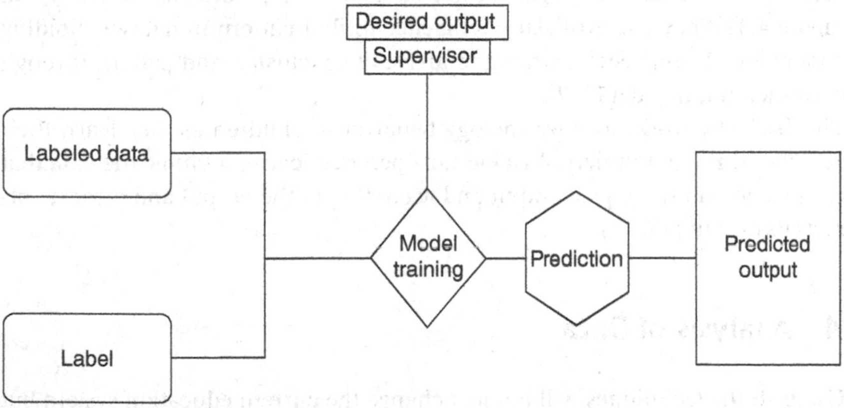

Figure 4.2 Basic block diagram for working of supervised learning.

4.3.2 Supervised Learning

- In supervised learning, we use models that use labeled datasets in which model learns about every type of data in dataset (as shown in Figure 4.2). After the completion of the training process, the testing of model is done based on test data which results in prediction of output [12].
- We can evaluate our model with our test data, the purpose of the model is to predict the probability of given output. After training, the machine is already trained with distinct types of datasets and when we find a new data and the basis of earlier data, prediction of output is done. Under neural network, discriminative (recognition) tasks use supervised methods [13–15].

4.3.3 Unsupervised Learning

- In unsupervised learning, the training of models is done through datasets that are neither classified nor labeled [16], in this the machine is provided with raw

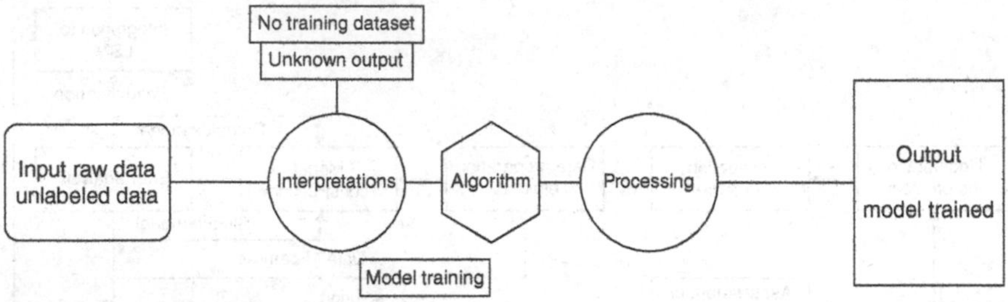

Figure 4.3 Basic block diagram for working of unsupervised learning.

data input that drives the machine to design an architecture for solution of the problem thus resulting in generation of model for prediction (as shown in Figure 4.3). They use artificial intelligence to find pattern in datasets holding data points. It uses deep learning to arrive at conclusion and pattern through unlabeled training data [17].

- This basically works as a psychology behavior of children as they learn their activities through mimicry. As a kid unsupervised learning mimic the data that is supplied and try to give output and according to the output and error it corrects its output [18, 19].

4.4 Analysis of Data

- Using all the techniques will not just change the current education system but also revolutionize it from ground to up. We tell students that they are unique in their own way, but we hand them to the generic way of learning. ML can work as a tutor, i.e. analyze their performance, while algorithm generates a curriculum different from others. It will not only just help students but also teachers, as it will understand the potential of everyone in the system [20–22].

4.5 Educational Data Mining

The processes in educational data mining are shown in Figure 4.4.

- This is used for finding specific type of data that come from education system or data that can be used for the betterment of education so that we can implement those changes in system so that we can incorporate with students and educational system efficiently [23].
- These techniques are useful for creating a range of aspects and phenomena affecting student learning on various platforms for conducting better accuracy and efficiency [8].

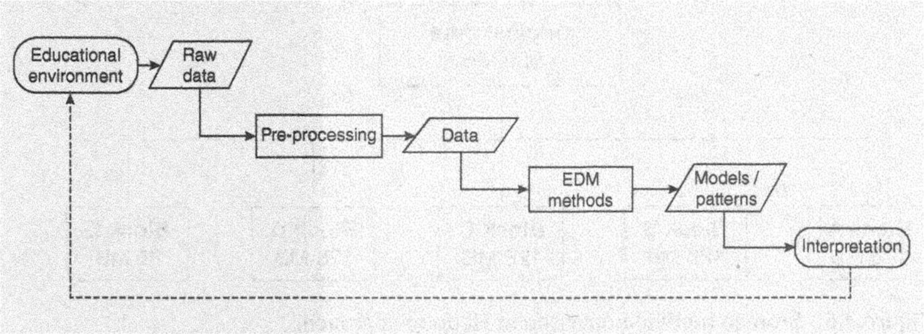

Figure 4.4 Processes in educational data mining [11].

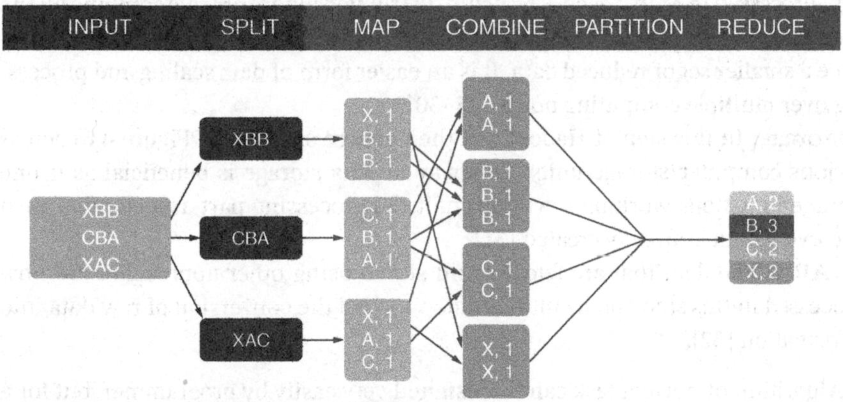

Figure 4.5 Basic working of Map-reduce processing technique.

- Data mining is used to collectively run-on large amounts of data to find hidden patterns and relationships, which is helpful in education domain as it is a data-driven decision organization [6].

4.6 Hadoop Approach

- Earlier when technology was not much advanced, data that was provided to computer or received was basically in form of rows and columns. So, fetching of data was not a hard task but as years passed by Internet gave rise to tons of data not only in size of data but also type of data. So, to tackle this problem of Big Data, Hadoop approach is applied that can incorporate vast amount of data efficiently [24–27].

Map Reduce: Whenever we must supply data for processing, we use the technique of MapReduce (Figure 4.5) which is mostly for computation of distributed

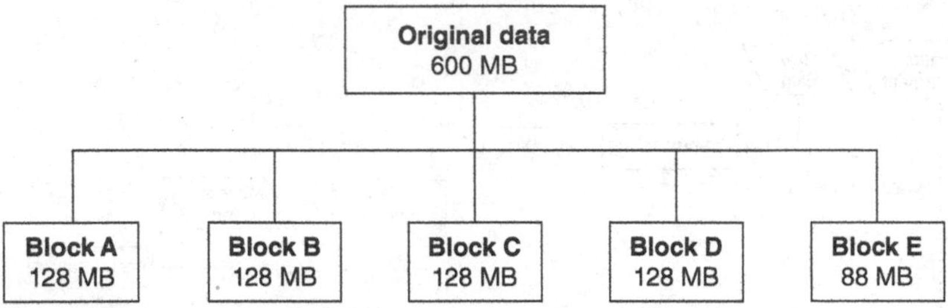

Figure 4.6 Storage methodology used in Hadoop approach.

data. In this, the dataset is split into independent blocks of data which are parallelly processed in Map. Second, by using distributed algorithm, we combine all the data that we have split and thus take input from map and combine them to produce a smaller set of reduced data. It is an easier form of data scaling and processing over multiple computing nodes [28–30].

Storage: In this step of Hadoop, all the data are stored (see Figure 4.6) across various computer/storage units. This way of data storage is beneficial as if one storage unit stops working it will not halt the processing part as a clone of earn and every data is already created [31].

YARN: The data that are fetched and stored using other approaches are now processed in this step and its ultimate step toward the conversion of raw data into information [32].

- Algorithm of normal task can be designed very easily by programmer, but for a complicated task that requires real-time upgradation of algorithm. We need ML so that we can update algorithm of problem through process of solving each step. ML focuses on making prediction using datasets. It can automatically improve through earlier data and experiences.
- ML is used in education system for learning analytics. It can have noteworthy influence on student performance. It can perform various operations without being explicitly programmed to do so.

4.7 Artificial Neural Network (ANN)

- ANNs (as shown in Figure 4.7) are computing systems adopted from biological neural network that constitutes of nervous system of every living organism. ANN model involves computational and mathematics which simulate the human-brain process [33].
- ANN is basically conducted by determining the comparative difference between the processed output of network (predicted output) and target/expected output [34].

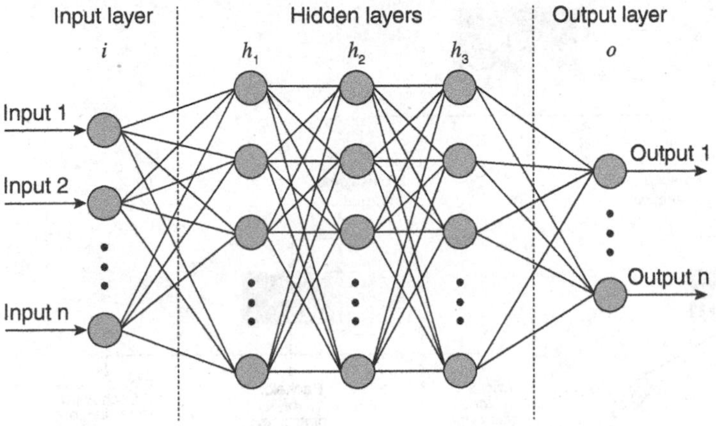

Figure 4.7 Basic block diagram of artificial neural network [16].

- Neurons and edges have weights that adjust during model creation. They automatically generate identifying characteristics from the examples that they process. After every output, there will be successive adjustment according to the learning rule and error, which will lead to new output increasingly like target output [35, 36].

4.8 Decision Tree

- The simplest and most adopted technique for classification and prediction is the decision tree (as depicted in Figure 4.8). In a decision tree, typically resembles a flowchart, each internal node shows a test on an attribute, each branch shows the test's result, and each leaf node (or terminal node) has a class label.
- Recursive partitioning method, which segments the source set into subsets in a recursive manner, is how decision trees are created. Their norms are simple to understand, which shows that their application is simple to understand in relation to their significance.

4.9 Results/Discussion

Using ML we can achieve some of the milestones that are listed below:

4.9.1 Personalized Learning Through Adaptive Learning

As we can easily understand from traditional method of teaching, we can also apply adaptive learning, where we can analyze student performance in real time.

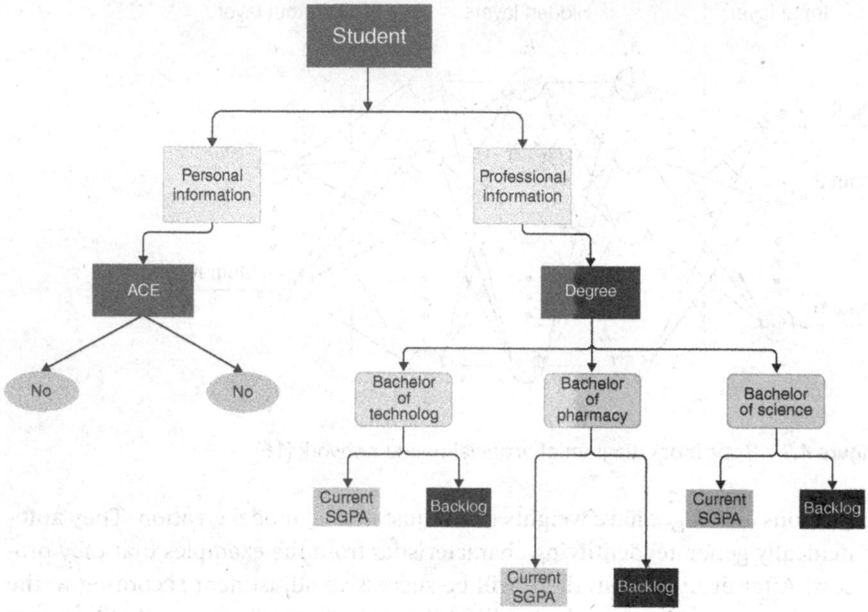

Figure 4.8 Diagram of decision tree for student database.

Thus, we can change the curriculum and teaching method according to the feedback received.

In this era of emerging technology, everything is customizable whether it is clothes or cars but education which becomes the building block of individual character and knowledge should also be customizable. People can have their own pace of curriculum what they want to learn by whom they want to learn rather than those patterns and standards they want to follow can be easily decided by students.

4.10 Increasing Efficiency Using Learning Analytics

Whenever we think about resources, we can see that comparatively we can have not only vast number of resources but also resources that are compatible to individual according to his/her interest or capability. Various features of ML can be used for better curation of content and curriculum. We can easily bifurcate our work according to our understanding toward the potential of distinct categories of students.

The analysis will not only be beneficial for students but also for teachers, who can analyze the domain in which they don't have deep knowledge or don't feel confident enough while teaching a topic. Thus, when they feel stuck on a topic, they can understand it from a student perspective and enhance their knowledge too.

4.11 Predictive Analysis for Better Assessment Evaluation

As mindset and needs vary from student to student, predictive analysis is a way to understand student using data from the past and present to predict the future of student. From day-to-day task to sub-exams, it will reflect which student will perform better in further exams and which will not.

Prior knowledge of the condition of a student will help teachers and parents to cope up with the condition before it worsens. When few inputs and tweaks are done in predefined model, the best result with higher validity and reliability with low chances of error is formed. As biasness of human can easily be corrected using ML.

4.12 Future Scope

One could plan to purpose a model suggesting only course-related colleges and students at the time of enrollment. A huge number of data from the previous year and the ML model will correlate to make an efficient algorithm. We can prepare a set of questionnaires by the model after each lecture to let students and teachers know if they have learned the concept accurately or not. If not so teacher would devote extra time for that specific problem which will lead to better understanding.

Through recursive clustering technique, one could divide students based on their scores and feedback from teachers. Students in the lower rank cluster are being looked after with their studies and study materials. With the help of ML, schools and colleges could get in touch with these students and decrease the risk as soon as possible. Through cluster method, students are classified based on high, medium, and low, and this segregation will help them in further studies as student retention is very important for school metrics, enrolment, and feedback.

4.13 Conclusion

The main aim of this study is to evaluate the various ML algorithms that are applicable in education area. Individualized educational experience can be achieved by personalized learning which can be achieved by using decision tree algorithm of

ML. Using support vector machine, we can work on student retention that can be easily done using data that are collected by institutions. Human biasness can easily be corrected using ML as it will not have inclinational toward an individual, thus it will be unbiased and rational. We can also use recursive clustering methods to group students on the basis of various earlier, current, and future courses. The correctness of proof to which we can resort can be automatically evaluated using supervised learning. We can use it for student dropout prediction as we will have the upper hand on prediction analysis of student academic performance also text classification to predict students' final course grade and for early detection of low performance. As realization and evolution of every domain takes its time thus our traditional education system and educators will realize the full extent of ML gradually. As they will realize it with its proper use, they can revolutionize education domain thus the minds of nation.

References

1 Kučak, D., Juričić, V., and Đambić, G. (2018). Machine learning in education – a survey of current research trends. *Ann. DAAAM Proc. Int. DAAAM Symp.* 29 (1): 0406–0410. https://doi.org/10.2507/29th.daaam.proceedings.059.

2 Nedeva, V. and Pehlivanova, T. (2021). Students' performance analyses using machine learning algorithms in WEKA. In: *IOP Conference Series: Materials Science and Engineering*, vol. 1031, 012061. IOP Publishing https://doi.org/10.1088/1757-899X/1031/1/012061.

3 Halde, R.R. (2016). Application of machine learning algorithms for betterment in education system. *Stud. Big Data* 19: 161–168. https://doi.org/10.1007/978-3-319-30315-4_14.

4 Mduma, N., Kalegele, K., and Machuve, D. (2019). A Survey of Machine Learning Approaches and Techniques for Student Dropout Prediction, pp. 1–10.

5 Sharma, Y., Pandey, S., and Raheja, R. (2022). Machine learning: assisting modern education. *Int. Res. J. Mod. Eng. Technol. Sci.* 4: 21–29.

6 Sharma, A., Mahapatra, R.P., and Kumar Sharma, V. (2022). An exploration of Fog procedures in comparison with IoT, design, and assessment issues. In: *10th International Conference on Reliability, Infocom Technologies and Optimization (Trends and Future Directions) (ICRITO)*, 1–6. IEEE https://doi.org/10.1109/ICRITO56286.2022.9964742.

7 Iatrellis, O., Savvas, I., Fitsilis, P., and Gerogiannis, V.C. (2021). A two-phase machine learning approach for predicting student outcomes. *Educ. Inf. Technol.* 26 (1): 69–88. https://doi.org/10.1007/s10639-020-10260-x.

8 Sharma, A., Vashishta, A., Shahi, A. et al. (2022). Study of video suggestions based on calendar events. In: *6th International Conference on Intelligent*

Computing and Control Systems (ICICCS), Madurai. https://doi.org/10.1109/ICICCS53718.2022.9788466, 1572–1579. IEEE.

9 Hussain, M., Zhu, W., Zhang, W. et al. (2019). Using machine learning to predict student difficulties from learning session data. *Artif. Intell. Rev.* 52 (1): 381–407. https://doi.org/10.1007/s10462-018-9620-8.

10 Rodríguez-Hernández, C.F., Musso, M., Kyndt, E., and Cascallar, E. (2021). Artificial neural networks in academic performance prediction: systematic implementation and predictor evaluation. *Comput. Educ. Artif. Intell.* 2 (December): https://doi.org/10.1016/j.caeai.2021.100018.

11 Liñán, L.C. and Pérez, Á.A.J. (2015). Educational data mining and learning analytics: differences, similarities, and time evolution. *RUSC Univ. Knowl. Soc. J. 12* (3): 98–112. https://rusc. uoc.edu/rusc/ca/index.php/rusc/article/view/v12n3-calvet-juan/2746.html.

12 Villegas-ch, W. and Palacios-pacheco, X. (2020). Improvement of an online education model with the integration of machine learning and data analysis in an LMS. *Appl. Sci.* 10 (15): 5371.

13 Rashid, J., Batool, S., Kim, J. et al. (2022). An augmented artificial intelligence approach for chronic diseases prediction. *Front. Public Health* 10: 860396.

14 Juneja, A., Juneja, S., Soneja, A., and Jain, S. (2021). Real time object detection using CNN based single shot detector model. *J. Inf. Technol. Manage.* 13 (1): 62–80.

15 Dhiman, G., Juneja, S., Viriyasitavat, W. et al. (2022). A novel machine-learning-based hybrid CNN model for tumor identification in medical image processing. *Sustainability* 14 (3): 1447.

16 Facundo, B., Juan, G., and Fachinotti, V.D. (2017). Prediction of wind pressure coefficients on building surfaces using Artificial Neural Networks. *Energy Build.* 158. https://doi.org/10.1016/j.enbuild.2017.11.045: 1429–1441.

17 Dhilipan, J., Vijayalakshmi, N., Suriya, S., and Christopher, A. (2021). Prediction of students performance using machine learning. *IOP Conf. Ser. Mater. Sci. Eng.* 1055 (1): 012122. https://doi.org/10.1088/1757-899x/1055/1/012122.

18 Saxena, H., Joshi, D., Singh, H., and Anand, R. (2022). Comparison of classification algorithms for Alzheimer's disease prediction. *2022 Seventh International Conference on Parallel, Distributed and Grid Computing (PDGC)*. pp. 687–692. IEEE.

19 Man, I., Ho, K., Cheong, K.Y., and Id, A.W. (2021). Predicting student satisfaction of emergency remote learning in higher education during COVID-19 using machine learning techniques. *PLoS One* 16 (4): e0249423. https://doi.org/10.1371/journal.pone.0249423.

20 Janani, S., Sivarathinabala, M., Anand, R. et al. (2023). Machine learning analysis on predicting credit card forgery. In: *International Conference on Innovative Computing and Communications. ICICC 2023*, Lecture Notes in Networks and

Systems, vol. 537 (ed. A.E. Hassanien, O. Castillo, S. Anand, and A. Jaiswal). Singapore: Springer. https://doi.org/10.1007/978-981-99-3010-4_12.

21 Juneja, S., Juneja, A., Dhiman, G. et al. (2021). An approach for thoracic syndrome classification with convolutional neural networks. *Comput. Math. Methods Med.* 2021: 1–10.

22 Kharb, L. and Singh, P. (2020). Role of machine learning in modern education and teaching. In: *Impact of AI Technologies on Teaching, Learning, and Research in Higher Education*, 99–123. IGI Global https://doi.org/10.4018/978-1-7998-4763-2.ch006.

23 Kaddoura, S., Popescu, D.E., and Hemanth, J.D. (2022). A systematic review on machine learning models for online learning and examination systems. *PeerJ. Comput. Sci.* 8: https://doi.org/10.7717/PEERJ-CS.986.

24 Sharma, S., Gupta, S., Gupta, P. et al. (2022). Deep learning model for the automatic classification of white blood cells. *Comput. Intell. Neurosci. 2022.*

25 Sharma, S., Gupta, S., Gupta, D. et al. (2022). Recognition of gurmukhi handwritten city names using deep learning and cloud computing. *Sci. Prog. 2022*: 1–16.

26 Juneja, S., Juneja, A., Dhiman, G. et al. (2021). Computer vision-enabled character recognition of hand gestures for patients with hearing and speaking disability. *Mobile Inf. Syst. 2021*: 1–10.

27 Dhiman, G., Juneja, S., Mohafez, H. et al. (2022). Federated learning approach to protect healthcare data over big data scenario. *Sustainability 14* (5): 2500.

28 Aggarwal, S., Kannan, R., Ahuja, R. et al. (2022). A convolutional neural network-based framework for classification of protein localization using confocal microscopy images. *IEEE Access 10*: 83591–83611.

29 Sharma, S., Gupta, S., Gupta, D. et al. (2022). Performance evaluation of the deep learning based convolutional neural network approach for the recognition of chest X-ray images. *Front. Oncol.* 12.

30 Sharma, S., Gupta, S., Gupta, D. et al. (2022). Optimized CNN-based recognition of district names of Punjab state in Gurmukhi script. *J. Math. 2022*: 1–10.

31 Dhall, A., Upadhyay, H.K., Juneja, S., and Juneja, A. (2022). Machine learning algorithms for industry using image sensing. In: *Healthcare Solutions Using Machine Learning and Informatics*, 75–97. Auerbach Publications.

32 Aggarwal, S., Gupta, S., Gupta, D. et al. (2023). An artificial intelligence-based stacked ensemble approach for prediction of protein subcellular localization in confocal microscopy images. *Sustainability 15* (2): 1695.

33 Dewani, A., Memon, M.A., Bhatti, S. et al. (2022). Detection of cyberbullying patterns in low-resource colloquial roman urdu microtext using natural language processing, machine learning and ensemble techniques. *Appl. Sci.* 13 (4): 2062; https://doi.org/10.3390/app13042062.

34 Shen, Y.B. and Gadekallu, T.R. (2022). Resource search method of mobile intelligent education system based on distributed hash table. *Mobile Networks Appl.* 27 (3): 1199–1208.

35 Xiang, C.Z., Fu, N.X., and Gadekallu, T.R. (2022). Design of resource matching model of intelligent education system based on machine learning. *EAI Endorsed Trans. Scalable Inf. Syst.* 9 (6): e1–e1.

36 Rajab, K., Hamdi, M., Al Reshan, M.S. et al. (2022). Implementation of virtual training: on the example of the a faculty of computer science during COVID-19 for sustainable development in engineering education. *Electronics* 11 (5): 1–20. https://doi.org/10.3390/electronics11050694.

5

Approaches and Methodologies for Distributed Systems: Threats, Challenges, and Future Directions

Bhawna and Veena Parihar

KIET Group of Institutions, Ghaziabad, Uttar Pradesh, India

5.1 Introduction

In the era of digital transformation, distributed systems (DSs) have become an essential part of our daily lives. They offer the ability to connect and share data, resources, and computational power across multiple devices and locations, providing a flexible and scalable solution for various applications such as cloud computing, big data processing, and the Internet of Things (IoTs). However, the increased connectivity of these systems also brings new security challenges that must be addressed. The security of DSs is threatened by a wide range of attacks [1], including hacking, malware, and denial of service (DoS) attacks. These threats can result in unauthorized access to sensitive information, data theft, and disruption of normal system operations. In addition, the use of wireless communication and the integration of DSs into existing networks introduce new security challenges that must be addressed, such as the risk of eavesdropping and man-in-the-middle (MitM) attacks.

To mitigate these security threats, various access control methods have been proposed and implemented in DSs. These methods, such as role-based access control (RBAC), discretionary access control (DAC), and mandatory access control (MAC), aim to restrict access to sensitive information and resources to authorized users only. Authentication and authorization are also crucial components in

Meta-Heuristic Algorithms for Advanced Distributed Systems, First Edition. Edited by Rohit Anand, Abhinav Juneja, Digvijay Pandey, Sapna Juneja, and Nidhi Sindhwani.

ensuring the security of DSs [2], since they allow for the identification of users and the determination of their access. The collection and transmission of data by DSs also raise concerns about privacy, as personal information may be at risk of being disclosed or misused. To address these concerns, various privacy [3]-enhancing technologies have been proposed, including data encryption, privacy-preserving data mining, and differential privacy.

Despite the efforts to secure distributed [4] systems, security breaches are still a common occurrence. Real-world examples, such as the Target data breach, the WannaCry ransomware attack, and the Equifax data breach, highlight the need for continued efforts to improve the security of these systems.

In this chapter, we will provide a comprehensive overview of the current state of security in DSs. We will examine the various types of security threats that these systems face, the access control methods that can be applied, and the importance of authentication and authorization. We will also discuss the privacy risks associated with the collection and transmission of data by DSs and possible solutions to address these concerns. Finally, we will summarize the key issues and challenges in securing DSs and provide insights into future directions for research and development in this field.

5.2 Distributed Systems

DSs (as shown in Figure 5.1) are a type of computer system that consists [5] of multiple, independent components that work together to perform a common task. These components are typically connected through a network, and they communicate and coordinate their actions to achieve a shared goal. DSs are

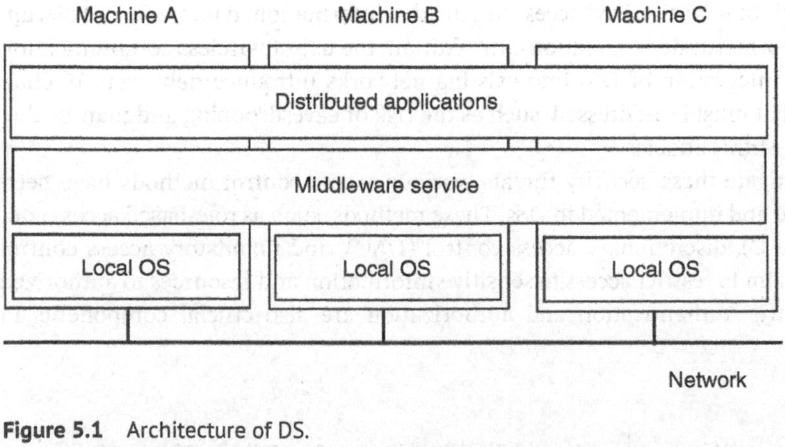

Figure 5.1 Architecture of DS.

designed to be scalable, fault-tolerant, and highly available, and they are used in a wide range of applications, including data centers, cloud computing, and the IoTs [6].

In a DS, each component can operate independently and can also be connected to other components in different geographic locations. The system is designed to work as a single entity, but it can also function even if some of its components fail. A DS's components are linked through a network, allowing for communication and data sharing [7]. This network can be local, such as a local area network (LAN), or it can be global, such as the Internet.

A DS's architecture is intricate and necessitates careful consideration of many different aspects, such as communication protocols, security, and data management. The selection of suitable algorithms and protocols for communication and coordination amongst the components is crucial to ensuring the performance and dependability of the system. In order to defend against harmful attacks like hacking, malware, and DoS attacks, the system must also be secure.

One of the major challenges in designing and managing a DS is ensuring the consistency of the data stored in its components [8]. In order to maintain consistency, the system must implement appropriate protocols for data synchronization and conflict resolution. Additionally, the system must be designed to handle failures and to continue to operate even if some of its components are unavailable.

5.3 Literature Review

Wide-ranging connections between digital and physical "things" are made possible by the IoT. Nevertheless, "big data" problems including enormous data volumes, data redundancy, a lack of scalability, and other concerns are brought on by the streaming data from IoT devices. Monitoring IoT systems under huge data conditions becomes difficult. Additionally, IoT security threats from cyberattacks are challenging to find. An online distributed IoT security monitoring technique was proposed by F. Li et al. (offender data information system [ODIS]) [9]. The suggested ODIS algorithm showed promising performance in terms of monitoring and detection.

Critical problems with straggler effects and communication burden plague distributed computing. In particular, communication overheads are greatly increased since computing nodes must share intermediate results with one another in order to calculate the ultimate result. J. S. Ng et al. [10] employed coded distributed computing (CDC), which combines distributed computing and coding theoretic methods, to overcome these problems. The authors of this survey began by outlining the foundations of CDC before moving on to basic CDC strategies. Then, they examine and evaluate several CDC strategies put forth to save communication costs, lessen straggler impacts, and ensure privacy and security.

When using machine learning algorithms for large-scale systems, over-fitting is a common problem that J. Shi et al. [11] suggested distributed intrusion detection technique that avoids. To start, a distributed state estimation technique is used in each area to estimate the state of the entire system. Following that the trained neural network input for each local area is used to detect the covert false data injection (FDI) attacks. The suggested method not only lowers the risk of over-fitting but also can identify the attacked areas, according to simulation findings on the Institute of Electrical and Electronics Engineers (IEEE) 118-bus system.

Cyber-physical systems (CPSs) [2] have received a lot of interest recently because of the wide range of possible uses they may have. However, due to their heavy reliance on communication networks, CPSs are exposed to deliberate cyber-attacks [12]. As a result, numerous attack detection techniques have been suggested to ensure the security of CPSs. Multiple bogus data injection attack detection methods for CPSs were explored and assessed by S. Tan et al. [13].

A comparative analysis of DSs and the security challenges relating to those systems was offered by M. Firdhous [14]. Four widely used DSs were taken into consideration for a thorough investigation of the technologies utilized, the security challenges they encountered, and the solutions suggested to get around those issues.

5.4 Threats to Distributed Systems Security

DSs are susceptible to many different types of security risks, such as:

5.4.1 Hacking

Unauthorized access to a DS or one of its components is referred to as hacking. Hackers can gain access to a system through a variety of methods, such as exploiting vulnerabilities in software, using weak passwords, or social engineering tactics [15]. Once inside a system, hackers can steal sensitive information, disrupt operations, or even take control of the system.

5.4.2 Malware

Malware is a term used to describe any software that is designed to damage a computer system [3, 16]. This can include viruses, worms, and Trojan horses. In a DS, malware can spread quickly from one component to another, causing widespread damage.

5.4.3 Denial of Service (DoS) Attacks

A DoS attack aims to prevent the targeted users from accessing a system or network. This might be accomplished by flooding the system with traffic or by focusing on its crucial components. DSs are particularly vulnerable to DoS attacks because they often rely on communication between multiple components, and a disruption in one component can have a cascading effect on the entire system [17].

5.4.4 Man-in-the-Middle (MitM) Attacks

When an attacker eavesdrops on a conversation between two participants, MitM attacks happen. When an attacker intercepts communication between various system components of a DS, they are able to steal sensitive data or interfere with operations [18].

5.4.5 Advanced Persistent Threats (APTs)

Advanced Persistent Threats (APTs) are sophisticated hacking attacks that are typically launched by nation-states or other powerful actors. These attacks are designed to infiltrate a system and remain undetected for long periods of time, allowing the attacker to steal sensitive information or disrupt operations [19–21].

5.4.6 Insider Threats

Insider threats are security breaches that occur when an individual with authorized access to a system uses that access to cause harm. Insider threats can include employees or contractors who steal sensitive information, disrupt operations, or sabotage the system.

5.4.7 Phishing

Phishing is a type of social engineering attack where targets are persuaded to divulge personal information or click on a malicious link through email, text messaging, or other means of communication. Phishing can be used to fool staff members or other authorized users into giving access to a DS [22].

5.4.8 Ransomware

A form of virus known as ransomware encrypts files on a computer and demands money in return for the decryption key. Ransomware can be used to encrypt files on numerous systems in a DS, causing extensive damage.

It's critical to remember that this is not a complete list of all security risks that DSs encounter. Additionally, it's critical to keep in mind that new dangers are continually developing and growing in terms of their nature. To protect a DS from these and other types of security threats, it's essential to implement robust security measures and to stay vigilant against new and emerging threats

5.5 Security Standards and Protocols

There are several security standards and protocols that have been proposed and adopted by industry groups and government organizations to secure DSs. Some of the most widely used include:

5.5.1 ISO/IEC 27001

The International Organization for Standardization (ISO) produced this standard to provide a foundation for an information security management system. It addresses the best practices for handling sensitive data and aids businesses in preserving the privacy, accuracy, and accessibility of their information assets [23, 24].

5.5.2 NIST SP 800-53

The National Institute of Standards and Technology (NIST) produced this standard, which offers a thorough set of security measures for government information systems [24]. Access control, incident response, and security management are just a few of the many security-related subjects it addresses.

5.5.3 SOC 2

The American Institute of Certified Public Accountants (AICPAs) produced this standard, which offers a framework for evaluating the security, accessibility, processing integrity, confidentiality, and privacy of a service organization's system. Many cloud service providers and businesses that offer cloud-based services have adopted this standard.

5.5.4 PCI DSS

This standard offers a framework for protecting payment card data and was created by the Payment Card Industry Security Standards Council (PCI SSC) [25]. Access control, incident response, and encryption are just a few of the many security-related subjects it addresses.

5.5.5 IEC 62443

This standard, developed by the International Electrotechnical Commission (IEC), provides a framework for securing ICSs. It covers best practices for the management of sensitive information and helps organizations to ensure the confidentiality, integrity, and availability of their ICS [26].

5.5.6 OWASP

The top ten web application security vulnerabilities are compiled and updated by the nonprofit Open Web Application Security Project (OWASP). Organizations frequently use this list as a reference for securing their online applications because it is frequently updated to reflect the most recent threats and vulnerabilities [27].

5.5.7 Control Objectives for Information and Related Technologies (COBIT)

This standard, developed by the ISACA (Information Systems Audit and Control Association), provides a framework for the governance and management of enterprise IT [28]. It covers best practices for the management of sensitive information and helps organizations to ensure the confidentiality, integrity, and availability of their IT systems.

These are some of the major standards and protocols that have been developed to secure DSs. It's important to note that these standards and protocols are constantly evolving, and new standards and protocols are constantly emerging. Organizations should stay informed about the latest standards and protocols and implement them as appropriate to ensure the security of their DSs.

5.6 Network Security

DSs pose several security challenges, which can make it difficult to secure the systems and protect them from attacks [15]. Some of the key security challenges of DSs include:

- *Wireless communication*: Wireless communication is widely used in DSs, but it also presents security risks. Wireless communication is vulnerable to various types of attacks, such as MitM attacks, eavesdropping, and denial-of-service attacks.
- *Integration with existing networks:* DSs must often be integrated with existing networks, which can create additional security risks. Integrating a new system with an existing network can increase the attack surface, making it easier for attackers to find vulnerabilities and exploit them.

- *Lack of centralized control:* DSs lack a central point of control, which can make it difficult to enforce security policies and implement security measures. In a DS, security measures must be implemented at each node, making it challenging to manage security consistently across the entire system.
- *Scalability and performance:* DSs are designed to scale to handle large amounts of data and users. However, this scalability can create security challenges, as the larger the system, the more difficult it is to secure. The security measures must be designed to maintain performance and scalability, even as the system grows.
- *Node heterogeneity:* DSs are often composed of nodes with different hardware, software, and operating systems, which can create security challenges. The heterogeneity of the nodes can make it difficult to implement consistent security measures and manage security across the system.
- *Lack of trust:* In a DS, nodes may not trust each other, which can create security risks. The lack of trust can lead to security breaches, as nodes may not authenticate each other properly, leading to unauthorized access to sensitive data.

These are some of the major security challenges that DSs face. Organizations must be aware of these challenges and implement appropriate security measures to protect their systems and the sensitive data they store and process.

5.7 Access Control

Discuss the various access control methods such as RBAC, DAC, and MAC that can be applied to DSs.

Access control is a crucial component of security in DSs, and various access control methods can be applied to secure these systems. Some of the most commonly used access control methods in DSs include:

5.7.1 Role-based Access Control (RBAC)

RBAC (see Figure 5.2) is a popular access control method that assigns permissions to roles rather than individual users [29, 30].

In RBAC, users are assigned to roles based on their job responsibilities, and the roles are given specific permissions [31]. This method is useful in large organizations, where many users have similar access requirements.

5.7.2 Discretionary Access Control (DAC)

DAC (as shown in Figure 5.3) is a flexible access control method that gives users the discretion to decide who has access to the resources they own [32].

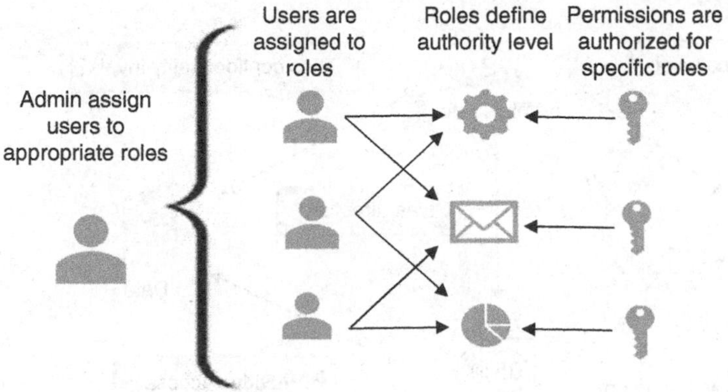

Figure 5.2 Role-based access control.

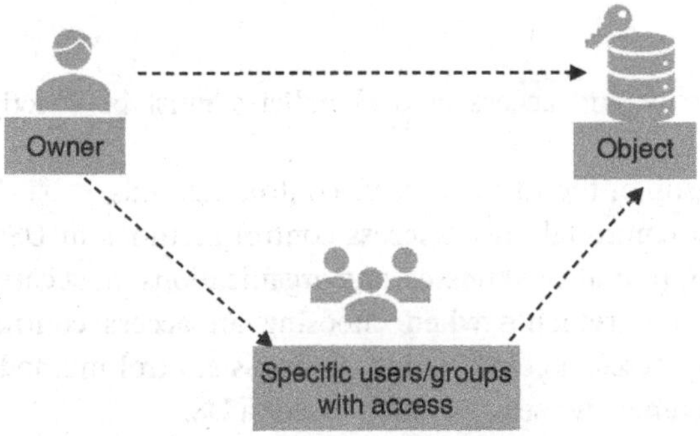

Figure 5.3 Discretionary access control (DAC).

In DAC, the owner of a resource can grant or revoke access to the resource as they see fit. This method is useful in environments where users have control over the resources they own and need to have the ability to control access to these resources.

5.7.3 Mandatory Access Control (MAC)

MAC (as shown in Figure 5.4) is a rigid access control method that enforces a strict set of security policies based on the security level of the resources and the security clearance of the users [31, 32].

In MAC, access is granted or denied based on the security level of the resource and the security clearance of the user. This method is useful in environments

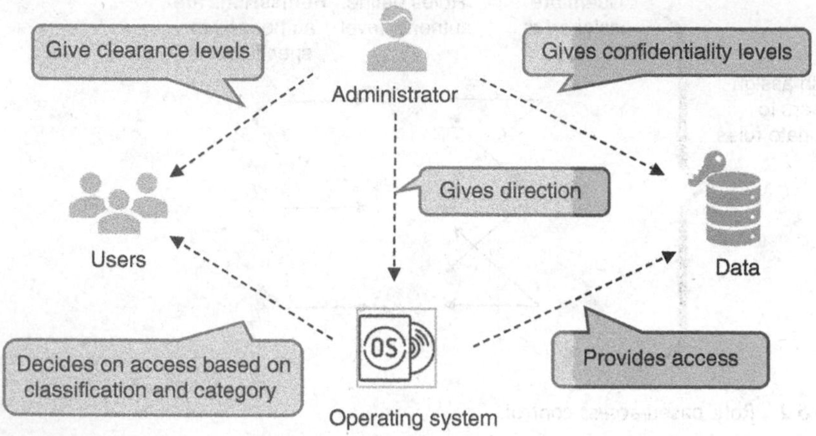

Figure 5.4 Mandatory access control (MAC).

where security is a high priority and access control policies must be strictly enforced.

Table 5.1 shows the comparison of the various access control methods.

These are some of the most commonly used access control methods in DSs. Each method has its own strengths and weaknesses, and organizations must carefully consider their security requirements when choosing an access control method for their DSs. In many cases, a combination of access control methods may be used to provide a comprehensive security solution for a DS.

5.8 Authentication and Authorization

Authentication and authorization are two critical components of security in DSs. These two processes help ensure that only authorized users have access to sensitive resources and data in the system.

Authentication refers to the process of verifying the identity of a user or device in a DS. This can be done using a variety of techniques such as passwords, digital certificates, biometrics, and others. The goal of authentication is to confirm that the user or device trying to access the system is indeed who they claim to be.

Authorization refers to the process of determining what resources and data a user or device is allowed to access in a DS. Once a user or device has been authenticated, authorization is used to determine the level of access that the user or device is granted. This can include access to specific files, applications, data, and other resources in the system.

Table 5.1 Comparative table of access control methods.

Access control method	Description	Advantages	Disadvantages
Role-based access control (RBAC)	Used for managing user access to one or more systems	• The simplicity of updating the security policy contributes to the model's ease of administration, which also includes the benefits of the DAC and MAC models • The fact that this model is built on the concepts of constraints and inheritance makes it applicable in complicated and scattered regions	• It is impossible to articulate the norms without knowing the context, and the line between the role and group concepts is hazy. It is also difficult to express prohibitions, recommendations, or responsibilities
Discretionary access control (DAC)	Least restrictive model	• Flexible; utilized in settings where information sharing is more important than protection	• Costly to update the security policy; prone to Trojans and channel conversion; unable to communicate prohibitions, suggestions, or obligations
Mandatory access control (MAC)	Most restrictive model	• Rigid; distinguishes between users and subjects; developed in a setting where user hierarchy is more significant than information sharing	• Costly to update the security policy, vulnerable to channel changes, unable to allow information to move between levels, and unable to express prohibitions, recommendations, or duties

DSs need both authentication and authorization because they help prevent unauthorized access to sensitive resources and data. By verifying the identity of users and devices and limiting access to only those who have been granted permission, organizations can reduce the risk of security breaches and protect their critical information.

In addition, authentication and authorization are important for regulatory compliance. Many regulations, such as Health Insurance Portability and Accountability Act (HIPAA) and PCI Distributed Storage System (DSS), require organizations to implement strong authentication and authorization controls to protect sensitive information.

In conclusion, authentication and authorization are essential components of security in DSs and play a critical role in ensuring that sensitive resources and data are protected from unauthorized access.

5.9 Privacy Concerns

The collection and transmission of data by DSs raise serious privacy concerns for individuals and organizations. The nature of DSs, which often involve the sharing of data across multiple devices and networks, increases the risk of unauthorized access, theft, and misuse of personal information.

- One of the biggest privacy risks in DSs is the unauthorized collection and storage of personal data. This can occur when organizations collect data for one purpose, but then use or share it for another purpose without the individual's consent. For instance, a health monitoring device might gather private data about a person's health and send it to the maker for examination, but the maker might subsequently use this data for marketing.
- Another privacy risk is the transmission of personal data over public networks. When data is transmitted over public networks, it can be intercepted by unauthorized parties and used for malicious purposes. This risk is particularly high in wireless networks, where data can be intercepted without the user's knowledge.
- In addition, the use of cloud-based storage and computing can also pose privacy risks. When organizations store personal data in the cloud, they are often relying on third-party providers to secure that data. If the provider experiences a security breach, the data can be compromised.

To address these privacy concerns, it is important for organizations to implement privacy-by-design principles in the design and development of DSs. This can involve incorporating privacy-enhancing technologies, such as encryption [33], into the system and ensuring that privacy policies are in place to govern the collection, storage, and transmission of personal data.

In order to monitor and trace access to personal data, organizations should also build robust access restrictions and audit trails. This can help prevent unauthorized access and ensure that personal data is only used for its intended purpose.

In conclusion, the collection and transmission of data by DSs pose significant privacy risks to individuals and organizations. To address these concerns, organizations should implement privacy-by-design principles, use privacy-enhancing technologies, and implement strong access controls and audit trails.

5.10 Case Studies

DSs have become a critical component of modern society, powering everything from online banking to connected medical devices. Unfortunately, these systems are also vulnerable to security breaches that can result in the theft of sensitive information and disruption of critical services.

Here are a few real-world examples of security breaches in DSs:

5.10.1 Equifax Data Breach

One of the biggest credit reporting companies, Equifax, experienced a data breach in 2017 that exposed the personal and financial data of 143 million people. A flaw in Equifax's website software allowed hackers to access private data kept in the company's systems, which led to the breach.

5.10.2 Target Data Breach

In 2013, a data breach at the major retail company Target revealed the credit card details of 40 million consumers. Malware that was planted on Target's point-of-sale systems led to the breach, which made it possible for hackers to take credit card data while it was being processed.

5.10.3 WannaCry Ransomware Attack

In 2017, the WannaCry ransomware attack affected more than 200 000 computers in 150 countries. The attack was carried out through a worm that spread rapidly through unpatched computers running Microsoft Windows.

These examples highlight the importance of implementing strong security measures in DSs. To prevent similar incidents in the future, organizations can implement the following best practices:

- *Keep software up-to-date:* Regularly updating software is one of the most effective ways to prevent security breaches. Known vulnerabilities are frequently addressed by security patches included in software upgrades.
- *Implement strong access controls:* Access controls, such as password protection and two-factor authentication, can help prevent unauthorized access to sensitive information.
- *Monitor networks and systems:* Network and system monitoring on a regular basis can speed up the detection and response of security events for enterprises.
- *Educate employees:* Employees can be a weak link in the security chain, so it's important to educate them about the importance of security and best practices for keeping sensitive information safe.

- *Conduct regular security assessments*: Regular security assessments can help organizations identify potential security vulnerabilities and implement measures to address them.

Security breaches in DSs can have serious consequences for individuals and organizations. To prevent similar incidents in the future, organizations should implement strong security measures and regularly assess and update their security posture.

5.11 Conclusion

DSs, which are becoming increasingly prevalent in modern society, pose unique security challenges due to their decentralized and interconnected nature. Some of the key issues and challenges in securing DSs include:

- *Complexity:* DSs are often complex, making it difficult to identify and address security vulnerabilities.
- *Interoperability:* DSs often rely on multiple components and technologies, making it difficult to ensure that they all work together securely.
- *Wireless communication:* DSs often use wireless communication, which can be more vulnerable to attack than wired communication.
- *Data privacy:* DSs often collect and transmit sensitive information, raising concerns about privacy.
- *Integration with existing networks:* DSs must often be integrated into existing networks, which can introduce security risks.

To address these challenges, future research and development in the field of DSs security will likely focus on:

- *Improved security protocols:* Researchers are working to develop more secure and efficient protocols for DSs.
- *Better access control:* Researchers are exploring ways to improve access control in DSs, including the use of biometrics and blockchain technology [34].
- *Enhanced data privacy:* Researchers are developing new techniques to protect the privacy of data collected and transmitted by DSs.
- *Robust security testing:* Researchers are exploring ways to more effectively test the security of DSs, including the use of artificial intelligence and machine learning.
- *Integrating security into the design process:* Researchers are working to integrate security considerations into the design process for DSs so that security is built in from the start.

Securing DSs will continue to be a major challenge for the foreseeable future. However, by focusing on these key issues and challenges and leveraging advances in technology, researchers and practitioners can work to make DSs more secure and trustworthy.

5.12 Future Scope

The future scope of research in the area of security issues in DSs is very promising and holds great potential for advancements in this field. With the increasing integration of DSs in various sectors, including healthcare, finance, transportation, and many others, the importance of ensuring the security of these systems is paramount. The current landscape of security solutions for DSs is far from perfect and still has many areas for improvement.

In the coming years, researchers are expected to focus on developing more advanced and efficient security solutions that cater to the unique requirements of different types of DSs. Some of the key areas that are likely to see significant progress include:

- The development of more secure protocols and standards for DSs, especially those that use wireless communication.
- The integration of artificial intelligence and machine learning algorithms in security solutions to make them more effective and efficient.
- The development of privacy-preserving solutions that can prevent the unauthorized collection and transmission of data.
- The exploration of new and innovative security solutions that can cater to the unique requirements of different types of DSs.
- The development of secure solutions for the integration of DSs with existing networks and infrastructure.

The future of research in the area of security issues in DSs is very promising and holds great potential for advancements in this field [35]. The current landscape of security solutions for DSs still has many areas for improvement, and researchers are expected to focus on developing more advanced and efficient solutions in the coming years.

References

1 Kada, B., Khalid, M., and Shaikh, M.S. (2020). Distributed cooperative control of autonomous multi-agent UAV systems using smooth control. *J. Syst. Eng. Electron.* 31 (6): 1297–1307. https://doi.org/10.23919/JSEE.2020.000100.

2 Ding, D., Han, Q.-L., Wang, Z., and Ge, X. (2021). Recursive filtering of distributed cyber-physical systems with attack detection. *IEEE Trans. Syst. Man Cybern.: Syst.* 51 (10): 6466–6476. https://doi.org/10.1109/TSMC.2019.2960541.

3 Anand, R., Juneja, S., Juneja, A., Jain, V., and Kannan, R. (eds.) (2023). *Integration of IoT with Cloud Computing for Smart Applications*. CRC Press. https://doi.org/10.1080/03772063.2022.2038288.

4 Wang, L., Zhou, Q., Xiong, Z. et al. (2022). Security constrained decentralized peer-to-peer transactive energy trading in distribution systems. *CSEE J. Power Energy Syst* 8 (1): 188–197. https://doi.org/10.17775/CSEEJPES.2020.06560.

5 Deng, C., Wang, Y., Wen, C. et al. (2021). Distributed resilient control for energy storage systems in cyber–physical microgrids. *IEEE Trans. Ind. Inf.* 17 (2): 1331–1341. https://doi.org/10.1109/TII.2020.2981549.

6 Juneja, S., Dhiman, G., Kautish, S. et al. (2021). A perspective roadmap for IoMT-based early detection and care of the neural disorder, dementia. *J. Healthc. Eng.* 2021: 6712424. https://doi.org/10.1155/2021/6712424.

7 Song, A., Chen, W.-N., Gu, T. et al. (2021). Distributed virtual network embedding system with historical archives and set-based particle swarm optimization. *IEEE Trans. Syst. Man Cybern.: Syst.* 51 (2): 927–942. https://doi.org/10.1109/TSMC.2018.2884523.

8 Zhang, Y., He, D., Obaidat, M.S. et al. (2021). Efficient identity-based distributed decryption scheme for electronic personal health record sharing system. *IEEE J. Sel. Areas Commun.* 39 (2): 384–395. https://doi.org/10.1109/JSAC.2020.3020656.

9 Li, F., Xie, R., Wang, Z. et al. (2020). Online distributed IoT security monitoring with multidimensional streaming big data. *IEEE Internet Things J.* 7 (5): 4387–4394. https://doi.org/10.1109/JIOT.2019.2962788.

10 Ng, J.S., Lim, W.Y.B., Luong, N.C. et al. (2021). A comprehensive survey on coded distributed computing: fundamentals, challenges, and networking applications. *IEEE Commun. Surv. Tutor.* 23 (3): 1800–1837. https://doi.org/10.1109/COMST.2021.3091684.

11 Shi, J., Liu, S., Chen, B., and Yu, L. (2021). Distributed data-driven intrusion detection for sparse stealthy FDI attacks in smart grids. *IEEE Trans. Circuits Syst. II Express Briefs* 68 (3): 993–997. https://doi.org/10.1109/TCSII.2020.3020139.

12 Zhou, Q., Shahidehpour, M., Alabdulwahab, A., and Abusorrah, A. (2020). A cyber-attack resilient distributed control strategy in islanded microgrids. *IEEE Trans. Smart Grid* 11 (5): 3690–3701. https://doi.org/10.1109/TSG.2020.2979160.

13 Tan, S., Guerrero, J.M., Xie, P. et al. (2020). Brief survey on attack detection methods for cyber-physical systems. *IEEE Syst. J.* 14 (4): 5329–5339. https://doi.org/10.1109/JSYST.2020.2991258.

14 Firdhous, M. (2011). Implementation of security in distributed systems – a comparative study. *Int. J. Comput. Inf. Syst.* 2 (2): https://doi.org/10.48550/arXiv.1211.2032.

15 Bhagwath, S. and Mallikarjun Math, D. (2016). Distributed systems and recent innovations: challenges benefits and security issues in distributed systems. *Bonfring Int. J. Softw. Eng. Soft Comput.* 6 (Special Issue): 37–42. https://doi.org/10.9756/bijsesc.8239.

16 Singamaneni, K. K., Dhiman, G., Junejaet, S. et al. (2022). A novel QKD approach to enhance IIOT privacy and computational knacks. *Sensors* 22 (18) (2022): 6741. https://doi.org/10.1080/03772063.2022.2043788.

17 Juneja, S., Juneja, A., Bali, V., and Upadhyay, H. (2021). 9 Cyber Security. *Industry 4.0, AI, and Data Science: Research Trends and Challenges*, 135. https://doi.org/10.1080/03772063.2021.1982418.

18 Dhiman, G., Juneja, S., Mohafez, H. et al. (2022). Federated learning approach to protect healthcare data over big data scenario. *Sustainability* 14 (5): 2500.

19 Mittal, S., Bansal, A., Gupta, D. et al. (2022). Using identity-based cryptography as a foundation for an effective and secure cloud model for e-health. *Comput. Intell. Neurosci.* 2022: 7016554. https://doi.org/10.1155/2022/7016554.

20 Uppal, M., Gupta, D., Juneja, S. et al. (2022). Cloud-based fault prediction for real-time monitoring of sensor data in hospital environment using machine learning. *Sustainability* 14 (18): 11667.

21 Juneja, A., Juneja, S., Bali, V. et al. (2021). Artificial intelligence and cybersecurity: current trends and future prospects. In: *The Smart Cyber Ecosystem for Sustainable Development*, 431–441. https://doi.org/10.1002/9781119761655.ch22.

22 Juneja, S., Juneja, A., and Anand, R. (2019). Reliability modeling for embedded system environment compared to available software reliability growth models. In: *2019 International Conference on Automation, Computational and Technology Management (ICACTM)*, pp. 379–382. IEEE.

23 Guo, H., Wei, M., Huang, P., and Chekole, E.G. (2021). Enhance enterprise security through implementing ISO/IEC 27001 standard. In: *2021 IEEE International Conference on Service Operations and Logistics, and Informatics (SOLI)*, pp. 1–6. Singapore. https://doi.org/10.1109/SOLI54607.2021.9672401.

24 Roy, P.P. (2020). A high-level comparison between the NIST cyber security framework and the ISO 27001 information security standard. In: *2020 National Conference on Emerging Trends on Sustainable Technology and Engineering Applications (NCETSTEA)*, pp. 1–3. Durgapur, India. https://doi.org/10.1109/NCETSTEA48365.2020.9119914.

25 Liu, J., Xiao, Y., Chen, H. et al. (2010). A survey of payment card industry data security standard. *IEEE Commun. Surv. Tutor.* 12 (3): 287–303. https://doi.org/10.1109/SURV.2010.031810.00083.

26 Tanveer, A., Sinha, R., and Kuo, M.M.Y. (2021). Secure links: secure-by-design communications in IEC 61499 industrial control applications. *IEEE Trans. Ind. Informatics* 17 (6): 3992–4002. https://doi.org/10.1109/TII.2020.3009133.

27 Kiruba, B., Saravanan, V., Vasanth, T., and Yogeshwar, B.K. (2022). OWASP attack prevention. In: *2022 3rd International Conference on Electronics and Sustainable Communication Systems (ICESC)*, pp. 1671–1675. Coimbatore, India. https://doi.org/10.1109/ICESC54411.2022.9885691.

28 Yasin, M., Akhmad Arman, A., Edward, I.J.M., and Shalannanda, W. (2020). Designing Information Security Governance Recommendations and Roadmap Using COBIT 2019 Framework and ISO 27001:2013 (Case Study Ditreskrimsus Polda XYZ). In: *2020 14th International Conference on Telecommunication Systems, Services, and Applications*, TSSA, Bandung, Indonesia, 2020, pp. 1–5. https://doi.org/10.1109/TSSA51342.2020.9310875.

29 Bacon, J. and Moody, K. (2006). Access control in distributed systems. https://doi.org/10.1007/0-387-21821-1_4.

30 Nazerian, F., Motameni, H., and Nematzadeh, H. (2019). Emergency role-based access control (E-RBAC) and analysis of model specifications with alloy. *J. Inf. Secur. Appl.* 45: 131–142. https://doi.org/10.1016/j.jisa.2019.01.008.

31 Delessy, N., Fernández, E., Petrie, L. et al. (2007). Patterns for access control in distributed systems, 3. https://doi.org/10.1145/1772070.1772074.

32 Kashmar, N., Adda, M., and Atieh, M. (2019). From access control models to access control metamodels: a survey. In: *Proceedings of the 14th Conference on Pattern Languages of Programs*, Lecture Notes in Networks and Systems, 892–911. New York: ACM https://doi.org/10.1007/978-3-030-12385-7_61.

33 Kautish, S., Juneja, S., Mohiuddin, K. et al. (2023). Enhanced cloud storage encryption standard for security in distributed environments. *Electronics* 12 (3): 714.

34 Singh, S., Hosen, A.S.M.S., and Yoon, B. (2021). Blockchain security attacks, challenges, and solutions for the future distributed IoT network. *IEEE Access* 9: 13938–13959. https://doi.org/10.1109/ACCESS.2021.3051602.

35 Uppal, M., Gupta, D., Juneja, S. et al. (2021). Cloud-based fault prediction using IoT in office automation for improvisation of health of employees. *J. Healthcare Eng.* 2021: 8106467. https://doi.org/10.1155/2021/8106467.

6

Efficient-driven Approaches Related to Meta-Heuristic Algorithms using Machine Learning Techniques

Ashima Arya, Swasti Singhal, and Rashika Bangroo

Department of Computer Science and Information Technology, KIET Group of Institutions, Ghaziabad, Uttar Pradesh, India

6.1 Introduction

The optimization approach is a vital tool that may be used to acquire the design parameters that are sought as well as the optimal operating circumstances. This would provide direction for the experimental effort and lessen the risks as well as the costs associated with designing and managing the system. Optimization is the process of identifying the values of the decision variables that produce the highest or lowest value of one or more desired outcomes. The design of objective functions and the optimization approach that is chosen both have a role in determining the reliability of optimal solutions. For optimization, a mathematical model is required that both describes and analyses the behavior of the mechanism. When dealing with complicated nonlinear systems, optimization search may be able to assist in the estimation of unknown parameters. In dynamic processes, robust optimization might be used to find the uncertainty variables. The approach of scale-up and the design of multiphase reactors and flow systems might both benefit from the application of optimization as a tool. Manufacturing and engineering activities will not have the same level of efficiency that they do right now if the designs and operations are not optimized [1].

Figure 6.1 shows the various types of optimization approaches.

Meta-Heuristic Algorithms for Advanced Distributed Systems, First Edition. Edited by Rohit Anand, Abhinav Juneja, Digvijay Pandey, Sapna Juneja, and Nidhi Sindhwani.

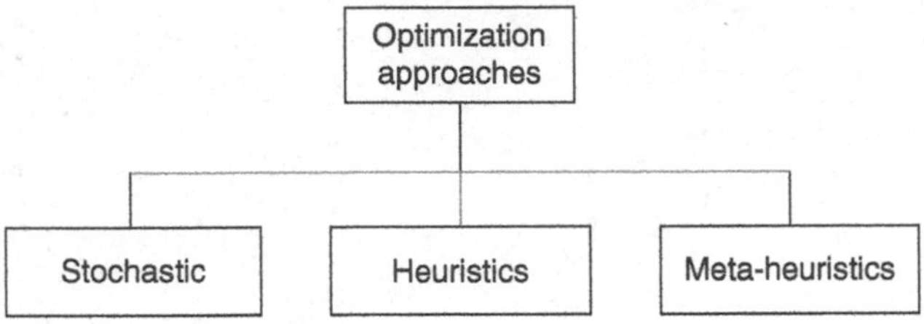

Figure 6.1 Types of optimization approaches.

6.2 Stochastic Optimization

Stochastic optimization techniques are those that create random variables and use them in their optimization processes. When an optimization problem is phrased stochastically, it may incorporate random objective functions or random constraints. This is how the random variables are introduced into the problem. Stochastic optimization approaches also involve random iteration techniques as one of their component parts. Some strategies for stochastic optimization integrate the two definitions of stochastic optimization by employing random iterates as a means of addressing stochastic concerns. The application of stochastic optimization techniques can generalize the use of deterministic approaches for determining solutions to deterministic issues.

Stochastic optimization is a method that can assist in either the maximization or minimization of objective functions when stochastic difficulties are taken into consideration. Throughout the course of the last several decades, it has been claimed that these methodologies are essential tools for the fields of engineering, business, computer science, and statistics. Particularly, these methods may be applied in a wide variety of different domains. Approaches to stochastic optimization often categorize issues based on one of two contexts: the objective functions (also known as cost functions), or the limitations. Using stochastic optimization methodologies, one may find solutions to a wide variety of statistical problems [2].

There are a number of different stochastic optimization algorithms (as shown in Figure 6.2). Some of them are as follows, provided for the experience:

The use of simulated annealing as a method for improving model parameters is becoming more widespread. The physical annealing process underpins the use of this approach. The process of heating a material to its annealing temperature and then allowing it to cool slowly in order to obtain the desired crystal structure is referred to as physical annealing. The purpose of simulated annealing is to replicate the results of genuine annealing so that parameters may be optimized.

The optimization problem-solving strategy known as simulated annealing may be used to find optimal solutions for both unconstrained and bound-constrained

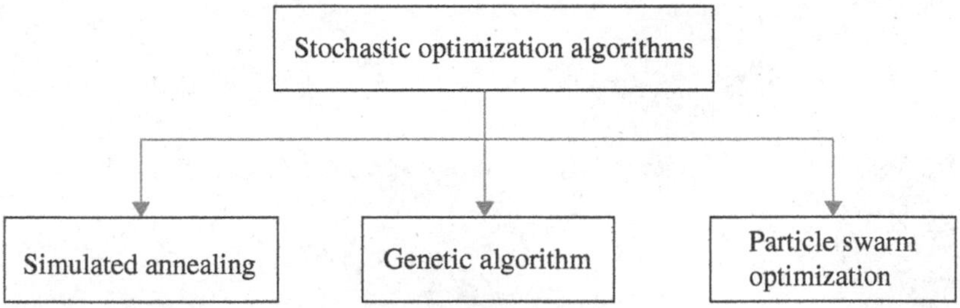

Figure 6.2 Types of stochastic optimization approaches.

problems. The method of simulated annealing creates a new point at random after each iteration of the procedure. A temperature-proportional probability distribution calculates the distance between the new location and the old point and the search region. At a specified pace, the algorithm will accept additional points that move the target closer to zero and further away from zero. When an algorithm is given the ability to accept points that increase the aim, it is able to explore worldwide for a greater number of alternative solutions rather than being trapped in the local minimum.

6.2.1 Genetic Algorithm

Genetic algorithms (GAs), which are adaptive heuristic search algorithms, make up the great bulk of evolutionary algorithms (EAs). Natural selection and genetics serve as the foundation for GAs. To focus the search on areas of the solution space that have better performance, these novel applications of random search are supported by historical data. They are frequently utilized to produce practical solutions to issues relating to search and optimization. The Traveling Salesman Problem, the Knapsack Problem, and the Multi-processor Work Scheduling Problem have all been solved by the GA, surpassing more traditional optimization techniques. To have a better understanding of the GA, let's begin by being acquainted with certain fundamental terminology, which includes the following phrases:

Population: Population is a subset of all potential or likely answers that can address the issue at hand.

Chromosomes: Genes come together to form a chromosome, which is one of the population's answers to the situation at hand.

Gene: A chromosome is divided into various genes, or it is a chromosomal component.

Allele: An allele is a value given to a gene located on a specific chromosome.

Determine the individual's degree of fitness in relation to the population using the fitness function. It refers to a person's capacity for conflict with others. Individuals are assessed based on their fitness function during each iteration.

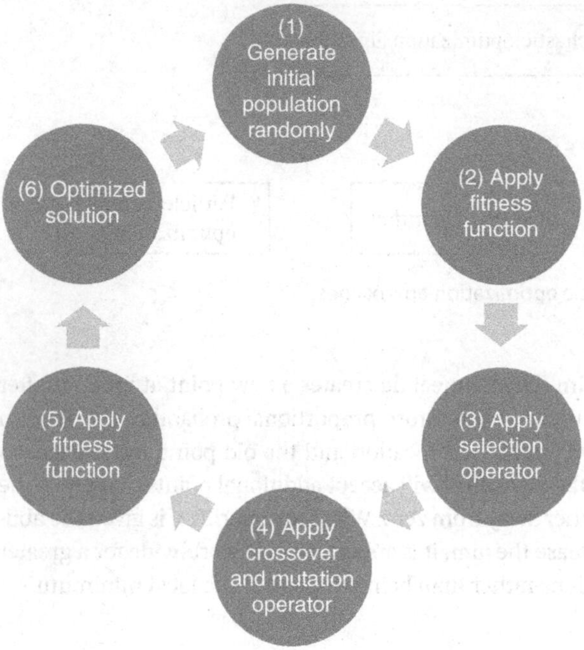

Figure 6.3 Steps of genetic algorithm.

The steps to implement GAs are (Figure 6.3) as follows:

1) Generate initial population
2) Apply fitness function
3) Apply mutation and crossover operators
4) Calculate fitness using fitness function
5) Terminating condition

6.2.2 Particle Swarm Optimization

One of the bio-inspired algorithms, particle swarm optimization (PSO), searches the problem space in a straightforward manner for the best answer. It differs from standard optimization techniques because it simply requires the objective function and does not involve the gradient or any differential form of the fitness function. The best solution found by the flock while simulating a flock of birds is also the best solution in the space, thus making it possible to suppose that each bird is assisting in our search for the perfect answer in a high-dimensional problem space. This is a heuristic approach because we can never be certain that the genuine global optimal solution can be found – and generally, it isn't. Nonetheless, the PSO solution is typically very close to the overall ideal [3, 4].

- This technique is based on how swarms move and function.
- Social interaction is only the optimum solution to resolve a conflict.
- It uses a swarm of particulate, also known as agents, that move about the search space in an effort to find the most appropriate response.
- In order to find the positional coordinates, the algorithm finds "pbest" value which gives the best solution that member of the swarm has created so far.
- The PSO maintains a record of yet another best value, which it refers to as the "gbest" or "global best." To this day, no other adjacent particle has been able to establish a value that is higher than this one.

6.3 Heuristic Search

A heuristic is a strategy for solving a problem more quickly than traditional approaches, or for finding an approximate answer in situations when traditional methods are unable to do so. This might be seen as a form of shortcut, given that we often sacrifice completeness, correctness, precision, or optimality in favor of speed. An examination of search procedures is what a heuristic, often called a heuristic function, does. At each fork in the path, it analyses the data at hand in order to determine which path it should take next and then proceeds accordingly. It achieves this by assigning rankings to the various options. The term "heuristic" refers to any method or tool that has a good track record but cannot promise success in every circumstance. One of the reasons for this is to be able to provide a solution that is adequate for the situation at hand within a fair length of time. It is not necessary for it to be the most accurate answer; given the time constraints, an approximation will serve. Most issues are exponential. Due to heuristic search, researchers were able to reduce this number to a polynomial.

6.3.1 Heuristic Search Techniques

Heuristic approaches can be categorized into two ways:

a) Direct Heuristic Search Techniques in Artificial Intelligence (AI)

Blind Control Strategy, Blind Search, and Uninformed Search are similar concepts. They need too much time or memory, making them unworkable. They randomly organize processes and seek the state space for a solution. Examples are Breadth-first and Depth-first searches.

Table 6.1 Techniques of heuristic search used in AI.

• Best First Search	Before moving further with the study, Best First Search will employ an evaluation tool to decide which location in the vicinity has the most potential. Both Breadth- and Depth-First Searches investigate potential paths in an ignorant manner, paying no attention to the cost function [6]
• Hill climbing	A strategy for numerically optimizing various activities is shown here. It is necessary to choose input values that either maximize or minimize the effect of an actual function. It is not necessary for the response to be the local maximum optimal value [7]
• Simulated annealing	Random search is conducted at a high temperature in this technique. As it continues through the process, however, the temperature is gradually lowered until it reaches its final state [7]
• Constraint satisfaction problems	To put it more simply, a constraint is the same thing as a limitation or restriction. When dealing with artificial intelligence, it is possible that it will be required to adhere to specific boundaries in order to address problems [8]

b) Weak Heuristic Search Techniques in AI

These are useful if they are applied appropriately to the appropriate kinds of jobs, and they often need information that is domain specific [5].

For the purpose of computing preference among child nodes to investigate and extend, we need this additional information. A heuristic function is linked with each of the nodes in the graph. Some examples include the acronym "A*" and "Best First Search."

Let's begin by examining the strategies that are most often used by opponents before moving on to elucidate specific tactics.

Table 6.1 provides an explanation of a few heuristics search approaches used in AI.

6.4 Meta-Heuristic

Simulations and nature-inspired meta-heuristic algorithms optimize globally. Meta-heuristic algorithms use simulations and natural methods for global optimization.

Meta-heuristics optimize globally. Meta-heuristic algorithms solve difficulties in several disciplines. There are numerous concurrent concerns in these domains, such as biological signal processing, image processing analysis, classification, and clustering.

There are various beneficial characteristics of meta-heuristic algorithms that can be used to explain the universal acceptance and extensive use of existence algorithms to address a wide range of real-world optimization issues, including (1) their fluidity and mobility; (2) the fact that they are gradient free; and (3) avoiding regionally optimum solutions. The use of meta-heuristic methods solves such problems by taking into consideration just input and output parameters are directly responsible for the first two attributes. Underscoring the notion that optimization is a process that determines the optimum solution for a particular optimization problem, given a set of constraints that change depending on the complexity and nature of the problem, is of the utmost importance. This definition of optimization is vital. Meta-heuristic algorithms, in the most literal sense, operate on the assumption that optimization problems are closed boxes. As a result, computing the derivative of the search domain is not something that has to be done. Because of this, meta-heuristic algorithms may be used for a very wide variety of optimization issues [9].

6.4.1 Structures of Meta-Heuristic

Meta-heuristic algorithms are distinguished by a number of main properties, two of which are intensification and variety (as shown in Figure 6.4). During the phase of intensification, the best existing candidates or solutions are sifted through, and the most promising ones are selected. In order to ensure that the algorithm efficiently navigates the search space, the diversification step is implemented.

There are primarily two categories of meta-heuristics, which are as follows: architecture of algorithms based on single and population elements [10].

Type1: Types of single-based meta-heuristics (as shown in Figure 6.5) are:

Type 2: Types of population-based meta-heuristics are shown in Figure 6.6 [11] (Figure 6.7):

EAs is the name given to the first subdivision of population-based algorithms. These algorithms use the three main operators of selection, recombination, and mutation and are modeled after the natural processes of evolution. Population-based algorithms include EAs (Figure 6.8).

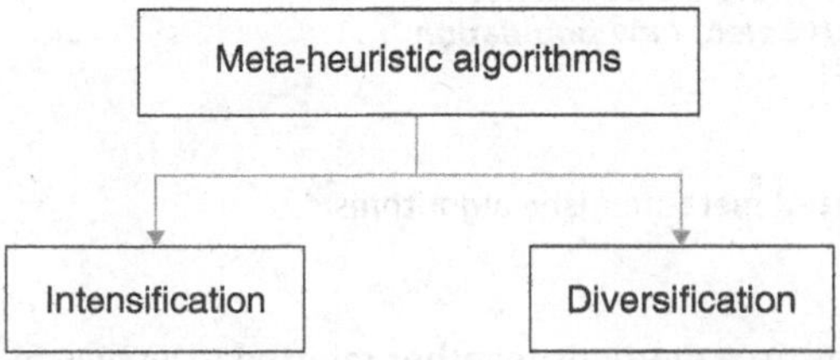

Figure 6.4 Structure of the meta-heuristic algorithms.

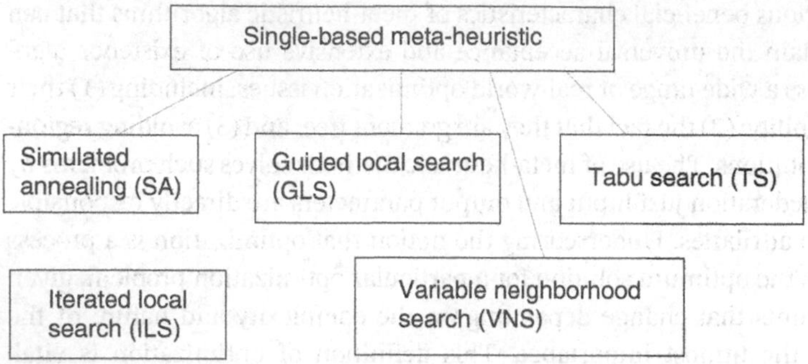

Figure 6.5 Types of single-based meta-heuristic algorithms.

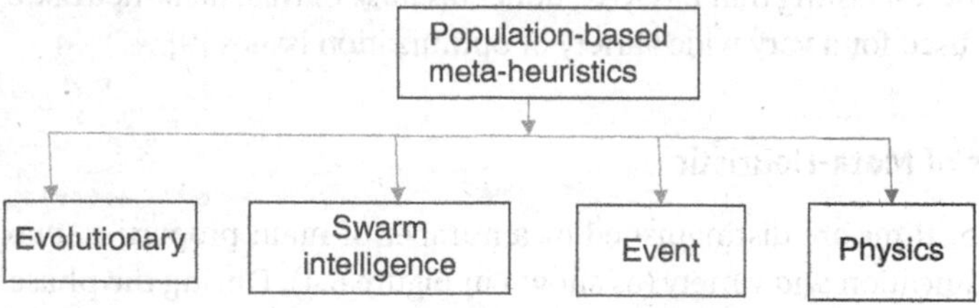

Figure 6.6 Types of population-based meta-heuristic algorithms.

Algorithm 1: A high-level framework for meta-heuristics that are based on a single solution,
s = s0;
/* Generation of the initial solution */
t = 0; Continue /* Develop alternative alternatives from st */
Generate(C(st)); /* Choose a resolution from C(st) to replace the existing solution
****** t = t + 1 ; Until Stopping requirements are met; st */ st+1 = Select(C(st));***
Output: Best solution found.

Figure 6.7 Algorithm of single-based meta-heuristic algorithms.

Algorithm 2 : High-level template of P-meta-heuristics
P = P0; /* Generation of the initial population */
t = 0; Repeat Generate(P ' t); /* Generation a new population */
Pt+1 = Replace-Population(Pt U P ' t); /* Select new population */
t = t+1; Until Stopping criteria satisfied
Output: Best solution(s) found.

Figure 6.8 Algorithm of population-based meta-heuristic algorithms.

The second category consists of multiple methods together referred to as swarm intelligence (SI), which derives knowledge from the coordinated behaviors of living things in their natural habitats (for instance, ants, bees, and birds).

The third family's main sources of inspiration are human deeds rather than natural phenomena. For instance, the teaching learning-based algorithm (TLBA) imitates the teaching and learning process that occurs in classrooms. The harmony search (HS) algorithm is influenced by musical ideas, while the imperialist competitive algorithm (ICA) is driven by imperialism in various civilizations.

Algorithms based on physics make up the final class of meta-heuristics. The idea of several universes serves as the inspiration for the multi-verse optimizer (MVO), while the gravitational search algorithm (GSA) simulates the gravitational interactions that occur between masses.

Algorithms based on physics make up the final class of meta-heuristics (PA). The motivation behind the MVO.

Table 6.2 shows the arrangement of population-based algorithms into categories.

Table 6.2 Arrangement of population-based algorithms into categories.

<table>
<tr><th>Swarm-based</th><th>Physic-based</th><th>Evolutionary-based</th><th>Human-based</th></tr>
<tr>
<td>• Particle Swarm Optimization (PSO)
• Ant Colony Optimization (ACO)
• Artificial Bee Colony (ABC) Algorithm
• Cuckoo Search Algorithm (CS)
• Firefly Algorithm (FA)
• Bat Algorithm (BA)
• Krill Herd (KH)
• Grey Wolf Optimizer
• Genetic Programming (GP)
• Moth-Flame Optimization (MFO) Algorithm
• Dragonfly Algorithm (DA)
• Whale Optimization Algorithm (WOA)
• Crow Search Algorithm (CSA)
• Salp Swarm Algorithm (SSA)
• Grasshopper Optimization Algorithm (GOA)</td>
<td>• Big-Bang Big-Crush (BBBC) Magnetic Charged System Search (MCSS)
• Electromagnetic Field Optimization (EFO)
• Gravitational Search Algorithm (GSA)
• Central Force Optimization (GFO)
• Optics Inspired Optimization (OIO)
• Multi-Verse Optimizer (MVO)
• Thermal Exchange Optimization (TEO)
• Henry Gas Solubility Optimization (HGSO)
• Arithmetic Optimization Algorithm (AOA)</td>
<td>• Genetic Algorithm (GA)
• Differential Evolution (DE)
• Evolutionary Programming (EP)
• Evolution Strategy (ES)
• Probability Based Incremental Learning (PBIL)
• Genetic Programming (GP)
• Biogeography-Based Optimizer (BBO)</td>
<td>• Harmony Search (HS)
• Imperialist Competitive Algorithm (ICA)
• Football Game Inspire Algorithm (FGIA)
• Fire Work Algorithm (FWA)
• Human Group Formation (HGF)</td>
</tr>
</table>

There are no limitations placed on the sources of inspiration that may be used by meta-heuristic algorithms. However, nature is the major source of inspiration for the creation of new meta-heuristic procedures, and algorithms that are heavily inspired by nature have been widely employed for the construction of systems and the resolution of issues.

In general, the bio-inspired algorithms may be divided into one of three separate categories:

1) EAs,
2) SI, and
3) Bacterial foraging algorithms.

The process of biological evolution served as an inspiration for the development of the EAs.

The PSO and ant colony optimization (ACO) are the two most often used paradigms in the field of SI. The social behavior of groups of animals, such as flocking birds or schooling fish, served as the model for the population-based algorithm known as PSO. The ACO algorithm was conceived after seeing how ant colonies go about their food gathering. When it comes to dealing with optimization problems, the research literature relies heavily on these methods.

The behavior of bacteria as they search for food has led to the creation of an innovative bio-inspired optimization approach that has been given the name bacterial foraging algorithm. Computing systems of microbial interactions and communications and rule-based bacterial modeling (RUBAM) are the two most well-known bacterial foraging algorithms.

Table 6.3 demonstrates several algorithms that may be derived from the previous three.

6.5 Machine Learning

Machine learning (ML) is a key AI research area. Over the last decade, ML has grown into a powerful analytical tool for large data applications. ML finds hidden patterns in a large training dataset. ML jobs vary by model output. Usually, learning is supervised, semi-supervised, or unsupervised [11].

With the help of a collection of attributes (continuous variables for regression and discrete variables for classification), this supervised ML task predicts a category or class. It is common practise to approach this class of issues using the Gaussian process, linear regression, K-nearest neighbors, artificial neural network (ANN), support vector machine (SVM), random forests, decision trees, logistic regression, naive Bayes, and deep learning [22–25].

Table 6.3 Various algorithms.

Flower pollination algorithm [12]	The scope of the FPA has been broadened to include the optimization of many objectives simultaneously. For the sake of clarity, the following four rules are utilized: 1. The methods of global pollination include biological and cross-pollination, and the movement of pollen-carrying pollinators is determined by Lévy flights (Rule 1) 2. Abiotic pollination and self-pollination are both employed to accomplish local pollination (Rule 2) 3. It is possible for pollinators, such as insects, to develop floral constancy, which causes a reproduction probability that is proportional to how similar two blooms are (Rule 3) 4. A switch probability that spans from 0 to 1 may be used to regulate the interaction between local and global pollination, also known as switching, with a slight preference for the former (Rule 4)	2012
Krill herd [13]	When determining the objective function for krill migration, the shortest distances between individual krill and sources of food as well as the highest possible population densities are taken into consideration. There are three key elements that decide where each individual krill will be found at any given point in time: 1. motion that is brought about by the presence of other creatures 2. behavior that is associated with foraging, 3. random diffusion	2012
Mine blast algorithm [14]	It takes into account the actual detonations of mine bombs as its primary source of data. The theory underlying the suggested method was inspired by the sight of a mine bomb explosion in which shrapnel fragments hit with other mine bombs around the explosion region, forcing those mine bombs to explode as well. This phenomenon was observed during one particular mine bomb explosion. To have a better understanding of this condition, picture yourself in a minefield where your mission is to clear out all of the mines.	2013
Lightning search algorithm [15]	LSA to optimize constraints. Its pillars are lightning and step leader dissemination via projectiles. To represent the transition projectiles that produce the initial step leader population, the space projectiles that compete to become the leader, and the lead projectile shot from the step leader in the best location, three projectile types are constructed	2015
Artificial algae algorithm [16]	This is inspired by the biological behaviors of microalgae, which are creatures that produce their own food via photosynthesis, is presented. The evolutionary process, the adaption process, and the mobility of microalgae all played a part in the development of the algorithm	2015

(Continued)

Table 6.3 (Continued)

Ant lion optimizer [17]	The ALO algorithm is designed to function similarly to the way that antlions hunt in the wild. In the process of hunting prey, there are five basic processes that are carried out. These actions include the random movement of ants, the construction of traps, the capture of prey, and the rebuilding of traps	2015
Shark smell optimization [18]	This article outlines the shark smell optimization (SSO) approach, which takes its name from the shark's acute capacity for detecting odors	2016
Virus colony search algorithm [19]	The virus's strategies for infection and diffusion to live and spread within the host cell environment are replicated by VCS	2016
Crow search algorithm [20]	It is a novel swarm intelligence optimization algorithm that simulates the clever behavior of crows in concealing and collecting food. The technique has a basic structure, few control parameters, and is straightforward to implement	2016
Grasshopper optimization algorithm [10]	A new Swarm Intelligence approach based on grasshopper swarming	2017
Selfish herd optimizer [21]	SHO simulates the selfish herd behavior seen in animals under danger of predation. In SHO, people behave like greedy herd members and ravenous predators	2017
Electro-search algorithm [22]	Electro-Search algorithm, based on electron orbits around atom nuclei. Electro-search (ES) algorithm uses Bohr model, Rydberg formula, and three-phase scheme	2017
Squirrel search algorithm [21]	The nature-inspired Squirrel Search Algorithm (SSA) was presented lately (Jain et al. 2019). Flying squirrels' gliding inspired SSA. The SSA has never been used for portfolio optimization before	2019
Coral reefs optimization [12]	The CRO algorithm simulates coral reef growth and reproduction. The CRO algorithm simulates coral reproduction and competition for reef space, resulting in an efficient approach for tackling challenging optimization problems	2019
Capuchin search algorithm (CapSA) [11]	This novel algorithm models capuchins' social behavior while browsing over trees and riverbanks in woods for food	2020

- *Clustering:* Using unsupervised ML, this challenge subsets similar data (clusters) the most common algorithms used in this type of techniques, hierarchical clustering, distance-based similarity measures partitioning, partitioning methods (K-means, K-medoids, Mean-Shift), and density-based approaches, are the most prominent clustering methods (e.g. DBSCAN, Optics, and Denclue) [26].

- *Association rules:* In datasets from various databases, association rule mining identifies patterns, correlations, relationships, and causal structures. The most efficient algorithms include Apriori, FP-growth, and Eclat.
- The number of characteristics, or the dimensionality of the dataset, is something that may be reduced as part of the process of feature selection. The task at hand is very important due to the fact that selecting essential variables paves the way for the creation of simpler, more accurate models and cuts down on overfitting [27, 28].

Filter methods, such as linear discriminant analysis (LDA), analysis of variance (ANOVA), and chi-square tests, as well as wrapper methods, which include forward selection, backward selection, recursive feature removal, and embedding methods [29], which also include forward selection, backward selection, and recursive feature removal, are examples of traditional strategies for feature selection (e.g. mRMR, Greedy) [30].

- *Reinforcement learning:* is a technique that asks the learner to interact continuously with an unknowing environment in an effort to learn the best behaviors from a limited selection of accessible actions. The most important parts are the various states, the acts, and the rewards. An RL agent goes from their current state to a new state, completes an activity from their current state, and receives a reward. The level of the challenge that was completed will determine the award. The term "dynamic programming approximation" (RL) [31–33] is another name for it. The goal of the agent should be to accumulate as many rewards as possible during the course of their work. Principal RL approaches may be broken down into the following categories:
- *Model free:* Prior to the explicit learning of a model, the best control policy is learned.
- *Model based:* the control policy is learned explicitly. Methods such as these include policy search (such as meta-heuristics and policy gradient), as well as value-function-based approaches that are connected to dynamic programming principles (e.g. temporal difference [TD] learning).

Research into the application of ML to create efficient, effective, and robust meta-heuristics has become more and more popular in recent years.

Many of these data-driven meta-heuristics have produced excellent outcomes and are cutting-edge approaches to optimization. In spite of the fact that a variety of methods have been proposed, this research problem does not have a systematic survey or categorization. Throughout the course of this investigation, we will investigate a variety of strategies for integrating ML into meta-heuristics.

In most cases, meta-heuristics do not make use of the explicit knowledge gathered by more complex ML models while the search is being conducted. Meta-heuristics are responsible for the generation of a significant volume of search-related data. The data can be considered static in regard to the problem that has to be addressed and the instance characteristics at hand. The iterative search process also generates a wide range of dynamic data, including solutions in both the choice space and the goal space, sequences of solutions or trajectories, successive populations of solutions, movements, recombination, local optimums, elite solutions, poor solutions, and so forth. As a result, ML may be useful when analyzing these data and coming to pertinent conclusions. These guidelines and improvements to the search performance brought forth by this information will make meta-heuristics "smarter" and "more knowledgeable." It has been shown that data-driven meta-heuristics are advantageous in terms of the speed of convergence, the quality of the solution, and the durability of the system.

The survey found that there are three different hierarchical ways to use ML in meta-heuristics, and they are as follows:

- *Data-driven problem-level meta-heuristics:* ML is able to provide a hand in the modeling of the optimization issue that has to be addressed (e.g. objective function, constraints). It is also possible that it will help in the examination of the landscape and the breakdown of the problem.
- *Data-driven meta-heuristics at a low level:* A meta-heuristic is a collection of various search elements. Each step of the search process, including initializing the solution (s) and search variation operators, may be driven by ML (e.g. neighborhoods in local search, mutation, and crossover in EAs). It could also be used to change a meta-heuristic's parameters.
- *High-level data-driven meta-heuristics:* The selection and creation of meta-heuristics, as well as the design of hybrid and parallel cooperative meta-heuristics, are all topics covered in this subcategory of data-driven meta-heuristics [14].

6.5.1 Applications of Meta-Heuristic

Because of the sometimes nonlinear and very unpredictable nature of traffic patterns, particularly during peak hours, the application of such systems is severely constrained. This research aims to develop intelligent traffic management solutions for isolated signalized crossings by using meta-heuristics as a foundation. Through the use of a GA and differential evolution(DE), the level of service (LOS) at the junction was brought up to par by enhancing the signal timing plan.

The method was put to the test by applying it to the optimization challenge presented by the design of pressure vessels, which is one of the optimization issues that is faced the most often.

It is recommended that an application of the multi-objective shark smell optimization approach using composite angle cosine be used for the operation of autonomous trains (ATO). To be more precise, the shark smell optimization approach, which has a huge searching capacity, is used in conjunction with the composite angle cosine to tackle the issue of the autonomous train operation velocity trajectory optimization easily attaining a local optimum. Moreover, the shark population aggregation problem is avoided by using the dual-population evolution approach, which prevents it at the end of each cycle. To do this, the aggregation phenomenon is suppressed in both shark populations. As a result, the assessment index is the composite angle cosine, which takes into account both the numerical difference and the preference difference. This lessens the impact of the usual evaluation's lack of objectivity and rationality.

Application meta-heuristic algorithms are population-based techniques that create novel solutions based on the behavior of living things by using a set of tuning parameters. Many issues can be addressed using these novel techniques.

The primary driving force for the creation of CapSA was the kinetic behavior of capuchin monkeys. This unique algorithm's core optimization features are modeled after the social behavior of capuchin monkeys as they search for food by traveling and foraging across forest trees and riverbanks. Capuchin monkeys search for food by traveling and foraging across forest trees and riverbanks. This algorithm takes into account some of the most common foraging behaviors of capuchin monkeys, such as leaping, climbing, and hanging from branches. The capuchin's ability to jump helps it accomplish its remarkable feat of climbing from one tree to the next. Swinging and climbing are the two methods of foraging used by capuchins. These methods allow capuchins to traverse trees, tree branches, and the tips of tree branches over relatively short distances. In the end, these methods of locomotion result in feasible solutions to the problems associated with global optimization The suggested method is evaluated on a set of hard and computationally expensive engineering scenarios and 23 well-known benchmark functions.

References

1 Alwan, G.M. (2016). *Optimization Technique* https://doi.org/10.13140/RG.2.2.16302.56643.

2 Abraham, A., Muhuri, P., Muda, A., and Gandhi, N. (ed.) (2017). Hybrid Intelligent Systems. HIS 2017. In: *Advances in Intelligent Systems and Computing*, vol. 734. Cham: Springer https://doi.org/10.1007/978-3-319-76351-4_13.

3 Bangroo, R., Kumar, N., and Sharma, R. (2018). A model for multi-processor task scheduling problem using quantum genetic algorithm. In: *Advances in Intelligent Systems and Computing book series (AISC)*, vol. 734 (ed. A. Abraham, P.K. Muhuri, A.K. Muda, and N. Gandhi), 126–135. Cham: Springer.

4 Ardizzon, G., Cavazzini, G., and Pavesi, G. (2015). Adaptive acceleration coefficients for a new search diversification strategy in particle swarm optimization algorithms. *Inf. Sci.* 299: 337–378.
5 Lange, S., Gebert, S., Zinner, T. et al. (2015). Heuristic approaches to the controller placement problem in large scale sdn networks. *IEEE Trans. Netw. Serv. Manag.* 12 (1): 4–17.
6 Sulistiani, H, Wardani, F, and Sulistyawati, A. (2019). Application of Best First Search Method to Search Nearest Business Partner Location (Case Study: PT Coca Cola Amatil Indonesia, Bandar Lampung) Proc. ICOMITEE 2019, October 16th-17th 2019, Jember, Indonesia, 978-1-7281-3436-9/19/$31.00 ©2019 IEEE.
7 Saqib Nawaz, M., Philippe Fournier, V., Unil, Y. et al. (2021). Mining high utility itemsets with hill climbing and simulated annealing. *ACM Trans. Manag. Inform. Syst.* 13 (1): 1–22.
8 Brailsford, S.C., Potts, C.N., and Smith, B.M. (1999). Constraint satisfaction problems: algorithms and applications. *Eur. J. Operation. Res.* 119 (3): 557–581.
9 Braik, M., Sheta, A., and Al-Hiary, H. (2021). A novel meta-heuristic search algorithm for solving optimization problems: capuchin search algorithm. *Neural Comput. Appl.* 33: 2515–2547.
10 Meraihi, Y., Benmessaoud Gabis, A., Mirjalili, S., and Ramdane-Cherif, A. (2021). Grasshopper optimization algorithm: theory, variants, and applications. *IEEE* 9: 50001–50024. doi: 10.1109/ACCESS.2021.3067597. ISSN: 2169-3536.
11 Li, X., Hua, S., Liu, Q., and Li, Y. (2023). A partition-based convergence framework for population-based optimization algorithms. *Inf. Sci.* 627: 169–188.
12 Abdel-Basset, M. and Shawky, L.A. (2018). Flower pollination algorithm: a comprehensive review. *Artif. Intell. Rev.* 52: 2533–2557.
13 Hossein Gandomi, A. and Hossein, A. (2012). Krill herd: a new bio-inspired optimization. *Commun. Nonlinear Sci. Numer. Simul.* 17 (12): 4831–4845.
14 Sadollah, A., Bahreininejad, A., Eskandar, H., and Hamdi, M. (2013). Mine blast algorithm: a new population based algorithm for solving constrained engineering optimization problems. *Appl. Soft Comput.* 13 (5): 2592–2612.
15 Shareef, H., Ibrahim, A., and Hussein Mutlag, A. (2015, 2013). Lightning search algorithm. *Appl. Soft Comput.* 36 (5): 2592–2612.
16 Uymaz, A., Tezel, G., and Yel, E. (2015). Artificial algae algorithm (AAA) for nonlinear global optimization. *Appl. Soft Comput.* 31: 153–171.
17 Mirjalili, S. (2015). The ant lion optimizer. *Adv. Eng. Softw.* 83: 80–98.
18 Mohammad-azari, S., Bozorg-Haddad, O., and Chu, X. (2018). Shark smell optimization (SSO) algorithm. In: *Studies in Computational Intelligence*. https://doi.org/10.1007/978-981-10-5221-7_10.
19 Zilfikri Yulfiandi Rachmat, Z. and Mandala, R. (2022). Improving virus colony search performance on travelling salesman problem case. In: *2022 5th International Conference on Information and Communications Technology (ICOIACT)*. 10.1109/ICOIACT55506.2022.9971896.

20 Cheng, Q., Huang, H., and Chen, M. (2021). A novel crow search algorithm based on improved flower pollination. 2021: 1048879. doi: 10.1155/2021/1048879.

21 Yimit, A., Iigura, K., and Hagihara, Y. (2020). Refined selfish herd optimizer for global optimization problems. *Expert Syst. Appl.* 139: 112838.

22 Tabar, A. and Ahmad, A. (2017). A new optimization method: electro-search algorithm. *Comput. Chem. Eng.* 103 (4): 1–11.

23 Juneja, A., Juneja, S., Soneja, A., and Jain, S. (2021). Real time object detection using CNN based single shot detector model. *J. Inf. Technol. Manag.* 13 (1): 62–80.

24 Viriyasitavat, W., Mohafez, H., Hadizadeh, M. et al. (2022). A novel machine-learning-based hybrid CNN model for tumor identification in medical image processing. *Sustainability* 14 (3): 1447.

25 Kaur, S. and Kumar, V. (2021). Predicting diabetes mellitus with machine learning techniques using multi-criteria decision making. *Int. J. Inf. Retr. Res.* 11 (2): 38–52.

26 Dhankhar, A. and Bali, V. (2021). Kernel parameter tuning to tweak the performance of classifiers for identification of heart diseases. *Int. J. E-Health Med. Commun.* 12 (4): 1–16.

27 Rashid, J., Batool, S., Kim, J. et al. (2022). An augmented artificial intelligence approach for chronic diseases prediction. *Front. Public Health* 10: 860396.

28 Amin, S. U., Alsulaiman, M., Muhammad, G. Mekhtiche, M. A. and Hossain, M. S. (2019). Deep Learning for EEG motor imagery classification based on multi-layer CNNs feature fusion. *Future Generation computer systems,* 101: 542–554.

29 Aggarwal, S., Gupta, S., Kannan, R. et al. (2022). A convolutional neural network-based framework for classification of protein localization using confocal microscopy images. *IEEE Access* 10: 83591–83611.

30 Sharma, S., Gupta, S., Gupta, D. et al. (2022). Performance evaluation of the deep learning based convolutional neural network approach for the recognition of chest X-ray images. *Front. Oncol.* 12: 932496.

31 Rashid, J., Kim, J., Hussain, A., and Naseem, U. (2022). A novel multiple kernel fuzzy topic modeling technique for biomedical data. *BMC Bioinf.* 23 (1): 275.

32 Aggarwal, S., Gupta, S., Gupta, D. et al. (2023). An artificial intelligence-based stacked ensemble approach for prediction of protein subcellular localization in confocal microscopy images. *Sustainability* 15 (2): 1695.

33 Upadhyay, C. and Upadhyay, H.K. (2022). Plant disease detection using imaging sensors, deep learning and machine learning for smart farming. In: *Healthcare Solutions Using Machine Learning and Informatics* (ed. P. Gupta, D.K. Saini, and R. Verma), 173–185. Auerbach Publications.

7

Security and Privacy Issues in Distributed Healthcare Systems – A Survey

Manish Bhardwaj[1], *Samad Noeiaghdam*[2], *and Yu-Chen Hu*[3]

[1] *KIET Group of Institutions, Ghaziabad, Uttar Pradesh, India*
[2] *Industrial Mathematics Laboratory, Baikal School of BRICS, Irkutsk National Research Technical University, Irkutsk, Russia*
[3] *Department of Computer Science and Information Management, Providence University, Taichung City, Taiwan*

7.1 Introduction

It is clear that businesses want to reduce their reliance on a centralized data center without sacrificing the efficiency of their regionally dispersed database, application, and user infrastructure [1]. Today's web-based systems and apps (also known as WEBAPPS) have highly developed computer tools that can not only do basic tasks alone but can also communicate with and access data from other systems.

In today's rapidly evolving world, wireless Internet access in rural and outlying areas is an absolute necessity [2]. It is web access via wireless mobile device. According to a survey, an Internet-based or electronic health system is not readily available in India's rural areas. The evidence suggests that wireless technology is not being widely adopted in these regions.

Even though Primary Health Centres (PHCs) are located all across the region, current methods of communication are far from ideal and have several flaws [3, 4]. The healthcare (HC) environment is poor in rural places, and doctors and nurses spend more time gathering data and writing reports than really talking with patients. Services, advice, and supply of basic HC suffer as a result of their increased administrative duties [5]. As a result, it is recommended that a Diversity Workbench (DWB) model be implemented for such Indian businesses. That's why

Meta-Heuristic Algorithms for Advanced Distributed Systems, First Edition. Edited by Rohit Anand, Abhinav Juneja, Digvijay Pandey, Sapna Juneja, and Nidhi Sindhwani.

when we're designing and developing distributed system models, we count each PHC as a single client node [6]. As such, we believe these models will prove fruitful. The models can be lightweight, portable, and self-sufficient clients that connect to a server over a network [7, 8].

Telemedicine plays an important part in the modern HC system. A major benefit of telemedicine is that it makes high-quality medical care available even in remote locations, where it is desperately needed. It helps keep medical expenses low while still enhancing treatment [9]. Users, such as doctors, nurses, and allied health professionals, are less likely to feel alone with the help of this system. Telemedicine is "the application of electronic and telecommunications technologies to the practice of medicine with the goal of extending the reach of HC to patients in geographically isolated or otherwise inaccessible areas."

According to our research, telemedicine faces a number of drawbacks. Principally, it poses risks if used by unauthorized personnel [10].

The development of the Internet has contributed to the expansion of such fields as medicine, engineering, and information and communication technologies. Thanks to the advancements in Internet technology, we now have access to more thorough, accurate, and up-to-date patient health records and information. In the medical industry, it is crucial for users (patients and physicians, doctors and other doctors) to be able to interact with one another face to face [11–13]. The created models serve a crucial role in getting information regarding better therapies in instances where face-to-face meetings are not possible. Also included is any method of interaction between users, such as between medical staff and patients using electronic devices.

There are things called "communication lines" that can be used to transfer data. Computer networks are created when individual computers are linked together by means of carrier lines. In a network, one computer acts as the sending unit (Sender Computer) and another as the receiving unit (Receiver Computer). Topologies for establishing connections between computers come in a wide variety of forms. Local area networks (LANs), like Ethernet, were the first distributed system to be developed in the 1970s.

The study of distributed systems is the focus of distributed computing. Distributed computing is the practice of employing multiple computers to work on a single task [14]. In this setup, the problem is broken down into smaller, more manageable pieces that can be handled by individual computers.

A distributed system is made up of many separate computers that operate together and share information across a network. Those machines collaborate with one another to complete a task. A distributed program is any application or software that operates in a distributed environment. Distributed programming refers to the methodology of creating a program that runs across multiple computers [15].

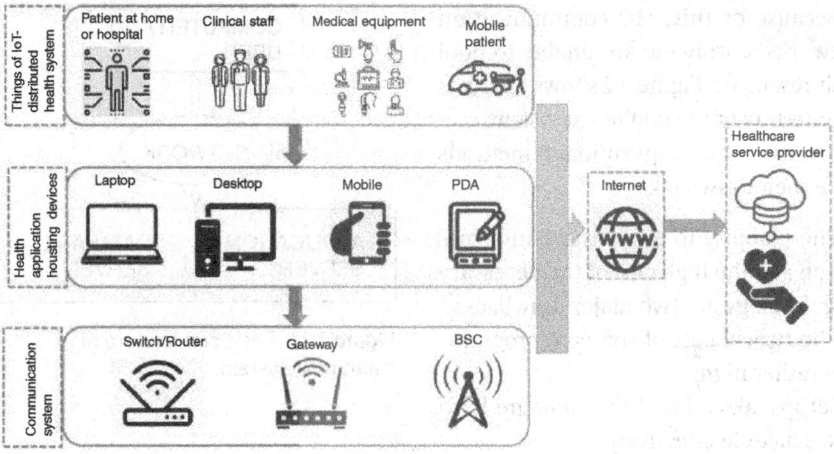

Figure 7.1 Basic architecture of distributed healthcare system.

A distributed system is one in which the processing of data is dispersed over multiple computers rather than being limited to just one. To put it simply, distributed systems are any Internet-based applications that require two distinct kinds of computers, a server node and a client node, to function properly [16]. The term "Simply Distributed System" refers to a computer system that functions through the cooperation of multiple computers linked together by digital communications networks. Figure 7.1 shows the basic architecture of distributed HC system.

Consolidation in early data warehouses led to complicated databases. Databases can be accessed by multiple users at once, but all processing takes place on the central server. One-tier, or host, systems, and two-tier architecture, both of which have their own set of problems, are examples of classic systems. Users' requirements today aren't region specific; rather, they're world spanning, with the user desiring constant access to fresh content. Users need to access data from off-site locations or mobile devices that can be linked via wired or wireless networks [17–19]. Users of older systems can only consume data in a passive reading capacity. Cases like this prevent the server side from gaining logical access to the client side computing environment via global or remote networks.

7.1.1 Traditional Systems

Database management systems and relational database management systems are examples of classic computer architectures. The data processing and decision-making functions of these systems are not supported by Internet-based applications since they are centralized.

Because of this, HC communication networks worldwide are unable to pool their resources. Figure 7.2 shows the basic architecture of the traditional system.

It's true that conventional methods have their drawbacks.

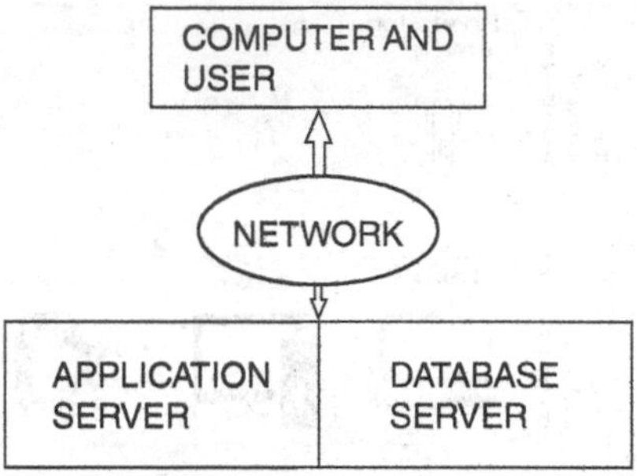

Figure 7.2 Basic architecture of traditional system.

- The inability to easily share information and the high cost of the necessary technology are two major drawbacks.
- The typical cost of software programs is rather high.
- Setups take a lot of time and are hard to schedule effectively.
- Individual licenses are too expensive.
- Both new installations and upgrades are labor intensive and time-consuming.
- Only client terminals can perform read activities.

We also believe another system is required to improve the overall efficiency of information transfer, its interpretation, and decision-making activities at the appropriate. For this reason, we think a distributed system is the best option [20].

7.1.2 Distributed Systems

Applications and infrastructure that are hosted and accessed solely via the Internet are examples of distributed systems. The web facilitates these. This type of technology allows for both regional and worldwide resource sharing [21]. Currently, the Internet is one of the most popular ways to send data. Distributed system's client–server architecture is depicted in Figure 7.3.

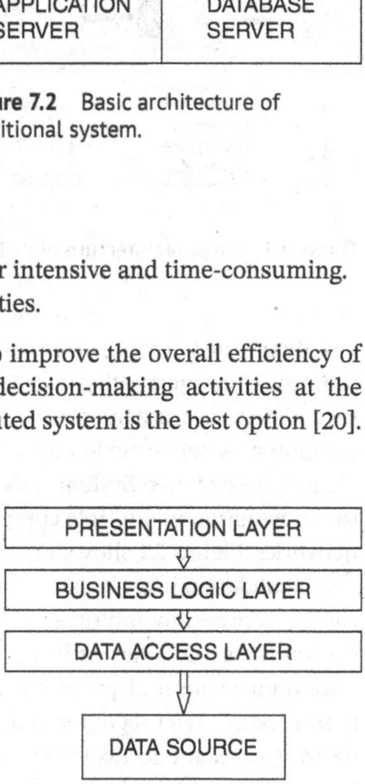

Figure 7.3 3-Tier basic architecture of distributed system.

7.2 Previous Study

Several studies have been undertaken in recent years to examine the current state of security and privacy threats to HC systems. However, without taking into account broader security and privacy concerns in HC systems, these works either focus on specific assaults or security solutions for specific devices. We provide a summary of these polls and comment on how they differ from our own here.

Current polls. Privacy and security considerations around implantable medical devices (IMDs) have been the primary focus of existing surveys, [22] conducted a thorough study of security and privacy issues related to telemetry interfaces and software, security frameworks, and best practices for bolstering the safety of IMDs. When considering how to improve remote health monitoring, [23] analyzed existing studies and identified gaps that must be filled. In their paper [24–28], David and Jeyachandran provided a comprehensive overview of WM-SNs, cryptographic methods for protecting health data, and the compromise between these two factors. An example of the difficulties in ensuring the safety of medical gadgets was documented. Several other helpful studies have concentrated on the uses of big data in today's HC systems. Using the HC business as a case study, Patil and Seshadri examined the most recent developments in security and privacy concerns related to big data. From a privacy and security perspective, Ref. [29] provided an overview of HC apps that made use of machine learning (ML) approaches.

Ref. [30] provided a comprehensive analysis of the current state of development of wearable biosensor devices for health monitoring. In their presentation of a HC information flow, zeroed in on the role that the Internet of Things (IoT) plays. Ref. [31] analyzed the current state of HC apps and addressed the risks, weaknesses, and repercussions of cyberattacks on HC infrastructure. Possible attack pathways and security flaws were presented, and assaults that might be applied to networked medical devices were shown to function. The privacy and safety measures built into IoT devices were also analyzed by the researchers.

The latest developments in IoT-based HC technologies, network topologies, and industrial trends were surveyed. Refs. [32–34] offered an introduction to the characteristics and concepts relevant to the security requirements for IoT in a HC system.

Variations from earlier polls. The following are some of the significant distinctions between our work and previous surveys. First, whereas most recent studies have concentrated on the safety and confidentiality of IMDs and implantable and wearable medical devices (IWMDs), our study has widened its scope to include the entire HC system, from medical devices and sensors to communication systems and HC practitioners [35]. Second, we propose a formal HC architecture and highlight its key components to define protection and confidentiality requirements. Third, using a standard vulnerability assessment system, we classify the various threats to HC data security and privacy. While previous studies paid little attention to the shortcomings of preexisting security measures, our work does just that. Fifth, our research provides researchers with a set of prioritized categories to follow as they investigate solutions to the most prevalent security flaws in HC IT.

7.2.1 Background and Definitions

Here, we break down the many HC systems' parts in order to better explain why security and privacy are such essential concerns in the medical field. The majority of modern HC systems consist of a network of interconnected medical devices, each of which is equipped with a variety of sensors to monitor a patient's vitals and determine the best course of action in terms of diagnosis and treatment.

How a HC system is structured as a whole? We single out five core elements that are normally required for a HC system to carry out its basic functions. The HC provider, network, data processing, medical sensors, and sensors on medical devices make up the other five parts.

In a medical sense, this is a gadget. A medical device is any implement, tool, appliance, or gadget used for medical purposes such as diagnosis, monitoring, treatment, or relief. Medical devices can range from tongue depressors to complex programmable implantable cardioverter-defibrillators (ICDs), as stated by the US Food and Drug Administration (FDA). The FDA establishes classification criteria for medical devices according to the potential for harm to patients in the event of device malfunction or malicious attacks [36].

Class I medical devices include items like elastic bandages and dental floss that pose minimal risk and are subject to limited regulation. Class II devices, which include pregnancy test kits, powered wheelchairs, and other similar products, are more complicated and riskier than Class I equipment, necessitating stricter regulatory oversight.

Class III device has some examples like implantable pacemakers and breast implants that pose the highest risk and complexity and hence are subject to the strictest regulatory regulations.

Sensor: Sensors are commonly employed to track and record a patient's vital signs in the medical field. Various physiological sensors are used to initiate the automation of various HC system capabilities (diagnostic, monitoring, etc.).

Networking: The networking elements of a HC system think about how various medical devices and sensors talk to one another and to the rest of the system. Data transmission over small distances can be handled by either wired or wireless means [37]. However, the patient's mobility and comfort may be compromised by the use of wired communication.

It is possible for a body area network (BAN) to be formed by a collection of autonomous sensor nodes that adhere to a primary star topology network and send information to a centralized node by means of this topology.

Wireless LANs have a division of groups that depend on the frequency of work like IEEE 802.15.1 (Bluetooth) and 802.15.4 (Zigbee) which are widely employed in BANs (WPAN). Bluetooth is a standard in the business world for wireless communication over short distances using radio frequency (RF) technology. It operates in the unlicensed 2.4 GHz frequency and requires nothing in the way of power output or expense.

To prevent interference, it employs a frequency hopping scheme across 79 channels in the ISM (industrial, scientific, and medical) band, allowing for data rates of up to 3 mbps in enhanced data rate mode and a range of up to 100 m. Zigbee is standardized to provide long-lasting, low-cost solutions with low data rates. Using offset quadrature phase shift keying (OQPSK) modulation at 250 kbps, it can operate on 16 channels in the 2.4 GHz ISM band, 10 channels in the 915 MHz band, and a single channel in the 868 MHz band [38–40].

Short-range intra-BAN communication can also be achieved through the use of other technologies, such as infrared data association, ultra-wideband (UWB), and medical implant communication service (MICS).

UWB is an inexpensive protocol for exchanging data using infrared light over short distances. MICS stands for "medical implant communication service," and it's an unlicensed mobile radio service that transmits low-rate data to aid in the diagnostic or therapeutic capabilities of medical devices. The frequency range it operates in is between 402 and 405 MHz, and the channel width is 300 kHz.

With the introduction of low-power communication protocols like Z-Wave and BLE, more products employing these standards are likely to flood the market soon.

Manipulation of information: The data processing section amasses information from various sensors and devices. The medical device and sensor components interact with a central data processing unit through communication and control modules [41]. A data processing device and a local database are included for storing preliminary patient information. It has an alert system that will notify the doctor or patient if something is wrong. A wireless communication module facilitates connectivity to the HC provider's health server.

Supplier of medical care: The HC provider component includes HC professionals and health servers. Through a wireless transmission module, they are able to communicate with the data processing element. The health server stores medical records online. Doctors and nurses can use this information whether they are treating a patient in person or not.

7.3 Security and Privacy Needs

The overarching privacy and safety objectives of the HC system are depicted in Figure 7.4. Here, a patient wears or is somehow equipped with a number of invasive and noninvasive medical devices that continuously record data from a wide range of physiological and environmental sources (e.g. ambient temperature and humidity).

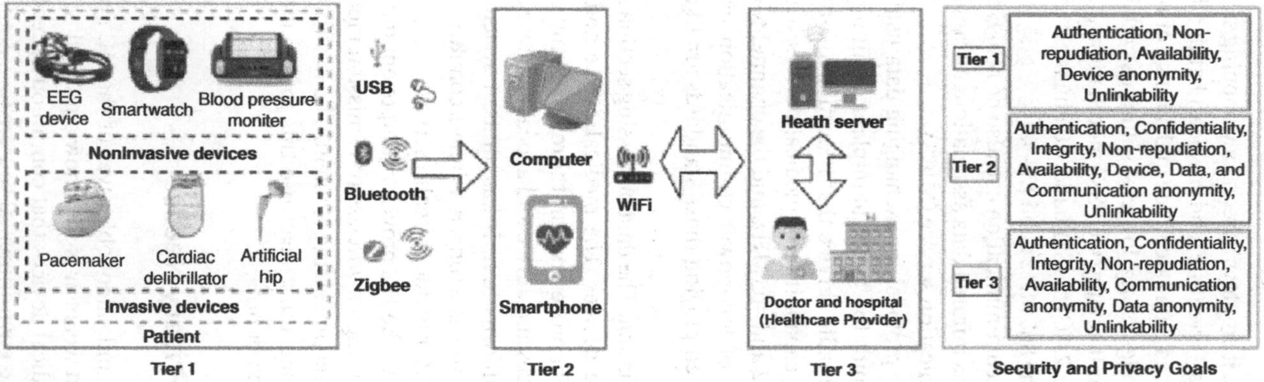

Figure 7.4 Healthcare architecture security and privacy in 3-tier format.

Patient-related data refers to the sum of sensor readings and patient profiles that are gathered and sent to various devices, such as cellphones and computers. The information collected by these gadgets can be processed, aggregated, or stored in a decentralized manner. Data pertaining to a patient can be transmitted to HC providers and the hospital for ongoing monitoring of the patient's physical status, as well as to a central HC server for permanent records [42, 43]. In conclusion, a personal HC system's overall architecture is composed of three distinct layers. Invasive and noninvasive medical gadgets make up Tier 1, whereas Tier 2 includes consumer electronics like cellphones and PCs. The third layer consists of HC providers and servers [44].

All three levels of authentication (Tiers 1, 2, and 3) are necessary for safety reasons. Authorization at each layer is required before any patient data is sent from a personal device to a health server. Information and data stored on medical devices should be accessible only by trained medical personnel and should not be editable by any third parties. Tiers 2 and 3 should likewise have safeguards in place to protect sensitive information [45]. Due to the sensitive nature of the data and processes that medical devices undertake, it is important that any access logs be maintained securely.

Because of the potential consequences for patient care if device data is unavailable, it is critical that medical devices be accessible at all times. All three levels must keep non-repudiation and availability intact [46].

Maintaining device anonymity is also necessary for achieving privacy goals, as only the patient and authorized users should be aware of the exact medical equipment that a patient is using [47]. To protect patients' and doctors' privacy, it is important that their personal information is concealed during data transmission between Tiers 1 and 2. Achieving anonymity and unlinkability in patient communications with HC providers and hospitals via the HC system should be possible. Figure 7.5 shows the cycle of a smart path automated HC system [48].

Security issues of the HC system are an important aspect for the success of the newly designed HC system. Figure 7.6 shows the process cycle of development of IT security task force [49].

7.4 Security and Privacy Goals

Taking into account the above debate, we arrive at the following HC system security objectives. In order to accomplish these objectives, it is important to take into account the following characteristics of a HC system during its whole lifespan:

Considerations for the environment configuration, one layered factor and several layered factor substantiations, elegance stages, and substitute circumstances

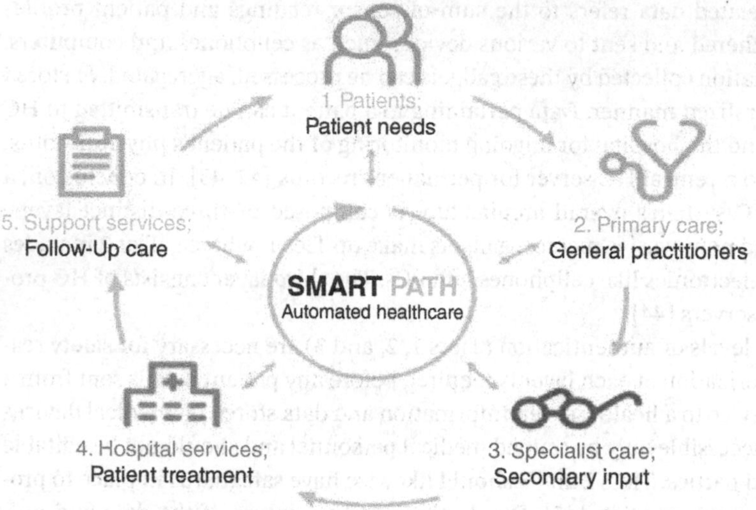

Figure 7.5 Cycle of smart path automated healthcare system.

are all part of a strong authentication system, which is a crucial component for safeguarding HC systems [50, 51].

The majority of today's grouped therapeutic strategies (e.g. IMDs and IWMDs) use apprehensive keyword substantiation mechanisms, such as storing password files locally on the device's hard drive.

Therefore, a malicious actor with sufficient access can alter any of the actions taken by the authenticated user. It can also have made the changes in the status of the software installed within the systems.

(a) Matters of ecology: It is important to choose an authentication method that works for the specific architecture of the HC environment in question.

Proximity cards, for instance, might be convenient and work well for everyday use with patients, but they wouldn't pass muster for vetting surgical suites.

(b) With the help of previous studies and the information of control system, it is easier to take decision of deployment of the single layer or multi-layer authentication. Blood pressure and temperature readings, for instance, might just need a single element of authentication, while accessing data stored on HC servers might necessitate a pair of additional factors.

(c) This is because continuous authentication requires HC providers to repeatedly enter their credentials in order to gain access to their patient's records.

However, any unauthorized individual can access the device during the grace time, which can lead to malicious circumstances. Using various

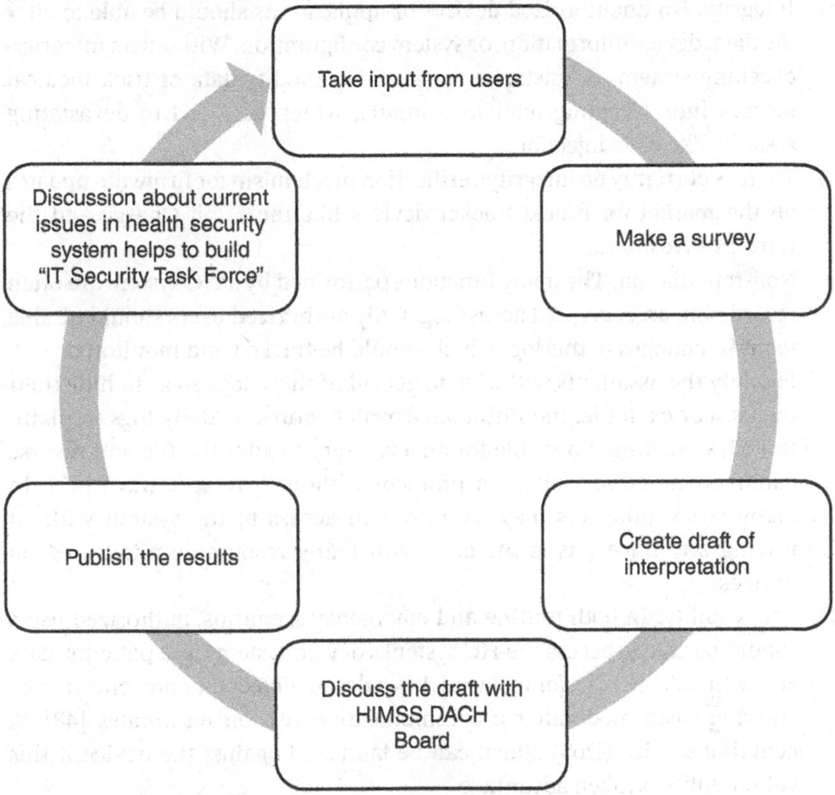

Figure 7.6 Process cycle of IT security task force.

approaches, such as wearable-assisted or sensor-assisted authentication, can help with continuous authentication.

(d) In the case of an emergency, it is important to plan for a variety of possible ways to gain access to necessary medical equipment. For instance, in the case of a patient's health, a medical device may be permitted access in any emergency situation but may only be considered to transmit data after authentication.

(e) Information about devices, system setup, and patient health records should be kept private. Any time these organizations attempted to access protected health information, they were first required to prove their identity.

(f) Nonetheless, patient data and device-related information can be gleaned through eavesdropping on current HC devices, such as an insulin pump's communication route.

(g) Integrity: No unauthorized devices or applications should be able to alter the data, device information, or system configuration. Without an integrity-checking system, for instance, hackers can modify data or trick medical devices into accepting malicious inputs, which can lead to devastating assaults like code injection.

(h) There is currently no integrity verification mechanism for firmware updates on the market for fitness tracker devices like the Fitbit Charge and the Garmin Vivosmart.

(i) Non-repudiation: The many functions performed by a HC system are often recorded in an encrypted access log. Only authorized users should be able to make changes to this log, which should be tracked and monitored.

(j) Possibly the assailants will wish to get rid of these logs so as to hide their tracks. For example, the Fitbit smartwatch stores its daily logs in plain-text files, making it possible for an adversary to alter the file and reverse engineer the communication protocol without leaving a trace [47]. In many cases, attackers may try to obtain access to the system without leaving any traces, as is the case with many resource-limited medical devices.

(k) Accessibility: In both routine and emergency scenarios, authorized users should be able to access the HC system's device systems and patients' data at any time. One ICD, for instance, has a design defect that prevents it from entering sleep mode after a communication session terminates [48]. A denial-of-service (DoS) attack can be launched against the device if this vulnerability is taken advantage.

7.5 Type of Attacks in Distributed Systems

As it stands, attackers can take advantage of various parts of HC systems due to the fact that present HC equipment and applications do not adequately protect patient data and privacy.

Here, we detail the intentions behind several types of assaults on HC systems, taking into account the attacker's resources and methods. We also highlight the ways in which the security and privacy of HC systems might be compromised by discussing a variety of attacks against various HC system components (e.g. sensor, device, and network).

We provide a formal taxonomy of the malicious action on the HC architecture. This final information is provided to communities related to academics and higher decision-making authorities. With the help of the above process, malicious activity is detected and also known for its categories.

7.5.1 Malicious Hardware

Attacks that take advantage of a flaw in the hardware of a device are known as hardware attacks. Such attacks can be launched either locally or remotely. Data corruption caused by hardware Trojans (HTs) inserted during chip fabrication is a severe threat to medical equipment. An attacker who knows or gains access to the device's internal hardware architecture might do this.

As most ICs are now made in outsourced fabrication facilities, HTs have become a major security risk. Untrusted intellectual property cores HTs provided by third-party vendors have the potential to be utilized for nefarious purposes, such as the disclosure of sensitive data stored on medical devices.

Physical qualities (such as chip architecture and activation) and action characteristics (such as logic functions and chip activities) can be used to categorize HTs. Trojans are characterized by their physical characteristics, and they can be introduced during chip fabrication by the addition or removal of transistors or gates.

The term "action characteristics" is used to describe an HT that alters a chip's operation by adding to or removing the chip's existing logic.

There have been a number of studies from the FDA on the topic of altering patient health records by tampering with hardware in medical devices. In recent research, scientists revealed an HT assault on the Bacillus Calmette–Guérin (BCG) titer. They compromised the system by inserting malicious code onto the input bus, which altered the operation of an XOR gate.

7.5.2 Malicious Programs

Software assaults are maliciously coded programs that target HC IT infrastructure, systems, or devices. With the rapid rise of embedded and modifiable software in the HC industry, patients are receiving better care and being monitored more closely than ever before.

However, there is currently no foolproof method for ensuring the reliability and validity of HC software.

Malware, ransomware, stale operating systems, fake firmware updates, and electroencephalography attacks are just some of the software- and app-related dangers that HC systems must contend with today.

Malware: Malware refers to any type of software or program that has been designed to harm its users. Malware can cause a HC device to malfunction in ways it wouldn't normally, such as by reducing its processing speed or even shutting it down entirely.

As a result, an unauthenticated, remote attacker may potentially run whatever code they pleased on the compromised system. In January 2010, malware in the computer systems forced the temporary closure of a Veterans Affairs catheterization laboratory in New Jersey. Since this was the case, the hospital's patients had no way of receiving treatment. Some reputable manufacturers of X-ray machines and laboratory equipment had a gadget that was compromised. In addition, viruses like Kwampirs can cause equipment failure or delays in obtaining information, hence introducing instability into HC systems.

Ransomware: Ransomware is a type of malicious software that encrypts files and systems and demands a ransom in exchange for unlocking them. An estimated fifty British hospitals were hit by ransomware in May of 2017, prompting several to shut down their networks in anticipation of an attack.

Care delivery was impacted, patient safety was jeopardized, and trust could have been damaged as a result. Patient information was encrypted and locked, with the ransomware's threat of exposure or deletion until a ransom was paid.

The network of Hollywood Presbyterian Medical Center in Los Angeles, California, was inaccessible for 10 days in 2016 due to ransomware. Until the hospital paid the ransom of $17,000, its employees were blocked from accessing patient records and medical equipment.

British freedom of information requests revealed that as many as half of National Health Services of England and Wales (NHS) trusts experienced ransomware attacks in 2015 and 2016. Hancock Health and Erie County Medical Center, both in the United States, were also struck by SamSam ransomware and ultimately paid the ransom.

The average time to recover restricted system access is 12 days and full access is 6 weeks in all of these occurrences.

7.6 Recommendations and Future Approaches

The following application scenario from a futuristic HC system is taken into account to indicate potential future research topics and recommendations. Let's pretend that Alice, a patient, decides to invest in a high-tech medical gadget (a pulse oximeter, for example) in order to track her oxygen saturation and heart rate. Alice gets the pulse oximeter app for the phone, writes the media access control (MAC) address of the medical equipment on her body, and connects the phone to the device wirelessly (through Wi-Fi, BLE, or ZigBee).

The data from the pulse oximeter, including blood oxygen saturation and heart rate, can be accessed by medical professionals via a mobile app and cloud storage. A number of security issues arise in this context, including (in no particular order): (1) system failures caused by counterfeit/faulty hardware; (2) information leakage from the app and cloud server; (3) eavesdropping during data transmission from the device to the app; (4) unauthorized access to the sensitive data via a backdoor in the installed app; (5) DoS due to open, accessible device information and subpar security standards; and (6) eavesdropping during data transmission from the device to the app.

Our suggestions for device makers, patients, HC practitioners, programmers, and the academic research community are based on this scenario.

Both patients and doctors need each other. Since patients (Alice) and HC providers typically lack technical understanding on various attacks (e.g. software, hardware, and communication channel), they are the primary targets of various malicious attempts.

As a result, both consumers and HC professionals need to be alert to the risks associated with HC devices and apps before making any purchases. Good security measures, such as refusing access from suspect devices or turning off automatic data sharing between apps, should also be implemented to further protect the devices and the data stored on them.

HC information protection: HC data has clinical, financial, and operational value in the market, and it is being generated rapidly by the HC business. It is imperative to implement robust security measures, such as cryptographic methods to protect the collection of nodes in particular manner and memories the secured information to the local system or server system, to prevent unauthorized access to this sensitive HC data.

To prevent spoofing and privilege elevation attacks, symmetric and lightweight cryptographic protocols can be used to restrict access to medical equipment. To implement cryptographic techniques in HC devices, however, would require either the complete replacement of existing devices like IMDs or a significant redesign.

There may be times when communicating with unapproved persons is necessary, but this is made more difficult by cryptographic safeguards. Therefore, researchers should work on creating medically centric cryptography solutions to fulfill the HC industry's specific security requirements.

7.7 Conclusion

The purpose of this chapter was to provide a synopsis of the literature on HC system security and privacy. Common trends in HC device applications include improving Procedural complication, Easiness for developing programs, and expanding the connection with the collection of nodes in the network [49–51]. However, these developments often come with unintended consequences that increase the risk of security and privacy breaches in HC devices and apps. We looked at many parts of the dangers and how the existing solutions counteract them. In light of the vital nature of the work done by HC equipment, the community as a whole must take an active role in resolving these problems. This research is providing the collection of number of attacks that occurred in a recent manner. This information helps to make the secure environment for the secured HC units or systems. We expect this poll to have a positive effect on the medical community.

References

1 Pantelopoulos, A. and Bourbakis, N.G. (2010). A survey on wearable sensor-based systems for health monitoring and prognosis. *IEEE Trans. Syst. Man Cybern. Part C* 40 (1): 1–12.

2 Zhang, M., Raghunathan, A., and Jha, N.K. (2014). Trustworthiness of medical devices and body area networks. *Proc. IEEE* 102 (8): 1174–1188.

3 Kailas, A. and Ingram, M.A. (2009). Wireless communications technology in telehealth systems. In: *Proceedings of the 2009 1st International Conference on Wireless Communication, Vehicular Technology, Information Theory, and Aerospace & Electronic Systems Technology*, 926–930. Los Alamitos, CA: IEEE.

4 Solanas, A., Patsakis, C., Conti, M. et al. (2014). Smart health: a context-aware health paradigm within smart cities. *IEEE Commun. Mag.* 52 (8): 74–81.

5 Lakkadi, S., Mishra, A., and Bhardwaj, M. (2015). Security in ad hoc networks. *Am. J. Networks Commun.* 4 (3–1): 27–34.

6 Jain, I. and Bhardwaj, M. A survey analysis of COVID-19 pandemic using machine learning (July 14, 2022). In: *Proceedings of the Advancement in Electronics & Communication Engineering 2022*, Available at SSRN: https://ssrn.com/abstract=4159523 or https://doi.org/10.2139/ssrn.4159523.

7 Razaque, A., Amsaad, F., Khan, M.J. et al. (2019). Survey: cybersecurity vulnerabilities, attacks and solutions in the medical domain. *IEEE Access* 7 (2019): 168774–168797.

8 Sikder, A.K., Petracca, G., Aksu, H. et al. (2018). A survey on sensor-based threats to Internet-of-Things (IoT) devices and applications. *arXiv*: 1802.02041.

9 Sharma, A., Tyagi, A., and Bhardwaj, M. (2022). Analysis of techniques and attacking pattern in cyber security approach: a survey. *Int. J. Health Sci.* 6 (S2): 13779–13798. https://doi.org/10.53730/ijhs.v6nS2.8625.

10 Tyagi, A., Sharma, A., and Bhardwaj, M. (2022). Future of bioinformatics in India: a survey. *Int. J. Health Sci.* 6 (S2): 13767–13778. https://doi.org/10.53730/ijhs.v6nS2.8624.

11 Sikder, A.K., Aksu, H., and Uluagac, A.S. (2019). A context-aware framework for detecting sensor-based threats on smart devices. *IEEE Trans. Mob. Comput.* 19 (2): 245–261.

12 Zhang, X., Jiang, H., Chen, X. et al. (2009). An energy efficient implementation of on-demand MAC protocol in medical Wireless Body Sensor Networks. In: *Proceedings of the International Symposium on Circuits and Systems*. Los Alamitos, CA: IEEE.

13 24x7. (2018). Global medical device market to grow 4.5%. https://www.24x7mag.com/medical-equipment/global-medical-device-market-grow-4-5/ Retrieved 25 May, 2021.

14 Pourush, N.S. and Bhardwaj, M. (2015). Enhanced privacy-preserving multi-keyword ranked search over encrypted cloud data. *Am. J. Networks Commun.* 4 (3): 25–31.

15 Wu, J., Haider, S.A., Bhardwaj, M. et al. (2022). Blockchain-based data audit mechanism for integrity over big data environments. *Security Commun. Netw.* 2022: 1–9. https://doi.org/10.1155/2022/8165653.

16 Ronquillo, J.G. and Zuckerman, D.M. (2017). Software-related recalls of health information technology and other medical devices: implications for FDA regulation of digital health. *Milbank Q.* 95 (3): 535–553.

17 Shahriar, M.H., Haque, N.I., Rahman, M.A., and Alonso, M. (2020). G-IDS: Generative adversarial net- works assisted intrusion detection system. In: *Proceedings of the 2020 IEEE 44th Annual Computers, Software, and Applications Conference (COMPSAC'20)*, 376–385. Los Alamitos, CA: IEEE.

18 Anand, R., Singh, J., Pandey, D. et al. (2022). Modern technique for interactive communication in LEACH-based ad hoc wireless sensor network. In: *Software Defined Networking for Ad Hoc Networks*, Part of the EAI/Springer Innovations in Communication and Computing Book Series (EAISICC) (ed. M.M. Ghonge, S. Pramanik, and A.D. Potgantwar), 55–73. Springer https://doi.org/10.1007/978-3-030-91149-2_3.

19 Chen, M., Hao, Y., Kai Hwang, L., and Wang, and Lin Wang. (2017). Disease prediction by machine learning over big data from healthcare communities. *IEEE Access* 5 (2017): 8869–8879.

20 Bhardwaja, M. and Ahlawat, A. (2019). Evaluation of maximum lifetime power efficient routing in ad hoc network using magnetic resonance concept. *Recent Patents on Engineering* 13 (3): 256–260.

21 Bhardwaj, M. and Ahalawat, A. (2019). Improvement of lifespan of ad hoc network with congestion control and magnetic resonance concept. In: *International Conference on Innovative Computing and Communications*, 123–133. Singapore: Springer.

22 Anand, R., Shrivastava, G., Gupta, S. et al. (2018). Audio watermarking with reduced number of random samples. In: *Handbook of Research on Network Forensics and Analysis Techniques* (ed. G. Shrivastava, P. Kumar, B. Gupta, et al.), 372–394. IGI Global https://doi.org/10.4018/978-1-5225-4100-4.ch020. www.igi-global.com/chapter/audio-watermarking-with-reduced-number-of-random-samples/201622.

23 Bhardwaj, M. and Ahlawat, A. (2017). Enhance lifespan of WSN using power proficient data gathering algorithm and WPT. *DEStech Transactions on Computer Science and Engineering.*

24 Finlayson, S.G., Chung, H.W., Kohane, I.S., and Beam, A.L. (2018). Adversarial attacks against medical deep learning systems. *arXiv*: 1804.05296.

25 Newaz, A.K.M., Haque, N.I., Sikder, A.K. et al. (2020). Adversarial attacks to machine learning-based smart healthcare systems. In: *Proceedings of the IEEE Global Communications Conference (GLOBE-COM'20)*, 1–6. IEEE.

26 Malasri, K. and Wang, L. (2009). Design and implementation of a securewireless mote-based medical sensor network. *Sensors (Basel)* 9 (8): 6273–6297.

27 Khera, M. (2017). Think like a hacker: insights on the latest attack vectors (and security controls) for medical device applications. *J. Diabetes Sci. Technol.* 11 (2): 207–212.

28 Williams, P.A.H. and Woodward, A.J. (2015). Cybersecurity vulnerabilities in medical devices: a complex environment and multifaceted problem. *Medical Devices (Auckland, NZ)* 8 (2015): 305.

29 Sharma, M., Rohilla, S., and Bhardwaj, M. (2015). Efficient routing with reduced routing overhead and retransmission of manet. *Am. J. Networks Commun.* 4 (3–1): 22–26. https://doi.org/10.11648/j.ajnc.s.2015040301.15.

30 Bhardwaj, M. and Ahlawat, A. (2018). Wireless power transmission with short and long range using inductive coil. *Wireless Eng. Technol.* 9: 1–9. https://doi.org/10.4236/wet.2018.91001.

31 Kaur, K.D. and Bhardwaj, M. (2015). Effective energy constraint routing with on-demand routing protocols in MANET. *Am. J. Networks Commun.* 4 (2): 21–24. https://doi.org/10.11648/j.ajnc.20150402.12.

32 Petlovana, Y.2018). Privacy and security in healthcare: a must-read for healthtech entrepreneurs. https://steelkiwi.com/blog/privacy-and-security-in-healthcare/ Retrieved May 25, 2021.

33 Baldus, H., Corroy, S., Fazzi, A. et al. (2009). Human-centric connectivity enabled by body-coupled communications. *IEEE Commun. Mag.* 47 (6, 2009): 172–178.

34 Bagade, P., Banerjee, A., Milazzo, J., and Gupta, S.K.S. (2013). Protect your BSN: noo handshakes, just namaste! In: *Proceedings of the 2013 IEEE International Conference on Body Sensor Networks*, 1–6. IEEE.

35 Bhardwaj, M. (2020). Research on IoT governance, security, and privacy issues of internet of things. In: *Privacy Vulnerabilities and Data Security Challenges in the IoT*, vol. 115. CRC Press.

36 Kumar, A., Rohilla, S., and Bhardwaj, M. (2019). Analysis of cloud computing load balancing algorithms. *Int. J. Comput. Sci. Eng.* 7: 359–362.

37 Bhardwaj, M., Ahlawat, A., and Bansal, N. (2018). Maximization of lifetime of wireless sensor network with sensitive power dynamic protocol. *Int. J. Eng. Technol.* 7 (3.12): 380–383.

38 Rasmussen, K.B., Castelluccia, C., Heydt-Benjamin, T.S., and Capkun, S. (2009). Proximity-based access control for implantable medical devices. In: *Proceedings of the 16th ACM Conference on Computer and Communications Security*. New York, NY: ACM.

39 Lu, S., Li, M., Yu, S., and Yuan, J. (2013). BANA: body area network authentication exploiting channel characteristics. *IEEE J. Sel. Areas Commun.* 31 (9): 1803–1816.

40 Rostami, M., Juels, A., and Koushanfar, F. (2013). Heart-to-heart (H2H): Authentication for implanted medical devices. In: *Proceedings of the 2013 ACM SIGSAC Conference on Computer and Communications Security (CCS'13)*, 1099–1112. ACM Publisher.

41 Jurik, A.D. and Weaver, A.C. (2011). Securing mobile devices with biotelemetry. In: *Proceedings of the 20th International Conference on Computer Communications and Networks (ICCCN'11)*, 1–6. IEEE.

42 Cherukuri, S., Venkatasubramanian, K.K., and Gupta, S.K.S. (2003). Biosec: a biometric based approach for securing communication in wireless networks of biosensors implanted in the human body. In: *Proceedings of the International Conference on Parallel Processing Workshops*. Los Alamitos, CA: IEEE https://doi.org/10.1109/ICPPW.2003.1240399.

43 Chizari, H. and Lupu, E.C. (2019). Extracting randomness from the trend of IPI for cryptographic operators in implantable medical devices. *IEEE Trans. Dependable Secure Comput.* 18 (2): 875–888.

44 Uppal, M. and Kautish, S. (2021). Cloud-based fault prediction using IoT in office automation for improvisation of health of employees. *J. Healthcare Eng.* 2021: 8106467.

45 Bhattacharya, S., Maddikunta, P.K.R., and Kaluri, R. (2020). A novel PCA-firefly based XGBoost classification model for intrusion detection in networks using GPU. *Electronics.* 9: 219.

46 Mittal, S. et al. (2022). Using identity-based cryptography as a foundation for an effective and secure cloud model for e-health. *Comput. Intell. Neurosci.* 2022.

47 Mohafez, H., El-Bayoumy, I., Sharma, L.K. et al. (2022). Federated learning approach to protect healthcare data over big data scenario. *Sustain. For. 14* (5): 2500.

48 Singamaneni, K.K., Muhammad, G., AlQahtani, S.A., and Zaki, J. (2022). A novel QKD approach to enhance IIOT privacy and computational knacks. *Sensors 22* (18): 6741.

49 Bali, V., Jain, V., and Upadhyay, H. (2021). Artificial intelligence and cybersecurity: current trends and future prospects. *Smart Cyber Ecosys. Sustainable Dev.* 431–441.

50 Uppal, M., Mahmoud, A., Elmagzoub, M.A. et al. (2023). Fault prediction recommender model for IoT enabled sensors based workplace. *Sustain. For. 15* (2): 1060.

51 Kautish, S., Juneja, S., Mohiuddin, K. et al. (2023). Enhanced cloud storage encryption standard for security in distributed environments. *Electronics 12* (3): 714.

8

Implementation and Analysis of the Proposed Model in a Distributed e-Healthcare System

Manish Bhardwaj, Sanjiv Sharma, and Amit K. Gupta

KIET Group of Institutions, Ghaziabad, Uttar Pradesh, India

8.1 Introduction

Clearly, businesses want to achieve information integration across their geographically dispersed systems of databases, apps, and end users, but they also want to decentralize their processes.

As time has progressed, the systems and apps available on the web (also known as WEBAPPS) have become increasingly complex computing tools, able to not only do tasks independently for users but also to interact with other systems and databases in a business setting. With the world evolving at such a rapid rate, wireless Internet access in all outlying areas is an absolute necessity.

Internet access via wireless mobile device. Benefits in the field of medicine were immediately put to use, thanks to developments in analog telephony in the late nineteenth and early twentieth centuries. By means of this development, people could get in touch with medical help when they needed it. It was also put to use in hospitals, where it was used to send electrocardiograms over the phone [1]. All of them fall under the category of telemedicine or the delivery of medical services over long distances. Just as there is a downside to every upside. The centralization of these methods is hindered by their limited bandwidth, slow pace of data transfer across copper cables, and interference and other sounds. Since then, the use of computers, digital networks, and electronic health records has expanded far beyond the realm of traditional telemedicine.

Meta-Heuristic Algorithms for Advanced Distributed Systems, First Edition. Edited by Rohit Anand, Abhinav Juneja, Digvijay Pandey, Sapna Juneja, and Nidhi Sindhwani.

There are PHCs spread out around the region, but current methods of communication are inefficient and hampered by a number of barriers. It has been noted that healthcare (HC) providers in rural areas spend more time gathering data and writing up reports than they do actually speaking with patients. Poorer services, consultation, and provision of fundamental HC are all made more difficult by their increased administrative participation [2]. Therefore, it is recommended that the distributed web-based model be implemented in such businesses.

We represent the entire PHC network as if it were composed of individual client nodes, and this allows us to create distributed system designs and models. These models, we believe, will prove helpful. Depending on the design, the models can be lightweight, portable, and self-reliant clients that connect to a server over a network [3].

Telemedicine plays an important part in the modern HC system. Telemedicine's benefits include bringing better medical attention to persons in remote locations. The quality of care is increased while costs are decreased. Most notably, it helps HC professionals including specialists, nurses, and allied health professionals feel less alone in their work. When we talk about "tele-medicine," we're referring to the practice of combining medical knowledge with telecommunication and computer information technology in order to provide HC and other medical services to geographically dispersed patients.

Despite the importance of precise record keeping and communication, the HC industry falls behind other sectors in its use of computing and networking technology [4].

Despite the consensus that accurate record keeping and clear communication are critical to providing quality HC, many in the HC industry and their patients remain uncomfortable using computers and do not view them as fundamental to their purpose.

The existing HC system relies on handwritten notes and face-to-face communication between doctors and nurses. In the United States, for instance, doctors and pharmacies rarely use electronic means of communication; instead, patients often receive paper prescriptions from their doctors.

The patient must next bring the prescription to the pharmacy, stand in line to provide it to a pharmacist, and then wait for the pharmacist to fill the order. Voice-enabled human–computer interfaces for doctors, nurses, pharmacists, and others in the HC industry would greatly enhance this procedure by allowing for the computerized transmission of prescriptions from the doctor to the pharmacist [5].

As many as 7000 people each year die as a result of improper prescriptions, claims Carmen Catizone of the National Association of Boards of Pharmacy. An estimated 5% of the approximately 3 billion prescriptions filled annually are incorrect, according to a Washington Post report. All of these figures point to the critical importance of finding ways to cut down on medical mistakes [6]. Workplace mistakes are addressed in the paper To Err is Human: Building a Safer Health System:

> Humans are fallible, and that's true in any industry."

When building systems, make it difficult for people to do the wrong thing while making the correct thing easy to accomplish, and you'll reduce the likelihood of human error [7]. Large HC systems face problems in managing individual patients' data, standardizing that data, extracting knowledge from it, and federating databases. These issues highlight the need to enhance HC quality, broaden patients' access to care and information, and lower HC costs.

8.2 Outmoded Systems

Management information systems that have been around for a while include relational databases. Data processing and decision-making applications built for use on the Internet are not supported by these centralized systems. As a result, the resources needed for global HC communication remain siloed within these systems. Certain drawbacks of this system are mentioned as follows:

- High cost of hardware.
- The cost of software projects is typically very high.
- Frustratingly slow communication.
- Separate licenses are expensive and unnecessary.
- Only client terminals are permitted to perform read activities.

These are a two-tiered, non-distributed system. Figure 8.1 shows the basic architecture of outmoded system before the distributed system.

Even though PHCs are located all across the region, current methods of communication are far from ideal and have several flaws. The HC environment is poor in rural places, and doctors and nurses spend more time gathering data and writing reports than really talking with patients. Services, advice, and supply of basic HC suffer as a result of their increased administrative duties. As a result, it is recommended that a Dynamical Wasserstein Barycenters (DWB) model be implemented for such Indian businesses [8]. That's why when we're designing and developing distributed system models, we count each PHC as a single client node. As such, we believe these models will prove fruitful. The models can be lightweight, portable, and self-sufficient clients that connect to a server over a network.

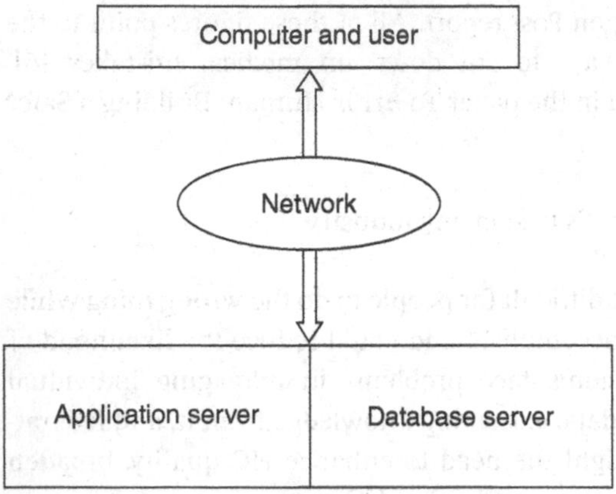

Figure 8.1 Basic architecture of outmoded system before the distributed system.

8.3 Distributed Systems

A distributed system is made up of many independent computers that are all connected and able to exchange information with one another. These machines collaborate with one another to do a specific task. A distributed program is a computer application or program that operates in a distributed environment [9]. Distributed programming refers to the method used to create such software. Distributed computing is a method of processing data using multiple computers rather than a single supercomputer. Distributed systems are web-based applications that require a server node and a client node in order to function.

Centralization in early database systems led to complicated databases. The databases can be accessed by multiple users at once, but all processing takes place on the server. Single-tier or host systems, as well as two-tier architectures, both fall within the category of classic systems, and both have their share of drawbacks. Users' requirements today aren't region specific; rather, they're universal: they demand constant access to the latest information, wherever it may be located [10]. Users of older systems can do nothing but read data. It is not possible to logically connect the client side of computing in these scenarios to the server side of computing via networks anywhere in the world or remotely.

A distributed system is made up of many separate computers that operate together and share information across a network. Those machines collaborate with one another to complete a task. A distributed program is any application or software that operates in a distributed environment. Distributed programming refers to the methodology of creating a program that runs across multiple computers.

A distributed system is one in which the processing of data is dispersed over multiple computers rather than being limited to just one [11–13]. To put it simply, distributed systems are any Internet-based applications that require two distinct kinds of computers, a server node and a client node, to function properly. The term "Simply Distributed System" refers to a computer system that functions through the cooperation of multiple computers linked together by digital communications networks. Figure 8.2 shows the 3-tier architecture of distributed system [14].

Consolidation in early data warehouses led to complicated databases. Databases can be accessed by multiple users at once, but all processing takes place on the central server. One-tier, or host, systems, and two-tier architecture, both of which have their own set of problems, are examples of classic systems [15–18]. Users' requirements today aren't region specific; rather, they're world spanning, with the user desiring constant access to fresh content. Users need to access data from off-site locations or mobile devices that can be linked via wired or wireless networks. Users of older systems can only consume data in a passive reading capacity.

Distributed system is divided into two types of architecture:

1) Peer-to-Peer (P2P) architecture
2) Client–server architecture

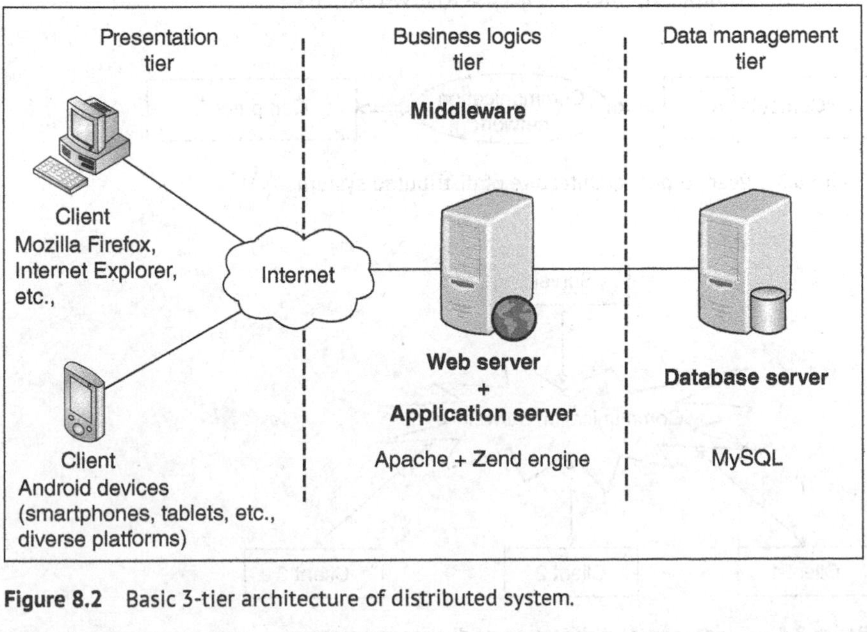

Figure 8.2 Basic 3-tier architecture of distributed system.

8.3.1 Peer-to-Peer Architecture

In this architecture, the nodes are connected directly with the help of a communication network. no other node acts as the intermediate node in the type of architecture. Figure 8.3 shows this architecture.

It's a design for exchanging data between two computers: a sender (the client) and a receiver (the server), using a protocol like transmission control protocol/internet protocol (TCP/IP).

Other sorts of architectures include distributed object architecture and multi-processor architecture. Figure 8.4 shows the client–server architecture of the distributed system.

The term "health information technology (HIT)" is used to refer to the overarching framework that describes the secure administration and interchange of patient data between consumers, providers, governments, and insurance companies via electronic means [19]. More and more people believe that HIT has the greatest potential to boost the HC system's quality, safety, and efficiency.

- Extensive and regular use of HIT will.
- The quality of HC must be increased.
- To avoid medical mistakes.
- Spend less on HC.
- Boost organizational effectiveness.
- Reduce red tape and increase access to low-cost HC.

Figure 8.3 Peer-to-peer architecture of distributed system.

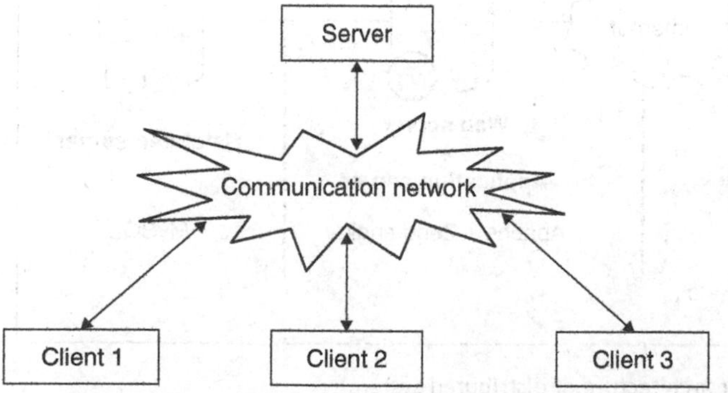

Figure 8.4 Client–server architecture of distributed system.

If a population has specific HC needs, a health system (also known as a HC system) is the network of providers, facilities, and funds put in place to address those demands.

Recent developments in Internet technology have facilitated the expansion of fields including medicine, engineering, and IT [20]. Thanks to the advancements in Internet technology, we now have access to more thorough, accurate, and up-to-date patient health records and information [21]. There is no substitute for in-person interactions between HC providers and their patients or between HC providers themselves [22]. When face-to-face encounters are not an option, the knowledge gained from these models is crucial in determining how to provide better medical care [23]. It also includes any and all means through which users, such as patients and HC providers, can interact remotely via technological technology [24].

To be interoperable, two or more parts, programs, or systems must be able to communicate with one another and share data [25]. Each hospital department or medical clinic may employ many applications to transmit clinical and administrative information among applications, making interoperability between applications from different suppliers a key concern for the HC business today.

It enhances the convenience and availability of health professionals access to electronic health records and other health-related information at any time and from any location. Health administrators benefit from enhanced data gathering and simplified opportunities for statistical and economic analysis [26]. The quantity of readily accessible medical data has grown, which is a boon to the field of health sciences.

When it comes to managing dispersed patient records, distributed solutions are crucial. The patient's information is stored in a decentralized manner, with a local database on each client computer. Data in a distributed database is not kept in a single location but rather is dispersed over a group of computers that are all linked together by some sort of communication mechanism.

As a result, we have a robust, accessible, and adaptable database. The primary benefit is that distributed databases can decrease network traffic and improve response times for local queries.

8.4 Previous Work

There has been a lot of effort put into the creation of e-HC systems [27]. The limitations and difficulties of creating a versatile, process-oriented architecture for an integrated HC network are discussed [28].

They single out malleability, versatility, robustness, the incorporation of preexisting systems and standards, semantic compatibility, security, and process orientation as significant concerns. Computer-assisted HC workflow [29] cover most of the ground. They include an overview of workflow properties and needs as well as a definition of workflow properties for frequently performed HC procedures. We intend to further examine the topic of HC workflow as a business process execution language (BPEL) process.

Records and databases have been the primary focus of e-HC system development [30]. The social consequences of capturing and sharing HC information have also been the subject of research, in addition to access and security [31].

Human–computer interfaces and usability testing by HC workers and patients have received less attention. Using electronic communication and record keeping, as well as providing user-friendly input and output capabilities, our e-HC system strives to decrease human error.

Though the United States Department of Health and Human Services [32] and the California HC Foundation have advocated for the use of electronic HC records, both institutions tend to favor highly centralized or centrally administered systems.

More distributed and interoperable solutions based on open international standards are required due to the splintered state of HC in the United States and the increasingly transnational nature of HC services and patients [33].

There are other e-HC Web portals, systems, and phones available from commercial companies including Aurora Healthcare Systems, Medseek, and Palm, but none of them offers all the capabilities that our e-HC system provides.

To make our e-HC system accessible to both humans and software, we make use of cutting-edge techniques to publish its features as Web Services in line with the service-oriented architecture (SOA) [34].

Using the SOA, other academics have created e-HC systems. [35] has used the SOA in conjunction with grid computing technology to create a sensor and actuator framework that monitors a patient's health state and provides feedback.

Since their framework is narrowly focused on the usage of medical monitoring devices, our e-HC system provides services that engage patients, doctors, nurses, and pharmacists.

Ref. [36] details a SOA for a data network used in medical research that allows for granular management of data access and utilization. Care2x is a free and open-source web-based university project that implements a cutting-edge hospital information system, used for the education of future medical professionals and engineers in the HC industry.

It makes use of the Apache web server, the PHP scripting language, and the MySQL database system to build its central data server and health exchange protocol [37]. Instead of concentrating on a health research data network or HC training for the hospital setting, our e-HC system prioritizes interactions between patients, doctors, nurses, pharmacists, and medical monitoring equipment.

Weiss [38] has created a model for patient-centered HC services that employ the utilization of a mobile device to push and draw data to and from a data analysis engine based on the SOA; this is related to our use of Atom/respiratory syncytial virus (RSS) [39, 40].

According to the software service paradigm, it has created a data integration broker for HC systems that gathers and combines data from autonomous HC agencies.

Our infrastructure for Consistent Data Replication and Reliable Data Distribution can also be used for this. How to address semantic interoperability issues across medical data systems that use incompatible standards to express the same data is an exciting area of unanswered study [41].

8.5 Service-Oriented Architecture of e-Healthcare

Our created electronic HC system makes use of Web Services and Atom/RSS and is based on the SOA. Principles of software architecture including abstraction, encapsulation, modularization, and software reuse are all bolstered by the SOA. It separates the interfaces from the implementations and provides well-defined interfaces for client applications [42]. A set of procedures can be used to implement the service's capabilities and interfaces. Each process delivers an independent service or set of capabilities. Because of this standardized interface, the underlying implementation of each service can evolve independently of how it is consumed. Not only do technological aspects of service delivery and consumption fall under the purview of the SOA, but so do the guiding principles and operational procedures that make this possible [43].

Thus, the SOA is a good framework for creating a decentralized e-HC system [44]. Our electronic HC system has a three-tiered SOA. The Web Service interfaces are provided by the top layer. The HC services discussed to make up the lowest layer. In the system, communications traveling between the Web Services interfaces and the HC services are coordinated by the services coordinator located in the middle layer [45]. The rest of the architecture's pieces are not HC-specific but rather "application neutral."

Safety and confidentiality are of paramount concern in the medical field. Only authenticated and authorized individuals should have access to sensitive personal health information. Data storage security is just as important as data transmission security [46, 47]. Using a SOA is crucial for implementing such regulations. Figure 8.5 shows the layered architecture of SOA.

We have taken these concerns into account while developing our electronic HC system. Service requests are recorded and user sessions are tracked to ensure security. Data in the system is linked to its original developer, and only authorized

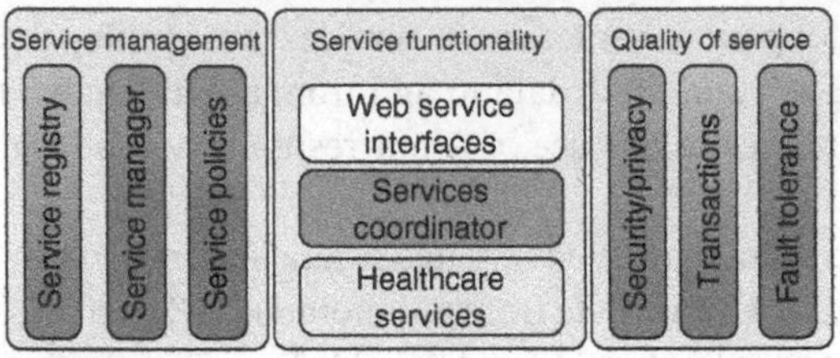

Figure 8.5 Layered diagram of SOA.

users have access to the data. Authentication and session management are strictly enforced for apps installed on devices like personal digital assistants (PDAs) [48].

Our electronic HC system's Clinic component delivers the system's medical services to patients. Patients, doctors, nurses, and pharmacists can all access the system through specialized user interfaces. These modules can be accessed from any device, including regular computers, servers, handheld devices, and even smartphones. It's also possible for them to serve as blood pressure monitors and similar medical monitoring devices.

The clinicians, patients, and health trackers at the clinic can access the Clinic module's features via a Web Server and a Web Service. Those who would rather utilize a web browser to access the HC services can do so through the Web Server interface.

Humans and machines alike can talk to the e-HC system through its Web Service interface. Data is accessed by the Web Server via the Web Services. The Clinic section helps the doctor out with daily tasks. It stores data like the doctor's daily or weekly schedule, a list of patients who have been seen, any relevant notes, etc. As was previously mentioned, patients' personal information is protected by strong access controls and security measures.

Using the given Web Service, the Clinic component transmits doctor's orders to the chosen pharmacies across the global Internet. In order to find a pharmacy near a user's current location, it queries the Yahoo! LocalSearch Web Service.

Whether working from a desktop computer or a portable device, the doctor can use the Web Server interface to gain access to the electronic HC system. Doctors can utilize PDAs to record and retrieve patient information during and after appointments.

It is challenging for the doctor to enter patient data using a PDA due to the small keyboard. For this reason, we've equipped the PDA with speech recognition software that lets the doctor enter and retrieve data just by speaking to it.

We also use speech synthesis software to give the doctor some feedback. These speech technologies make it easier for doctors to do their work, and they also serve to promote the usage of PDAs.

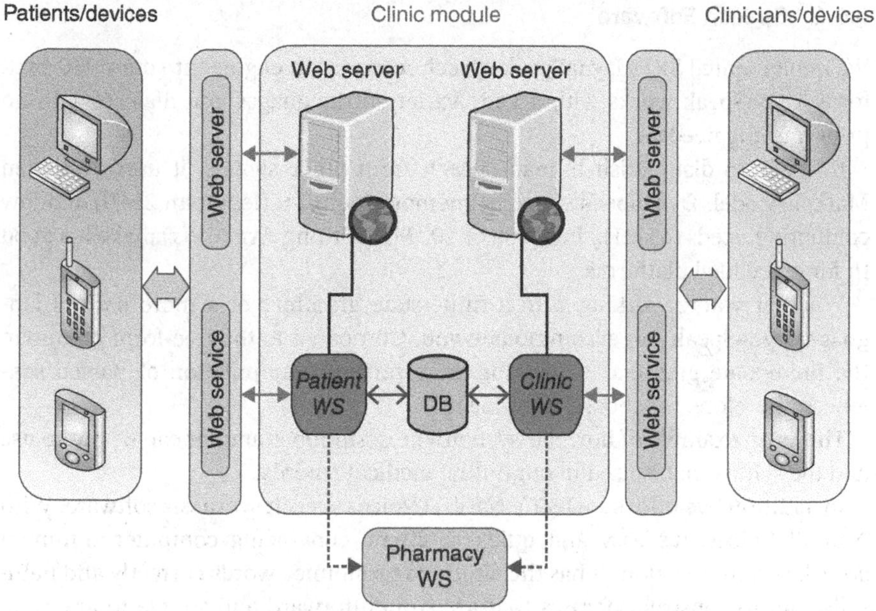

Figure 8.6 Three-layered architecture of clinical module of the system.

Clinic Web Service receives data from a variety of medical monitoring devices that use wired or wireless networks to collect and transfer data. Our blood pressure monitor has Bluetooth connectivity, allowing for data to be wirelessly communicated from the patient to the e-HC system and then on to the doctor for review (Figure 8.6).

8.6 Implementation of the Proposed Model

As part of our solution, we used PCs with 3 GHz processors and 2 GB of RAM to host the Web Services. We used 2 GB RAM, 2 GHz processors, and installed our client apps. Over the global Internet, client programs exchange data with a Web Server or Web Services. The OQO device, a full-featured personal computer measuring just 3″ × 5″, was utilized as the PDA. An embedded speech recognition engine and our physician application are both supported by the 1 GHz Transmeta Crusoe processor found in the OQO gadget. The screen has a resolution of 800 by 480, which is high enough to display graphical data in great detail. The PDA is equipped with WiFi for wireless connection to a home or office computer.

8.6.1 Speech Software

We implemented SRI's DynaSpeak speech recognition engine into our e-HC platform. DynaSpeak works with a wide variety of languages and dialects with no prior training needed.

In order to distinguish human speech from other signals, it uses a Hidden Markov Model. DynaSpeak's modest memory footprint (less than 2 MB) and low computing needs (66 MHz Intel x86 or 200 MHz Strong Arm CPU) make it a good fit for embedded platforms.

Whether you're working with a finite-state grammar or a more natural language, DynaSpeak can accommodate you. Compared to the free-form grammar, the finite-state grammar allows for more precise manipulation of parsed sentences; therefore, we choose to utilize it.

This is an example of how our system's prescription grammar can be put to use and the syntax that is used in our online medical records.

In addition, we utilized AT&T's Natural Voices speech synthesis software. With Natural Voices, it's easy and quick to create convincing computer-to-human speech communication. It has the ability to pronounce words correctly and naturally, and to construct phrases that are straightforward and simple to grasp, all without giving off the impression that a machine is doing the talking.

Several languages, both male and female voices, and the SAPI, VoiceXML, and JSAPI interface standards are all supported by Natural Voices. We built text-to-speech software using Natural Voices for the prototype device; it operates in the background and understands VoiceXML messages.

8.7 Evaluation of the Proposed Model Performance

We timed how long it took for a doctor's app to get confirmation from a pharmacy app that it had received a prescription sent by a doctor's app (the latency of the Pharmacy Web Service) as part of our performance evaluation.

Prescriptions were sent at several speeds (0.1, 0.2, 0.5, 1, 2, and 3 per second) and dosages in the studies (1, 2, 3, 4, and 5 medicines). Experimental results are depicted in Figure 8.7; specifically, the average time it takes to fill a prescription for a set amount of medications (expressed in seconds) over a 300-second period.

As may be expected, the latency grows as the pace at which prescriptions are sent grows.

Since more people are using the Pharmaceutical Web Service, its response times have slowed down. Just as the latency grows as the number of medications in a prescription grows, so does the rate at which that prescription is sent, due to the bigger message size and longer processing time for the XML.

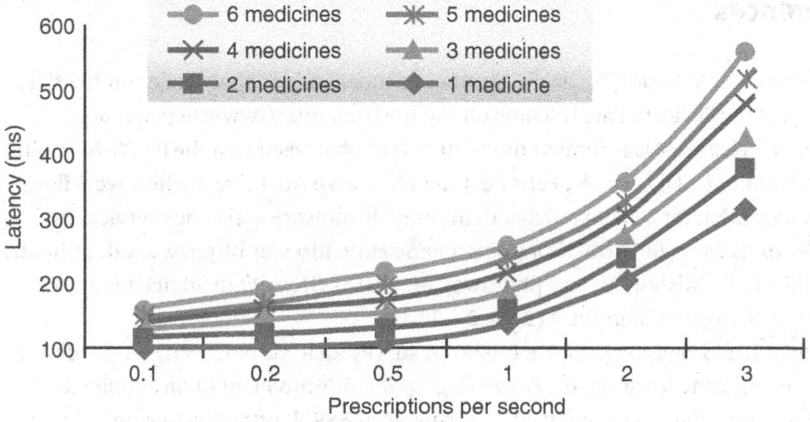

Figure 8.7 Graphical representation of latency of the model (ms) vs prescriptions per second.

8.8 Conclusion and Future Work

In this study, we introduce a decentralized e-HC system that employs the SOA for its service-centric operations (i.e. service design, deployment, management, and invocation). HC calls for cutting-edge answers, crafted and put into practice using cutting-edge technologies, that inspire medical staff and patients to embrace novel practices that enhance the quality of care provided.

The utilization of multimedia for both input and output, especially visuals and sound, makes the system more approachable to people who are not tech savvy.

The relationships between patients, doctors, nurses, and pharmacists are currently the main emphasis of our electronic HC system. As an example, laboratory technicians who carry out and report on tests and analyses requested by physicians will soon be able to use the system. Epocrates Rx is just one example of a pharmaceutical company-supplied application that can be interfaced with our Clinic and Pharmacy modules to provide additional information about drugs, doses, and potential drug interactions.

We also intend to look into drug delivery technologies, such as electronic pillboxes, that encourage and track the timely and correct intake of medication. We are currently having discussions with manufacturers of such medical equipment regarding the merits of making available open interfaces that would allow their products to be integrated into a SOA-based electronic HC system. We're also consulting with medical experts to hone our e-HC platform to perfection and address concerns raised by practitioners in the field.

References

1 Alexandria, V. (April 28, 2006). Number of independent pharmacies on the rise, Impact of Medicare Part D looms on the horizon. http://www.ncpanet.org/media/releases/2006/number of independent pharmacies on the 04-28-2006.php.

2 Ardissono, L., Di Leva, A., Petrone, G. et al. (2005). Adaptive medical workflow management for a context-dependent home healthcare assistance service. In: *Electronic Notes in Theoretical Computer Science*. Elsevier http://www.di.unito.it/.

3 Lakkadi, S., Mishra, A., and Bhardwaj, M. (2015). Security in ad hoc networks. *Am. J. Networks Commun.* 4 (3–1): 27–34.

4 Ishita, J. and Bhardwaj, M. Dr. (2022). A survey analysis of COVID-19 pandemic using machine learning. In: *Proceedings of the Advancement in Electronics & Communication Engineering 2022*, Available at SSRN: https://ssrn.com/abstract=4159523 or http://dx.doi.org/10.2139/ssrn.4159523.

5 Andersen, R., Rice, T.H., and Kominski, G.F. (2001). *Changing the U.S. Health Care System: Key Issues in Health Services, Policy and Management*. Josswey-Bass.

6 Sharma, A., Tyagi, A., and Bhardwaj, M. (2022). Analysis of techniques and attacking pattern in cyber security approach: a survey. *Int. J. Health Sci.* 6 (S2): 13779–13798. https://doi.org/10.53730/ijhs.v6nS2.8625.

7 Anderson, R.J. (1996). *Security in Clinical Information Systems*. British Medical Association.

8 Tyagi, A., Sharma, A., and Bhardwaj, M. (2022). Future of bioinformatics in India: a survey. *Int. J. Health Sci.* 6 (S2): 13767–13778. https://doi.org/10.53730/ijhs.v6nS2.8624.

9 Beyer, M., Kuhn, K.A., Meiler, C. et al. (2004). Towards a flexible, process-oriented IT architecture for an integrated healthcare network. In: *Proceedings of the 2004 ACM Symposium on Applied Computing, Nicosia, Cyprus, March 2004*, 264–271. ACM.

10 Chauhan, P. and Bhardwaj, M. (2017). Analysis the performance of interconnection network topology C2 torus based on two dimensional torus. *Int. J. Emerging Res. Manage. Technol.* 6 (6): 169–173.

11 Bloomfield, B.P. (1991). The role of information systems in the UK national health service: action at a distance and the fetish of calculation. *Social Stud. Sci.* 21: 701–734.

12 Pourush, N.S. and Bhardwaj, M. (2015). Enhanced privacy-preserving multi-keyword ranked search over encrypted cloud data. *Am. J. Networks Commun.* 4 (3): 25–31.

13 Budgen, D., Rigby, M., Brereton, P., and Turner, M. (2007). A data integration broker for healthcare systems. *IEEE Comput.* 40 (4): 34–41.

14 Detmer, D.E. (2003). Building the national health information in-frastructure for personal health, health care services, public health and research. *BMC Med. Inf. Decis. Making* 3: 1–40.

15 Grimson, J., Grimson, W., and Hasselbring, W. (2000). The SI challenge in health care. *Communi. ACM* 43 (6): 48–55.

16 Jain, S., Sindhwani, N., Anand, R., and Kannan, R. (2022). COVID Detection Using Chest X-Ray and Transfer Learning. In: *Intelligent Systems Design and Applications. ISDA 2021*, Lecture Notes in Networks and Systems, vol. 418 (ed. A. Abraham, N. Gandhi, T. Hanne, et al.), 933–943. Cham: Springer https://doi.org/10.1007/978-3-030-96308-8_87.

17 Wu, J., Haider, S.A., Bhardwaj, M. et al. (2022). Blockchain-Based Data Audit Mechanism for Integrity over Big Data Environments. Security and Communication Networks. Hindawi Publisher.

18 Bhardwaja, M. and Ahlawat, A. (2019). Evaluation of maximum lifetime power efficient routing in Ad hoc network using magnetic resonance concept. *Recent Pat. Eng.* 13 (3): 256–260.

19 Bhardwaj, M. and Ahalawat, A. (2019). Improvement of lifespan of Ad hoc network with congestion control and magnetic resonance concept. In: *International Conference on Innovative Computing and Communications*, 123–133. Singapore: Springer.

20 Meivel, S., Sindhwani, N., Anand, R. et al. (2022). Mask detection and social distance identification using internet of things and faster R-CNN algorithm . *Comput. Intell. Neurosci.* 2022: 2103975. https://doi.org/10.1155/2022/2103975.

21 Wehde, M. (2019). Healthcare 4.0. *IEEE Eng. Manag. Rev.* 47 (3): 24–28. https://doi.org/10.1109/EMR.2019.2930702.

22 Omar, W.M. and Taleb-Bendiab, A. (2006). Service oriented architecture for e-health support services based on grid computing. In: *Proceedings of the IEEE International Conference on Services Oriented Computing, Chicago, IL*, 135–142.

23 Song, X., Hwong, B., Matos, G. et al. (May 2006). Understanding requirements for computer-aided healthcare workflows: experiences and challenges. In: *Proceedings of the 28th International Conference on Software Engineering, Shanghai, China*, 930–934.

24 Schwiegelshohn, U., Badia, R.M., Bubak, M. et al. (2010). Perspectives on grid computing. In: *Future Generation Computer Systems*, vol. 26 (ed. M. Taufer), 1104–1115. Elsevier https://doi.org/10.1016/j.future.2010.05.010.

25 Sharma, M., Rohilla, S., and Bhardwaj, M. (2015). Efficient routing with reduced routing overhead and retransmission of manet. *Am. J. Networks Commun.* 4 (3-1): 22–26. https://doi.org/10.11648/j.ajnc.s.2015040301.15.

26 Bhardwaj, M. and Ahlawat, A. (2018). Wireless power transmission with short and long range using inductive coil. *Wireless Eng. Technol.* 9: 1–9. https://doi.org/10.4236/wet.2018.91001.

27 Kaur, K.D. and Bhardwaj, M. (2015). Effective energy constraint routing with on-demand routing protocols in MANET. *Am. J. Networks Commun.* 4 (2): 21–24. https://doi.org/10.11648/j.ajnc.20150402.12.

28 Bhardwaj, M. (2020). 7 Research on IoT Governance, Security, and Privacy Issues of Internet of Things. Privacy Vulnerabilities and Data Security Challenges in the IoT, 115–134. CRC Press.

29 Kumar, A., Rohilla, S., and Bhardwaj, M. (2019). Analysis of cloud computing load balancing algorithms. *International Journal of Computer Sciences and Engineering* 7: 359–362.

30 Bhardwaj, M., Ahlawat, A., and Bansal, N. (2018). Maximization of lifetime of wireless sensor network with sensitive power dynamic protocol. *Int. J. Eng . Technol.* 7 (3-12): 380–383.

31 Subramanian, M., Ali, A.S., Rana, O. et al. (2006). Healthcare@Home: research models for patient-centered healthcare services. In: *Proceedings of the 2006 International Symposium on Modern Computing*, 107–113.

32 Taylor, K.L., Colton, C.M., Baxter, R. et al. (2004). A Service Oriented Architecture for a health research data network. In: *Proceedings of the International Conference on Scientific and Statistical Database Management, Santorini, Greece*, 443–444.

33 Tsiknakis, M., Chronaki, C.E., Kapidakis, S. et al. (1997). An integrated architecture for the provision of health telematic services based on digital library technologies. *Int. J. Digital Libraries* 1 (3): 257–277.

34 Toseland, R.W., McCallion, P., Gerber, T., and Banks, S. (2002). Predictors of health and human services use by persons with dementia and their family caregivers. *Soc. Sci. Med.* 55 (7): 1255–1266. https://doi.org/10.1016/S0277-9536(01)00240-4.

35 U.S. Institute of Medicine (1997). *The Computer-Based Patient Record, an Essential Technology for Health Care* (ed. R.S. Dick, E.B. Steen, and D.E. Detmer). National Academy Press.

36 Mahrous, M.S. (2018). Patient safety culture as a quality indicator for a safe health system: experience from Almadinah Almunawwarah, KSA. *J. Taibah Univ. Med. Sci.* 13 (4): 377–383. https://doi.org/10.1016/j.jtumed.2018.04.002.

37 Lee, E., Daugherty, J.A., and Hamelin, T. (2019). Reimagine health care leadership, challenges and opportunities in the 21st century. *J. Perianesth. Nurs.* 34 (1): 27–38. https://doi.org/10.1016/j.jopan.2017.11.007.

38 Weiss, R. (November 30, 1999), Medical errors blamed for many deaths: As many as 98,000 a year in U.S. linked to mistakes, The Washington Post, A01.

39 Sharma, S. et al. (2022). Deep learning model for the automatic classification of white blood cells. *Comput. Intell. Neurosci.* 2022: 7384131.

40 Juneja, S. et al. (2021). An approach for thoracic syndrome classification with convolutional neural networks. *Comput. Math. Methods Med.* 2021.

41 Kaur, S. and Kumar, V. (2021). Predicting diabetes mellitus with machine learning techniques using multi-criteria decision making. *Int. J. Inf' Retr. Res. 11* (2): 38–52.

42 Dhankhar, A. and Bali, V. (2021). Kernel parameter tuning to tweak the performance of classifiers for identification of heart diseases. *Int. J. e-Health Med. Commun. 12* (4): 1–16.

43 Juneja, S., Juneja, A., Dhiman, G. et al. (2021). Computer vision-enabled character recognition of hand gestures for patients with hearing and speaking disability. *Mobile Inf. Syst. 2021*: 1–10.

44 Rashid, J., Batool, S., Kim, J. et al. (2022). An augmented artificial intelligence approach for chronic diseases prediction. *Front. Public Health 10*: 860396. https://doi.org/10.3389/fpubh.2022.860396.

45 Aggarwal, S., Gupta, S., Kannan, R. et al. (2022). A convolutional neural network-based framework for classification of protein localization using confocal microscopy images. *IEEE Access 10*: 83591–83611.

46 Sharma, S., Gupta, S., Gupta, D. et al. (2022). Performance evaluation of the deep learning based convolutional neural network approach for the recognition of chest X-ray images. *Front. Oncol.* 12: 932496. https://doi.org/10.3389/fonc.2022.932496.

47 Viriyasitavat, W., Mohafez, H., Hadizadeh, M. et al. (2022). A novel machine-learning-based hybrid CNN model for tumor identification in medical image processing. *Sustainability 14* (3): 1447.

48 Kanwal, S., Rashid, J., Anjum, N. et al. (2022). Feature selection for lung and breast cancer disease prediction using machine learning techniques. In: *2022 1st IEEE International Conference on Industrial Electronics: Developments & Applications (ICIDeA)*, 163–168. IEEE.

9

Leveraging Distributed Systems for Improved Educational Planning and Resource Allocation

S. Durga[1], Priti Gupta[2], Latika Kharb[3], P.S. Ranjit[4], Venkata Harshavardhan Reddy Dornadula[5], Kali Charan Modak[6], and Geetha Manoharan[7]

[1] *Koneru Lakshmaiah Education Foundation, Vaddeswaram, Andhra Pradesh, India*
[2] *P.G. Department of Economics, Bhupendra Narayan Mandal University (West Campus) P.G. Centre, Saharsa, India*
[3] *Jagan Institute of Management Studies, Rohini, Sector-5, Delhi, India*
[4] *Department of Mechanical Engineering, Aditya Engineering College Surampalem, Kakinada, Andhra Pradesh, India*
[5] *Startups and IIC, Chairman Office, Sree Venkateswara College of Engineering, Nellore, Andhra Pradesh, India*
[6] *IPS Academy, Institute of Business Management and Research, Indore, Madhya Pradesh, India*
[7] *School of Business, SR University, Hyderabad, Telangana, India*

9.1 Introduction

In recent years, educational planning and resource allocation have become increasingly complex tasks, with a growing need for innovative approaches to address the challenges faced by educational institutions. Leveraging distributed systems, a class of computer systems that are composed of multiple, autonomous computing entities that communicate and coordinate their actions via a network, presents a promising solution for improving the efficiency, effectiveness, and sustainability of educational planning and resource allocation. Distributed systems have already been widely adopted in various domains, including finance, healthcare, transportation, and entertainment, due to their ability to offer superior performance, scalability, fault tolerance, and flexibility compared to traditional centralized systems. Moreover, distributed systems can support a wide range of applications, such as real-time data processing, machine learning, and cloud computing, which are essential for meeting the demands of modern education. In this review chapter, we

Meta-Heuristic Algorithms for Advanced Distributed Systems, First Edition. Edited by Rohit Anand, Abhinav Juneja, Digvijay Pandey, Sapna Juneja, and Nidhi Sindhwani.

explore the potential benefits of leveraging distributed systems for improved educational planning and resource allocation. We focus on the theoretical and practical aspects of distributed systems in education, as well as the challenges and opportunities for future research. Our research question is: How can distributed systems be used to improve educational planning and resource allocation? To answer this question, we first provide a theoretical framework that describes the main concepts and principles of distributed systems and their relevance to education. We then present a set of case studies and examples of successful implementations of distributed systems for educational planning and resource allocation, with a particular emphasis on their technical and practical aspects. We also analyze the challenges and limitations of implementing distributed systems in education, including infrastructure requirements, security and privacy concerns, and data management and analysis. Finally, we discuss future directions and opportunities for research and practice, such as identifying new applications of distributed systems in education, developing new methodologies for evaluating the performance and impact of distributed systems in education, and addressing ethical, legal, and social issues related to the use of distributed systems in education. Our chapter contributes to the literature on educational planning and resource allocation by providing a comprehensive and systematic review of the potential benefits and challenges of leveraging distributed systems. We hope that our work will inspire researchers, practitioners, and policymakers to consider the use of distributed systems as a viable and effective solution for addressing the complex and evolving needs of education [1–3].

9.1.1 Overview of the Current State of Educational Planning and Resource Allocation

Educational planning and resource allocation are critical components of the education system that play a key role in ensuring that students have access to high-quality education. In recent years, the increasing demand for education, combined with limited resources and changing demographics, has made educational planning and resource allocation more complex and challenging.

In many countries, educational planning and resource allocation are primarily centralized, with decisions made by government bodies or education authorities at the national or regional level. These centralized systems typically rely on a top-down approach to planning, where decisions are made based on centralized data, policies, and guidelines.

However, centralized systems can also face a number of challenges, such as inefficiencies, inflexibility, and lack of responsiveness to local needs. For example, centralized planning can result in inadequate distribution of resources, with certain regions or schools receiving less funding or support than others. Additionally, centralized planning may not effectively address the unique needs and challenges of specific schools or communities, leading to reduced effectiveness and quality of education.

In recent years, there has been a growing recognition of the importance of decentralized and participatory approaches to educational planning and resource allocation. Decentralized systems, which delegate decision-making power to local authorities, teachers, and communities, can offer a more responsive and flexible approach that better reflects the local context and needs.

However, even with decentralized systems, there are still challenges and limitations to educational planning and resource allocation. These challenges can include inadequate data and information systems, insufficient resources or funding, and limited community participation and engagement.

In light of these challenges, there is a need for innovative and effective approaches to educational planning and resource allocation. Leveraging distributed systems presents a promising solution that can improve the efficiency, effectiveness, and sustainability of educational planning and resource allocation. Distributed systems can provide a more flexible and scalable approach that allows for decentralized decision-making and data-driven planning and allocation.

In the following sections of this review chapter, we will explore the potential benefits of leveraging distributed systems for educational planning and resource allocation, with a particular emphasis on the technical and practical aspects of these systems in education. We will also examine the challenges and limitations of implementing distributed systems in education and identify future directions and opportunities for research and practice in this field [4, 5].

9.1.2 The Potential Benefits of Leveraging Distributed Systems in Education

Leveraging distributed systems in education can offer a wide range of potential benefits, including increased efficiency, scalability, and flexibility. Here are some of the key benefits:

- *Decentralized decision-making:* Distributed systems can support decentralized decision-making, allowing local authorities, teachers, and communities to have more control over educational planning and resource allocation. This can lead to a more responsive and adaptive approach that better reflects the local context and needs.
- *Improved data-driven planning:* Distributed systems can provide more accurate and timely data, enabling better-informed decision-making and more efficient allocation of resources. With real-time data, educational planners can monitor and adjust plans as needed, ensuring that resources are directed where they are needed most.

- *Enhanced scalability:* Distributed systems are inherently scalable, meaning that they can handle large amounts of data and processing power. This can be particularly beneficial for large-scale educational institutions, such as universities or school districts, that need to manage complex data and resources across multiple locations.
- *Increased efficiency and reduced costs:* By automating certain tasks and reducing the need for manual intervention, distributed systems can help educational institutions become more efficient and cost-effective. This can free up resources for other important activities, such as improving curriculum, hiring more teachers, or investing in technology infrastructure.
- *Enhanced collaboration:* Distributed systems can support collaborative learning, allowing students and teachers to work together regardless of their physical location. This can help to foster a sense of community and shared learning experiences, enhancing the overall quality of education.

9.2 Theoretical Framework

Overall, the potential benefits of leveraging distributed systems in education are significant and can help to improve the quality, accessibility, and sustainability of education for students and institutions alike. However, implementing distributed systems in education also presents several challenges and limitations, which we will explore in the next section of this review chapter.

The theoretical framework for leveraging distributed systems in education can draw on several disciplines, including computer science, education, and organizational theory.

From a computer science perspective, distributed systems are defined as a set of autonomous computers that communicate and coordinate with each other to perform a task or solve a problem. These systems are characterized by their ability to handle large amounts of data and processing power and distribute resources across multiple nodes. In education, distributed systems can be applied to a variety of tasks, such as student assessment, curriculum development, and resource allocation.

From an educational perspective, distributed systems can be seen as a way to empower teachers, students, and communities to have more control over educational planning and resource allocation. By leveraging the power of technology and data, distributed systems can provide more accurate and timely information, enabling better-informed decision-making and more efficient allocation of resources. This can lead to a more responsive and adaptive approach that better reflects the local context and needs.

Organizational theory can also provide insights into the implementation of distributed systems in education. In particular, the concept of organizational change can help to explain the challenges and opportunities associated with implementing distributed systems in educational institutions. Organizational change refers to the process of transitioning from one state to another and can involve a range of factors such as leadership, culture, and communication. Implementing distributed systems in education requires significant organizational change and can present challenges such as resistance to change, lack of resources or support, and difficulty in coordinating across multiple stakeholders.

Overall, the theoretical framework for leveraging distributed systems in education can draw on a range of disciplines and can help to identify the key opportunities and challenges associated with this approach. By understanding the underlying concepts and theories, educational institutions can develop more effective strategies for implementing distributed systems and improving educational planning and resource allocation [6–8].

9.2.1 Overview of Distributed Systems and their Key Concepts

Distributed systems are a collection of autonomous computers connected through a network, designed to work together to perform complex tasks. The computers in a distributed system have their own memory and processing capabilities, allowing them to work in parallel and share data and resources. These systems are commonly used in a variety of applications, including web applications, cloud computing, and scientific computing.

Scalability is a key concept in distributed systems. Distributed systems are designed to be highly scalable, meaning they can handle large workloads and accommodate changes in demand without a significant impact on performance. This is achieved by dividing the workload across multiple nodes, allowing for parallel processing and resource sharing [9–13].

Another key concept in distributed systems is fault tolerance. Because distributed systems rely on multiple nodes working together, it is important to ensure that the system can continue to operate even if individual components fail. This is achieved through redundancy and replication of data and resources, so that if one component fails, another component can take over without interrupting the operation of the system.

Consistency is also an important concept in distributed systems. Ensuring consistency of data across multiple nodes is a significant challenge, as data may be updated simultaneously on multiple nodes. Various techniques, such as locking and distributed transaction management, can be used to maintain consistency across the system.

Finally, security is an essential consideration in distributed systems. Because multiple nodes are involved, security risks can arise at various points in the system. Distributed systems must be designed with security in mind, including secure communication protocols, access control mechanisms, and secure data storage and transmission [14–18].

In summary, distributed systems are a powerful tool for handling complex tasks that require large amounts of processing power and resources. Scalability, fault tolerance, consistency, and security are key concepts that must be addressed to ensure the efficient and effective operation of distributed systems [19–21].

9.2.2 Theoretical Basis for the Use of Distributed Systems in Education

Distributed system use in education is theoretically supported by a number of fields, including computer science, education, and organizational theory. In order to facilitate more effective and efficient educational planning and resource allocation, the essential ideas of scalability, fault tolerance, consistency, and security in distributed systems can be used in education. From a computer science perspective, distributed systems provide a platform for managing large and complex datasets, enabling efficient processing and analysis of data. In the field of education, this can be used to collect and analyze data on student performance, curriculum development, and resource allocation. With a distributed system, data can be collected and shared across multiple nodes, enabling more accurate and timely decision-making.

From an educational perspective, the use of distributed systems can help to empower teachers, students, and communities to have more control over educational planning and resource allocation. By leveraging the power of technology and data, distributed systems can provide more accurate and timely information, enabling better-informed decision-making and more efficient allocation of resources. This can lead to a more responsive and adaptive approach that better reflects the local context and needs.

Organizational theory can also provide insights into the implementation of distributed systems in education. In particular, the concept of organizational change can help to explain the challenges and opportunities associated with implementing distributed systems in educational institutions. Implementing distributed systems in education requires significant organizational change and can present challenges such as resistance to change, lack of resources or support, and difficulty in coordinating across multiple stakeholders. The theoretical basis for the use of distributed systems in education highlights the potential benefits of this approach, including more efficient and effective educational planning and resource allocation. By understanding the underlying concepts and theories, educational institutions can develop more effective strategies for implementing distributed systems and improving education outcomes [22, 23].

9.2.3 Comparison of Different Distributed Systems Architectures

Distributed systems can use different architectures are shown in Table 9.1, each with its own strengths and weaknesses. A client–server architecture divides the system into two parts, the client and the server, and is simple to implement and scalable, but can suffer from performance issues. In a peer-to-peer architecture, each node is both a client and a server, making it highly scalable and fault tolerant, but difficult to maintain consistency across the system. A hybrid architecture combines both client–server and peer-to-peer elements, providing the benefits of both architectures, while minimizing their drawbacks. A microservices architecture is composed of independent services that communicate through application programming interfaces (APIs), making it highly scalable and flexible, but complex to manage and requiring careful coordination. Cloud computing architecture uses remote servers to store, manage, and process data and is highly scalable and cost-effective, but requires a reliable internet connection and can be vulnerable to security risks.

Table 9.1 Comparison of different distributed systems architectures.

Architecture	Description	Advantages	Disadvantages
Client–server	The system is divided into two main parts: the client and the server	Simple to implement, highly scalable	Performance issues if the server becomes overloaded
Peer-to-peer	Each node in the system is both a client and a server	Highly scalable, fault tolerant	Difficult to maintain consistency across the system
Hybrid	Combines elements of both client–server and peer-to-peer architectures	Provides benefits of both architectures, minimizes drawbacks	May still suffer from performance issues or consistency challenges
Microservices	The system is composed of independent services that communicate with each other through APIs	Highly scalable, flexible	Can be complex to manage and require careful coordination
Cloud computing	Remote servers are used to store, manage, and process data	Highly scalable, cost-effective	Requires a reliable Internet connection, vulnerable to security risks

When choosing an architecture for a distributed system, it is important to consider the specific requirements of the system, including scalability, fault tolerance, consistency, and security, as well as the available resources and expertise. Each architecture has its own advantages and disadvantages, and the suitability of each will depend on the specific needs of the system. Ultimately, the chosen architecture should be one that meets the requirements of the system while minimizing its drawbacks, to ensure the success and longevity of the distributed system [24–26].

9.3 Distribution System in Education

Distributed systems have the potential to revolutionize education by improving educational planning and resource allocation. By using distributed systems, educational institutions can streamline their processes and maximize their resources, resulting in better outcomes for students. One of the primary benefits of using distributed systems in education is their ability to connect students and teachers from different locations, making education more accessible to people around the world.

Distributed systems can also improve resource allocation by allowing educational institutions to share resources such as teaching materials, equipment, and expertise. This can be especially beneficial for institutions with limited resources, enabling them to provide high-quality education to their students. Moreover, distributed systems can enable educational institutions to monitor and assess student progress more effectively, providing valuable feedback to teachers and students, and allowing for more personalized learning experiences.

There are several distributed systems in education, including learning management systems (LMSs), online course platforms, and educational apps. LMSs are web-based applications that allow for the administration, documentation, tracking, and reporting of educational courses and training programs. Online course platforms provide access to courses and materials through the Internet, allowing students to study and learn from anywhere at any time. Educational apps provide a range of functions, from language learning to virtual field trips, and can be accessed through smartphones and tablets.

By leveraging distributed systems in education, institutions can overcome traditional barriers to learning, such as location, time, and resource constraints. However, it is important to note that the successful implementation of distributed systems requires careful planning and consideration of factors such as infrastructure, user experience, and data security. Ultimately, the integration of distributed systems in education has the potential to enhance the quality and accessibility of education, making learning more engaging and effective for students of all ages and backgrounds [27, 28].

9.4 Technical Aspects of Distributed Systems in Education

The technical aspects of distributed systems in education are essential to their successful implementation [29–31]. These technical aspects include the hardware, software, networking, and security components of the system. The following are some of the critical technical aspects of distributed systems in education:

1) *Hardware:* The hardware components of distributed systems include servers, storage devices, and end-user devices. Educational institutions need to ensure that they have the necessary hardware to support the distributed system. They should also consider factors such as capacity, scalability, and redundancy to ensure the system can accommodate the expected traffic and avoid downtime.
2) *Software:* The software components of distributed systems include the operating system, applications, and middleware. Educational institutions need to select software that is compatible with the hardware and meets the needs of the system. They should also consider the licensing requirements, as well as the training and support available for the software.
3) *Networking:* The Internet, routers, switches, firewalls, and other network devices are among the distributed systems' networking components. The network infrastructure of educational institutions must be strong and trustworthy in order to support the distributed system. To make sure the system is responsive and secure against cyber threats, they should also take into account variables like bandwidth, latency, and security.
4) *Security:* The security components of distributed systems include access control, authentication, encryption, and other security measures. Educational institutions need to ensure that the system is protected from cyber threats and that student and faculty data is secure. They should also consider the regulations and laws governing data privacy and security.
5) *Interoperability:* The ability of different systems to work together is critical to the success of distributed systems in education. Educational institutions need to ensure that the different components of the system can communicate with each other and that data can be exchanged seamlessly.

The technical aspects of distributed systems in education are shown in Figure 9.1, essential to their successful implementation. Educational institutions need to consider hardware, software, networking, security, and interoperability when designing and implementing distributed systems. By addressing these technical aspects, educational institutions can ensure that their distributed systems are reliable, scalable, secure, and effective.

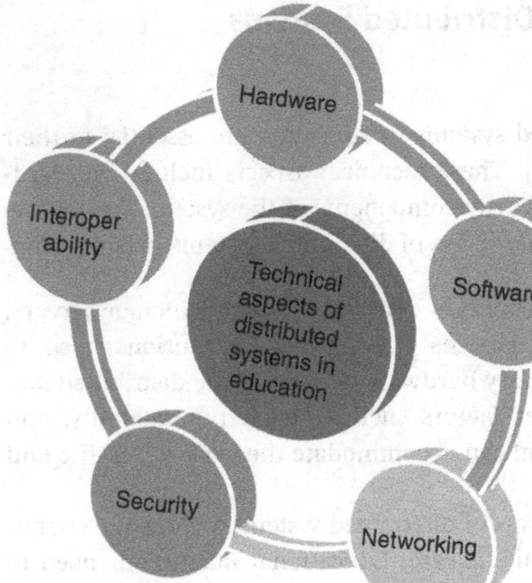

Figure 9.1 Technical aspects of distributed systems in education.

9.4.1 Infrastructure Requirements for Implementing Distributed Systems in Education

Implementing distributed systems in education requires a robust infrastructure that can support the hardware, software, and networking components of the system. The following are some of the critical infrastructure requirements for implementing distributed systems in education:

- *Bandwidth:* Distributed systems in education require high-speed Internet connectivity to enable seamless communication between the different components of the system. Educational institutions need to ensure that they have sufficient bandwidth to accommodate the expected traffic, including streaming video and audio.
- *Cloud computing:* Cloud computing can provide educational institutions with the necessary storage and processing power to support their distributed systems. Cloud computing can also provide additional scalability, redundancy, and accessibility to the system.
- *Data centers:* Educational institutions can also implement distributed systems in education by setting up their data centers. This will require the necessary hardware, software, and networking components to ensure the system is reliable and secure.

- *Virtual private networks (VPNs):* VPNs can be used to establish secure connections between different components of the distributed system, enabling safe and reliable data exchange.
- *Mobile connectivity:* Mobile devices such as smartphones and tablets can be used to access distributed systems in education. Educational institutions need to ensure that their system is compatible with mobile devices and that the necessary infrastructure is in place to support mobile connectivity.
- *Redundancy:* The ability of the system to continue operating even if one or more components fail is referred to as redundancy. Redundancy measures must be put in place by educational institutions to guarantee that the system can still run in the case of hardware or software failure.

A strong infrastructure that can support high-speed internet connectivity, cloud computing, data centers, VPNs, mobile connectivity, and redundancy is needed to implement distributed systems in education. For their distributed systems to be dependable, scalable, and secure, educational institutions must take these infrastructural needs into account while building and putting them into practise. Educational institutions can guarantee that their distributed systems can offer students a high-quality education regardless of location or time constraints by satisfying certain infrastructural requirements.

9.4.2 Security and Privacy Concerns in Distributed Systems for Education

As with any system that involves the exchange of data, security and privacy concerns are critical when implementing distributed systems in education. The following are some of the key security and privacy concerns that educational institutions need to address when implementing distributed systems in education:

1) *Access control:* Educational institutions need to ensure that only authorized users can access the system. They need to implement robust authentication and access control measures, including strong passwords, two-factor authentication, and biometric authentication.
2) *Data encryption:* Data encryption is essential to protect student and faculty data from unauthorized access. Educational institutions should use encryption technologies to secure the data in transit and at rest.
3) *Firewall and network security:* Firewall and network security measures can help protect the system from cyber threats. Educational institutions should implement firewalls, intrusion detection, and prevention systems to detect and prevent unauthorized access and malicious activities.
4) *Data privacy:* Educational institutions need to comply with regulations and laws governing data privacy. They need to ensure that the system collects,

stores, and processes student and faculty data in compliance with applicable laws and regulations.

5) *Cyber threats:* Distributed systems in education are vulnerable to cyber threats such as malware, viruses, and ransomware. Educational institutions need to implement anti-malware and anti-virus software and train faculty and staff on how to identify and avoid cyber threats.
6) *Third-party services:* Educational institutions often use third-party services such as cloud storage, email, and collaboration tools in their distributed systems. Educational institutions need to ensure that these third-party services are secure and comply with applicable laws and regulations.

When using distributed systems in education, security and privacy issues are crucial. To safeguard student and faculty data and stop unauthorized access and malicious actions, educational institutions need to adopt effective access control, data encryption, firewall and network security, data privacy, and cyber threat prevention measures. Educational institutions can make sure that their distributed systems are dependable, secure, and in compliance with relevant laws and regulations by addressing these security and privacy issues.

9.4.3 Data Management and Analysis in Distributed Systems for Education

Critical components of adopting distributed systems in education include data management and analysis. Massive volumes of data are produced by educational institutions and can be used to enhance teaching and learning results. However, the value of data depends on the conclusions that can be drawn from it. To make the most of the data created, educational institutions must make sure they have a solid data management and analysis plan.

One of the primary considerations for data management is data collection. Educational institutions need to collect data that is relevant and can be used to improve teaching and learning outcomes. This data can be collected through various means, including surveys, assessments, and student feedback.

Once the data is collected, it needs to be stored in a secure and accessible manner. Educational institutions can store the data in cloud storage, data centers, or on-premise storage systems. They need to ensure that the data is appropriately protected, backed up, and accessible to authorized personnel.

Data analysis is the process of deriving insights from the collected data. This analysis can be achieved through various means, including statistical analysis, machine learning, and artificial intelligence. The insights derived from data analysis can be used to identify areas for improvement in teaching and learning outcomes, provide feedback to faculty, and help students identify areas where they need to focus. Data visualization is an essential aspect of data management and analysis. Data visualization techniques can be used to communicate the results of data analysis to stakeholders. These techniques can include charts, graphs, and dashboards that are easy to understand and use. Data visualization can help educational institutions identify patterns, trends, and outliers that can help them make data-driven decisions.

Privacy and security are critical considerations in data management and analysis in distributed systems for education. Educational institutions need to ensure that the data is appropriately protected and that only authorized personnel can access it. They also need to comply with privacy and security regulations to ensure that student and faculty data is appropriately protected. Finally, data governance is essential to ensure that educational institutions use the data they collect appropriately. Data governance includes policies, processes, and standards for managing data, including how data is collected, stored, analyzed, and shared. A robust data governance strategy can help educational institutions ensure that they get the most out of their data while complying with regulations and protecting student and faculty data.

9.5 Challenges and Limitations

Despite the potential advantages of using distributed systems in education, there are also considerable obstacles and restrictions that must be taken into account. Some of the main issues and restrictions [32, 33] are:

1) *Technical challenges:* Implementing and maintaining distributed systems in education can be technically challenging, particularly for smaller educational institutions with limited resources. Technical challenges can include infrastructure requirements, software compatibility, and interoperability issues.
2) *Cost:* Implementing and maintaining distributed systems in education can be costly. Educational institutions may need to invest in new hardware, software, and infrastructure, which can be a significant financial burden, particularly for smaller institutions.
3) *Security and privacy concerns:* Distributed systems in education require the transfer and storage of sensitive student and faculty data, which can be a significant security and privacy concern. Educational institutions need to ensure that they have robust security and privacy protocols in place to protect the data and comply with regulations.
4) *Faculty and staff training:* Implementing and maintaining distributed systems in education requires a significant amount of training for faculty and staff.

Without adequate training, faculty and staff may struggle to use the systems effectively, which can impact teaching and learning outcomes.
5) *Resistance to change:* Resistance to change can be a significant challenge when implementing distributed systems in education. Faculty and staff may be resistant to new technology and processes, which can impact adoption rates and the effectiveness of the system.
6) *Limited access to technology:* Educational institutions in developing countries or remote regions may have limited access to technology, which can limit their ability to implement distributed systems.

Overall, the challenges and limitations of leveraging distributed systems in education need to be carefully considered to ensure that educational institutions can effectively implement and maintain these systems. By addressing these challenges and limitations, educational institutions can take advantage of the benefits of distributed systems to improve teaching and learning outcomes for students and faculty.

9.5.1 Merits of Distributed Systems for Educational Planning and Resource Allocation

Distributed systems offer several advantages for educational planning and resource allocation, but they also have some disadvantages that must be considered. Some of the key advantages of leveraging distributed systems in education include:

- *Improved resource allocation:* Distributed systems make it possible for educational institutions to better allocate both human and physical resources, such as teachers and staff, as well as physical resources like equipment and classrooms. This may result in institutions using their resources more effectively and spending less money.
- *Enhanced collaboration:* Distributed systems can facilitate collaboration among faculty, staff, and students across different locations and time zones. This can lead to improved communication and collaboration, which can enhance the learning experience for students and improve outcomes.
- *Increased access to education:* Distributed systems can increase access to education by giving students distant access to educational resources and online learning opportunities. Students who live in rural areas or have limited access to conventional educational institutions may find this to be especially helpful.
- *Customized learning:* Distributed systems can facilitate customized learning experiences for students by providing access to personalized learning materials and resources. This can improve student engagement and learning outcomes.

9.5.2 Demerits of Distributed Systems for Educational Planning and Resource Allocation

However, there are also several disadvantages of leveraging distributed systems in education that need to be considered, including:

- *Technical complexity:* Because of their technical complexity, distributed systems can be extremely difficult to design, build, and maintain. For smaller educational institutions with fewer resources, this can be difficult.
- *Security and privacy risks:* Sensitive student and teacher data are sent and stored using distributed systems, where there is a risk of privacy and security breaches. To protect this data, educational institutions must make sure they have strong security and privacy measures in place.
- *Limited interaction:* Distributed systems may restrict in-person interactions between students and instructors, which may have an effect on how well students learn. The self-discipline needed for online learning may also be difficult for some students, which can have a detrimental effect on outcomes.
- *Resistance to change:* When implementing distributed systems in education, resistance to change can be a major obstacle. The success of the system may be hampered by faculty and staff resistance to new methods and technology.

Distributed systems offer several advantages for educational planning and resource allocation, including improved resource allocation, enhanced collaboration, increased access to education, and customized learning. However, they also have some disadvantages, including technical complexity, security and privacy risks, limited interaction, and resistance to change. Educational institutions need to carefully consider these advantages and disadvantages when deciding whether to implement distributed systems in their institutions.

9.6 Discussion

As educational institutions seek to enhance their planning and resource allocation procedures, the use of distributed systems in education has grown in popularity in recent years. Distributed systems are a group of separate computers or "nodes" that collaborate to create a single, cohesive system that enables information to be processed in a decentralized and collaborative way.

In the context of education, distributed systems have a number of benefits, including the capacity to enhance collaboration, better allocate resources, expand educational access, and enable students' personalized learning experiences. By utilizing distributed systems, educational institutions can more effectively allocate resources, such as physical and human resources, leading to cost savings and resource use that is more efficient. In addition, distributed systems make it possible for staff, students, and faculty to collaborate regardless of their geographical location or time zone, which improves communication and collaboration and results in better learning outcomes. The expanded access to education that distributed systems can offer is one of their most important advantages in the field of education. Distributed systems make it possible to create online learning opportunities and provide remote access to learning materials, which is especially useful for students living in remote areas or those who have little access to conventional educational institutions. Distributed systems can also help students have individualized learning experiences by giving them access to personalized learning materials and resources, which can boost student engagement and academic results. Despite these benefits, distributed systems have some drawbacks and difficulties that must be taken into account. The biggest difficulties with implementing distributed systems in education are related to technical complexity, security and privacy risks, limited face-to-face interaction between students and faculty, and resistance to change. While security and privacy risks can be a major concern for educational institutions due to the transfer and storage of sensitive student and faculty data, technical complexity can be a challenge for smaller educational institutions with constrained resources. Additionally, a lack of student–faculty interaction can affect how well students learn, and some students might find it difficult to maintain the self-discipline needed for online learning. In conclusion, the use of distributed systems in education has a number of benefits that can improve educational planning and resource allocation, improve collaboration, increase access to education, and provide students with more personalized learning experiences. The drawbacks and difficulties of distributed systems, such as their technical complexity, security and privacy risks, low interactivity, and resistance to change, must be carefully taken into account by educational institutions. Overall, distributed systems can significantly benefit educational institutions and their students when properly planned, implemented, and managed.

9.7 Conclusion

In conclusion, the use of distributed systems has the potential to significantly enhance educational planning and resource allocation and improve the learning outcomes for students. By leveraging distributed systems, educational institutions can allocate their resources more efficiently and effectively, while providing personalized and customized learning experiences for their students. Furthermore, distributed systems can enable collaboration and communication among faculty, staff, and students regardless of their location or time zone, which can lead to improved learning outcomes.

However, the implementation of distributed systems also presents challenges and limitations that must be carefully considered. Technical complexity, security and privacy risks, limited interaction, and resistance to change are some of the most significant challenges associated with distributed systems in education. These challenges must be addressed through careful planning, management, and implementation. Overall, the benefits of using distributed systems in education outweigh the challenges, making them an attractive option for educational institutions seeking to improve their planning and resource allocation processes, enhance collaboration and communication, and increase access to education. With proper planning and management, distributed systems can lead to better educational outcomes for students and improved operational efficiency for educational institutions. The use of distributed systems in education is a promising trend that has the potential to transform the education landscape in the years to come.

References

1 Sahin, F. and Robinson, E.P. Jr. (2005). Information sharing and coordination in make-to-order supply chains. *J. Oper. Manage. 23*: 579–598.
2 Fayezi, S. and Zomorrodi, M. (2015). Supply chain management: developments, theories and models. In: *Handbook of Research on Global Supply Chain Management* (ed. B. Christiansen), 313–340. Hershey, PA, USA: IGI Global.
3 Zantalis, F., Koulouras, G., Karabetsos, S., and Kandris, D. (2019). A review of machine learning and IoT in smart transportation. *Future Internet 11*: 94.
4 Svorobej, S., Takako Endo, P., Bendechache, M. et al. (2019). Simulating fog and edge computing scenarios: an overview and research challenges. *Future Internet 11*: 55.
5 Li, Y. (2018). An integrated platform for the internet of things based on an open source ecosystem. *Future Internet 10*: 105.
6 Treiblmaier, H. (2019). Combining blockchain technology and the physical internet to achieve triple bottom line sustainability: a comprehensive research agenda for modern logistics and supply chain management. *Logistics 3*: 10.
7 Kharlamov, A. and Parry, G. (2018). Advanced supply chains: visibility, blockchain and human behaviour. In: *Innovation and Supply Chain Management* (ed. A.C. Moreira, L.M.D.F. Ferreira, and R.A. Zimmermann), 321–343. Cham, Switzerland: Springer International Publishing. ISBN 978-3-319-74303-5.
8 Rejeb, A., Sűle, E., and Keogh, J.G. (2018). Exploring new technologies in procurement. *Transp. Logist. Int. J. 18*: 76–86.
9 Saxena, H., Joshi, D., Singh, H., and Anand, R. (2022). Comparison of classification algorithms for Alzheimer's disease prediction. In: *2022 Seventh International Conference on Parallel, Distributed and Grid Computing (PDGC)*, 687–692. IEEE.

10 Sindhwani, N., Anand, R., Vashisth, R. et al. (2022). Thingspeak-based environmental monitoring system using IoT. In: *2022 Seventh International Conference on Parallel, Distributed and Grid Computing (PDGC)*, 675–680. IEEE.

11 Pandey, B.K., Pandey, D., Anand, R. et al. (2022). The impact of digital change on student learning and mental anguish in the COVID era. In: *An Interdisciplinary Approach in the Post-COVID-19 Pandemic Era* (ed. D. Pandey, B.K. Pandey, N. Sindhwani, et al.), 197–206. NOVA.

12 Singh, H., Pandey, B.K., George, S. et al. (2022). Effective overview of different ML models used for prediction of COVID-19 patients. In: *Artificial Intelligence on Medical Data: Proceedings of International Symposium, ISCMM 2021*, 185–192. Singapore: Springer Nature Singapore.

13 Anand, R., Nirmal, V., Chauhan, Y., and Sharma, T. (2023). An image-based deep learning approach for personalized outfit selection. In: *2023 10th International Conference on Computing for Sustainable Global Development (INDIACom)*, 1050–1054. IEEE.

14 Govindaraj, V., Dhanasekar, S., Martinsagayam, K. et al. (2023). Low-power test pattern generator using modified LFSR. *Aerosp. Syst.* 1–8.

15 Kumar Pandey, B., Pandey, D., Nassa, V.K. et al. (2021). Encryption and steganography-based text extraction in IoT using the EWCTS optimizer. *Imaging Sci. J. 69* (1–4): 38–56.

16 Jain, N., Chaudhary, A., Sindhwani, N., and Rana, A. (2021). Applications of wearable devices in IoT. In: *2021 9th International Conference on Reliability, Infocom Technologies and Optimization (Trends and Future Directions)(ICRITO)*, 1–4. IEEE.

17 Sindhwani, N., Rana, A., and Chaudhary, A. (2021). Breast cancer detection using machine learning algorithms. In: *2021 9th International Conference on Reliability, Infocom Technologies and Optimization (Trends and Future Directions)(ICRITO)*, 1–5. IEEE.

18 Bruntha, P.M., Dhanasekar, S., Hepsiba, D. et al. (2023). Application of switching median filter with L 2 norm-based auto-tuning function for removing random valued impulse noise. *Aerosp. Syst. 6* (1): 53–59.

19 Hofstede, G.J. (2007). Trust and transparency in netchains: a contradiction? In: *Supply Chain Management: Issues in the New Era of Collaboration and Competition* (ed. W.Y.C. Wang, M.S.H. Heng, and P.Y.K. Chau), 105–126. Hershey, PA, USA; London, UK: Idea Group Inc.

20 New, S. (2010). The transparent supply chain. *Harv. Bus. Rev. 88*: 1–5.

21 Dorsemaine, B., Gaulier, J.-P., Wary, J.-P. et al. Internet of things: a definition & taxonomy. In: *Proceedings of the 2015 9th International Conference on Next Generation Mobile Applications, Services and Technologies*, Cambridge, UK, 9–11 September 2015, 72–77.

22 Lelli, F. (2019). Interoperability of the time of industry 4.0 and the internet of things. *Future Internet 11*: 36.

23 Hsiao, H.-I. and Huang, K.-L. (2016). Time-temperature transparency in the cold chain. *Food Control 64*: 181–188.

24 Óskarsdóttir, K. and Oddsson, G.V. (2019). Towards a decision support framework for technologies used in cold supply chain traceability. *J. Food Eng. 240*: 153–159.

25 Knickle, K. (2018). Manufacturing and manufacturing technologies–evolutions in convergence. https://www.i-scoop.eu/industry-4-0/manufacturing-sector-manufacturing-technology-evolutions/ (accessed 21 November 2018).

26 Barboutov, K., Furuskär, A., Inam, R. et al. (2017). *Ericsson Mobility Report*. Sweden: Niklas Heuveldop https://www.ericsson.com/assets/local/mobility-report/documents/2017/ericsson-mobility-report-june-2017.pdf (accessed 25 June 2019).

27 World Economic Forum. (2016). The Internet of Things and connected devices: making the world smarter. http://wef.ch/2ihHIY2 (accessed 29 April 2019).

28 Atzori, L., Iera, A., and Morabito, G. (2018). The internet of things: a survey. *Comput. Networks 54*: 2787–2805.

29 Gubbi, J., Buyya, R., Marusic, S., and Palaniswami, M. (2013). Internet of Things (IoT): a vision, architectural elements, and future directions. *Future Gener. Comput. Syst. 29*: 1645–1660.

30 Shrouf, F., Ordieres, J., and Miragliotta, G. (2014). Smart factories in Industry 4.0: A review of the concept and of energy management approached in production based on the Internet of Things paradigm. In: *Proceedings of the IEEE International Conference on Industrial Engineering and Engineering Management*, Bandar Sunway, Malaysia, 9–12 December 2014, 679–701.

31 Sikorski, J.J., Haughton, J., and Kraft, M. (2017). Blockchain technology in the chemical industry: machine-to-machine electricity market. *Appl. Energy 195*: 234–246.

32 Skowroński, R. (2019). The open blockchain-aided multi-agent symbiotic cyber–physical systems. *Future Gener. Comput. Syst. 94*: 430–443.

33 Yang, X., Wang, G., He, H. et al. (2019). Automated demand response framework in ELNs: decentralized scheduling and smart contract. *IEEE Trans. Syst. Man Cybern.: Syst. 50*: 58–72.

10

Advances in Education Policy Through the Integration of Distributed Computing Approaches

W. Vinu[1], Luigi P.L. Cavaliere[2], K. Suresh Kumar[3], Y. Venkata Ramana[4], Kunjan Shah[5], Kapil Joshi[6], and Nadanakumar Vinayagam[7]

[1] *Department of Physical Education and Sports, Pondicherry University, Pondicherry, India*
[2] *Department of Economics, University of Foggia, Foggia, Italy*
[3] *MBA Department, Panimalar Engineering College, Chennai, Tamil Nadu, India*
[4] *KL Business School, Koneru Lakshmaiah Education Foundation, Guntur, Andhra Pradesh, India*
[5] *Unitedworld School of Computational Intelligence, Karnavati University, Gandhinagar, Gujarat, India*
[6] *Uttaranchal Institute of Technology, Uttaranchal University, India*
[7] *Department of Automobile Engineering, Hindustan Institute of Technology and Science, Chennai, Tamil Nadu, India*

10.1 Introduction

Education policy is a constantly evolving field that aims to improve the quality and accessibility of education. In the present digital era, traditional methods of education policy may not be sufficient to keep up with the changing times. Advancements in technology have revolutionized teaching and learning, and it has become essential for policymakers to adapt and incorporate new techniques. The integration of a network of computers that work together to complete a task, known as distributed computing, presents a promising solution to improving education policy and enhancing learning outcomes. It is highly scalable, efficient, and reliable. The technique has been applied to several fields, including scientific research and e-commerce, and has been successful in solving complex problems. Incorporating distributed computing approaches in education policy has a lot of advantages. Cloud computing, for example, enables educators to share educational resources and data globally, providing a flexible learning experience for students. Similarly,

Meta-Heuristic Algorithms for Advanced Distributed Systems, First Edition. Edited by Rohit Anand, Abhinav Juneja, Digvijay Pandey, Sapna Juneja, and Nidhi Sindhwani.

grid computing can be used to analyze a vast amount of educational data, which can help make informed decisions and develop better policies. Besides the advantages, distributed computing approaches can also help to address the most pressing challenges that education policy is currently facing. For instance, the digital divide, a significant obstacle to educational equity, still exists. However, policymakers can use distributed computing to provide equal access to educational resources and support services, thereby bridging this gap. The potential benefits of distributed computing, several challenges need to be addressed when implementing these approaches in education policy. Data privacy and security are some of the critical concerns to consider when using distributed computing solutions in education. Additionally, technical expertise and specialized knowledge requirements can make it challenging for educators and policymakers to adopt these approaches. The incorporation of distributed computing approaches presents an excellent opportunity to advance education policy and improve learning outcomes. By leveraging the benefits of distributed computing, policymakers can create more effective and efficient systems for delivering education while addressing the current challenges. Although there are challenges that need to be overcome, the benefits of these approaches cannot be ignored, and policymakers should work together to explore their full potential in education policy [1–3].

10.1.1 Technology in Education Policy

Technology has become an integral part of modern society, and education is no exception. Technology has transformed the way we teach and learn, and it has also had a significant impact on education policy. Incorporating technology in education policy has provided a range of benefits, including enhancing learning outcomes, improving access to education, and increasing educational equity. Technology provides a wealth of educational resources, including online textbooks, videos, and interactive software. These resources can be accessed anywhere and anytime, allowing students to learn at their own pace and style. Technology also facilitates collaboration and communication, enabling teachers and students to interact beyond the traditional classroom setting. This increased engagement can lead to better academic performance and improved learning outcomes. Enhancing learning outcomes, technology has also improved access to education. Technology has made it possible to provide education to people in remote and rural areas where traditional education may not be available. Online learning platforms and digital resources have made it possible for students to access education regardless of their location, making education more accessible and inclusive. Another advantage of technology in education policy is that it has increased educational equity.

Technology has also transformed the way education policy is developed and implemented. Policymakers can use data analytics and machine learning techniques to analyze large amounts of educational data, allowing them to make informed decisions about education policy. Additionally, technology can help policymakers to monitor and evaluate the effectiveness of educational programs, providing insights into how to improve education policy and programs. One of the most significant challenges is ensuring that technology is used in a way that enhances education rather than replacing traditional teaching methods. It is crucial to balance the use of technology with effective teaching strategies to ensure that students receive a well-rounded education. This requires policymakers to address the digital divide and provide resources to underserved communities. Furthermore, there is a need to address the privacy and security concerns associated with technology use in education, particularly regarding student data. However, policymakers must balance the use of technology with traditional teaching methods and address the challenges associated with technology use in education. By doing so, we can create an education system that is inclusive, accessible, and effective for all students [4–6].

10.1.2 Advances in Education Policy through Distributed Computing

It refers to a network of computers that work together to solve complex problems. Integrating distributed computing approaches in education policy presents an opportunity to create more efficient and effective systems for delivering education while addressing current challenges.

It can facilitate the sharing of educational resources and data globally. Cloud computing, for example, enables educators to store and share educational resources, making them more accessible to students and teachers worldwide. This allows for more flexible learning experiences and can help to increase the quality and effectiveness of education policy. Grid computing, in particular, can be used to process vast amounts of data quickly and efficiently [7, 8]. This can lead to better-informed policies and improved educational outcomes. By using distributed computing approaches, policymakers can provide access to educational resources and support services to underserved communities, thereby bridging this gap and promoting educational equity. One of the significant concerns is data privacy and security [9–12]. The use of distributed computing requires the sharing of data among multiple computers, and there is a risk that sensitive data may be compromised. Policymakers must take steps to ensure that data privacy and security are maintained and that personal information is not misused. Technical expertise and specialized knowledge are required to implement distributed computing approaches in education policy. Policymakers and educators may not have the necessary skills or resources to incorporate these techniques into their work. Training programs and educational resources can help address this challenge, but policymakers must be willing to invest in these initiatives. Advances in distributed computing present an opportunity to improve education policy and enhance learning outcomes. By leveraging the benefits of distributed computing, policymakers can create more effective and efficient systems for delivering education while addressing the current challenges. Policymakers must also be mindful of the challenges associated with distributed computing, such as data privacy and security concerns and the need for specialized knowledge and expertise [13–16]. By addressing these challenges, we can harness the full potential of distributed computing and create a more equitable and inclusive education system [17, 18].

10.2 Distributed Computing Approaches

Researchers and organizations tackle complex problems that were previously impossible or too expensive to solve using traditional computing methods. This is because distributed computing allows for the pooling of resources, such as processing power, storage, and memory, from multiple computers to work toward a common goal. The potential to transform the way we teach and learn. By leveraging the benefits of distributed computing, educators can develop more effective and efficient systems for delivering education. For example, cloud computing can enable educators to store and share educational resources, making them more accessible to students and teachers worldwide. This can help to increase the quality and effectiveness of education policy. Gamification involves the use of game design elements and principles to engage and motivate students in the learning process. Distributed computing can be used to support gamification by enabling the creation of complex games that require the pooling of resources from multiple computers. This can lead to more engaging and immersive learning experiences that promote better educational outcomes. By using distributed computing approaches, policymakers can provide access to educational resources and support services to underserved communities, thereby bridging this gap and promoting educational equity. One of the most significant challenges is the need for technical expertise and specialized knowledge to implement these techniques effectively. Educators and policymakers may not have the necessary skills or resources to incorporate distributed computing into their work. This requires investment in training programs and educational resources to address this challenge. Another challenge is the issue of data privacy and security. The use of distributed computing requires the sharing of data among multiple computers, which increases the risk of data breaches and cyberattacks. Policymakers must take steps to ensure that data privacy and security are maintained and that personal information is not misused. By leveraging the benefits of distributed computing, educators can develop more effective and efficient systems for delivering education while addressing current challenges. Policymakers must also be mindful of the challenges associated with distributed computing [19, 20].

Distributed computing refers to the use of multiple computers connected by a network to work together toward a common goal. Rather than relying on a single computer to perform a task, distributed computing allows for the sharing of computational resources, such as processing power, storage, and memory, to achieve a faster and more efficient result. In this context, distributed computing is used to train and test machine learning models by breaking down the computation into smaller tasks that can be distributed across multiple computers. It has numerous applications in various fields, including science, finance, healthcare, and education [21, 22].

10.2.1 Benefits of Education Policy

Distributed computing approaches offer a range of benefits that can transform the way education policy is developed, implemented, and evaluated.

- One of the primary benefits of distributed computing in education policy is the ability to pool resources and expertise to tackle complex educational challenges. By leveraging distributed computing, educators and policymakers can access vast computational power, storage, and memory to develop and implement more effective and efficient education policies.
- One application of distributed computing in education policy is the development of cloud-based educational resources. Cloud computing allows educators to store and share educational resources, making them more accessible to students and teachers worldwide. This can help to increase the quality and effectiveness of education policy, as it enables educators to collaborate and share best practices, improving the delivery and outcomes of education programs.
- Another application of distributed computing in education policy is the use of gamification. Gamification involves the use of game design elements and principles to engage and motivate students in the learning process. Distributed computing can be used to support gamification by enabling the creation of complex games that require the pooling of resources from multiple computers. This can lead to more engaging and immersive learning experiences that promote better educational outcomes.
- Moreover, distributed computing can also address the digital divide, which refers to the gap between those who have access to technology and those who do not. By using distributed computing approaches, policymakers can provide access to educational resources and support services to underserved communities, thereby bridging this gap and promoting educational equity.

- Another benefit of distributed computing in education policy is the ability to analyze and process large amounts of data. With the growth of digital learning platforms and online educational resources, there is an increasing amount of data available that can be used to inform and improve education policy. Distributed computing enables policymakers and educators to analyze and process this data quickly and accurately, providing insights that can inform more effective policy development and implementation.

However, there are also challenges associated with distributed computing approaches in education policy. One of the most significant challenges is the need for technical expertise and specialized knowledge to implement these techniques effectively. Educators and policymakers may not have the necessary skills or resources to incorporate distributed computing into their work. This requires investment in training programs and educational resources to address this challenge. The use of distributed computing requires the sharing of data among multiple computers, which increases the risk of data breaches and cyberattacks. Policymakers must take steps to ensure that data privacy and security are maintained and that personal information is not misused. Policymakers and educators must also be mindful of the challenges associated with distributed computing, such as the need for technical expertise and the importance of data privacy and security.

10.2.2 Types of Distributed Computing Approaches

Table 10.1 provides information on four types of distributed computing approaches, including their descriptions, examples, and advantages.

The first type of approach, grid computing, involves a network of computers working together toward a common goal, such as data processing or scientific research. Advantages of grid computing include the ability to handle large-scale computing tasks, reduce the cost of computing resources, and can lead to breakthrough scientific discoveries.

The second type of approach, cloud computing, involves the use of remote servers to store, manage, and process data, making it accessible from anywhere with an Internet connection. Examples of cloud computing include Amazon Web Services and Microsoft Azure. Advantages of cloud computing include scalability, cost-effectiveness, accessibility from anywhere, and no need for physical infrastructure.

The third type of approach, peer-to-peer (P2P) networking, enables computers to share resources, such as processing power or storage, with each other without relying on a central server. Examples of P2P networking include BitTorrent and Skype. Advantages of P2P networking include reducing the cost of computing resources, improving data sharing, and being more resilient than centralized systems.

Table 10.1 Types of distributed computing approaches.

Approach	Description	Examples	Advantages
Grid computing	A network of computers works together toward a common goal, such as data processing or scientific research	SETI@Home, Folding@ Home	Ability to handle large-scale computing tasks, reduces the cost of computing resources, can lead to breakthrough scientific discoveries
Cloud computing	Involves the use of remote servers to store, manage, and process data, making it accessible from anywhere with an internet connection	Amazon Web Services, Microsoft Azure	Scalability, cost-effective, accessibility from anywhere, no need for physical infrastructure
Peer-to-peer (P2P) networking	Enables computers to share resources, such as processing power or storage, with each other without relying on a central server	BitTorrent, Skype	Reduces the cost of computing resources, improves data sharing, more resilient than centralized systems
Distributed processing	Tasks are divided and processed by multiple computers, each contributing a portion of the overall computation	BOINC, Hadoop	High performance, efficient processing, fault-tolerant, cost-effective

The fourth type of approach, distributed processing, involves tasks being divided and processed by multiple computers, with each contributing a portion of the overall computation. Examples of distributed processing include BOINC and Hadoop. Advantages of distributed processing include high performance, efficient processing, fault tolerance, and cost-effectiveness.

10.3 Advances in Education Policy Through Distributed Computing Approaches

The use of multiple computers working together toward a common goal, often sharing resources such as processing power, storage, or data. This integration has allowed for increased efficiency, scalability, and accessibility in education policy. The ability to handle large-scale data processing tasks. For example, distributed computing can be used to analyze large datasets to identify trends and patterns in student performance or resource allocation. This can be particularly beneficial for educators and policymakers who need to access data from different locations or who work in remote areas with limited resources. With cloud computing, data can be easily shared and analyzed by multiple stakeholders, leading to more informed decision-making and policy development. Grid computing involves the use of a network of computers working together toward a common goal, such as data processing or scientific research. In education policy, grid computing has been used to simulate and model educational scenarios, allowing policymakers to explore different options and test the potential outcomes of policy decisions before implementing them in real-world settings. This approach enables computers to share resources, such as processing power or storage, with each other without relying on a central server. In education policy, this could potentially be used to share data and resources between different schools or educational institutions, allowing for more efficient and cost-effective use of resources. Distributed processing is a fourth type of distributed computing approach that has been utilized in education policy. This approach involves tasks being divided and processed by multiple computers, with each contributing a portion of the overall computation. This can lead to more efficient processing of large datasets and can help to reduce the cost of computing resources. These approaches have the potential to revolutionize education policy by allowing for more informed decision-making, more efficient resource allocation, and more effective implementation of educational programs [23–25].

10.3.1 Significant Impact on Education Policy

As technology continues to evolve, it is likely that distributed computing will continue to play an important role in shaping education policy and improving educational outcomes for students around the world. Distributed computing approaches have had a significant impact on education policy, particularly in terms of improving access to educational resources and opportunities [26].

10.3.2 Improved Access

Distributed computing can also help to bridge the digital divide by providing access to technology and resources to individuals and communities who might not have had access otherwise. For example, cloud computing allows educators and policymakers to access data and resources from anywhere with an internet connection. This can be particularly beneficial for those working in remote or underserved areas, where access to educational resources and technology may be limited. With cloud computing, educators and policymakers can collaborate in real time, share resources and data, and access a wealth of educational materials. Other forms of distributed computing, such as grid computing and P2P networking, can also provide improved access to educational resources. Grid computing, for example, allows for the sharing of computing power and data across multiple machines, which can help to increase the availability of resources and reduce costs. This can be particularly useful for distance learning programs, where students may be located in different parts of the world. This can be particularly important in developing countries or areas with limited resources, where access. As technology continues to advance, it is likely that distributed computing will continue to play an important role in improving access to education and reducing the digital divide [27, 28].

10.3.3 Personalized Learning

Personalized learning is an educational approach that seeks to tailor instruction and learning experiences to meet the individual needs and preferences of each student. Rather than using a one-size-fits-all approach, personalized learning recognizes that students have different learning styles, interests, and strengths and aims to create a learning environment that is responsive to those differences.

Personalized learning can take many different forms, depending on the needs and preferences of individual students and the goals of the educational program. Some common approaches to personalized learning include:

- *Adaptive learning technology:* The use of computer programs and algorithms to adapt the learning experience to the individual student. Adaptive learning technology can help to identify areas where a student may be struggling or excelling, and adjust the pace and difficulty of the learning experience accordingly.
- *Project-based learning:* In this approach, students work on projects and assignments that are tailored to their interests and strengths, rather than following a predetermined curriculum. This approach allows students to engage in hands-on learning experiences that are personally meaningful to them.
- *Competency-based learning:* This approach focuses on mastery of specific skills or competencies, rather than on completing a certain number of tasks or assignments. Students work at their own pace, progressing through the material only once they have demonstrated mastery of the targeted competencies.
- *Personal learning plans:* The creation of individualized learning plans for each student, based on their interests, learning style, and academic goals. These plans may include specific learning objectives, personalized resources and materials, and a timeline for completing assignments and assessments.

The benefits of personalized learning are many. Research has shown that students who engage in personalized learning experiences tend to have higher levels of academic achievement, greater motivation and engagement, and increased confidence in their own learning abilities. However, there are also challenges associated with personalized learning. While personalized learning can be highly effective at engaging students and promoting individualized learning, it is important to ensure that students are still developing the foundational skills and knowledge they need to succeed academically and in their future careers. In order to successfully implement personalized learning, educators and policymakers must work together to develop effective strategies and approaches that meet the needs of individual students while also promoting broader educational goals. This may require ongoing assessment and evaluation of personalized learning programs, as well as investments in teacher training and professional development to ensure that educators have the skills and resources, they need to support personalized learning in the classroom. Personalized learning is a powerful educational approach that has the potential to transform the way we think about teaching and learning.

10.3.4 Data-Driven Decision-Making

Data-driven decision-making is an approach to decision-making that relies on the analysis of data to inform and guide the decision-making process. In the context of education policy, data-driven decision-making involves using data to identify areas of need, evaluate the effectiveness of educational programs, and make informed decisions about resource allocation and policy development. This has led to a growing emphasis on data-driven decision-making in education policy, as policymakers and educators seek to use data to improve student outcomes and promote equitable access to high-quality education. For example, by analyzing data on student performance and demographic characteristics, policymakers and educators can identify schools or districts that are struggling and allocate resources to those areas more strategically. This can help to ensure that students who are most in need of support receive the resources and assistance they require to succeed. It can also be used to evaluate the effectiveness of educational programs and interventions. By collecting and analyzing data on program outcomes and student performance, educators can assess the impact of different interventions and adjust their approach accordingly. This can help to promote continuous improvement and ensure that educational programs are meeting the needs of students and achieving their intended outcomes. It can help to promote accountability and transparency in education policy. By making data publicly available and using it to inform policy decisions, policymakers and educators can demonstrate their commitment to evidence-based decision-making and help to build trust with stakeholders. Collaboration and engagement among educators, policymakers, and members of the community create a more responsive and effective education system.

Another challenge is ensuring that data is used in a way that is meaningful and relevant to educators and policymakers. It is important to ensure that data is presented in a way that is accessible and easy to understand and that it is used to inform decisions that will have a tangible impact on student outcomes.

To successfully implement data-driven decision-making in education policy, policymakers and educators must work together to develop effective data collection and analysis strategies, as well as policies and procedures for protecting student privacy and ensuring that data is used ethically and responsibly. This may require investments in technology and infrastructure to support data collection and analysis, as well as ongoing professional development and training for educators and policymakers. Data-driven decision-making is a powerful approach to education policy that has the potential to improve student outcomes, promote equity and accountability, and build trust with stakeholders [29, 30].

10.4 Challenges: Privacy Concerns

One of the key challenges of integrating distributed computing approaches in education policy is related to privacy concerns. These concerns arise from the collection, storage, and sharing of sensitive data about students, teachers, and educational institutions.

A vast amount of data can be collected and analyzed to help make informed decisions about student learning and progress. This data can include student academic records, personal information such as names and addresses, and even sensitive data such as medical records or disciplinary records. However, the collection and analysis of this data can also raise concerns about the privacy of individuals involved in the educational process. The main concern is that the collection and storage of student data can be vulnerable to security breaches and hacking attempts. If unauthorized individuals gain access to this data, it can be used for malicious purposes such as identity theft or cyberbullying. Therefore, it is essential for educational institutions to implement robust security measures and data protection protocols to ensure that sensitive information is not compromised. While these technologies have the potential to improve educational outcomes, they can also reinforce existing biases and perpetuate inequalities. For example, if an algorithm is trained on data that is biased against certain groups, such as low-income students or students of color, it may lead to biased or unfair decisions about these groups.

Additionally, the use of data analytics and machine learning in education can also lead to concerns about the transparency of decision-making processes. Educational institutions must ensure that the decisions made based on student data are transparent and easily understandable by all stakeholders involved. This includes making sure that the algorithms used are explainable and that decision-making processes are not influenced by hidden biases or interests. Furthermore, privacy concerns can also arise from the use of online educational tools and platforms, such as learning management systems and educational apps. These tools can collect data about students' online behavior, such as their browsing history, location data, and communication patterns. Educational institutions must ensure that these tools are following relevant data privacy regulations, such as the Family Educational Rights and Privacy Act in the United States. It is essential for educational institutions to prioritize data security and privacy and implement robust measures to protect sensitive information. Data analysis and machine learning algorithms are also critical to ensuring that the integration of distributed computing approaches in education policy is beneficial for all stakeholders involved [31].

10.4.1 Technical Requirements

In addition to privacy concerns, technical requirements present another significant challenge to integrating distributed computing approaches in education policy. These challenges are related to the infrastructure and hardware needed to support the collection, storage, and analysis of data. One of the main technical challenges of distributed computing approaches in education is the need for high-performance computing systems to manage the large amount of data generated. This requires the development of complex and specialized hardware and software systems to handle the processing and storage of data. Furthermore, these systems must be scalable and adaptable to meet the ever-increasing demand for processing power and storage capacity. Many educational institutions may have older systems in place that are not designed to handle the amount of data generated by newer systems. Therefore, there may be a need to upgrade or replace older systems to ensure that they are compatible with distributed computing approaches. These systems require specialized knowledge and expertise to manage, and it may be challenging to find personnel with the necessary skills to operate and maintain these systems. Moreover, the cost associated with developing and maintaining distributed computing systems can also present a significant challenge. The development of high-performance computing systems and the necessary infrastructure can be costly, and educational institutions may not have the resources to invest in these systems. Additionally, the cost of maintaining and upgrading these systems can also be a significant burden. High-performance computing systems, interoperability of systems, and the need for trained personnel are some of the technical challenges that must be addressed to ensure that distributed computing approaches can be effectively implemented in education. Additionally, the cost associated with the development and maintenance of these systems can also be a significant barrier. Educational institutions must address these challenges to ensure that they can effectively integrate distributed computing approaches into their education policy to improve educational outcomes for students.

10.4.2 Impact of Emerging Technologies and Use of Distributed Computing

The integration of emerging technologies such as artificial intelligence (AI) and blockchain with distributed computing approaches has the potential to revolutionize education policy and transform the way educational institutions collect, store, and analyze data. AI can be used to analyze large amounts of data and provide insights that can inform decision-making in education policy. Additionally, AI can be used to develop personalized learning programs that are tailored to individual student needs, allowing students to learn at their own pace and in a way that suits their learning style.

Blockchain technology, on the other hand, can be used to create secure, decentralized systems for storing and sharing data. For instance, blockchain can be used to create digital credentials that are tamper-proof and can be easily verified, eliminating the need for traditional paper-based transcripts and reducing the risk of fraud. such as AI and blockchain. Additionally, distributed computing can facilitate the interoperability of different systems and enable the seamless exchange of data between different educational institutions.

The integration of emerging technologies and distributed computing approaches in education policy can have a significant impact on student outcomes. For instance, personalized learning programs developed using AI can help students to learn at their own pace and in a way that suits their learning style, improving engagement and reducing the risk of students falling behind. The integration of emerging technologies and distributed computing approaches can help to reduce costs associated with education. For instance, the use of AI to develop personalized learning programs can reduce the need for expensive one-on-one tutoring, making education more accessible to students who may not have the financial resources to access traditional tutoring services. Additionally, the use of blockchain technology can reduce the cost of administering traditional paper-based transcripts, making it easier for students to access their educational records and reducing the need for administrative staff to manually process transcript requests. The use of AI to develop personalized learning programs and analyze student data, and the use of blockchain technology to create secure, decentralized systems for storing and sharing educational data, are just a few examples of how emerging technologies can be used to improve education. However, challenges such as technical requirements and privacy concerns must be addressed to ensure that these emerging technologies can be effectively integrated into education policy. Educational institutions must work together to identify and address these challenges to ensure that emerging technologies and distributed computing approaches can be leveraged to improve education for all students [32, 33].

10.5 Conclusion

In conclusion, the integration of distributed computing approaches has brought significant advances in education policy. It has resulted in improved access to education, personalized learning experiences, and data-driven decision-making. The benefits of using distributed computing approaches are numerous and have the potential to revolutionize education systems globally. However, there are also challenges that need to be addressed, such as privacy concerns and technical requirements. It is essential to address these challenges and continue to develop and improve distributed computing approaches to ensure that the benefits outweigh the risks. The impact of emerging technologies such as AI and blockchain has also contributed to the advances in education policy through distributed computing approaches. The use of AI can help personalize learning and provide more effective teaching methods, while blockchain technology can enhance the security and privacy of student data. Education policy has the potential to transform education systems by providing greater access to education, improving learning outcomes, and facilitating data-driven decision-making. It is essential to continue exploring and refining these approaches to ensure that they are secure, efficient, and effective in meeting the needs of students and educators.

References

1 Marcum, D. (**2014**). The digital transformation of information, education, and scholarship. *Int. J. Humanit. Arts Comput. 8*: 1–11.

2 Alenezi, M. (**2021**). Deep dive into digital transformation in higher education institutions. *Educ. Sci. 11*: 770.

3 Akour, M., Alenezi, M., Sghaier, H.A., and Shboul, Y.A. (**2021**). The COVID-19 pandemic: when e-learning becomes mandatory not complementary. *Int. J. Technol. Enhanc. Learn. 13*: 429–439.

4 Mahlow, C. and Hediger, A. (**2019**). Digital transformation in higher education-buzzword or opportunity? *eLearn Mag. 2019*: 13.

5 Gurung, B. and Rutledge, D. (**2014**). Digital learners and the overlapping of their personal and educational digital engagement. *Comput. Educ. 77*: 91–100.

6 Pandey, D., Pandey, B.K., Sindhwani, N. et al. (2022). *An Interdisciplinary Approach in the Post-COVID-19 Pandemic Era*, 1–290. New York: NOVA.

7 Saxena, H., Joshi, D., Singh, H., and Anand, R. (2022). Comparison of classification algorithms for Alzheimer's disease prediction. In: *2022 Seventh International Conference on Parallel, Distributed and Grid Computing (PDGC)*, 687–692. IEEE.

8 Sindhwani, N., Anand, R., Vashisth, R. et al. (2022). Thingspeak-based environmental monitoring system using IoT. In: *2022 Seventh International Conference on Parallel, Distributed and Grid Computing (PDGC)*, 675–680. IEEE.
9 Pandey, B.K., Pandey, D., Anand, R. et al. (2022). The impact of digital change on student learning and mental anguish in the COVID era. In: *An Interdisciplinary Approach in the Post-COVID-19 Pandemic Era*, 197–206. New York: NOVA.
10 Singh, H., Pandey, B.K., George, S. et al. (2022). Effective overview of different ML models used for prediction of COVID-19 patients. In: *Artificial Intelligence on Medical Data: Proceedings of International Symposium, ISCMM 2021*, 185–192. Singapore: Springer Nature Singapore.
11 Anand, R., Nirmal, V., Chauhan, Y., and Sharma, T. (2023). An image-based deep learning approach for personalized outfit selection. In: *2023 10th International Conference on Computing for Sustainable Global Development (INDIACom)*, 1050–1054. IEEE.
12 Govindaraj, V., Dhanasekar, S., Martinsagayam, K. et al. (2023). Low-power test pattern generator using modified LFSR. *Aerosp. Syst.* 1–8.
13 Kumar Pandey, B., Pandey, D., Nassa, V.K. et al. (2021). Encryption and steganography-based text extraction in IoT using the EWCTS optimizer. *Imaging Sci. J. 69* (1–4): 38–56.
14 Bruntha, P.M., Dhanasekar, S., Hepsiba, D. et al. (2023). Application of switching median filter with L 2 norm-based auto-tuning function for removing random valued impulse noise. *Aerosp. Syst. 6* (1): 53–59.
15 Sindhwani, N., Rana, A., and Chaudhary, A. (2021). Breast cancer detection using machine learning algorithms. In: *2021 9th International Conference on Reliability, Infocom Technologies and Optimization (Trends and Future Directions)(ICRITO)*, 1–5. IEEE.
16 Jain, N., Chaudhary, A., Sindhwani, N., and Rana, A. (2021). Applications of Wearable devices in IoT. In: *2021 9th International Conference on Reliability, Infocom Technologies and Optimization (Trends and Future Directions)(ICRITO)*, 1–4. IEEE.
17 (a) Greenhow, C., Graham, C.R., and Koehler, M.J. (2022). Foundations of online learning: challenges and opportunities. *Educ. Psychol.* 57: 131–147. (b) Foster, I., Kesselman, C., and Tuecke, S. (2001). The anatomy of the grid: enabling scalable virtual organizations. *Int. J. High Perform. Comput. Appl.* 15: 200–222.
18 Lin, W.-M., Tu, C.-S., and Tsai, M.-T. (**2015**). Energy management strategy for microgrids by using enhanced bee colony optimization. *Energies 9*: 5.
19 El Baz, D. (2014). IoT and the need for high performance computing. In: *Proceedings of the 2014 International Conference on Identification, Information and Knowledge in the Internet of Things*, Beijing, China, 17–18 October, 1–6. IEEE.
20 Roche, R. and Miraoui, A. (**2017**). Microgrid sizing with combined evolutionary algorithm and MILP unit commitment. *Appl. Energy 188*: 547–562.

21 Liu, H., Abraham, A., and Hassanien, A.E. (**2010**). Scheduling jobs on computational grids using a fuzzy particle swarm optimization algorithm. *Futur. Gener. Comput. Syst. 26*: 1336–1343.

22 Bommareddy, S., Khan, J.A., and Anand, R. (2022). A review on healthcare data privacy and security. In: *Networking Technologies in Smart Healthcare* (ed. P. Singh, O. Kaiwartya, N. Sindhwani, et al.), 165–187. CRC Press.

23 Aghdam, F.H., Salehi, J., and Ghaemi, S. (**2018**). Contingency based energy management of multi-microgrid based distribution network. *Sustain. Cities Soc. 41*: 265–274.

24 Gabri, L.R., Agrawal, Y., and Srinivas, B. (**2020**). A survey on grid computing scheduling algorithms. *Int. J. Res. Appl. Sci. Eng. Technol. (IJRASET) 8*: 731–736.

25 Olivares, D.E., Canizares, C.A., and Kazerani, M. (**2014**). A centralized energy management system for isolated microgrids. *IEEE Trans. Smart Grid 5*: 1864–1875.

26 Elkazaz, M., Sumner, M., and Thomas, D. (**2020**). Energy management system for hybrid PV-wind-battery microgrid using convex programming, model predictive and rolling horizon predictive control with experimental validation. *Int. J. Electr. Power Energy Syst. 115*: 105483.

27 Tsikalakis, A.G. and Hatziargyriou, N.D. (**2011**). Centralized control for optimizing microgrids operation. In: *Proceedings of the 2011 IEEE Power and Energy Society General Meeting*, Detroit, MI, USA, 24–28 July 2011, 1–8. IEEE.

28 Warnier, M., Dulman, S., Koç, Y., and Pauwels, E. (**2017**). Distributed monitoring for the prevention of cascading failures in operational power grids. *Int. J. Crit. Infrastruct. Prot. 17*: 15–27.

29 Kermani, M., Carnì, D.L., Rotondo, S. et al. (**2020**). A nearly zero-energy microgrid testbed laboratory: centralized control strategy based on SCADA system. *Energies 13*: 2106.

30 Yamashita, D.Y., Vechiu, I., and Gaubert, J.-P. (**2020**). A review of hierarchical control for building microgrids. *Renew. Sust. Energ. Rev. 118*: 109523.

31 Mohamed Hashim, M.A., Tlemsani, I., and Matthews, R. (**2022**). Higher education strategy in digital transformation. *Educ. Inf. Technol. 27*: 3171–3195.

32 Selwyn, N. (**2015**). Minding our language: why education and technology is full of bullshit . . . and what might be done about it. *Learn. Media Technol. 41*: 437–443.

33 Pacansky-Brock, M. (2017). *Best practices for teaching with emerging technologies.* In: *Best Practices in Online Teaching and Learning*, 2e. London, UK: Routledge.

11

Revolutionizing Data Management and Security with the Power of Blockchain and Distributed System

Radha R. Chandan[1], Fred Torres-Cruz[2], Ernesto N.T. Figueroa[2], Charles I. Mendoza-Mollocondo[2], Dharini R. Sisodia[3], Tanweer Alam[4], and Mohit Tiwari[5]

[1] *School of Management Sciences (SMS), Department of Computer Science, Varanasi, Uttar Pradesh, India*
[2] *Academic Department of Statistics and Computer Engineering, Universidad Nacional del Altiplano de Puno, Puno, Peru*
[3] *Army Institute of Management & Technology, Department of Management, Greater Noida, Uttar Pradesh, India*
[4] *Islamic University of Madinah, Department of Computer Science, Faculty of Computer and Information Systems, Madinah, Saudi Arabia*
[5] *Department of Computer Science and Engineering, Bharati Vidyapeeth's College of Engineering, Delhi, India*

11.1 Introduction

In today's increasingly digital world, data management (DM) and security have become critical concerns for individuals and organizations alike. Furthermore, as data becomes more valuable, the need to ensure its integrity and authenticity becomes more important. To address these challenges, many researchers and practitioners have turned to emerging technologies such as blockchain and distribution system (DS). These technologies offer promising solutions to some of the key problems in DM and security, including the need for secure and reliable storage, efficient data sharing and access, and the ability to verify the authenticity and integrity of data. For its potential to transform DM and security, blockchain technology (BT) in particular has drawn a lot of interest in recent years. The technology has already been used extensively in a variety of industries, including

Meta-Heuristic Algorithms for Advanced Distributed Systems, First Edition. Edited by Rohit Anand, Abhinav Juneja, Digvijay Pandey, Sapna Juneja, and Nidhi Sindhwani.

finance, supply chain management (SCM), and healthcare. With fewer single points of failure, these systems can boost security, resilience, and transparency. We will examine the possibilities for blockchain and DS to revolutionize DM and security in this chapter. We'll start by giving a general review of these technologies, outlining both their benefits and drawbacks in terms of DM and security. Then, using examples from the real world, we will demonstrate how blockchain and DS can change DM and security. By exploring the advantages and disadvantages of these technologies, their real-world applications, and the challenges and limitations they face, we hope to provide a valuable resource for researchers, practitioners, and decision-makers in this critical area. Ultimately, we believe that the power of blockchain and DS can help to revolutionize DM and security, providing greater security, reliability, and trust in the digital world [1, 2].

11.1.1 Importance of Data Management and Security

Revolutionizing DM and Security with the Power of Blockchain and DS.

In today's increasingly digital world, DM and security have become critical concerns for individuals and organizations alike. We will explore the potential of blockchain and DS to revolutionize DM and security. As data becomes more valuable, the need to ensure its integrity and authenticity becomes more important. For its potential to transform DM and security, BT in particular has drawn a lot of interest in recent years. The technology has already been used extensively in a variety of industries, including finance, SCM, and healthcare. With fewer single points of failure, these systems can boost security, resilience, and transparency. We'll start by giving a general review of these technologies, outlining both their benefits and drawbacks in terms of DM and security. Then, using examples from the real world, we will demonstrate how blockchain and DS can change DM and security. We will also talk about some of the difficulties and restrictions associated with using DS and blockchain for DM and security. These include issues such as scalability, interoperability, and regulatory concerns. A comprehensive overview of the potential of blockchain and DS for DM and security. By exploring the advantages and disadvantages of these technologies, their real-world applications, and the challenges and limitations they face, we hope to provide a valuable resource for researchers, practitioners, and decision-makers in this critical area. Ultimately, we believe that the power of blockchain and DS can help to revolutionize DM and security, providing greater security, reliability, and trust in the digital world [3, 4].

11.1.2 Current State of Data Management and Security

As we continue to rely more and more on digital technology in our personal and professional lives, the importance of DM and security has become increasingly clear. The current state of DM and security is characterized by both the opportunities and challenges presented by this new digital landscape. On the one hand, advances in technology have made it easier to collect, store, and analyze large amounts of data, opening up new opportunities for innovation and growth. For example, organizations can use data analytics to gain insights into customer behavior, improve operational efficiency, and develop new products and services. However, this new digital landscape has also created new risks and challenges. Cybersecurity threats such as data breaches and cyberattacks have become more frequent and sophisticated, with potentially devastating consequences. Additionally, the sheer volume of data being generated and processed can make it difficult to manage and secure effectively, creating the risk of errors and oversights. The current state of DM and security is further complicated by the rapidly evolving technology landscape. In addition to presenting new potential for DM and analysis, emerging technologies like cloud computing, AI, and the Internet of Things also pose new challenges for security and privacy [5–9]. Notwithstanding these obstacles, businesses and people are making improvements to their DM and security procedures. This entails putting in place strong security mechanisms like firewalls, encryption, and two-factor authentication in addition to creating DM and governance policies and processes. Although new technologies create intriguing possibilities for DM and analysis, they also bring with them new hazards and difficulties that must be handled through efficient DM and security policies [10, 11].

11.2 Blockchain Technology

Data can be stored and transferred securely and transparently using BT, a decentralized distributed ledger. Blockchain was initially created for use in the cryptocurrency Bitcoin, but it has since found use in a wide range of sectors, including finance and healthcare as well as SCM and voting systems. A blockchain, at its heart, is a database that organizes information into a number of blocks, each of which contains a number of transactions. A record of all transactions that have taken place on the network is permanently and irrevocably produced when a block is created and added to the existing chain of blocks. The blockchain is less vulnerable to fraud and hacking since there is no need for a centralized authority to authenticate transactions. It is therefore a perfect instrument for use in fields like SCM, where stakeholders may monitor the flow of items and confirm their legitimacy. Blockchain also offers security and immutability in addition to transparency. It is incredibly challenging to change the contents of the blockchain without being noticed because each block in the chain is linked to the one before it. Because of this, BT is appealing for applications like digital identity verification. BT provides a

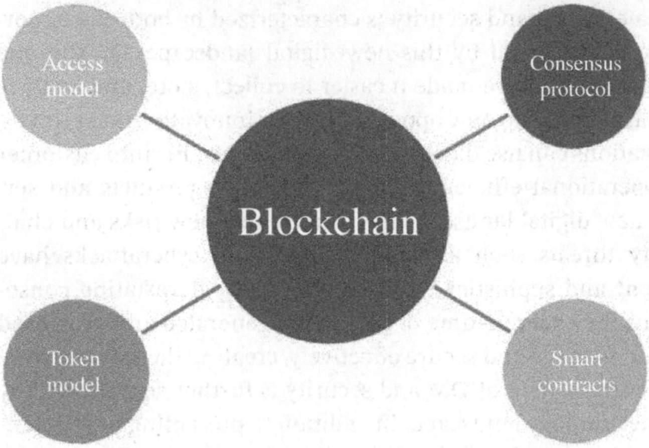

Figure 11.1 Basic elements of BT.

lot of advantages, but it also has certain drawbacks. Scalability is one of the key difficulties. There is a cap on the number of transactions that can be executed at once since each block needs to be confirmed by the network before it can be added to the chain. Moreover, the maintenance of the blockchain can demand a large amount of energy, making it less ecologically friendly than alternative technologies. It has the potential to transform how we manage and secure our data by enabling transparent, decentralized, and secure data storage and transit. Figure 11.1 depicts the essential components of BT [12–14].

11.2.1 Benefits of Using Blockchain for Data Management and Security

- *Decentralization:* Each node in the network has a copy of the entire blockchain and must reach a consensus before any changes can be made. Single point of control, data stored on a blockchain is less vulnerable to hacking and fraud. This makes it much more difficult for an attacker to compromise the network.
- *Immutability:* Any attempt to change one block would also involve modifying all following blocks because each block in the chain holds a hash of the block before it. This ensures the integrity and reliability of the data recorded on a blockchain and makes it nearly hard to tamper with it.
- *Transparency:* Everyone may view the transaction history and confirm that it is accurate and genuine because the blockchain is a public ledger. This openness is particularly helpful in fields like SCM, where stakeholders can follow the flow of commodities and confirm their legitimacy.

- *Security:* BT uses advanced cryptography to secure data stored on the network. Transactions are verified using complex algorithms that make it extremely difficult for attackers to compromise the network. In addition, sensitive data can be encrypted before it is stored on the blockchain, ensuring that it is protected even if the network is breached.
- *Data privacy:* While the blockchain is transparent, it is also possible to maintain privacy by encrypting data or using private blockchains that restrict access to authorized users. This makes BT useful for applications that require both security and privacy, such as healthcare or financial services.

Overall, the advantages of BT make it an attractive tool for DM and security. Its decentralized, immutable, and transparent nature is combined with advanced cryptography. As a result, blockchain is being used in a variety of industries and applications, from finance and healthcare to SCM and voting systems.

11.2.2 Limitations of Using Blockchain for Data Management and Security

- *Scalability:* The cost of the computer power needed to maintain the blockchain and validate transactions can rise to an unaffordable level. Because of the potential for lengthy transaction times and expensive fees, it may be challenging to scale the network to accommodate rising demand.
- *Energy consumption:* Another issue with BT is how much energy it uses. The blockchain needs a lot of computational power to run the network because it depends on a network of nodes to verify transactions. As a result, there have been worries raised regarding BT's potential negative effects on the environment.
- *Regulation and legal challenges:* Leading to legal and regulatory challenges, in some cases, this can create uncertainty around the use of BT for DM and security and may limit its adoption in certain industries or applications.
- *Complexity:* BT can be complex to implement and use, requiring specialized technical expertise to develop and maintain. This can make it challenging for organizations to adopt BT without significant investment in training and infrastructure.
- *Data privacy:* In applications where data privacy is important, the blockchain's transparency can be both an advantage and a disadvantage. On the blockchain, data can be encrypted, but it might be challenging to guarantee that private information won't be accessed by unauthorized users. While BT has a lot of potential advantages for DM and security, there are some drawbacks as well. When selecting whether to utilize blockchain for their DM and security purposes, organizations should thoroughly weigh the possible benefits and drawbacks of the technology.

11.3 Distributed System

DS refers to a network of independent computers that work together to achieve a common goal. These systems allow for the efficient sharing and processing of data and resources across multiple machines, rather than relying on a single centralized system. In a distributed system, each computer, or node, is connected to the network and can communicate with other nodes to perform specific tasks or share data. Cloud computing and data analytics to e-commerce and online gaming. They are designed to be highly scalable, flexible, and fault tolerant, allowing them to handle large amounts of data and traffic while remaining highly available. For example, a distributed system might be used to process millions of transactions per second, such as those required by a large e-commerce site or financial institution. There are several key characteristics of DS, including decentralization, interoperability, and resource sharing [15–19]. This means that if one node in the network fails or goes offline, the other nodes can continue to function without interruption. This is achieved by designing the system in a way that allows for redundancy and failover, so that if one node goes down, another node can take over its tasks without any disruption to the overall system. Interoperability is another important characteristic of DS. These systems are designed to work across multiple platforms and operating systems, allowing different nodes to communicate with each other regardless of their underlying technology. This means that developers can build applications that can run on any node in the network, regardless of the underlying hardware or software. Resource sharing is another key advantage of DS. These systems allow for the efficient sharing of computing resources such as processing power, memory, and storage across multiple nodes. This means that the resources of the entire network can be used to perform specific tasks or store data, rather than relying on a single machine to do everything. This can lead to significant improvements in efficiency and scalability, as the network can be scaled up or down to meet changing demands.

DS is a powerful tool for DM and security, as they allow for the efficient sharing and processing of data across multiple machines. They are designed to be highly scalable, fault tolerant, and interoperable. By combining the power of DS with BT, it is possible to create highly secure, decentralized networks that are capable of handling massive amounts of data and traffic with ease [20–24].

11.3.1 Benefits of Using Distributed Systems for Data Management and Security

- *Fault tolerance:* DS are designed to be fault tolerant, which means that if one node in the network fails or goes offline, the system can continue to function without interruption. This is achieved by implementing redundancy and failover mechanisms that ensure that critical data and applications are always available.

- *Security:* DS can improve security by using encryption and other security mechanisms to protect data at rest and in transit. They can also be designed to limit access to specific nodes in the network, which can help prevent unauthorized access and data breaches.
- *Cost-effectiveness:* Because DS require less infrastructure and can be scaled up or down more easily in response to demand, they may be more cost-effective than centralized systems. Organizations that need to manage vast amounts of data or process data in real time may find this to be especially helpful.

DS offers a range of benefits for DM and security, including improved performance, scalability, fault tolerance, security, and cost-effectiveness. By leveraging these advantages, organizations can build highly resilient and secure systems that are capable of handling massive amounts of data and traffic with ease.

11.3.2 Limitations of Using Distributed Systems for Data Management and Security

- *Complexity:* This is because they require more coordination and communication between nodes, as well as more sophisticated software and hardware to ensure data consistency and reliability.
- *Latency:* While DSs can improve performance in some cases, they can also introduce additional latency or delays in data processing. This can be a problem for applications that require very low latency, such as real-time analytics or financial trading systems.
- *Security risks:* While DSs can improve security in some ways, they can also introduce new security risks. For example, attacks on one node in the network can potentially compromise the entire system. Additionally, it can be challenging to manage security across multiple nodes with different hardware, software, and security configurations.
- *Data consistency:* It can be challenging to design and implement systems that maintain data consistency and integrity in a distributed environment. This is because there may be delays or inconsistencies in data updates, which can lead to conflicting or outdated data.
- *Cost:* While DSs can be more cost-effective in some cases, they can also be more expensive to design, implement, and manage than centralized systems. This is because they require more sophisticated hardware, software, and management tools, as well as specialized expertise to ensure they are designed and implemented correctly. DS offers many advantages for DM and security, but they also

come with some potential disadvantages. Organizations need to determine whether they are the right choice for their specific needs and requirements.

11.4 Revolutionizing Data Management and Security with Blockchain and Distributed Systems

Revolutionizing DM and security with blockchain and DS is a promising area of research and development, as both technologies offer significant benefits for managing and securing data. BT provides a secure and decentralized way of storing and sharing data, while DS offers improved performance, scalability, fault tolerance, and security. The combination of these two technologies has the potential to transform the way organizations manage and secure their data, transparent, and efficient way to store and process data. By leveraging blockchain's decentralized and tamper-resistant architecture and DS' scalability and fault tolerance, organizations can build highly resilient and secure DM systems that are capable of handling massive amounts of data and traffic with ease. The DS for DM and security is that they can provide a high degree of transparency and accountability. This can be especially helpful in applications like SCM where it's crucial to trace the flow of materials and goods. Data privacy and security can be increased by combining blockchain and DS for DM and security, which is another benefit. Moreover, blockchain and DS are more resistant to attacks due to their decentralized architecture. Organizations can safeguard sensitive data from unwanted access and make sure that only those with the necessary authorization have access to it by utilizing encryption and other security measures.

Yet, using blockchain and DS for DM and security may provide some difficulties. For some businesses, the difficulty of building and managing these systems may be a deterrent to adoption. Integration of blockchain and DS with current IT systems and infrastructure may also provide difficulties. DM and the secure, open, and effective manner to store and process data could be revolutionized by the use of BT and distributed ledger technology (DS). The advantages these technologies offer in terms of security, scalability, and accountability make them a viable field of study and development for organizations looking to enhance their DM and security practices, even though there are some possible difficulties and disadvantages [25–29].

11.4.1 Blockchain and Distributed Systems Can Revolutionize Data Management and Security

Blockchain and DS can revolutionize DM and security in several ways. This is achieved through the use of multiple nodes or servers, each of which is responsible for a portion of the data processing and storage. By distributing the workload in this way, the system can handle more traffic and data without becoming overloaded, which can improve performance and scalability. Furthermore, the decentralized and tamper-resistant architecture of blockchain and DS makes them more secure and resilient to attacks. In a traditional centralized DM system, a single point of failure can compromise the entire system. However, in a decentralized system, an attacker would need to compromise multiple nodes to gain access to the data, making it much more difficult to launch a successful attack. Another advantage of using blockchain and DS for DM and security is that they can improve data privacy. This can be particularly important for organizations that handle sensitive data such as personal information, financial data, or trade secrets. While there are some potential challenges and drawbacks to using these technologies, the benefits they offer in terms of security, scalability, and accountability make them a promising area of research and development for organizations seeking to improve their DM and security practices.

11.4.2 Real-World Examples of Blockchain and Distributed Systems in Data Management and Security

The usage of blockchain in the healthcare sector is one illustration. The healthcare industry is a highly regulated, intricate, and data-producing sector. By offering a transparent, impenetrable, and tamper-proof mechanism for maintaining records, BT has the ability to enhance the security and privacy of patient data. The application of DS in the financial sector is another such. Large volumes of sensitive data, including financial and personal data, are handled by financial organizations including banks and insurance firms.

By decentralizing data processing and storage, DS can enhance the security and scalability of financial DM. This can lower the danger of data breaches and cyberattacks while also enhancing the performance and accessibility of financial services. Another area where blockchain and DS are being utilized to boost DM and security is in SCM. Supply chain managers can increase the accountability and transparency of their operations by tracking and verifying the movement of goods and services using a distributed ledger counterfeiting while enhancing the precision and effectiveness of logistics and inventory control.

Utilities may increase the accuracy of their billing and reporting while also lowering the risk of mistakes and fraud by adopting a decentralized system to measure and manage energy production and usage. These real-world examples show how blockchain and DS have the ability to change DM and security in a variety of fields and applications. We may anticipate seeing even more cutting-edge applications of blockchain and DS in DM and security as these technologies continue to develop and mature [30, 31].

11.5 Challenges of Using Blockchain and Distributed Systems

As mentioned earlier, there are several challenges associated with using blockchain and DS for DM and security. Some of the main challenges are:

1) *Complexity:* Blockchain and DS are complex technologies that require specialized technical expertise to implement and manage. This can make it difficult for smaller organizations to adopt these technologies.
2) *Data privacy and governance:* The use of BT may make it difficult to delete or modify data, which can raise questions about data ownership and control. In addition, the use of DS may require new governance models to ensure that data is being managed in a fair and transparent way.
3) *Interoperability:* Blockchain and DS may have different standards, protocols, and technologies, which can make it difficult to integrate with existing systems or share data across different platforms. This can create barriers to adoption and collaboration, particularly in industries where there are many different stakeholders and systems in place.
4) *Security vulnerabilities:* While blockchain and DS can improve security by providing a tamper-proof and transparent record-keeping system, they are not immune to attacks. In fact, the use of blockchain and DS may create new attack vectors, such as 51% of attacks, which could compromise the integrity of the system. These challenges highlight the importance of careful planning, governance, and risk management when adopting blockchain and DS for DM and security. It is important to carefully weigh the potential benefits against the costs and risks and to develop a clear strategy for managing these challenges. Challenges in blockchain and DS for data security are shown in Figure 11.2.

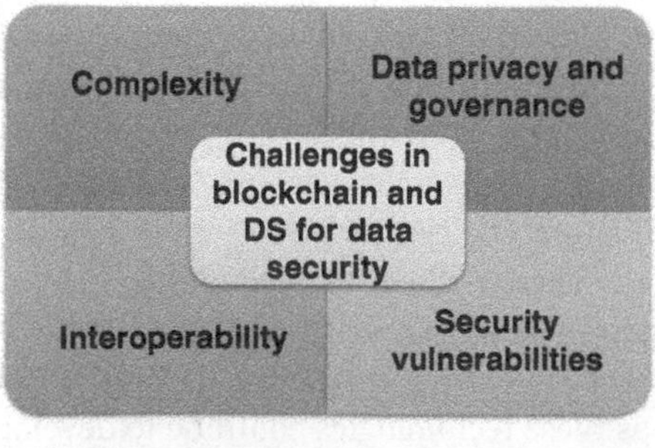

Figure 11.2 Challenges in blockchain and DS for data security.

11.5.1 Limitations of Using Blockchain and Distributed Systems

In addition to the challenges, there are several limitations associated with using blockchain and DS for DM and security. Some of the main limitations are:

1) *Cost:* Implementing and managing blockchain and DS can be expensive, particularly for smaller organizations. This may make it difficult for some organizations to justify the cost of adopting these technologies.
2) *Speed:* The consensus algorithms used by blockchain and DS can slow down the transaction processing speed, which may not be suitable for certain applications that require real-time processing.
3) *Regulatory concerns:* While blockchain and DS can improve security and transparency, they may also create regulatory challenges, particularly in industries that are highly regulated. This can create legal and compliance issues that may limit the adoption of these technologies.
4) *Environmental impact:* The energy consumption associated with the mining process used to validate transactions on some blockchain networks has been criticized for its negative impact on the environment. This has raised concerns about the sustainability of these technologies.
5) *Complexity and interoperability:* As mentioned earlier, the complexity and lack of interoperability associated with blockchain and DS can make it difficult to integrate with existing systems, which may limit their usefulness in certain industries.

These limitations demonstrate that blockchain and DS are not a panacea for all DM and security challenges. It is important to carefully consider the potential limitations when evaluating the suitability of these technologies for a particular use case [32, 33].

11.6 Discussion

As blockchain and DS continue to gain popularity, there is a growing need for research to explore the potential future directions for these technologies in DM and security. One important area of future research is the integration of these systems with existing technology infrastructure. This integration is necessary to leverage the benefits of these new technologies while also minimizing the costs associated with upgrading existing systems. Research in this area could focus on developing new standards and protocols that enable the seamless integration of these technologies with existing systems. Governance and regulation are another area of research that is critical for the adoption of blockchain and DS in DM and security. The use of these technologies raises new questions about data governance and regulation. Future research could focus on developing new governance models and regulatory frameworks that balance the need for security and transparency with the need for privacy and control. This will be particularly important in industries that are highly regulated, such as healthcare and finance. Privacy and confidentiality is another important area of future research. While blockchain and DS provide a tamper-proof and transparent record-keeping system, they may not be suitable for all applications where privacy and confidentiality are important. Future research could focus on developing new technologies that enable selective disclosure of data and provide greater privacy and confidentiality guarantees. This will be particularly important in applications where sensitive data is being stored or shared.

11.7 Conclusion

In conclusion, the combination of blockchain and DS has the potential to revolutionize DM and security. These technologies offer unique advantages, including immutability, transparency, decentralization, and enhanced security Future research directions for blockchain and DS in DM and security include integration with existing technology infrastructure, scalability and performance, governance and regulation, privacy and confidentiality, and interdisciplinary collaboration. By exploring these research directions, we can develop new standards, protocols, and frameworks that enable greater collaboration and innovation in this area. Overall, the adoption of blockchain and DS for DM and security represents an exciting new frontier in technology. As these technologies continue to evolve and mature, they have the potential to transform the way data is managed and secured. With ongoing research and innovation, we can unlock the full potential of blockchain and DS for DM and security, creating a more secure and transparent digital future.

References

1 Humayun, M., Jhanjhi, N., Hamid, B., and Ahmed, G. (**2020**). Emerging smart logistics and transportation using IoT and blockchain. *IEEE Internet Things Mag. 3*: 58–62.

2 Alamri, M., Jhanjhi, N., and Humayun, M. (**2019**). Blockchain for Internet of Things (IoT) research issues challenges & future directions: a review. *Int. J. Comput. Sci. Netw. Secur. 19*: 244–258.

3 Jun, M. (**2018**). Blockchain government—a next form of infrastructure for the twenty-first century. *J. Open Innov.: Technol. Mark. Complex. 4*: 7.

4 Cagigas, D., Clifton, J., Diaz-Fuentes, D., and Fernandez-Gutierrez, M. (**2021**). Blockchain for public services: a systematic literature review. *IEEE Access 9*: 13904–13921.

5 Saxena, H., Joshi, D., Singh, H., and Anand, R. (2022). Comparison of classification algorithms for Alzheimer's disease prediction. In: *2022 Seventh International Conference on Parallel, Distributed and Grid Computing (PDGC)*, 687–692. IEEE.

6 Sindhwani, N., Anand, R., Vashisth, R. et al. (2022). Thingspeak-based environmental monitoring system using IoT. In: *2022 Seventh International Conference on Parallel, Distributed and Grid Computing (PDGC)*, 675–680. IEEE.

7 Pandey, B.K., Pandey, D., Anand, R. et al. (2022). The impact of digital change on student learning and mental anguish in the COVID era. In: *An Interdisciplinary Approach in the Post-COVID-19 Pandemic Era*, 197–206. Nova Science.

8 Anand, R., Nirmal, V., Chauhan, Y., and Sharma, T. (2023). An image-based deep learning approach for personalized outfit selection. In: *2023 10th International Conference on Computing for Sustainable Global Development (INDIACom)*, 1050–1054. IEEE.

9 Singh, H., Pandey, B.K., George, S. et al. (2022). Effective overview of different ML models used for prediction of COVID-19 patients. In: *Artificial Intelligence on Medical Data: Proceedings of International Symposium, ISCMM 2021*, 185–192. Singapore: Springer Nature Singapore.

10 Themistocleous, M. (**2018**). Blockchain technology and land registry. *Cyprus Rev. 30*: 195–202.

11 Humayun, M., Jhanjhi, N.Z., Niazi, M. et al. (2022). Securing drug distribution systems from tampering using blockchain. *Electronics* 11 (8): 1195.

12 Kumar, R. and Tripathi, R. (2019). Traceability of counterfeit medicine supply chain through Blockchain. In: *Proceedings of the 2019 11th International Conference on Communication Systems & Networks (COMSNETS)*, Bengaluru, India, 7–11 January 2019, 568–570.

13 Wang, J., Gao, Y., Liu, W. et al. (**2019**). An intelligent data gathering schema with data fusion supported for mobile sink in WSNs. *Int. J. Distrib. Sens. Netw.*

14 Ge, C., Liu, Z., Xia, J., and Fang, L. (**2019**). Revocable identity-based broadcast proxy re-encryption for data sharing in clouds. *IEEE Trans. Dependable Secure Comput.* 18 (3): 1214–1226.

15 Sindhwani, N., Rana, A., and Chaudhary, A. (2021). Breast cancer detection using machine learning algorithms. In: *2021 9th International Conference on Reliability, Infocom Technologies and Optimization (Trends and Future Directions) (ICRITO)*, 1–5. IEEE.

16 Bruntha, P.M., Dhanasekar, S., Hepsiba, D. et al. (2023). Application of switching median filter with L 2 norm-based auto-tuning function for removing random valued impulse noise. *Aerosp. Syst. 6* (1): 53–59.

17 Kumar Pandey, B., Pandey, D., Nassa, V.K. et al. (2021). Encryption and steganography-based text extraction in IoT using the EWCTS optimizer. *Imaging Sci. J. 69* (1-4): 38–56.
18 Jain, N., Chaudhary, A., Sindhwani, N., and Rana, A. (2021). Applications of wearable devices in IoT. In: *2021 9th International Conference on Reliability, Infocom Technologies and Optimization (Trends and Future Directions) (ICRITO)*, 1–4. IEEE.
19 Govindaraj, V., Dhanasekar, S., Martinsagayam, K. et al. (2023). Low-power test pattern generator using modified LFSR. *Aerosp. Syst.* 1–8.
20 Wang, J., Gu, X., Liu, W. et al. (**2019**). An empower Hamilton loop based data collection algorithm with mobile agent for WSNs. *Hum.-Centric Comput. Inf. Sci.* 9 (1): 1–14.
21 Cao, D., Zheng, B., Ji, B. et al. (**2018**). A robust distance-based relay selection for message dissemination in vehicular network. *Wireless Netw.* 26: 1755–1771.
22 Dwyer, J.T., Coates, P.M., and Smith, M.J. (**2018**). Dietary supplements: regulatory challenges and research resources. *Nutrients 10*: 41.
23 Schöner, M.M., Kourouklis, D., Sandner, P. et al. (2017). *Blockchain Technology in the Pharmaceutical Industry*. Frankfurt, Germany: Frankfurt School Blockchain Center.
24 Erokhin, A., Koshechkin, K., and Ryabkov, I. (**2020**). The distributed ledger technology as a measure to minimize risks of poor-quality pharmaceuticals circulation. *PeerJ. Comput. Sci. 6*: e292.
25 Uddin, M. (**2021**). Blockchain medledger: hyperledger fabric enabled drug traceability system for counterfeit drugs in pharmaceutical industry. *Int. J. Pharm. 597*: 120235.
26 Ahmadi, V., Benjelloun, S., el Kik, M. et al. (2020). Drug governance: IoT-based blockchain implementation in the pharmaceutical supply chain. In: *Proceedings of the 2020 Sixth International Conference on Mobile And Secure Services (MobiSecServ)*, Miami Beach, FL, USA, 22–23 February 2020, 1–8.
27 Lokesh, M., Ahmed, S., and Khan, S. (**2021**). Block chain based SCM for counterfeit drugs in pharmaceutical industry. *Int. J. Sci. Res. Comput. Sci. Eng. Inf. Technol. 7*: 100–108.
28 Abbas, K., Afaq, M., Ahmed Khan, T., and Song, W.-C. (**2020**). A blockchain and machine learning-based drug SCM and recommendation system for smart pharmaceutical industry. *Electronics 9*: 852.
29 Humayun, M. (**2021**). Industrial revolution 5.0 and the role of cutting edge technologies. *Int. J. Adv. Comput. Sci. Appl. 12*: 605–615.
30 Siyal, A.A., Junejo, A.Z., Zawish, M. et al. (**2019**). Applications of blockchain technology in medicine and healthcare: challenges and future perspectives. *Cryptography 3*: 3.

31 Humayun, M. (**2020**). Role of emerging IoT big data and cloud computing for real time application. *Int. J. Adv. Comput. Sci. Appl. 11*: 494–506.

32 Uddin, M., Salah, K., Jayaraman, R. et al. (**2021**). Blockchain for drug traceability: architectures and open challenges. *Health Inform. J. 27*: 14604582211011228.

33 Bamakan, S.M.H., Moghaddam, S.G., and Manshadi, S.D. (**2021**). Blockchain-enabled pharmaceutical cold chain: applications, key challenges, and future trends. *J. Cleaner Prod. 302*: 127021.

12

Enhancing Business Development, Ethics, and Governance with the Adoption of Distributed Systems

Aarti Dawra[1], K.K. Ramachandran[2], Debasis Mohanty[3], Jitendra Gowrabhathini[4], Brijesh Goswami[5], Dhyana S. Ross[6], and S. Mahabub Basha[7]

[1] *Manav Rachna International Institute of Research and Studies, Faridabad, Haryana, India*
[2] *Management/Commerce/International Business, DR. G R D College of Science, Coimbatore, Tamilnadu, India*
[3] *School of Commerce Management and Research, ITM University, Raipur, Chhattisgarh, India*
[4] *K L Business School, Koneru Lakshmaiah Education Foundation, K L University, Vijayawada, Andhra Pradesh, India*
[5] *Institute of Business Management GLA University, Mathura, Uttar Pradesh, India*
[6] *Loyola Institute of Business Administration (LIBA), Chennai, Tamilnadu, India*
[7] *Department of Commerce, International Institute of Business Studies, Bangalore, Karnataka, India*

12.1 Introduction

Companies are continuously looking for new ways to innovate, stay competitive, and adapt to the changing needs of their clients in today's quickly changing business climate. Using distributed systems is one strategy that is growing in popularity, since it can aid firms in developing their businesses, encouraging moral behavior, and enhancing governance systems.

Distributed systems are a group of linked computers that collaborate to accomplish a single objective. They offer many advantages, including improved productivity, scalability, fault tolerance, and cost savings. Businesses may access enormous volumes of data and use sophisticated algorithms to acquire insights and make wise decisions by utilizing the power of distributed systems.

Distributed systems can also be very important in supporting ethical corporate practices. Distributed systems ethics is concerned with the ethical and accountable use of technology, making sure that the interests of all stakeholders are taken into

Meta-Heuristic Algorithms for Advanced Distributed Systems, First Edition. Edited by Rohit Anand, Abhinav Juneja, Digvijay Pandey, Sapna Juneja, and Nidhi Sindhwani.

account. As an illustration, a distributed system can be created to safeguard user privacy, stop data breaches, and provide equitable and open access to information. The use of distributed systems can also enhance organizational governance processes. Governance describes the procedures and frameworks used to direct, control, and hold organizations accountable.

By implementing governance mechanisms in distributed systems, businesses can ensure that their technology infrastructure is secure, reliable, and aligned with their overall business objectives. This can help organizations reduce risks, increase transparency, and improve decision-making processes. Despite the numerous benefits that distributed systems offer, their adoption also poses challenges and limitations. Companies need to be aware of the technological, organizational, and cultural barriers that can prevent the effective use of distributed systems. Moreover, businesses need to ensure that they have the necessary expertise and resources to implement and manage distributed systems effectively.

As the use of distributed systems continues to expand, it is essential for businesses to understand the opportunities and challenges associated with their adoption. This review chapter aims to explore how distributed systems can enhance business development, promote ethical practices, and improve governance mechanisms in organizations. By analyzing relevant case studies and best practices, the chapter provides insights and recommendations for businesses that are considering adopting distributed systems. By leveraging the benefits of distributed systems, companies can improve their business development, promote ethical practices, and improve their governance mechanisms. However, businesses need to be aware of the challenges and limitations associated with the adoption of distributed systems and take a strategic and proactive approach to their implementation. This review chapter aims to provide a comprehensive overview of the topic and to guide businesses toward the effective adoption of distributed systems in their operations [1–3].

12.1.1 Distributed Systems for Business Development

Distributed systems refer to a network of interconnected computers that work together to achieve a common goal. In a distributed system, tasks are distributed among the participating computers, which work together to complete a task in a decentralized manner. This approach allows for increased scalability, efficiency, fault tolerance, and cost savings compared to centralized systems.

The relevance of distributed systems to business development lies in their ability to provide businesses with access to vast amounts of data and leverage sophisticated algorithms to gain insights and make informed decisions. By leveraging the power of distributed systems, businesses can also improve their customer service, increase their speed to market, and better adapt to changing market conditions.

In terms of ethics, distributed systems play a critical role in promoting ethical practices in business. Ethics in distributed systems is concerned with the responsible and accountable use of technology, ensuring that the interests of all stakeholders are considered. For example, a distributed system can be designed to protect user privacy, prevent data breaches, and ensure fair and transparent access to information. Finally, distributed systems can also improve governance mechanisms in organizations. Governance refers to the processes and structures by which organizations are directed, controlled, and held accountable. By implementing governance mechanisms in distributed systems, businesses can ensure that their technology infrastructure is secure, reliable, and aligned with their overall business objectives. This can help organizations reduce risks, increase transparency, and improve decision-making processes.

Overall, the adoption of distributed systems can provide significant benefits to businesses, such as increased efficiency, scalability, and improved decision-making. At the same time, businesses need to be aware of the challenges and limitations associated with the adoption of distributed systems and take a strategic and proactive approach to their implementation. By doing so, businesses can leverage the power of distributed systems to enhance their business development, promote ethical practices, and improve governance mechanisms in their organizations [4, 5].

12.2 Applications of Distributed Systems in Business Development

- Distributed systems are computer networks that are designed to work together to accomplish a common goal. They are composed of a collection of interconnected nodes, each of which operates independently, with the nodes communicating with each other to exchange information and work collaboratively. The geographical distribution of the nodes enables distributed systems to operate across several places, opening up a wide range of applications.
- Distributed systems have several uses in the growth of businesses. The fact that distributed systems enable more scalability and flexibility is one of their main benefits. Businesses may quickly scale up and down operations as needed using distributed systems, free from the constraints of a centralized one. Businesses that are expanding swiftly need to be able to scale up and down easily in order to be able to respond quickly to shifting market conditions [6, 7].
- Increased fault tolerance is another important advantage of distributed systems in business development. Because each node in a distributed system runs independently, any downtime or interruption caused by a failed node will have a little effect on the system as a whole. This adaptability is crucial for companies whose operations primarily rely on technology.

- Distributed systems can be utilized to speed up data processing and decision-making in corporate development. Distributed systems can be utilized to get insights into consumer behavior, market trends, and other crucial business data because of their capacity to analyze enormous amounts of data fast and effectively. Businesses can decide on their operations and strategy by using distributed systems to evaluate and process data [8, 9].
- There are, however, some challenges associated with the adoption of distributed systems in business development. One of the key challenges is the need for specialized expertise and resources to implement and maintain these systems. Distributed systems are complex, and businesses need to have the necessary technical expertise to design and operate them effectively. Additionally, because distributed systems are often used to process large amounts of data, businesses need to have the necessary resources to support these operations.
- In conclusion, distributed systems have numerous applications in business development, including scalability, fault tolerance, and data analysis. However, they also present challenges, including the need for specialized expertise and resources. Businesses that are considering adopting distributed systems should carefully evaluate their needs and capabilities and take a strategic and proactive approach to their adoption. By doing so, they can leverage the power of distributed systems to enhance their operations and gain a competitive advantage in their respective industries [10–12].

12.2.1 Characteristics of Distributed Systems

Distributed systems are computer systems that are composed of multiple autonomous computers or nodes that work together as a single system to provide a common set of functionalities. In a distributed system, these nodes are physically located at different locations, often connected to each other through a network. These systems enable organizations to scale their operations, increase fault tolerance, and achieve better performance and resource utilization.

There are several key characteristics of distributed systems. These include:

1) *Decentralization:* In a distributed system, there is no central node or server that controls the entire system. Instead, the system is composed of multiple nodes, each with its own processing power and storage, and they work together to provide the desired functionality.
2) *Autonomy:* Each node in a distributed system is autonomous and can perform its own tasks independently. This autonomy allows the system to be fault tolerant, as if one node fails, the other nodes can continue to operate independently.
3) *Heterogeneity:* Nodes in a distributed system can have different hardware, operating systems, and software, allowing for greater flexibility and easier integration of legacy systems.

4) *Scalability:* Distributed systems can be easily scaled by adding or removing nodes as the demand for services changes. This enables organizations to handle large-scale computing tasks that would be difficult or impossible to accomplish with a single system.
5) *Concurrency:* Distributed systems must be able to handle concurrent requests from multiple nodes. This requires careful management of resources and coordination between nodes to ensure that tasks are executed in an orderly and efficient manner.
6) *Security:* Distributed systems must be designed with security in mind to prevent unauthorized access to the system or data.
7) *Transparency:* Distributed systems must provide transparency to users and applications, hiding the complexity of the underlying infrastructure and allowing users to interact with the system as if it were a single entity.

Distributed systems are composed of multiple autonomous nodes that work together to provide a common set of functionalities. They are characterized by decentralization, autonomy, heterogeneity, scalability, concurrency, security, and transparency [13–15]. Understanding these characteristics is essential to designing and operating distributed systems effectively.

12.2.2 Benefits of Distributed Systems in Business Development

- Distributed systems offer several key benefits to businesses that are looking to improve their development processes. One of the primary benefits is scalability. As businesses grow and their customer base expands, they need to handle increasing volumes of data and users. Distributed systems allow businesses to scale up or down by adding or removing nodes in the network, enabling them to handle variable workloads. This scalability is critical to ensuring that businesses can keep pace with the demands of their customers and remain competitive.
- Another advantage of using distributed systems in business development is improved performance. By distributing computing tasks across multiple nodes, distributed systems can achieve higher levels of performance and faster processing times. This means businesses can deliver products and services to their customers more quickly, reducing wait times and improving customer satisfaction. Improved performance is especially important for businesses that rely on their systems to provide critical services, such as online shopping or financial transactions.
- Distributed systems also offer better fault tolerance than traditional centralized systems [16, 17]. If one node fails, the rest of the network can continue to operate, ensuring that the business can continue to provide its services without

interruption. This fault tolerance is critical for businesses that rely on their systems to provide continuous services to customers. Distributed systems can also help businesses recover from disasters more quickly by distributing data across multiple nodes, ensuring that critical information is always available.

12.2.3 Applications in Business Development

Distributed systems have a wide range of applications in business development. Here are a few examples:

1) *E-commerce:* Online marketplaces and retailers rely on distributed systems to handle high volumes of traffic, process transactions, and manage inventory. Distributed systems allow these businesses to handle large numbers of users and transactions in real time, ensuring a seamless shopping experience for customers.
2) *Data analytics:* Big data analytics requires the processing of massive volumes of data, and distributed systems can handle this data more efficiently than traditional centralized systems. By using distributed systems, businesses can analyze data faster, make data-driven decisions, and gain a competitive edge in their industries.
3) *Cloud computing:* Cloud computing relies on distributed systems to provide on-demand access to computing resources such as storage, processing, and applications. This allows businesses to access the resources they need without having to invest in costly on-premise hardware and software.
4) *Supply chain management:* Distributed systems can be used to manage complex supply chains, allowing businesses to track inventory and shipments across multiple locations and systems. This enables businesses to reduce inefficiencies, improve delivery times, and ensure that their products are delivered to customers in a timely manner.

12.3 The Importance of Ethics in Distributed Systems

It's crucial to think about the ethical ramifications of using distributed systems as more firms adopt them for their development procedures. It is crucial to make sure that distributed systems are utilized ethically and responsibly. Ethics are the rules of right and wrong that guide our actions and judgments. Data privacy is one of the main ethical issues with distributed systems. Businesses must take precautions to safeguard the privacy of their customers and employees as they gather and handle massive volumes of data utilizing distributed technologies.

This includes putting robust security measures in place to stop unauthorized access to sensitive information, such as encryption and access limits.

Another ethical consideration when using distributed systems is transparency. Businesses must ensure that their use of these systems is transparent, with clear and open communication about how the systems are used and what benefits they provide [18–20]. Transparency is essential to building trust with customers and stakeholders, as it ensures that they understand how their data is being used and how it benefits them.

Businesses must take into account the ethical ramifications of their use of distributed systems on the environment in addition to privacy and transparency. Businesses must take into account the environmental impact of their use of distributed systems because they consume a lot of energy to run. This can be done by utilizing energy-saving devices and implementing sustainable habits, like the utilization of renewable energy sources. The ethical use of distributed systems also takes into account the ethical application of artificial intelligence (AI) [21, 22]. Businesses must make sure that AI is used ethically and responsibly as it is integrated into dispersed systems more and more.

In conclusion, ethics is a critical consideration in the use of distributed systems in business development. Businesses must ensure that they use these systems in a responsible and ethical manner, with a focus on data privacy, transparency, environmental impact, and the responsible use of AI. By doing so, businesses can build trust with customers and stakeholders and ensure that their use of distributed systems contributes to a more ethical and sustainable business environment [23, 24].

12.3.1 Ethics in Distributed Systems

Ethics in distributed systems refers to the principles and guidelines that govern the responsible and ethical use of distributed systems in a business context. It involves identifying and addressing ethical issues related to the collection, processing, and use of data, as well as ensuring the responsible and sustainable use of computing resources.

In the context of distributed systems, ethics includes ensuring that data privacy and security measures are in place to protect sensitive information. This includes implementing appropriate access controls, encryption, and other security measures to prevent unauthorized access and use of data. Additionally, it entails being open and honest about how data is collected and utilized, as well as making sure that stakeholders and customers are aware of how their data is being used and safeguarded.

Ethics in distributed systems also includes the responsible use of computing resources, particularly in terms of energy consumption and environmental impact.

As distributed systems require a significant amount of energy to operate, businesses must consider the environmental impact of their use, and take steps to minimize energy consumption and adopt sustainable practices. The proper application of AI and other automated decision-making systems is a component of DS. This entails making sure AI is utilized in an open and accountable manner, preventing the use of biased or discriminating algorithms, and making sure human beings aren't negatively impacted by AI. Businesses can increase trust with clients and stakeholders by employing distributed systems in a proactive and ethical manner. They can also make sure that their use of technology promotes a more moral and sustainable corporate environment [25–27].

12.3.2 Ethics to Business Development and Governance

In order to ensure that businesses function in a responsible, ethical, and sustainable way, ethics is extremely important to corporate development and governance. Businesses can enhance their reputation, foster stakeholder and customer trust, and achieve long-term success by incorporating ethical issues into corporate development and governance procedures.

The influence of ethics on innovation is one of the main ways in which company development can benefit from them. Businesses can identify new prospects for innovation and make sure that new products and services are produced in a responsible and ethical manner by taking ethical considerations into account. This entails taking into account how new technology might affect people, society, and the environment, as well as taking action to counteract any unfavorable effects.

Moreover, ethics is important to business governance because it offers a framework for ethical judgment and accountability. Businesses may make sure that their actions are in keeping with their values and mission and that they are held accountable for their decisions and actions by adopting explicit ethical guidelines and codes of conduct. This involves making sure companies are open and honest about how they operate and that they take action to resolve any ethical issues or infractions.

The manner that businesses deal with their stakeholders, such as employees, clients, suppliers, and the general public, is equally important in terms of ethics. Businesses may improve their reputation, establish a culture of trust and collaboration, and strengthen their connections with their stakeholders by giving ethical issues first priority.

The sustainability and long-term profitability of enterprises are also impacted by ethics. Businesses can add value for their stakeholders and advance the greater social and environmental good by pursuing a responsible and ethical approach to corporate development and governance. This entails implementing sustainable business practices, aiding neighborhood initiatives, and taking action to solve global issues like social inequality and climate change [28, 29].

12.3.3 Distributed Systems in Promoting Ethical Practices

Distributed systems can play a significant role in promoting ethical practices in business development and governance. By their very nature, distributed systems provide a decentralized and transparent way of sharing data and resources, which can help to ensure ethical practices are followed.

By utilizing blockchain technology, distributed networks can encourage moral behavior in a number of important ways. Blockchain is a distributed ledger technology that makes it possible to conduct secure, open, and direct transactions without the use of middlemen. Businesses can use blockchain to verify that information is recorded in an auditable and tamper-proof manner and that all stakeholders have access to the same data. This can aid in fostering accountability, openness, and trust while also assisting in the prevention of fraud and other unethical behavior. Decentralized apps are yet another way that distributed systems might encourage moral behavior (dApps).

dApps are applications that run on a blockchain network and are not controlled by any central authority. This decentralized approach can help to prevent censorship and promote transparency and can enable users to have greater control over their data and personal information.

Distributed systems can also promote ethical practices by enabling more sustainable and efficient use of computing resources. By using distributed computing, businesses can reduce their energy consumption and carbon footprint, which can contribute to a more sustainable business environment. This can also help to reduce costs and increase efficiency, which can be reinvested into ethical initiatives such as community development and social responsibility programs.

Finally, distributed systems can promote ethical practices by enabling more responsible and ethical use of AI. By using distributed computing and blockchain, businesses can ensure that AI algorithms are transparent, auditable, and accountable, which can help to prevent bias, discrimination, and other ethical concerns. This can also help to ensure that automated decision-making is aligned with ethical principles and values and that human oversight is in place to ensure that decisions are made in a responsible and ethical manner [30, 31].

12.4 Governance in Distributed Systems

Governance is an essential aspect of distributed systems, as it helps to ensure that the system is operating in a fair, transparent, and secure manner as shown in Figure 12.1. In the context of distributed systems, governance refers to the processes, policies, and rules that are put in place to manage the system and ensure that it is functioning as intended. Establishing defined guidelines and procedures for

Figure 12.1 Governance in distributed systems.

network participation is one of the main functions of governance in distributed systems. This entails articulating the rights and obligations of network participants, as well as defining the roles and duties of various network participants and the requirements for participation. Governance may help to ensure that the network runs in a fair and transparent manner and that all members are held accountable for their actions by defining these standards. Governance also plays a crucial role in ensuring the security of the distributed system. This includes establishing protocols for securing the network, such as implementing encryption and authentication mechanisms, defining procedures for managing security breaches, and responding to threats. Governance can aid in preserving the integrity of the system and preventing bad actors from undermining its functioning by making sure the network is safe.

Establishing procedures for decision-making and dispute resolution is a crucial function of governance in distributed systems. This entails developing protocols for resolving disputes amongst participants as well as describing the process for making decisions that have an impact on the network. By putting these systems in place, governance may aid in making sure that decisions are made fairly and openly and that disputes are settled swiftly and effectively.

Finally, governance plays a critical role in ensuring the sustainability and long-term viability of the distributed system. This includes establishing protocols for upgrading and maintaining the system, as well as defining procedures for managing the growth and evolution of the network. Governance can help to ensure that the system can continue to meet the needs of its users in the long run by ensuring that the network is scalable and sustainable.

A crucial component of distributed systems is governance, which helps to make sure the network is run in a just, open, and secure way. Governance can help to assure the long-term success and viability of the distributed system by creating explicit rules and protocols, ensuring the security of the network, providing procedures for making decisions and resolving conflicts, and assuring the sustainability of the network [32–34].

12.4.1 Importance of Governance in Distributed Systems

The term "governance" in the context of distributed systems refers to the collection of standards, guidelines, and practices implemented to control system operations and participant conduct. It may also entail laying up the requirements for joining the network, creating the guidelines for participation, and building processes for resolving disputes and making decisions.

The importance of governance in distributed systems is twofold. First, governance helps to ensure that the system operates in a fair, transparent, and secure manner. By defining the roles and responsibilities of participants and establishing clear rules for participation, governance can ensure that all participants are held accountable for their actions and that the network functions smoothly.

Second, governance is essential for establishing trust in the network. Distributed systems rely on the cooperation and coordination of multiple parties to function effectively, and trust is essential for maintaining this cooperation. By establishing clear rules and procedures for participation, governance can help to build trust among participants and ensure that the system is perceived as trustworthy and reliable. Effective governance is especially important for distributed systems, as they are often designed to operate in a decentralized and autonomous manner. In these systems, there may be no central authority or organization responsible for managing the network, and participants must rely on the governance structures in place to ensure that the system operates effectively and fairly.

Overall, governance is a critical component of distributed systems, as it helps to ensure that the system operates in a secure, transparent, and trustworthy manner. By defining clear rules and procedures for participation, governance can help to build trust among participants and ensure the long-term viability and success of the network [35].

12.4.2 The Benefits of Implementing Governance Mechanisms in Distributed Systems

Implementing governance mechanisms in distributed systems can bring several benefits, such as:

1) *Improved security:* Governance mechanisms can help to establish security protocols and best practices to safeguard the system from external threats and internal vulnerabilities. For example, governance can define access controls,

encryption standards, and auditing procedures to ensure the security of data and transactions.

2) *Increased transparency:* Governance mechanisms can promote transparency by ensuring that information is shared openly and that decisions are made in an accountable and responsible manner. This can help to build trust among participants and ensure that the network operates fairly and effectively.
3) *Better decision-making:* Governance mechanisms can provide a framework for making decisions and resolving conflicts among participants. By establishing clear processes for decision-making, governance can help to ensure that decisions are made in a timely, informed, and collaborative manner.
4) *Reduced risks:* Governance mechanisms can help to identify and mitigate risks associated with the operation of the system. For example, governance can establish risk management frameworks and contingency plans to address potential issues and minimize their impact on the network.
5) Enhanced innovation*:* Governance mechanisms can foster innovation by promoting collaboration, experimentation, and the sharing of ideas among participants. By creating a supportive environment for innovation, governance can help to drive the development of new products, services, and technologies.

12.4.3 Examples of Governance Mechanisms in Distributed Systems

There are several governance mechanisms that can be implemented in distributed systems to promote security, transparency, and effective decision-making. Some examples include:

1) *Access controls:* Access controls can be implemented to restrict access to certain parts of the distributed system based on roles, permissions, or other criteria. For example, a permissioned blockchain network may require participants to provide proof of identity and meet certain criteria before being granted access to the network.
2) *Auditing procedures:* Auditing procedures can be used to monitor the activity of participants in the distributed system and ensure that they are adhering to the rules and procedures established by governance. For example, auditing procedures may be used to track transactions on a blockchain network and ensure that they are valid and authorized.
3) *Dispute resolution mechanisms:* Dispute resolution mechanisms can be used to resolve conflicts among participants in the distributed system. For example, a decentralized autonomous organization may use a voting mechanism to resolve disputes among its members.
4) *Governance frameworks:* Governance frameworks can be used to establish the rules, policies, and procedures that govern the operation of the distributed

system. For example, the Ethereum Foundation has established a governance framework for the Ethereum network that includes a set of principles, a code of conduct, and a process for proposing and voting on changes to the network.

12.4.4 Limitations in Business and Governance

While there are many potential benefits to using distributed systems for business development, ethics, and governance, there are also several challenges and limitations (as shown in Figure 12.2) that should be considered. Some of these include [36, 37]:

1) *Technical complexity:* Distributed systems can be complex and difficult to implement, especially for organizations that lack the necessary technical expertise. This can lead to delays, cost overruns, and other challenges that may limit the effectiveness of the system.
2) *Interoperability:* Distributed systems may struggle to communicate and interact with other systems, especially those that use different technologies or protocols. This can limit the ability of the system to work effectively with other systems, potentially reducing its overall value.

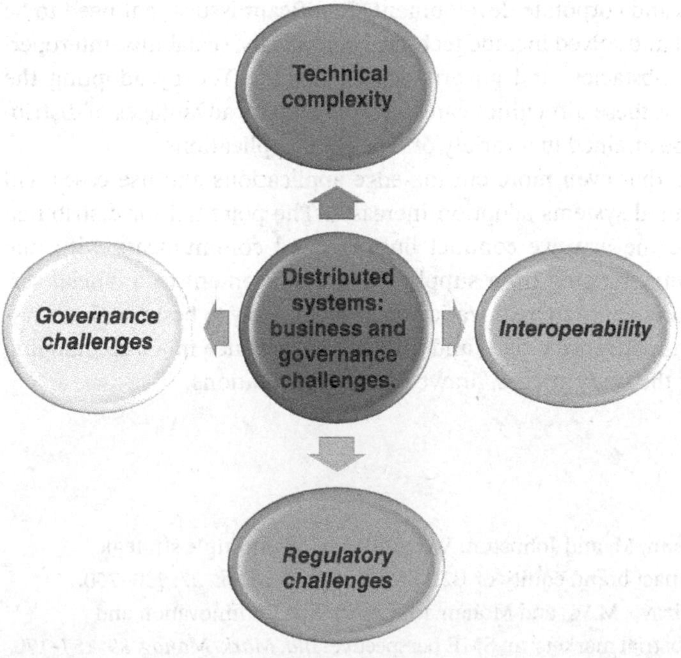

Figure 12.2 Distributed systems: business and governance challenges.

3) *Regulatory challenges:* Distributed systems may face regulatory challenges, especially in industries that are heavily regulated or where there are concerns about data privacy and security. This can result in additional costs, delays, and other challenges that may limit the effectiveness of the system.
4) *Governance challenges:* Implementing effective governance mechanisms in distributed systems can be challenging, especially when there are many participants with different interests and incentives. This can lead to disputes, conflicts, and other challenges that may limit the effectiveness of the system.

12.5 Conclusion

In conclusion, the adoption of distributed systems has the potential to fundamentally alter how companies are created, run, and governed, while simultaneously encouraging moral behavior and raising participant confidence. Organizations can enhance their operations, lower expenses, and boost efficiency by utilizing the advantages of distributed systems, such as decentralization, transparency, and security. Furthermore, the implementation of ethical and governance processes in distributed systems can aid in making sure that these advantages are attained in an ethical and long-lasting manner. Yet, there are also substantial obstacles and restrictions related to the implementation of distributed systems in terms of governance, morality, and corporate development. Significant issues that need to be properly evaluated and solved include technical complexity, scalability, interoperability, regulatory obstacles, and governance challenges. Yet, by adopting the appropriate strategy, these difficulties can be solved and the advantages of distributed systems can be attained in a variety of fields and applications.

It is conceivable that even more cutting-edge applications and use cases will develop as distributed systems adoption increases. The potential for distributed systems to change the way we conduct business and communicate with one another is enormous, ranging from supply chain management to financial services, healthcare, and energy. Organizations can decide how to best use these systems to spur growth, advance ethics, and improve governance in a fast-changing world by knowing their advantages, drawbacks, and limitations.

References

1 Anees-ur-Rehman, M. and Johnston, W.J. **(2019)**. How multiple strategic orientations impact brand equity of B2B SMEs. *J. Strat. Mark. 27*: 730–750.

2 Casidy, R., Nyadzayo, M.W., and Mohan, M. **(2019)**. Service innovation and adoption in industrial markets: an SME perspective. *Ind. Mark. Manag. 89*: 157–170.

3 Seifzadeh, M., Salehi, M., Abedini, B., and Ranjbar, M.H. **(2021)**. The relationship between management characteristics and financial statement readability. *EuroMed J. Bus. 16*: 108–126.

4 Muñoz-Pascual, L., Curado, C., and Galende, J. (1689). The triple bottom line on sustainable product innovation performance in SMEs: a mixed methods approach. *Sustainability* **2019:** *11*.

5 Valaei, N., Rezaei, S., and Ismail, W.K.W. **(2017)**. Examining learning strategies, creativity, and innovation at SMEs using fuzzy set qualitative comparative analysis and PLS path modeling. *J. Bus. Res. 70*: 224–233.

6 Malik, K. and Jasińska-Biliczak, A. **(2018)**. Innovations and other processes as identifiers of contemporary trends in the sustainable development of SMEs: the case of emerging regional economies. *Sustainability 10*: 1361.

7 Vrontis, D., Basile, G., Andreano, M.S. et al. **(2020)**. The profile of innovation driven Italian SMEs and the relationship between the firms' networking abilities and dynamic capabilities. *J. Bus. Res. 114*: 313–324.

8 Widya-Hasuti, A., Mardani, A., Streimikiene, D. et al. **(2018)**. The role of process innovation between firm-specific capabilities and sustainable innovation in SMEs: empirical evidence from Indonesia. *Sustainability 10*: 2244.

9 Al-Kwifi, O.S., Ongsakul, V., Abu Farha, A.K. et al. **(2021)**. Impact of product innovativeness on technology switching in global market. *EuroMed. J. Bus. 16*: 25–38.

10 Pandey, N., Tripathi, A., Jain, D., and Roy, S. **(2020)**. Does price tolerance depend upon the type of product in e-retailing? Role of customer satisfaction, trust, loyalty, and perceived value. *J. Strat. Mark. 28*: 522–541.

11 Bessant, J., Caffyn, S., and Gallagher, M. **(2001)**. An evolutionary model of continuous improvement behaviour. *Technovation 21*: 67–77.

12 Consoli, D. **(2012)**. Literature analysis on determinant factors and the impact of ICT in SMEs. *Procedia – Soc. Behav. Sci. 62*: 93–97.

13 Jain, N., Chaudhary, A., Sindhwani, N., and Rana, A. (2021). Applications of wearable devices in IoT. In: *2021 9th International Conference on Reliability, Infocom Technologies and Optimization (Trends and Future Directions) (ICRITO)*, 1–4. IEEE.

14 Sindhwani, N., Rana, A., and Chaudhary, A. (2021). Breast cancer detection using machine learning algorithms. In: *2021 9th International Conference on Reliability, Infocom Technologies and Optimization (Trends and Future Directions) (ICRITO)*, 1–5. IEEE.

15 Bruntha, P.M., Dhanasekar, S., Hepsiba, D. et al. (2023). Application of switching median filter with L 2 norm-based auto-tuning function for removing random valued impulse noise. *Aerosp. Syst. 6* (1): 53–59.

16 Kumar Pandey, B., Pandey, D., Nassa, V.K. et al. (2021). Encryption and steganography-based text extraction in IoT using the EWCTS optimizer. *Imaging Sci. J. 69* (1-4): 38–56.

17 Govindaraj, V., Dhanasekar, S., Martinsagayam, K. et al. (2023). Low-power test pattern generator using modified LFSR. *Aerosp. Syst.* 1–8.

18 Anand, R., Nirmal, V., Chauhan, Y., and Sharma, T. (2023). An image-based deep learning approach for personalized outfit selection. In: *2023 10th International Conference on Computing for Sustainable Global Development (INDIACom)*, 1050–1054. IEEE.

19 Singh, H., Pandey, B.K., George, S. et al. (2022). Effective overview of different ML models used for prediction of COVID-19 patients. In: *Artificial Intelligence on Medical Data: Proceedings of International Symposium, ISCMM 2021*, 185–192. Singapore: Springer Nature Singapore.

20 Pandey, B.K., Pandey, D., Anand, R. et al. (2022). The impact of digital change on student learning and mental anguish in the COVID era. In: *An Interdisciplinary Approach in the Post-COVID-19 Pandemic Era*, 197–206. Nova Science.

21 Saxena, H., Joshi, D., Singh, H., and Anand, R. (2022). Comparison of classification algorithms for Alzheimer's disease prediction. In: *2022 Seventh International Conference on Parallel, Distributed and Grid Computing (PDGC)*, 687–692. IEEE.

22 Sindhwani, N., Anand, R., Vashisth, R. et al. (2022). Thingspeak-based environmental monitoring system using IoT. In: *In 2022 Seventh International Conference on Parallel, Distributed and Grid Computing (PDGC)*, 675–680. IEEE.

23 Kapoor, K.K., Tamilmani, K., Rana, N.P. et al. **(2018)**. Advances in social media research: past, present and future. *Inf. Syst. Front. 20*: 531–558.

24 Ilavarasan, P.V. and Levy, M.R. (2010). ICTs and Urban Microenterprises: Identifying and Maximizing Opportunities for Economic Development Final Report. Human Communication Research.

25 Paris, C., Lee, W., and Paul, S. (2010). The role of social media in promoting special events: acceptance of Facebook 'Events'. In: *Information and Communication Technologies in Tourism* (ed. U. Gretzel, R. Law, and M. Fuchs), 531–541. Vienna, Austria: Springer.

26 Chung, A.Q.H., Andreev, P., Benyoucef, M. et al. **(2017)**. Managing an organization's social media presence: an empirical stages of growth model. *Int. J. Inf. Manage. 37*: 1405–1417.

27 Sundaram, R., Sharma, R., and Shakya, A. **(2020)**. Digital transformation of business models: a systematic review of impact on revenue and supply chain. *Int. J. Manage. 11*: 9–21.

28 Eller, R., Alford, P., Kallmünzer, A., and Peters, M. **(2020)**. Antecedents, consequences, and challenges of small and medium-sized enterprise digitalisation. *J. Bus. Res. 112*: 119–127.

29 Khanchel, H. **(2019)**. The impact of digital transformation on banking. *J. Bus. Adm. Res. 8*: 20.

30 Ying-Yu, K.C., Yi-Long, J., and Yu-Hsien, W. **(2016)**. Effect of digital transformation on organisational performance of SMEs: evidence from the Taiwanese textile industry's web portal. *Internet Res. 26*: 186–212.

31 Mubarak, M.F., Shaikh, F.A., Mubarik, M. et al. **(2019)**. The impact of digital transformation on business performance—a study of Pakistani SMEs. *Eng. Technol. Appl. Sci. Res. 9*: 5050–5061.

32 Downes, L. and Nunes, P.F. **(2013)**. Big-bang disruption. *Harv. Bus. Rev. 91*: 44–56.

33 Curraj, E. (2018). Business Digitalisation of SMEs in Albania: Innovative Approaches and Their Impact on Performance. Ph.D. Thesis, European University of Tirana, Tirana, Albania.

34 Gigova, T., Valeva, K., and Nikolova-Alexieva, V. (2019). Digital transformation—opportunity for industrial growth. In: *Proceedings of the 2019 International Conference on Creative Business for Smart and Sustainable Growth (CREBUS)*, Sandanski, Bulgari, 18–21 March 2019, 1–4.

35 Liu, D.Y., Chen, S.W., and Chou, T.C. **(2011)**. Resource fit in digital transformation: lessons learned from the CBC Bank global e-banking project. *Manag. Decis. 49*: 1728–1742.

36 Chen, Y. **(2020)**. Improving market performance in the digital economy. *China Econ. Rev. 62*.

37 Nambisan, S., Wright, M., and Feldman, M. **(2019)**. The digital transformation of innovation and entrepreneurship: Progress challenges and key themes. *Resour. Policy 48*: 1–9.

13

Leveraging Distribution Systems for Advanced Fraud Detection and Prevention in Finance

Venkateswararao Podile[1], Satish M. Dhoke[2], Shouvik K. Guha[3], Frakruddin A. Ahmed[4], T.V.N.J.L. Haritha[5], V. Abhinav[5], and M. Anirudh[5]

[1] *K. L. Business School, Koneru Lakshmaiah Education Foundation, Vaddeswaram, Andhra Pradesh, India*
[2] *Moreshwar Arts Science and Commerce College, Department of Commerce, Jalna, Maharashtra, India*
[3] *The West Bengal National University of Juridical Sciences, Kolkata, West Bengal, India*
[4] *School of Management, Presidency University, Bangalore, Karnataka, India*
[5] *Koneru Lakshmaiah Education Foundation, Vaddeswaram, Andhra Pradesh, India*

13.1 Introduction

Traditional fraud detection (FD) and prevention techniques have relied on rule-based systems and, more recently, machine learning-based systems. It can result in significant financial losses, undermine trust in financial institutions, and compromise the security of personal and sensitive information. However, these techniques have limitations, and as fraudsters become more sophisticated, it is necessary to explore new ways to combat financial fraud. We will provide an overview of distributed systems (DSs), discuss traditional FD and prevention techniques, explore how DSs can be used to enhance these techniques, and present case studies of DSs in action in the financial industry. We will also discuss future directions for leveraging DSs and conclude with a summary of the chapter. Fraud in finance is a persistent and significant problem that has been present in the financial industry for many years. Fraud is a purposeful misrepresentation or act of deception, frequently done for personal advantage, and it can take many different forms in the financial sector. Identity theft, credit card fraud, investment fraud, insider trading, money laundering, and embezzlement are a few typical examples of financial fraud. Financial

Meta-Heuristic Algorithms for Advanced Distributed Systems, First Edition. Edited by Rohit Anand, Abhinav Juneja, Digvijay Pandey, Sapna Juneja, and Nidhi Sindhwani.

fraud can have detrimental effects on both individuals and institutions, including considerable monetary losses, harm to one's reputation, legal repercussions, and a decline in the public's trust in the financial sector. It is getting harder for conventional FD and preventive tactics to keep up as fraudsters get more skilled and technology develops. Financial efficiently process large amounts of data and handle complex computations, offer a promising solution for enhancing FD and prevention in finance [1–3].

13.1.1 Background on Fraud in Finance

Fraud in finance is a persistent and significant problem that has been present in the financial industry for many years. Fraud is a deliberate act of deception or misrepresentation, often committed for personal gain, and it can take many forms in the financial industry. Identity theft, credit card fraud, investment fraud, insider trading, money laundering, and embezzlement are a few typical examples of financial fraud. Financial fraud can have detrimental effects on both individuals and institutions, including considerable monetary losses, harm to one's reputation, legal repercussions, and a decline in the public's trust in the financial sector. It is getting harder for conventional FD and prevention measures to keep up as fraudsters become cleverer and technology develops. Financial institutions are looking at cutting-edge strategies to fight financial fraud [4–6].

13.1.2 Importance of Fraud Detection and Prevention

Organizations in a variety of industries, including financial, take fraud seriously. Traditional techniques of FD and prevention are no longer effective due to the development of technology and the sophistication of fraudsters. By detecting fraudulent activities early, organizations can prevent or limit financial losses, maintain their reputation, and protect their customers' interests. Moreover, identify vulnerabilities in the organization's security systems and processes, allowing them to take corrective measures to prevent future attacks. Given the significant impact that fraud can have on an organization's financial stability and reputation, it is imperative that organizations prioritize FD and prevention. By doing so, they can help protect their stakeholders and their business operations from fraudulent activities.

13.1.3 Distributed Systems and Their Potential for Fraud Detection and Prevention

DSs are a collection of independent computers that work together to achieve a common goal. These computers communicate and coordinate with each other through a network to achieve complex tasks. DSs have many advantages, such as scalability, fault tolerance, and efficiency in processing large volumes of data [7, 8].

DSs have the potential to enhance FD and prevention in several ways:

1) *Efficient data processing:* DSs can efficiently process large volumes of data from various sources, making it easier to detect fraudulent activities. This is particularly important for financial institutions that handle a vast amount of data on a daily basis.
2) *Improved resilience:* This is critical for FD and prevention as it ensures that the system can continue to function even in the event of an attack.
3) *Advanced analytics:* Financial institutions can proactively spot and stop fraudulent actions with the aid of this. DSs provide a number of benefits that make them a viable option for improving FD and prevention in the financial sector. Financial organizations may more effectively, precisely, and quickly identify and stop fraudulent activity while maintaining the robustness of their systems by utilizing the power of DSs.

13.2 Benefits of Distributed Systems

DSs offer several benefits [9–11], including:

- *Scalability:* DSs can scale horizontally, meaning that they can add more nodes to handle an increase in workload. This makes it easier to handle large volumes of data and process complex tasks.
- *Efficiency:* DSs can distribute tasks across multiple nodes, making it easier to process data and handle complex computations. This can help reduce processing time and increase efficiency.
- *Flexibility:* DSs can be designed to meet specific requirements and can be customized to suit different needs. DSs are used in a variety of applications, including financial systems, e-commerce, and social networks.

13.2.1 Definition of Distributed Systems

These nodes communicate and coordinate with each other through a network, allowing them to distribute tasks and data across the system. This is achieved by replicating data and tasks across multiple nodes, ensuring that there is no single point of failure. DSs are used in a wide range of applications, including cloud computing, e-commerce, social networks, and financial systems. They offer several advantages over traditional centralized systems, including scalability, efficiency, resilience, and flexibility [12–14].

13.2.2 Advantages of Distributed Systems

DSs offer several advantages over traditional centralized systems, including:

- *Scalability:* DSs can scale horizontally, meaning that they can add more nodes to handle an increase in workload. This makes it easier to handle large volumes of data and process complex tasks.
- *Efficiency:* DSs can distribute tasks across multiple nodes, making it easier to process data and handle complex computations. This can help reduce processing time and increase efficiency.
- *Flexibility:* DSs can be designed to meet specific requirements and can be customized to suit different needs. This makes it easier to develop systems that are tailored to specific use cases.
- *Geographic distribution:* DSs can be geographically distributed, meaning that nodes can be located in different parts of the world. This can help reduce network latency and improve the user experience for global applications.
- *Cost-effectiveness:* DSs can be cost-effective, as they can use commodity hardware and can be designed to scale horizontally. DSs offer several advantages that make them a popular choice for a wide range of applications, including financial systems, e-commerce, social networks, and cloud computing.

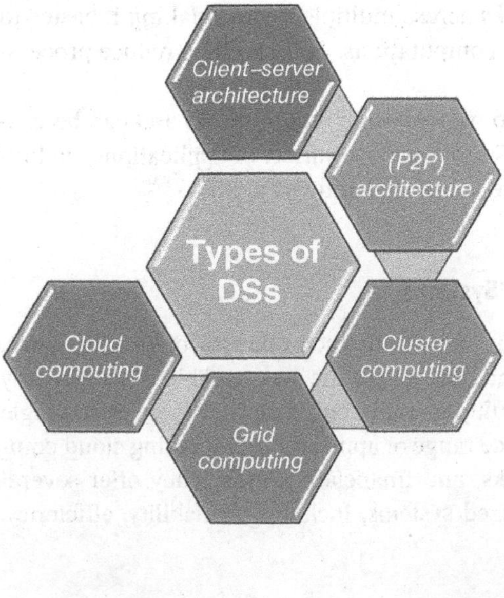

Figure 13.1 Types of DSs.

13.2.3 Types of Distributed Systems

Types of distribution systems have been shown in Figure 13.1.

1) *(P2P) architecture:* To accomplish a common objective, nodes collaborate and interact with one another. This is frequently employed in programs that allow users to exchange files.
2) *Client–server architecture:* In a client–server architecture, one or more servers provide services to one or more clients. Clients request services from servers, and servers respond to client requests. This is commonly used in web applications, where a web server provides services to web clients.
3) *Cluster computing:* Each computer in the cluster is capable of handling computations and data processing, and they are all connected by a fast network. This is frequently used in scientific computing when processing massive amounts of data.
4) *Grid computing:* In a grid computing architecture, resources are shared across multiple organizations. This is commonly used in scientific computing, where researchers can access and use resources from multiple institutions.
5) *Cloud computing:* A network is used to deliver resources as a service in a cloud computing architecture. Cloud service providers provide online access to resources including computer power, storage, and software [15, 16]. Web applications and data processing frequently use this.

13.3 Prevention Techniques

There are several FD and prevention techniques used in finance [17–20], including:

1) *Machine learning: ML* techniques can be used to identify fraudulent transactions by analyzing large amounts of data. These techniques can be used to detect patterns that are difficult for rule-based systems to identify and can also adapt to new types of fraud over time.
2) *Anomaly detection:* Anomaly detection techniques are used to identify transactions that are significantly different from normal transactions. For example, if a credit card is used in a location that is unusual for the cardholder, it may be flagged as a potential fraud.
3) *Network analysis:* Network analysis techniques can be used to identify fraudulent transactions by analyzing the relationships between different entities, such as customers, merchants, and bank accounts. By analyzing these relationships, it is possible to identify patterns that are indicative of fraudulent activity.

4) *Biometric authentication:* Biometric authentication techniques can be used to verify the identity of customers, reducing the risk of identity theft and fraudulent activity. Biometric techniques can include fingerprint, facial recognition, voice recognition, and other biometric data.

These techniques can be used individually or in combination to detect and prevent fraudulent activity in financial systems. The use of DSs can improve the effectiveness of these techniques by allowing the coordination of multiple detection and prevention methods across a distributed network.

Let's understand with a sample example. Suppose a financial institution has a DS that uses machine learning algorithms to monitor transactions for potentially fraudulent activity. The system is distributed across multiple nodes, with each node responsible for processing a subset of the institution's transaction data.

Table 13.1 Distribution of data processing across the nodes.

Node	Data subset	Transactions processed
1	Jan to Feb	5,00,000
2	Mar to Apr	6,00,000
3	May to Jun	4,50,000
4	Jul to Aug	5,50,000

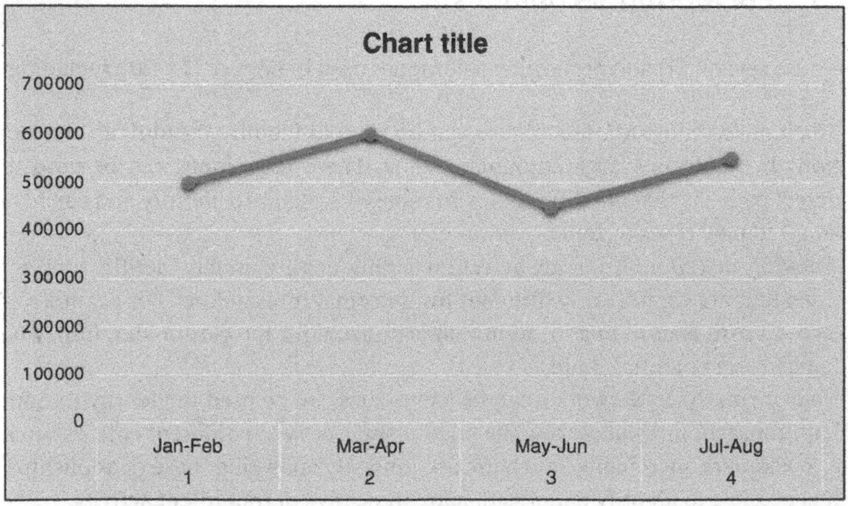

Figure 13.2 Data processing across the nodes.

Here's an example table (Table 13.1 and Figure 13.2) showing the distribution of data processing across the nodes.

In this example, the DS is designed to process four months' worth of transaction data, with each node responsible for processing two months of data. Node 1 processes transaction data from January to February, Node 2 processes data from March to April, and so on. Each node is equipped with a machine learning model that is trained to detect potentially fraudulent activity in transaction data. Once a model identifies a potentially fraudulent transaction, it can alert the relevant node, which can then flag the transaction for further investigation or action. The system can manage a huge volume of transactions while retaining high accuracy and speed in identifying and preventing fraud by dividing the processing of transaction data among numerous nodes. The system may swiftly detect and react to potentially fraudulent conduct by distributing the processing of transaction data across numerous nodes, lowering the risk of financial loss for the institution and its clients [21, 22].

13.3.1 Rule-Based Systems

These recommendations, which are based on historical data, are meant to identify patterns that might indicate fraud. The majority of the time rule-based systems are used to flag transactions that meet particular criteria, such as transactions that are above a certain value or that occur outside of regular business hours. For instance, a rule-based system for identifying credit card fraud may have rules that notify users of transactions that exceed a certain threshold, occur after regular business hours, or occur in a different country than the customer's usual location. With rule-based systems, a great deal of flexibility is also possible because rules can be added to as new fraud types are discovered and modified to fit specific use cases. But the rules themselves might limit rule-based systems. If the restrictions are applied too strictly, they may label legitimate transactions as fraudulent, which could lead to false positives. False negatives could result from rules that are too loose because they might overlook some fraudulent transactions.

13.3.2 Machine Learning-Based Systems

The first row in Table 13.2 describes natural language processing (NLP) systems, which are used to analyze human language using statistical and machine learning techniques. Example applications of NLP include language translation, sentiment analysis, and chatbot development. The techniques used in NLP systems include rule-based approaches, statistical models, and deep learning models like RNNs and transformers.

Table 13.2 Machine learning-based systems.

Machine learning-based systems	Description	Techniques used
Natural language processing (NLP)	Uses statistical and machine learning techniques to analyze human language	Rule-based, statistical, deep learning
Computer vision	Uses algorithms and deep learning techniques to interpret and understand images and videos	Convolutional neural networks (CNNs), object detection algorithms
Recommender systems	Uses machine learning algorithms to predict user preferences and make personalized recommendations	Collaborative filtering, content-based filtering
Predictive analytics	Uses machine learning algorithms to analyze data and make predictions about future events	Regression analysis, decision trees, time series forecasting
Autonomous vehicles	Uses machine learning algorithms to enable self-driving cars to navigate roads and avoid obstacles	Deep neural networks, reinforcement learning
Image recognition	Uses machine learning algorithms to identify objects and patterns in images	Convolutional neural networks (CNNs), object detection algorithms
Anomaly detection	Uses machine learning algorithms to identify unusual or unexpected patterns in data	Supervised learning, unsupervised learning, anomaly detection

The second row describes computer vision systems, which use algorithms and deep learning techniques to interpret and understand images and videos [23–25]. Example applications of computer vision include self-driving cars, facial recognition, and object detection. Techniques used in computer vision systems include Convolutional neural networks (CNNs) and object detection algorithms like YOLO.

The third row describes recommender systems, which use machine learning algorithms to predict user preferences and make personalized recommendations [26, 27]. Example applications of recommender systems include Netflix movie recommendations, Amazon product suggestions, and Spotify song recommendations. Techniques used in recommender systems include collaborative filtering and content-based filtering.

The fourth row describes predictive analytics systems, which use machine learning algorithms to analyze data and make predictions about future events. Example applications of predictive analytics include sales forecasting, inventory optimization, and risk management. Techniques used in predictive analytics systems include regression analysis, decision trees, and time series forecasting.

The fifth row describes autonomous vehicles systems, which use machine learning algorithms to enable self-driving cars to navigate roads and avoid obstacles. Example applications of autonomous vehicles include self-driving cars and delivery drones. Techniques used in autonomous vehicle systems include deep neural networks and reinforcement learning.

The sixth row describes image recognition systems, which use machine learning algorithms to identify objects and patterns in images. Example applications of image recognition include object recognition, image classification, and image segmentation. Techniques used in image recognition systems include CNNs and object detection algorithms.

The final row describes anomaly detection systems, which use machine learning algorithms to identify unusual or unexpected patterns in data. Example applications of anomaly detection include cybersecurity, predictive maintenance, and FD. Techniques used in anomaly detection systems include supervised learning, unsupervised learning, and anomaly detection algorithms [28, 29].

13.3.3 Hybrid Systems

A type of FD and prevention method that combines several techniques to increase accuracy is called a hybrid system. The strengths of each individual method can be maximized while minimizing the weaknesses of these systems. A hybrid system, for instance, might use a rule-based system to flag transactions that match particular requirements, like transactions over a certain value or transactions that take place outside of regular business hours. The system can then analyze these flagged transactions using a machine learning-based system to find more intricate patterns that might point to fraud. Depending on the particular use case and the types of data available, hybrid systems can be built in a variety of ways. Additionally, they can be modified over time to take into account changes in fraud patterns or adjustments to the data being studied. Hybrid systems can be more accurate and efficient than individual methods alone, which is one of their benefits. Hybrid systems can maximize the benefits of each method while reducing the drawbacks by combining several different approaches. Because they are less likely to be affected by a single method being compromised, hybrid systems can also be more resistant to attacks or attempts to trick the system. They call for knowledge in a variety of fields, including rule-based systems, machine learning, and DSs. They might also need extra resources, like computing power and data storage, to implement and maintain. In order to be effective and resilient, hybrid systems must be carefully designed and implemented. They can be a powerful tool for identifying and preventing financial fraud. The use of DSs enables the coordination of various detection and prevention techniques across a distributed network, which can enhance the efficacy of hybrid systems.

13.3.4 Limitations of Traditional Techniques

1) *Limited ability to detect new types of fraud:* Rule-based systems are based on pre-defined rules, which can make it difficult to detect new types of fraud that have not been previously encountered. Similarly, anomaly detection is based on detecting transactions that deviate from normal patterns, which can be less effective at detecting more sophisticated and targeted fraud attempts.
2) *High rate of false positives:* Rule-based systems and anomaly detection can generate a high rate of false positives, which can be costly and time-consuming to investigate.
3) *Limited scalability:* Traditional techniques can be limited in their ability particularly in real time. This can make it difficult to detect fraud in a timely manner, particularly in high-volume environments.
4) *Limited ability to adapt over time:* Traditional techniques can be less effective at adapting to changes in fraud patterns over time, particularly as fraudsters develop new and more sophisticated techniques for evading detection.
5) *Vulnerability to attacks:* Traditional techniques can be vulnerable to attacks that attempt to deceive the system, such as attacks that mimic normal behavior or attempt to bypass rule-based systems. They can be limited in their ability to detect and prevent fraud in a rapidly changing and complex financial environment. Some of these limitations improve the effectiveness of FD and prevention.

13.4 Leveraging Distributed Systems for Fraud Detection and Prevention

In finance, the use of DSs can enable the processing of large amounts of data in real time, allowing for more effective and timely detection of fraud. Real-time monitoring can be particularly effective in high-volume environments, where manual detection may be impractical or inefficient. DSs can also provide a more resilient architecture that can be more difficult to compromise, particularly if the system is designed to incorporate redundancy and failover mechanisms. This can help protect against attacks or attempts to deceive the system. Furthermore, DSs can be designed to analyze large amounts of data in parallel, leveraging the processing power of multiple nodes. This can enable the use of more sophisticated techniques, such as machine learning, for detecting and preventing fraud. One potential challenge in leveraging DSs for FD and prevention is the need for coordination and communication between different nodes. However, this can be addressed through the use of distributed consensus algorithms, such as the blockchain, that can enable nodes to work together to maintain a consistent view of the data. Leveraging DSs can be an effective approach to FD and prevention in finance, particularly in complex and high-volume environments. By combining the advantages of DSs with more sophisticated to develop more accurate and effective systems that can help protect against financial fraud [30, 31].

13.4.1 Advantages of Distributed Systems for Fraud Detection and Prevention

There are several advantages of using DSs for FD and prevention in finance, including:

1) *Real-time monitoring:* DSs can provide real-time monitoring of transactions, enabling immediate detection of potentially fraudulent activity.
2) *Scalability:* By expanding the number of nodes in the network, which can handle more data as transaction volumes rise, DSs can be scaled horizontally. As a result, massive amounts of data can be processed in real time without degrading system performance.
3) *Parallel processing:* By utilizing the computing capacity of numerous nodes, this can be created to analyze enormous volumes of data in parallel. This may make it possible to detect and prevent fraud using more advanced methods like machine learning.
4) *Flexibility:* This can be made to work with several data sources, allowing for the integration and uniform analysis of data from various sources. This could contribute to a more complete picture of fraud risk within an organization.

Using DSs for FD and prevention in finance can have a number of benefits, such as quicker detection and reaction times, increased scalability and resilience, and the capacity to use more sophisticated FD methodologies. Utilizing these benefits, businesses can strengthen their defences against financial fraud and lessen the negative effects that it has on their daily operations.

13.4.2 Applicability of Distributed Systems in Rule-Based Systems

This can help rule-based systems for FD and prevention function better and scale more easily. According to particular criteria, such as transaction amount, frequency, or location, it is characterized as the identification of possibly fraudulent transactions. To identify possibly fraudulent transactions and identify suspicious patterns, these criteria can be applied to big datasets. The burden can be split among several nodes, allowing the system to handle more transactions concurrently and speed up response times. DSs can also be used to enable real-time monitoring of transactions, allowing for immediate detection of potentially fraudulent activity. This can be particularly important in high-volume environments where manual detection may be impractical or inefficient. Furthermore, DSs can provide a more resilient architecture that can be more difficult to compromise. The use of

DSs can help improve the performance, scalability, and resilience of rule-based systems for FD and prevention in finance. By enabling real-time monitoring and analysis of large datasets, DSs can improve the accuracy helping to protect against financial fraud.

13.4.3 Applicability of Distributed Systems in Machine Learning-Based Systems

DSs can be leveraged to handle the processing and analysis of large amounts of data in parallel, which can improve the performance and scalability of machine learning-based systems. By distributing the workload across multiple nodes, the system can process more data in parallel, reducing the time required for analysis. DSs can also be used to enable real-time monitoring of transactions, allowing for immediate detection of potentially fraudulent activity. This can be particularly important in high-volume environments where manual detection may be impractical or inefficient. Furthermore, DSs can provide a more resilient architecture that can be more difficult to compromise. Another advantage of using DSs for machine learning-based FD is the ability to leverage multiple models in parallel. By training and deploying multiple models across negatives. The use of DSs can help improve the performance, scalability, and resilience of machine learning-based systems for FD and prevention in finance. By enabling real-time monitoring and analysis of large datasets, DSs can improve the accuracy and effectiveness of FD and prevention systems, helping to protect against financial fraud [32, 33].

13.4.4 Applicability of Distributed Systems in Hybrid Systems

The performance and scalability of hybrid systems can be enhanced by utilizing DSs to handle the processing and analysis of large amounts of data in parallel. The system can process more data in parallel by dividing the workload among several nodes, which shortens the time needed for analysis. Aside from enabling real-time monitoring of transactions, DSs can also be used to quickly spot potentially fraudulent activity. In environments with high volume, where manual detection might be difficult or ineffective, this can be especially crucial. A more resilient architecture that may be more difficult to compromise is another benefit of DSs. The system is able to function even in the event that a node fails or becomes compromised by incorporating redundancy and failover mechanisms. DSs can increase the precision and efficacy of FD and prevention systems, assisting in the fight against financial fraud by combining the advantages of rule-based and machine learning-based systems and enabling real-time monitoring and analysis of massive datasets.

13.4.5 Challenges in Implementing Distributed Systems for Fraud Detection and Prevention

1) One major challenge is the complexity of designing and deploying DSs. Building and maintaining a DS requires specialized expertise, including knowledge of distributed algorithms, networking, and fault tolerance.
2) The need for efficient data transfer and synchronization between nodes. As data is distributed across multiple nodes, it must be efficiently transferred and synchronized to ensure that all nodes have the same information for analysis. Security is another challenge in implementing DSs for FD and prevention. The distributed architecture can introduce new security risks, such as the potential for attacks on nodes or the need for secure communication between nodes. Strong security measures, such as encryption and authentication, must be put in place to protect against these risks.
3) Integrating a DS with existing systems and processes. This can require significant effort and coordination to ensure that the DS can effectively integrate with other systems and processes.
4) Cost considerations associated with the implementation of a DS, including the need for specialized hardware, software, and personnel. These costs must be carefully considered and balanced against the potential benefits of the system.

Overall, the challenges associated with implementing DSs for FD and prevention require careful consideration and planning to ensure that the system is effective, secure, and cost-efficient [34, 35].

13.5 Future Directions

The use of DSs for FD and prevention is an active area of research, and there are several future directions that hold promise for improving the effectiveness and efficiency of these systems. One potential direction is the use of blockchain technology for FD and prevention. Blockchain provides a secure and tamper-proof distributed ledger that can be used to store transaction data and verify the authenticity of transactions. Another potential direction is the use of edge computing for DSs. Edge computing involves processing data at or near the source, rather than in a centralized location, which can reduce the latency and bandwidth requirements of the system. By leveraging edge computing, DSs for FD and prevention may be able to process and analyze data more quickly and efficiently. Furthermore, the use of advanced analytics techniques, such as deep learning and NLP, may offer additional benefits for FD and prevention. Finally, the use of DSs for FD and prevention may expand beyond the finance industry, into areas such as healthcare and cybersecurity. As the amount of data generated by these industries continues to grow, the use of DSs may become increasingly important for effective FD and prevention. The future of DSs is likely to involve the continued exploration of advanced techniques and technologies, with a focus on improving the accuracy, efficiency, and security of these systems.

13.5.1 Current Trends in Fraud Detection and Prevention

There are several current trends in FD and prevention that are worth noting:

1) *Real-time monitoring:* One trend is the increasing use of real-time monitoring to detect and prevent fraud. Real-time monitoring can enable faster detection and response to potential fraud, allowing organizations to take action more quickly.
2) *Collaboration and information sharing:* Increasingly, organizations are recognizing the importance of collaboration and information sharing in FD and prevention. By sharing information and collaborating with other organizations, it may be possible to identify and prevent fraud more effectively.
3) *Blockchain technology:* As mentioned earlier, blockchain technology is a growing trend in FD and prevention, organizations to verify the authenticity of transactions and prevent fraudulent activity. These trends reflect a growing recognition of the importance of FD and prevention and the need for more advanced and effective techniques and technologies to address the ongoing challenge of fraud.

13.5.2 Future Directions for Leveraging Distributed Systems

There are several promising future directions for leveraging DSs for FD and prevention:

1) *Integration with other emerging technologies:* As new technologies continue to emerge, there may be opportunities to integrate DSs
2) For example, the integration of DSs with IoT (Internet of Things) devices may enable more accurate monitoring and analysis of financial transactions.
3) *Continued use of advanced analytics:* As mentioned earlier, the use of advanced analytics techniques such as deep learning and NLP may offer additional benefits for FD and prevention. Continued research and development in these areas may lead to new insights.
4) *Development of new DSs architectures:* The use of decentralized systems that enable nodes to process and analyze data independently may reduce the risk of fraud and improve the overall security of the system.
5) *Greater collaboration and information sharing:* As mentioned earlier, collaboration and information sharing are increasingly recognized as important for

effective FD and prevention. The development of new DSs that enable greater collaboration and information sharing between organizations may help to improve the overall effectiveness of these systems.

6) *Greater emphasis on privacy and security:* With the growing importance of data privacy and security, there may be a greater emphasis on developing DSs that are designed with privacy and security in mind. For example, the use of encryption and other security measures may be critical for ensuring the integrity of financial transactions and preventing fraud. These future directions for leveraging DSs suggest a continued focus on innovation and development, with a goal of improving effectiveness.

13.6 Conclusion

In conclusion, the use of DSs for advanced FD and prevention in finance offers significant advantages over traditional techniques. Organizations can improve the accuracy and efficiency of FD and prevention, enabling them to respond more quickly and effectively to potential threats.

While there are certainly challenges to implementing DSs for FD and prevention, such as the need for robust security measures and the potential for technical complexity, the benefits are clear. The use of DSs can enable faster, more accurate detection of potential fraud, and can provide a more comprehensive and secure approach to fraud prevention [36]. Looking to the future, the continued development of advanced analytics, integration with other emerging technologies, and a greater focus on privacy and security are likely to drive continued innovation in this area. The use of DSs for advanced FD and prevention in finance will undoubtedly continue to be a critical area of focus.

References

1 Katyara, S., Staszewski, L., and Leonowicz, Z. **(2018)**. Protection coordination of properly sized and placed distributed generations–methods, applications and future scope. *Energies 11*: 2672.

2 Katyara, S., Shah, M.A., and Iżykowski, J. **(2016)**. Power loss reduction with optimal size and location of capacitor banks installed at 132 kV grid station qasimabad Hyderabad. *Present Probl. Power Syst. Control.* 53–64.

3 Paliwal, P., Patidar, N.P., and Nema, R.K. **(2014)**. Planning of grid integrated distributed generators: a review of technology, objectives and techniques. *Renewable Sustainable Energy Rev. 40*: 557–570.

4 Katyara, S., Staszewski, L., and Chachar, F.A. **(2019)**. Determining the Norton's equivalent model of distribution system with distributed generation (DG) for stability analysis. *Recent Adv. Electr. Electron. Eng. 12*: 190–198.

5 Sultana, U., Khairuddin, A.B., Aman, M.M. et al. **(2016)**. A review of optimum DG placement based on minimization of power losses and voltage stability enhancement of distribution system. *Renewable Sustainable Energy Rev. 63*: 278–363.

6 Jang, S.I. and Kim, K.H. **(2004)**. An islanding detection method for distributed generations using voltage unbalance and total harmonic distortion of current. *IEEE Trans. Power Deliv. 19*: 745–752.

7 Katyara, S., Hashmani, A., Chowdhary, B.S. et al. **(2020)**. Wireless networks for voltage stability analysis and anti-islanding protection of smart grid system. *Wirel. Pers. Commun.* 116: 1361–1378.

8 Kanchev, H., Lu, D., Colas, F. et al. **(2011)**. Energy management and operational planning of a microgrid with a PV-based active generator for smart grid applications. *IEEE Trans. Ind. Electron. 58*: 4583–4592.

9 Palma-Behnke, R., Benavides, C., Lanas, F. et al. **(2013)**. A microgrid energy management system based on the rolling horizon strategy. *IEEE Trans. Smart Grid 4*: 996–1006.

10 Hilal, W., Gadsden, S.A., and Yawney, J. (2021). Financial fraud: a review of anomaly detection techniques and recent advances. *Expert Syst. Appl.* 193: 116429.

11 Ashtiani, M.N. and Raahemi, B. (2021). Intelligent fraud detection in financial statements using machine learning and data mining: a systematic literature review. *IEEE Access* 10: 72504–72525.

12 Sindhwani, N., Rana, A., and Chaudhary, A. (2021). Breast cancer detection using machine learning algorithms. In: *2021 9th International Conference on Reliability, Infocom Technologies and Optimization (Trends and Future Directions) (ICRITO)*, 1–5. IEEE.

13 Jain, N., Chaudhary, A., Sindhwani, N., and Rana, A. (2021). Applications of wearable devices in IoT. In: *2021 9th International Conference on Reliability, Infocom Technologies and Optimization (Trends and Future Directions) (ICRITO)*, 1–4. IEEE.

14 Bruntha, P.M., Dhanasekar, S., Hepsiba, D. et al. (2023). Application of switching median filter with L 2 norm-based auto-tuning function for removing random valued impulse noise. *Aerosp. Syst. 6* (1): 53–59.

15 Kumar Pandey, B., Pandey, D., Nassa, V.K. et al. (2021). Encryption and steganography-based text extraction in IoT using the EWCTS optimizer. *Imaging Sci. J. 69* (1-4): 38–56.

16 Govindaraj, V., Dhanasekar, S., Martinsagayam, K. et al. (2023). Low-power test pattern generator using modified LFSR. *Aerosp. Syst.* 1–8.

17 Albashrawi, M. (2016). Detecting financial fraud using data mining techniques: a decade review from 2004 to 2015. *J. Data Sci.* 14: 553–570.

18 Choi, D. and Lee, K. (2018). An artificial intelligence approach to financial fraud detection under IoT environment: a survey and implementation. *Secur. Commun. Netw.* 2018: 1–15.

19 Ngai, E.W.T., Hu, Y., Wong, Y.H. et al. (2011). The application of data mining techniques in financial fraud detection: a classification framework and an academic review of literature. *Decis. Support Syst.* 50: 559–569.

20 Ryman-Tubb, N.F., Krause, P., and Garn, W. (2018). How Artificial Intelligence and machine learning research impacts payment card fraud detection: a survey and industry benchmark. *Eng. Appl. Artif. Intell.* 76: 130–157.

21 Al-Hashedi, K.G. and Magalingam, P. Financial fraud detection applying data mining techniques: a comprehensive review from 2009 to 2019. *Comput. Sci. Rev.* 2021 (40): 100402.

22 Anand, R., Nirmal, V., Chauhan, Y., and Sharma, T. (2023). An image-based deep learning approach for personalized outfit selection. In: *2023 10th International Conference on Computing for Sustainable Global Development (INDIACom)*, 1050–1054. IEEE.

23 Singh, H., Pandey, B.K., George, S. et al. (2022). Effective overview of different ML models used for prediction of COVID-19 patients. In: *Artificial Intelligence on Medical Data: Proceedings of International Symposium, ISCMM 2021*, 185–192. Singapore: Springer Nature Singapore.

24 Pandey, B.K., Pandey, D., Anand, R. et al. (2022). The impact of digital change on student learning and mental anguish in the COVID era. In: *An Interdisciplinary Approach in the Post-COVID-19 Pandemic Era*, 197–206. Nova Science.

25 Sindhwani, N., Anand, R., Vashisth, R. et al. (2022). Thingspeak-based environmental monitoring system using IoT. In: *2022 Seventh International Conference on Parallel, Distributed and Grid Computing (PDGC)*, 675–680. IEEE.

26 Saxena, H., Joshi, D., Singh, H., and Anand, R. (2022). Comparison of classification algorithms for Alzheimer's disease prediction. In: *2022 Seventh International Conference on Parallel, Distributed and Grid Computing (PDGC)*, 687–692. IEEE.

27 Chaquet-ulldemolins, J., Moral-rubio, S., and Muñoz-romero, S. (2022). On the black-box challenge for fraud detection using machine learning (II): nonlinear analysis through interpretable autoencoders. *Appl. Sci.* 12: 3856.

28 Da'U, A. and Salim, N. (2019). Recommendation system based on deep learning methods: a systematic review and new directions. *Artif. Intell. Rev.* 53: 2709–2748.

29 Zeng, Y. and Tang, J. (2021). RLC-GNN: an improved deep architecture for spatial-based graph neural network with application to fraud detection. *Appl. Sci.* 11: 5656.

30 Delamaire, L., Hussein, A., and John, P. (2009). Credit card fraud and detection techniques: a review. *Banks Bank Syst.* 4: 57–68.

31 Nilsson, F. (2002). Strategy and management control systems: a study of the design and use of management control systems following takeover. *Account. Finance* 42: 41–71.

32 Cameron, E. and Green, M. (2019). *Making Sense of Change Management: A Complete Guide to the Models, Tools and Techniques of Organizational Change.* London, UK: Kogan Page Publishers.

33 Malmi, T. and Granlund, M. (2009). In search of management accounting theory. *Eur. Account. Rev.* 18: 597–620.

34 Merchant, K.A. and Van der Stede, W.A. (2007). *Management Control Systems: Performance Measurement, Evaluation and Incentives.* London, UK: Pearson Education.

35 Otley, D.T. (1980). The contingency theory of management accounting: Achievement and prognosis. In: *Readings in Accounting for Management Control*, 83–106. Berlin/Heidelberg, Germany: Springer.

36 Anand, R., Singh, B., and Sindhwani, N. (2009). Speech perception & analysis of fluent digits' strings using level-by-level time alignment. *Int. J. Inf. Technol. Knowl. Manage.* 2 (1): 65–68.

14
Advances in E-commerce Through the Integration of Distributed Computing Approaches

Venkateswararao Podile[1], K. Suresh Kumar[2], Luigi P.L. Cavaliere[3], Sri R.R. Annapureddy[4], Katakam V. Siva Praneeth[4], Kanamarlapudi P.S. Sabareesh[4], and Devati B. Sambasiva Rao[4]

[1] *K. L. Business School, Koneru Lakshmaiah Education Foundation, Vaddeswaram, Andhra Pradesh, India*
[2] *MBA Department, Panimalar Engineering College, Chennai, Tamil Nadu, India*
[3] *Department of Economics, University of Foggia, Foggia, Italy*
[4] *Koneru Lakshmaiah Education Foundation, Vaddeswaram, Andhra Pradesh, India*

14.1 Introduction

Electronic commerce, or E-commerce, has become an integral part of modern business operations in recent years. With the rise of the Internet, online shopping has grown exponentially, allowing businesses to reach customers globally, around the clock. However, the success of e-commerce also depends on the ability of businesses to provide efficient, secure, and seamless transactions to their customers. One of the challenges faced by businesses in e-commerce is the need for scalable and reliable computing infrastructure. As the volume of online transactions increases, so does the demand for computing resources to handle the increased workload. Traditional computing approaches often struggle to meet these demands, resulting in slower transaction times, system downtime, and other issues that can negatively impact customer experience. To address these challenges, businesses are increasingly turning to distributed computing approaches to enhance their e-commerce capabilities. distributed computing approaches refer to a range of technologies that allow computing resources to be spread across multiple locations, enabling more efficient use of resources and greater scalability. Fog computing is similar to edge computing but

Meta-Heuristic Algorithms for Advanced Distributed Systems, First Edition. Edited by Rohit Anand, Abhinav Juneja, Digvijay Pandey, Sapna Juneja, and Nidhi Sindhwani.

involves using a network of distributed devices to store and process data. Grid computing allows businesses to harness the processing power of multiple computers to complete complex tasks, while peer-to-peer computing enables devices to share processing power and other resources. By integrating distributed computing approaches into their e-commerce operations, businesses can enjoy numerous benefits. For example, they can achieve greater scalability and flexibility, enabling them to handle large volumes of transactions quickly and efficiently. They can also enhance security and privacy by using distributed systems that are more resilient to attacks and less vulnerable to single points of failure. Moreover, businesses can improve customer experience by providing faster transaction times, more reliable service, and personalized recommendations. They can also reduce costs by minimizing the need for expensive hardware and software infrastructure and streamline operations by automating various tasks and processes. However, integrating distributed computing approaches in e-commerce is not without its challenges. Businesses must carefully consider technical and organizational factors such as compatibility, data privacy, and regulatory compliance when implementing these approaches. Moreover, they must ensure that their staff is adequately trained to work with these systems and can manage them effectively. Despite these challenges, the future of e-commerce looks promising, with the integration of distributed computing approaches opening new possibilities for businesses of all sizes. With the potential to enhance scalability, performance, security, and customer experience, businesses embrace these approaches [1–3].

14.1.1 E-commerce and Its Growth

The rise of e-commerce has revolutionized the way businesses operate, providing them with a means to reach customers around the globe, 24/7, without the need for a physical presence in each location. The growth of e-commerce has been nothing short of phenomenal. This growth was driven by factors such as the COVID-19 pandemic, which forced many businesses to shift their operations online, as well as the increasing availability and accessibility of the Internet and mobile devices. In addition to its impact on retail sales, e-commerce has also transformed other sectors of the economy, including financial services, healthcare, and education. For instance, telemedicine has made it feasible for people to receive medical care remotely, while online banking and financial services have made it possible for consumers to access financial goods and services from anywhere in the globe. as well as direct-to-consumer sales, subscription-based services, and drop shipping. These business models give organizations more flexibility and creative freedom, as well as the ability to target niche markets and meet particular client demands. The expansion of e-commerce has had a significant impact on the world economy, changing how firms run and giving customers more convenience and options. In the upcoming years, it is probable that the expansion of e-commerce will continue to accelerate as technology advances and more people acquire access to the Internet [4, 5].

14.2 Distributed Computing Approaches for E-commerce

The integration of distributed computing approaches has revolutionized the way e-commerce operates. Distributed computing refers to the use of multiple computers working together as a unified system, often spread across different geographic locations, to solve complex computing problems. By utilizing this approach, businesses can improve the performance, scalability, and security of their e-commerce operations. One of the primary benefits of using distributed computing in e-commerce is improved performance. By leveraging distributed systems, businesses can distribute processing tasks across multiple machines, reducing the load on any one machine and improving overall system performance. This approach can also enable businesses to handle large volumes of traffic, ensuring that their e-commerce sites remain responsive even during periods of peak demand. In addition to performance benefits, distributed computing approaches can also enhance the scalability of e-commerce operations. By utilizing a distributed architecture, businesses can easily add or remove computing resources as needed, enabling them to scale their operations up or down as demand fluctuates. This approach can be particularly beneficial for businesses that experience seasonal spikes in traffic or those that need to quickly ramp up their operations to meet unexpected demand. Another key benefit of distributed computing in e-commerce is improved security. By spreading computing tasks across multiple machines, businesses can reduce the risk of a single point of failure, which can be a vulnerability for cyberattacks. The integration of distributed computing approaches has transformed the e-commerce landscape, providing businesses with a powerful tool for improving performance, scalability, and security. By leveraging these technologies, businesses can take advantage of new opportunities and stay competitive in an ever-changing digital marketplace [6–8].

14.2.1 Types of Distributed Computing Approaches

Distributed computing refers to the use of multiple computers working together as a unified system to solve complex computing problems. This approach can be used to improve the performance, scalability, and security of various computing systems, including those used in e-commerce.

There are several types of distributed computing approaches, including:

1) *Client–server architecture:* This approach involves dividing computing tasks between a client and a server. The client is responsible for initiating requests and processing user interfaces, while the server handles data processing and storage.
2) *Peer-to-peer architecture:* In this approach, all computers in a network share the processing load and act as both clients and servers. This approach is often used for file sharing and distributed computing tasks.
3) *Grid computing:* Coordinating the processing power of multiple computers to solve complex computing problems. This approach is often used in scientific research and data analysis. The type of distributed computing approach used will depend on the specific needs and requirements of the computing system in question. By utilizing these technologies, businesses can improve the efficiency, scalability, and security of their computing systems, including those used in e-commerce.

14.2.2 Comparative Analysis of Distributed Computing Approaches

Table 14.1 provides an analytical comparison of the advantages and disadvantages of four different distributed computing approaches: client–server, peer-to-peer, grid computing, cloud computing, and edge computing. Each approach is listed with its respective advantages and disadvantages. The advantages of the client–server approach include its simplicity and efficient use of resources, while its disadvantages include potential performance issues due to network latency and server capacity limitations. Peer-to-peer computing is praised for its decentralized architecture and high availability but can be difficult to manage and coordinate. Grid computing is used for complex problems and enables high-performance computing but can be complex and expensive to set up and manage. Cloud computing allows for scalable and cost-effective access to computing resources, but raises concerns about security, privacy, and unexpected costs.

Finally, edge computing is ideal for remote environments and real-time processing but is limited by its processing and storage capacity and requires specialized hardware and software. This table provides a clear comparison of the benefits and drawbacks of each distributed computing approach, allowing organizations to make informed decisions about which approach to use for their needs.

Table 14.1 Comparison of the advantages and disadvantages of four different distributed computing approaches.

Approach	Advantages	Disadvantages
Client–server	Simple and easy to implement. Centralized control and management. Allows for efficient use of resources	May suffer from performance issues due to network latency. Scalability may be limited by server capacity Requires maintenance of server infrastructure
Peer-to-peer	Decentralized architecture. No single point of failure. Provides high availability and fault tolerance	Can be difficult to manage and coordinate. Security may be compromised in open networks. May suffer from performance issues due to the overhead of peer communication and coordination
Grid computing	Enables high-performance computing for complex problems. Can leverage computing resources from multiple sources	Can be complex and expensive to set up and manage. Requires specialized software and infrastructure. May suffer from communication and synchronization issues
Cloud computing	Enables scalable and cost-effective access to computing resources. Flexible and can be easily customized to meet needs	Reliance on network connectivity and third-party providers. Security and privacy concerns. May be subject to unexpected costs and charges
Edge computing	Enables real-time processing and reduces network latency. Can operate autonomously in remote or disconnected environments	Limited processing and storage capacity compared to centralized systems. Complexity of managing distributed infrastructure. May require specialized hardware and software

14.3 Integration of Distributed Computing Approaches in E-commerce

The integration of distributed computing approaches in e-commerce is becoming important in recent years due to the growing demand for high-performance and scalable e-commerce platforms. The use of distributed computing approaches can provide a range of benefits, such as improved fault tolerance, increased processing power, and enhanced security. For example, peer-to-peer computing can enable faster and more efficient sharing of resources among e-commerce nodes, while grid computing can allow for high-performance computing for complex e-commerce operations. Cloud computing has emerged as a popular approach for integrating distributed computing in e-commerce due to its scalability, cost-effectiveness, and flexibility. By using cloud computing, e-commerce businesses can access computing resources on-demand, reducing the need for expensive on-premises infrastructure. Moreover, cloud computing allows for the easy deployment of e-commerce applications across different devices and platforms, making it easier for businesses to reach a wider audience. Edge computing is another promising approach for integrating distributed computing in e-commerce. By processing data and transactions closer to the source, edge computing can reduce network latency and improve real-time processing capabilities. This is particularly beneficial for e-commerce businesses that operate in remote or disconnected environments, such as in rural areas or on mobile devices. The integration of distributed computing approaches in e-commerce can provide significant benefits to businesses, such as improved scalability, fault tolerance, processing power, and security. By carefully selecting and integrating the appropriate distributed computing approach, e-commerce businesses can provide better services to their customers and gain a competitive advantage in the ever-evolving e-commerce landscape [9–11].

14.3.1 Benefits of Integrating Distributed Computing Approaches in E-commerce

1) *Improved scalability:* Distributed computing allows businesses to scale their e-commerce platforms more easily by distributing computing resources across multiple nodes or devices. This enables businesses to handle more traffic, users, and transactions without compromising performance or user experience.
2) *Increased fault tolerance:* By distributing computing resources across multiple nodes or devices, distributed computing can improve fault tolerance and minimize the risk of system failures or downtime. This ensures that e-commerce platforms always remain operational and available to users.
3) *Enhanced processing power:* Distributed computing can enable businesses to process large volumes of data or complex transactions more efficiently by distributing processing tasks across multiple nodes or devices. This enables businesses to improve processing speed and reduce latency, resulting in faster and more efficient e-commerce transactions.
4) *Improved security:* Distributed computing can improve the security of e-commerce platforms by distributing data and processing tasks across multiple nodes or devices. This reduces the risk of data breaches or cyberattacks, as it makes it more difficult for attackers to access or compromise sensitive data.
5) *Cost-effectiveness:* Distributed computing can reduce the cost of building and maintaining e-commerce platforms by enabling businesses to access computing

resources on-demand and reducing the need for expensive on-premises infrastructure. This allows businesses to save on hardware, software, and maintenance costs.

6) *Flexibility:* Distributed computing enables businesses to deploy e-commerce applications across multiple devices and platforms, making it easier to reach a wider audience and improve user experience. This enhances the flexibility and adaptability of e-commerce platforms, allowing businesses to respond quickly to changing market demands and trends.

14.3.2 Challenges in Integrating Distributed Computing Approaches in E-commerce

1) *Complexity:* Distributed computing can be complex and requires specialized expertise to implement and manage. Resources to effectively integrate and maintain distributed computing approaches in their e-commerce platforms.
2) *Security risks:* While distributed computing can improve security, it can also introduce new security risks, such as increased vulnerability to cyberattacks or data breaches [12–14]. Businesses must ensure that they have adequate security measures in place to protect their data and e-commerce platforms.
3) *Data management:* Distributed computing can create challenges for managing and storing large volumes of data across multiple nodes or devices [15, 16]. Businesses must ensure that they have effective data management strategies processed and accessed appropriately.
4) *Compatibility:* Different distributed computing approaches may not be compatible with each other or with existing e-commerce platforms. Businesses must ensure that they select and integrate distributed computing approaches that are compatible with their existing infrastructure and platforms.
5) *Cost:* Implementing and integrating distributed computing approaches in e-commerce platforms. Businesses must ensure that they have adequate budgets and resources to invest in distributed computing infrastructure.
6) *Regulatory compliance:* E-commerce platforms are subject to various regulations, such as data privacy and security regulations. Businesses must ensure that they comply with relevant regulations when integrating distributed computing approaches into their e-commerce platforms.

By carefully evaluating and addressing these challenges and considerations, businesses can effectively integrate distributed computing approaches in their e-commerce platforms and achieve the benefits of distributed computing.

14.4 Advancements in E-commerce Through the Integration of Distributed Computing Approaches

Figure 14.1 shows e-commerce and distributed computing advancements.

14.4.1 Improved Scalability and Flexibility

Improved scalability and flexibility are key benefits that businesses can achieve by integrating distributed computing approaches in their e-commerce platforms. Scalability refers to the ability of an e-commerce platform to handle increased traffic, users, and transactions without compromising performance or user experience. By distributing computing resources across multiple nodes or devices, businesses can improve the scalability of their e-commerce platforms. This allows them to handle increased traffic and users during peak periods, such as holiday seasons or promotional events, without experiencing performance issues or downtime. Users expect e-commerce platforms to be fast, responsive, and

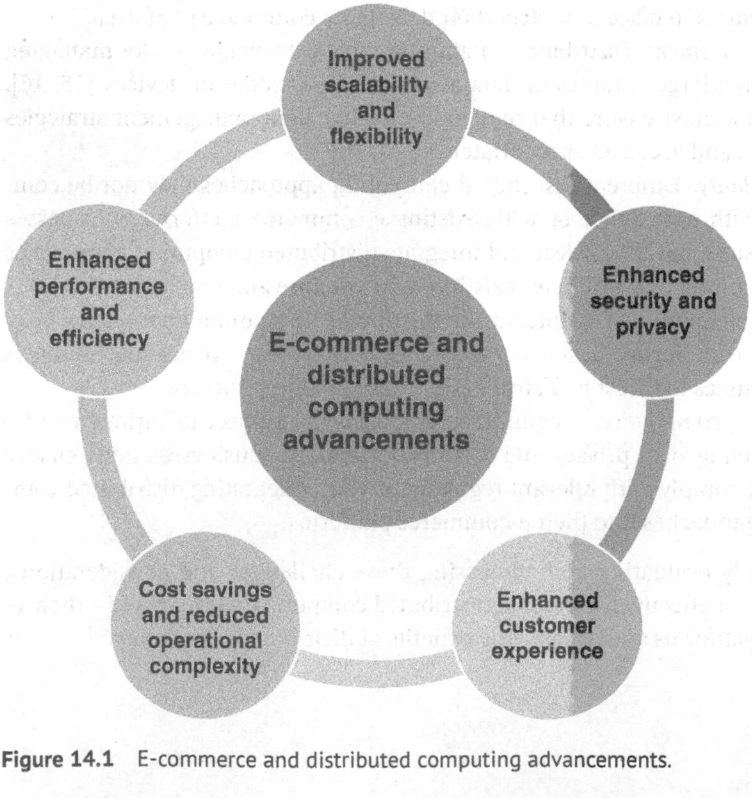

Figure 14.1 E-commerce and distributed computing advancements.

available always. If an e-commerce platform experiences performance issues or downtime, it can lead to user frustration, lost sales, and a damaged reputation. Improved scalability enables businesses to meet the performance demands of their users and provide a seamless user experience, regardless of the volume of traffic or transactions. Improved scalability can also help businesses to grow their e-commerce platforms over time. As businesses attract more users and transactions, they need to scale their infrastructure accordingly. By integrating distributed computing approaches, businesses can scale their infrastructure in a more efficient and cost-effective way. This can help businesses to expand their e-commerce platforms, enter new markets, and grow their customer base without experiencing performance issues or downtime. Flexibility refers to the ability of an e-commerce platform to adapt to changing market demands, trends, and user needs. By distributing computing resources across multiple nodes or devices, businesses can improve the flexibility of their e-commerce platforms. This enables them to deploy applications across multiple devices and platforms, reach a wider audience, and improve user experience. By improving flexibility, businesses can deploy new applications and features quickly, test new ideas and concepts, and respond to user feedback more effectively. Users expect e-commerce platforms to be accessible and easy to use across multiple devices and platforms, such as desktops, mobile devices, and tablets. By improving flexibility, businesses can ensure that their e-commerce platforms are accessible and easy to use across a wide range of devices and platforms. This can help businesses to improve user satisfaction, increase user engagement, and ultimately drive more sales. Improved scalability enables businesses to handle increased traffic and users without compromising performance or user experience, while improved flexibility enables businesses to adapt to changing market demands and trends and improve user experience across multiple devices and platforms. By achieving these benefits, businesses can stay competitive in the dynamic e-commerce landscape and grow their e-commerce platforms over time [17–19].

14.4.2 Enhanced Performance and Efficiency

Enhanced performance and efficiency are two additional benefits that businesses can achieve by integrating distributed computing approaches into their e-commerce platforms. Improved performance refers to the ability of an e-commerce platform to deliver faster response times and lower latency. By distributing computing resources across multiple nodes or devices, businesses can improve the performance of their e-commerce platforms. This allows them to deliver faster response times, reduce page load times and provide a more responsive user experience. It can increase user satisfaction and engagement. Users expect e-commerce platforms to be fast and responsive, and they are more likely to abandon slow or unresponsive platforms.

By improving the performance of their e-commerce platforms, businesses can reduce bounce rates, increase user engagement, and ultimately drive more sales. One of the main benefits of improved efficiency is that it can reduce operational costs and improve profitability. E-commerce platforms are typically resource intensive, and they require significant investments in hardware, software, and energy consumption. By improving efficiency, businesses can reduce these costs and improve profitability. This can help businesses to invest in new features and innovations, expand their e-commerce platforms, and ultimately drive growth and profitability. Enhanced performance and efficiency are two additional benefits that businesses can achieve by integrating distributed computing approaches into their e-commerce platforms. Improved performance can increase user satisfaction and engagement, while improved efficiency can reduce operational costs and improve profitability. By achieving these benefits, businesses can improve the overall performance and competitiveness of their e-commerce platforms [20, 21].

14.4.3 Enhanced Security and Privacy

Another important benefit of integrating distributed computing approaches in e-commerce is enhanced security and privacy. E-commerce platforms are often targets of cyberattacks and data breaches due to the large volumes of sensitive customer data they handle, such as personal and financial information. By leveraging distributed computing approaches, businesses can improve the security and privacy of their e-commerce platforms in several ways.

First, across multiple nodes or devices, businesses can improve the resilience of their e-commerce platforms against cyberattacks. In a distributed architecture, an attack on one node or device is unlikely to bring down the entire platform. This reduces the impact of potential cyberattacks and increases the overall security of the platform. Facilitate the implementation of advanced security and privacy technologies, such as blockchain and homomorphic encryption. These technologies enable businesses to store and process sensitive customer data securely, while maintaining the privacy and confidentiality of the data. By enhancing the security and privacy of their e-commerce platforms, businesses can build trust and confidence among customers, which is essential for long-term success in e-commerce. Customers are more likely to transact with businesses that can guarantee the security and privacy of their data, and businesses that can deliver on these promises are more likely to succeed in the competitive e-commerce landscape. Businesses can improve the resilience of their e-commerce platforms against cyberattacks, implement robust security measures, and facilitate the implementation of advanced security and privacy technologies. These benefits can help businesses to build trust and confidence among customers, and ultimately drive growth and success in e-commerce [22, 23].

14.4.4 Enhanced Customer Experience

Distributed computing approaches can be integrated into e-commerce to improve performance, security, scalability, flexibility, and customer experience in addition to other factors. Customer experience is a crucial component of e-commerce because it has a big impact on consumer advocacy, retention, and loyalty. Businesses can offer customers a seamless, customized, and convenient shopping experience through the use of distributed computing techniques, resulting in an increase in customer satisfaction and loyalty. It enables businesses to offer customers a quicker, more responsive purchasing experience. Businesses can spread traffic across a large number of nodes or devices to reduce latency and improve the responsiveness of their e-commerce platforms, resulting in quicker checkout, slicker navigation, and quicker load times. This can significantly improve the customer experience because it is more likely that customers will abandon e-commerce systems that are slow or unresponsive. Moreover, to provide customers with a more useful and accessible shopping experience. By utilizing cloud computing technologies, businesses can give customers access to their e-commerce platforms from any device or location without requiring them to install or download any software. Making online shopping simpler and more accessible can boost customer satisfaction and loyalty. Businesses can use chatbots and virtual assistants, which can enhance the customer experience, thanks to distributed computing strategies. Chatbots and virtual assistants can provide customers with individualized recommendations and guidance, adding interest and participation to the purchasing process. Utilize augmented reality (AR) and virtual reality (VR) technologies to produce a more dynamic and engaging purchasing experience. If AR and VR technologies enable customers to visualize products in more accurate and detailed ways, this may increase customer engagement and satisfaction. Using AR and VR technology, for example, customers could try on clothing or visualize furniture in their homes, making the purchasing process more personalized and meaningful. Businesses can use big data analytics, improve responsiveness, increase convenience and accessibility, implement chatbots and virtual assistants, use AR and VR technologies, and more to provide customers with a seamless, personalized, and convenient shopping experience that will boost satisfaction and loyalty [24, 25].

14.4.5 Cost Savings and Reduced Operational Complexity

Aside from the advantages, incorporating distributed computing techniques into e-commerce can also lead to significant cost savings and decreased operational complexity. Businesses can scale their IT infrastructure up or down as needed, based on shifting demand, without having to make sizable upfront investments. By employing this pay-as-you-go strategy, businesses can reduce capital expenditures while also gaining more management flexibility for their IT resources. Additionally, operational complexity can be decreased by automating a number of routine tasks, such as monitoring and maintenance. As a result, there will be less need for manual intervention, which can be time-consuming and error prone, and resources will be freed up to be used for higher-value tasks. To reduce operating costs, companies can also streamline their supply chain management processes. Distributed computing, for instance, can be used to improve inventory control, thereby lowering the need for excess inventory and the associated holding costs. Distributed computing can also enable real-time visibility into supply chain operations, allowing companies to spot and fix inefficiencies more quickly, which can eventually result in cost savings. Additionally, it facilitates increased data sharing and collaboration among various departments and stakeholders in order to reduce operational complexity. This may result in more effective decision-making procedures and, ultimately, better business results. Distributed computing, for instance, can enable real-time communication between the sales and marketing teams, resulting in more efficient customer engagement and ultimately higher sales. Businesses can streamline their IT infrastructure, cut down on the need for expensive hardware and software investments, and automate repetitive tasks by utilizing cloud computing services. Distributed computing can also aid companies in streamlining their supply chain management procedures, lowering excess inventory and the holding costs that go along with it, and enhancing collaboration and data sharing between various departments and stakeholders. These advantages can aid organizations in streamlining their processes, cutting expenses, and ultimately fostering growth and success in e-commerce [26, 27].

14.5 Future Trends in the Integration of Distributed Computing Approaches in E-commerce

Here are some potential future trends to watch for:

1) *AI & ML integration:* The use of AI and ML technologies in e-commerce is rising, and they will probably continue to be more closely integrated with distributed computing paradigms [28–30]. Businesses can improve product suggestions, personalize the customer experience, and enhance supply chain management procedures by utilizing these technologies to obtain a deeper understanding of client behavior and preferences.
2) *Blockchain technology integration:* To revolutionize e-commerce by enabling secure, transparent, and decentralized transactions. By integrating blockchain technology with distributed computing approaches, businesses can create a more secure and efficient e-commerce ecosystem, with reduced risk of fraud, lower transaction costs, and faster payment processing times.

3) *Edge computing integration:* Edge computing is the practice of processing data at the data's origin, at the network's edge. This strategy can aid in lowering latency and enhancing performance, which is crucial in applications like e-commerce. Businesses can optimize their IT infrastructure for quicker and more effective processing of e-commerce transactions by merging edge computing with distributed computing methodologies.
4) *Quantum computing integration:* It has the potential to revolutionize computing power, with the ability to solve complex problems at a speed that far surpasses traditional computing. Its integration with distributed computing approaches in e-commerce could lead to significant advancements in areas such as supply chain optimization, fraud detection, and customer personalization.
5) *Cloud-native applications:* Cloud-native applications are designed specifically to run on cloud infrastructure and are highly scalable, flexible, and resilient. By leveraging cloud-native applications with distributed computing approaches, businesses can optimize their IT infrastructure for e-commerce, with reduced costs, increased agility, and improved scalability.
6) *IOT integration:* Supply chain management and consumer experience can be greatly enhanced by combining IoT devices with distributed computing techniques in e-commerce. Businesses may receive real-time visibility into inventory levels, manage shipments, and monitor customer behavior by utilizing IoT devices, which can result in more effective and customized e-commerce experiences [31, 32].
7) *Virtual and augmented reality integration:* These technologies are becoming increasingly prevalent in e-commerce, with the ability to provide immersive and interactive shopping experiences. By integrating these technologies with distributed computing approaches, businesses can create more engaging and personalized e-commerce experiences, with improved product visualization, virtual try-ons, and interactive product demos.

The potential to revolutionize the industry, businesses that can stay ahead of these trends and leverage these technologies effectively will be well-positioned for success in the e-commerce landscape of the future.

14.6 Conclusion

In conclusion, the adoption of distributed computing strategies in e-commerce has fundamentally changed how companies conduct themselves in the world of the digital. This integration offers a wide range of advantages, including increased scalability and flexibility, improved performance and efficiency, improved security and privacy, cost savings, decreased operational complexity, and improved customer experience.

The benefits and difficulties of integrating distributed computing approaches have been discussed, and it has become clear that this technology is revolutionary for e-commerce companies. Businesses can quickly adapt to shifting market conditions and customer needs thanks to its scalability and flexibility. Faster transaction processing times and better resource utilization are outcomes of improved performance and efficiency. Distributed computing approaches help protect sensitive customer and business data, increasing trust and confidence in online transactions. These enhanced security and privacy features are provided by distributed computing approaches. Significant benefits of this integration include cost savings and decreased operational complexity, which let companies allocate resources more effectively and concentrate on core business functions. Finally, improved customer experiences brought about by the incorporation of distributed computing techniques increase client satisfaction, loyalty, and repeat business. Without a doubt, as technology advances, the use of distributed computing technologies will continue to have a significant impact on how e-commerce will evolve. The e-commerce industry is expected to benefit even more from advancements in big data, cloud computing, and artificial intelligence in the years to come [33, 34]. However, it is essential to consider the challenges and potential risks associated with this technology and put the necessary safeguards in place. E-commerce businesses can use distributed computing technologies by following the right plan of action in order to stay competitive and meet shifting customer demands in the digital age.

References

1 Pawłowski, M. **(2021)**. Machine learning based product classification for ecommerce. *J. Comput. Inf. Syst. 2*: 1–10.

2 Kumar, T. and Trakru, M. **(2020)**. The colossal impact of artificial intelligence. E-commerce: statistics and facts. *Int. Res. J. Eng. Technol. 6*: 570–572.

3 Aldayel, M., Ykhlef, M., and Al-Nafjan, A. **(2020)**. Deep learning for EEG-based preference classification in neuromarketing. *Appl. Sci. 10*: 1525.

4 Brei, V.A. **(2020)**. Machine learning in marketing: Overview, learning strategies, applications, and future developments. *Found. Trends Mark. 14*: 173–236.

5 Chopra, K. **(2019)**. Indian shopper motivation to use artificial intelligence: generating Vroom's expectancy theory of motivation using grounded theory approach. *Int. J. Retail. Distrib. Manage. 47*: 331–347.

6 Allal-Chérif, O., Simón-Moya, V., and Ballester, A.C.C. **(2021)**. Intelligent purchasing: how artificial intelligence can redefine the purchasing function. *J. Bus. Res. 124*: 69–76.

7 Lee, J., Jung, O., Lee, Y. et al. **(2021)**. A comparison and interpretation of machine learning algorithm for the prediction of online purchase conversion. *J. Theor. Appl. Electron. Commer. Res. 1*: 83.

8 Li, X., Dahana, W.D., Ye, Q. et al. **(2021)**. How does shopping duration evolve and influence buying behavior? The role of marketing and shopping environment. *J. Retail. Consum. Serv. 62*: 102607.

9 Li, J., Luo, X., Lu, X., and Moriguchi, T. **(2021)**. The double-edged effects of e-commerce cart retargeting: does retargeting too early backfire? *J. Mark. 85*: 123–140.

10 Panigrahi, D. and Karuna, M.A. **(2021)**. Review on leveraging artificial intelligence to enhance business engagement in ecommerce. *IJRPR 2582*: 2.

11 Pillarisetty, R. and Mishra, P. **(2022)**. A review of AI (artificial intelligence) tools and customer experience in online fashion retail. *Int. J. E-Bus. Res. 18*: 1–12.

12 Sindhwani, N., Anand, R., Vashisth, R. et al. (2022). Thingspeak-based environmental monitoring system using IoT. In: *2022 Seventh International Conference on Parallel, Distributed and Grid Computing (PDGC)*, 675–680. IEEE.

13 Saxena, H., Joshi, D., Singh, H., and Anand, R. (2022). Comparison of classification algorithms for Alzheimer's disease prediction. In: *2022 Seventh International Conference on Parallel, Distributed and Grid Computing (PDGC)*, 687–692. IEEE.

14 Pandey, B.K., Pandey, D., Anand, R. et al. (2022). The impact of digital change on student learning and mental anguish in the COVID era. In: *An Interdisciplinary Approach in the Post-COVID-19 Pandemic Era*, 197–206. Nova Science.

15 Anand, R., Nirmal, V., Chauhan, Y., and Sharma, T. (2023, March). An image-based deep learning approach for personalized outfit selection. In: *2023 10th International Conference on Computing for Sustainable Global Development (INDIACom)*, 1050–1054. IEEE.

16 Singh, H., Pandey, B.K., George, S. et al. (2022). Effective overview of different ML models used for prediction of COVID-19 patients. In: *Artificial Intelligence on Medical Data: Proceedings of International Symposium, ISCMM 2021*, 185–192. Singapore: Springer Nature Singapore.

17 Davenport, T., Guha, A., Grewal, D., and Bressgott, T. **(2020)**. How artificial intelligence will change the future of marketing. *J. Acad. Mark. Sci. 48*: 24–42.

18 Khrais, L.T. **(2020)**. Role of artificial intelligence in shaping consumer demand in e-commerce. *Future Internet 12*: 226.

19 Haenlein, M. and Kaplan, A. **(2019)**. A brief history of artificial intelligence: on the past, present, and future of artificial intelligence. *Calif. Manage. Rev. 61*: 5–14.

20 Eriksson, T., Bigi, A., and Bonera, M. **(2020)**. Think with me, or think for me? On the future role of artificial intelligence in marketing strategy formulation. *TQM J. 1*: 24–38.

21 Weber, F.D. and Schütte, R. **(2019)**. State-of-the-art and adoption of artificial intelligence in retailing. *Digit. Policy Regul. Gov. 1*: 12–27.

22 Giroux, M., Kim, J., Lee, J.C., and Park, J. **(2022)**. Artificial intelligence and declined guilt: Retailing morality comparison between human and AI. *J. Bus. Ethics 1*: 1027–1041.

23 André, Q., Carmon, Z., Wertenbroch, K. et al. **(2018)**. Consumer choice and autonomy in the age of artificial intelligence and big data. *Cust. Needs Solut.* *5*: 28–37.

24 Sima, V., Gheorghe, I.G., Subić, J., and Nancu, D. **(2020)**. Influences of the industry 4.0 revolution on the human capital development and consumer behavior: a systematic review. *Sustainability 12*: 4035.

25 Micu, A., Micu, A.E., Geru, M. et al. **(2021)**. The impact of artificial intelligence use on e-commerce in Romania. *Amfiteatru Econ. 23*: 137–154.

26 Libai, B., Bart, Y., Gensler, S. et al. **(2020)**. Brave new world? On AI and the management of customer relationships. *J. Interact. Mark. 51*: 44–56.

27 Bader, V. and Kaiser, S. **(2019)**. Algorithmic decision-making? The user interface and its role for human involvement in decisions supported by artificial intelligence. *Organization 26*: 655–672.

28 Govindaraj, V., Dhanasekar, S., Martinsagayam, K. et al. (2023). Low-power test pattern generator using modified LFSR. *Aerosp. Syst.* 1–8.

29 Bruntha, P.M., Dhanasekar, S., Hepsiba, D. et al. (2023). Application of switching median filter with L 2 norm-based auto-tuning function for removing random valued impulse noise. *Aerosp. Syst. 6* (1): 53–59.

30 Kumar Pandey, B., Pandey, D., Nassa, V.K. et al. (2021). Encryption and steganography-based text extraction in IoT using the EWCTS optimizer. *Imaging Sci. J. 69* (1-4): 38–56.

31 Jain, N., Chaudhary, A., Sindhwani, N., and Rana, A. (2021). Applications of wearable devices in IoT. In: *2021 9th International Conference on Reliability, Infocom Technologies and Optimization (Trends and Future Directions) (ICRITO)*, 1–4. IEEE.

32 Sindhwani, N., Rana, A., and Chaudhary, A. (2021). Breast cancer detection using machine learning algorithms. In: *2021 9th International Conference on Reliability, Infocom Technologies and Optimization (Trends and Future Directions) (ICRITO)*, 1–5. IEEE.

33 Sansanwal, K., Shrivastava, G., Anand, R., and Sharma, K. (2019). Big data analysis and compression for indoor air quality. In: *Handbook of IoT and Big Data*, 1–21. CRC Press.

34 Pandey, D., Pandey, B.K., and Wariya, S. (2019). Study of various techniques used for video retrieval. *J. Emerg. Technol. Innov. Res. 6* (6): 850–853.

15

The Impact of Distributed Computing on Online Shopping and Consumer Experience

K. Suresh Kumar[1], Luigi P.L. Cavaliere[2], Mano A. Tripathi[3], T.S. Rajeswari[4], S.S.C. Mary[5], G.H.A. Vethamanikam[6], and Nadanakumar Vinayagam[7]

[1] *MBA Department, Panimalar Engineering College, Chennai, Tamil Nadu, India*
[2] *Department of Economics, University of Foggia, Foggia, Italy*
[3] *Motilal Nehru National Institute of Technology, Department of Humanities and Social Sciences, Allahabad, India*
[4] *Koneru Lakshmaiah Education Foundation, Department of English, Vaddeswaram, Andhra Pradesh, India*
[5] *Loyola Institute of Business Administration, Business Analytics, India*
[6] *Department of Business Administration, Ayya Nadar Janaki Ammal College, Sivakasi, Tamil Nadu, India*
[7] *Department of Automobile Engineering, Hindustan Institute of Technology and Science, Chennai, Tamil Nadu, India*

15.1 Introduction

Over the past decade, the rise of e-commerce has revolutionized the way consumers shop, with online shopping becoming increasingly popular and convenient. As a result, companies have had to adapt to the changing landscape of retail by implementing new technologies to improve the online shopping experience for consumers. One such technology is distributed computing, which has had a significant impact on online shopping and consumer experience. The use of multiple computers or servers to solve complex computational problems or handle large amounts of data. In the context of online shopping, distributed computing is used to improve website performance, enhance security, and personalize the shopping experience for consumers. By distributing computing resources across multiple machines, online retailers can improve page load times, reduce server downtime,

Meta-Heuristic Algorithms for Advanced Distributed Systems, First Edition. Edited by Rohit Anand, Abhinav Juneja, Digvijay Pandey, Sapna Juneja, and Nidhi Sindhwani.

and ensure that customer data is kept secure. Consumer experience is a critical factor in the success of any online shopping platform, as consumers have come to expect fast and efficient browsing, personalized recommendations, and a secure checkout process. Distributed computing has enabled retailers to meet these expectations by providing the necessary computing power to deliver personalized recommendations, process transactions quickly and securely, and ensure that their websites remain up and running during periods of high traffic. Slow page load times can be a significant frustration for consumers and can lead to high bounce rates and lost sales. By using distributed computing, retailers can distribute the workload across multiple servers, allowing them to handle more requests simultaneously and reducing the time it takes to load web pages. Additionally, it can help ensure that online retailers' websites remain available during periods of high traffic, such as holiday shopping seasons or flash sales. By analyzing customer data, online retailers can use distributed computing to provide personalized product recommendations based on customers' purchase history, browsing behavior, and other data points. This personalized approach can lead to higher customer engagement, increased sales, and improved customer satisfaction.

Distributed denial-of-service (DDoS) attacks are a common threat to online retailers, where attackers overwhelm a server with requests, causing it to crash and rendering the website unavailable. Distributed computing can help mitigate the risk of DDoS attacks by spreading the workload across multiple servers, making it harder for attackers to take down the website. While it has brought many benefits to online shopping and consumer experience, it is not without its challenges and limitations. Technical challenges, such as ensuring data consistency across multiple servers and managing the complexity of distributed systems, can make implementing distributed computing challenging for some retailers. Additionally, there are limitations to the benefits of distributed computing, with some aspects of consumer experience, such as product selection and customer service, being less impacted by distributed computing than others. Despite these challenges and limitations, distributed computing is a powerful technology that has transformed online shopping and consumer experience. In this chapter, we will examine the impact of distributed computing on online shopping and consumer experience, including its benefits, challenges, and implications for the future of online retail. Ultimately, this chapter aims to provide a comprehensive understanding of the role of distributed computing in online shopping and consumer experience [1–3].

15.1.1 The Growing Trend of Online Shopping and the Importance of Consumer Experience

The growth of e-commerce has been one of the most significant trends in retail over the past decade. The convenience and accessibility of online shopping have made it an attractive option for consumers, who can browse and purchase products. However, as the number of online retailers has grown, so too has the competition for consumers' attention and loyalty. In this crowded marketplace, consumer experience has become a critical factor in the success of online retailers. Consumers have come to expect fast and efficient browsing, personalized recommendations, and a secure checkout process. Online retailers who fail to meet these expectations risk losing customers to competitors who can provide a better experience. The importance of consumer experience is reflected in the success of companies like Amazon, which has built its business around providing a seamless and personalized online shopping experience for its customers. Amazon's success has been driven in large part by its use of data and analytics to personalize product recommendations, streamline the checkout process, and improve customer service. Other online retailers have followed suit, investing in technology and innovation to improve the consumer experience and gain a competitive edge. In addition to improving customer experience, online shopping has also brought other benefits to consumers. For example, online shopping can offer a wider selection of products than traditional brick-and-mortar stores, as well as the ability to easily compare prices and read reviews from other customers. These benefits have made online shopping an attractive option for consumers, particularly for items that are hard to find or that require extensive research [4–6].

15.1.2 Distributed Computing in Online Shopping Applications

A computing model where multiple computers work together to solve a problem or perform a task. In distributed computing, each computer in the network performs a small part of the task, and the results are combined to produce the final output. This approach is used to improve the performance, reliability, and scalability of computing systems. In the context of retail, e-commerce has become increasingly popular due to its convenience and accessibility. However, as the number of online retailers has grown, so too has the competition for consumers' attention and loyalty. To provide a better shopping experience, retailers are leveraging technology to improve their websites and infrastructure. For example, retailers are investing in cloud computing, which is a type of distributed computing that allows for the use of remote servers to store, manage, and process data. Cloud computing can help retailers to scale their operations, reduce costs, and improve the performance and reliability of their websites. Another way that retailers are using technology to improve the shopping experience is through the use of artificial intelligence (AI) and machine learning (ML) [7–12]. AI and ML can be used to analyze consumer data and behavior to provide personalized recommendations, improve search results, and optimize pricing strategies. By leveraging AI and ML, retailers can create a more engaging and relevant shopping experience for their customers. Retailers are also investing in cybersecurity measures to protect their customers' personal and financial data. Cybersecurity threats, such as data breaches and hacking attempts, can undermine consumer trust and damage a retailer's reputation. Retailers are using technology, including distributed computing, cloud computing, AI, ML, and cybersecurity, to improve the shopping experience for consumers. These technologies allow retailers to deliver a fast, reliable, and personalized experience that meets the changing needs and expectations of their customers [13, 14].

15.2 Benefits of Distributed Computing for Online Shopping

Distributed computing can bring a number of benefits to the online shopping experience. Table 15.1 highlights three main benefits of distributed computing for online shopping.

Faster page load times are critical for online retailers because slow-loading pages can negatively impact customer experience and lead to lost sales. By utilizing distributed computing, retailers can distribute the workload across multiple servers, reducing downtime and maintaining fast page load speeds, even during peak traffic periods.

Improved security is also a key benefit of distributed computing for online shopping. With the increasing threat of data breaches and cyberattacks, retailers need to take steps to protect their customers' personal and financial information.

Table 15.1 Benefits of distributed computing.

Benefits of distributed computing	Explanation
Faster page load times	By utilizing distributed computing, retailers can distribute the workload across multiple servers, reducing downtime and maintaining fast page load speeds, even during peak traffic periods.
Improved security	Distributed computing can spread the encryption and decryption of customer data across multiple servers, reducing the risk of data breaches or cyberattacks. Additionally, distributed computing can enable real-time monitoring and detection of security threats.
Personalized recommendations	Retailers can use machine learning algorithms to analyze customer data and provide tailored product recommendations and promotions, increasing the likelihood of customer loyalty and repeat purchases.

Distributed computing can spread the encryption and decryption of customer data across multiple servers, reducing the risk of data breaches or cyberattacks. Additionally, distributed computing can enable real-time monitoring and detection of security threats, allowing retailers to quickly respond and mitigate any potential risks.

Finally, personalized recommendations can improve the overall customer experience and increase customer loyalty and repeat purchases. By analyzing customer data using ML algorithms, retailers can provide tailored product recommendations and promotions that are more likely to resonate with customers.

15.2.1 Distributed Computing for Improvising Online Shopping Experiences

Distributed computing has a significant impact on the online shopping experience, providing benefits such as improved performance, enhanced security, personalized marketing, and cost savings. Let's explore these benefits in more detail:

First, improve the performance of online shopping websites. By using multiple servers, retailers can distribute the workload across the network and avoid overwhelming any single server. This approach helps to reduce downtime and maintain fast page load speeds, even during peak traffic periods such as holidays or flash sales. Additionally, by leveraging cloud-based solutions, retailers can quickly scale up their infrastructure as their traffic grows, ensuring that they can continue to provide a seamless shopping experience to their customers.

Second, it can enhance the security of online shopping. Retailers need to keep sensitive customer data such as credit card details and personal information safe and secure. By utilizing distributed computing, retailers can spread the encryption and decryption of this data across multiple servers, reducing the risk of data breaches or cyberattacks. Additionally, distributed computing can also enable real-time monitoring and detection of security threats, allowing retailers to quickly respond and mitigate any potential risks.

Third, by analyzing customer data from various sources, retailers can better understand their customers' interests and preferences and provide tailored product recommendations and promotions. For example, retailers can use ML algorithms to analyze past purchase and history that are relevant and appealing to each customer. This helps to create a more engaging shopping experience and increases the likelihood of customer loyalty and repeat purchases.

Fourth, by using cloud-based solutions, retailers can avoid the high costs associated with building and maintaining their IT infrastructure. This allows retailers to focus on their core business activities such as marketing, product development, and customer service. Additionally, retailers can take advantage of the pay-as-you-go model offered by cloud computing providers. This enables retailers to scale their infrastructure up or down based on their current needs, resulting in significant cost savings over time.

Finally, by utilizing cloud computing and other distributed computing technologies, retailers can quickly and easily scale their operations to reach customers around the world. For example, retailers can use cloud-based services to host their websites in multiple regions, allowing them to serve customers in different countries with localized content and currency options. Additionally, distributed computing can enable retailers to provide multilingual support and flexible payment options, making it easier for customers to shop from anywhere in the world. By providing improved performance, enhanced security, personalized marketing, cost savings, and global expansion opportunities, distributed computing is helping to transform the online shopping experience. As retailers continue to adopt these technologies, we can expect to see further innovations that will improve the overall shopping experience even more. [15–17].

15.2.2 Impact of Distributed Computing on Consumer Experience

The benefits of distributed computing, such as faster page load times, improved security, and personalized recommendations, have a significant impact on the consumer experience in online shopping. Faster page load times mean that customers can access and browse products quickly and efficiently, without experiencing any lag or delays. This creates a positive experience for customers and can increase the likelihood of completing a purchase. When a website is slow, it can be frustrating for customers, causing them to abandon their shopping cart and look for other options. By utilizing to ensure faster page load times, retailers can improve the customer experience and increase the likelihood of customer satisfaction. Improved security is also critical for consumer experience in online shopping. Customers want to feel safe when making online purchases, and they expect their personal and financial information to be protected. Distributed computing can spread the encryption and decryption of customer data across multiple servers, reducing the risk of data breaches or cyberattacks. This helps to build trust with customers and create a positive experience, making them more likely to return to the retailer for future purchases. This helps customers feel more connected to the retailer and can increase the likelihood of repeat purchases. It also creates a more engaging shopping experience, where customers feel that the retailer understands their needs and preferences. By ensuring faster page load times, improved security, and personalized recommendations, retailers can create a more positive and engaging shopping experience, increase customer satisfaction and loyalty, and ultimately drive sales and revenue [18–20].

15.3 Limitations of Distributed Computing in Online Shopping

- *Complexity and cost:* Implementing a distributed computing system can be complex and costly. Retailers need to invest in hardware and software to support the system, and they need skilled IT staff to manage and maintain the system.
- *Integration with legacy systems:* Retailers may face challenges integrating a distributed computing system with existing legacy systems, such as inventory management, customer relationship management, and order processing systems.
- *Data privacy and compliance:* Distributed computing involves the processing and storage of large amounts of customer data, which raises concerns around data privacy and compliance with regulations such as General Data Protection Regulation (GDPR) and California's Consumer Privacy Act (CCPA). Retailers need to ensure that customer data is protected and that they are compliant with relevant regulations.
- *Network latency and bandwidth:* Distributed computing relies on a network of servers, and network latency and bandwidth can impact the performance of the system. Retailers need to ensure that their network infrastructure can support the demands of the system and provide reliable and fast connectivity to customers.
- *Scalability:* Distributed computing can be more scalable than traditional computing systems, but retailers need to ensure that the system can scale effectively to meet changing demands, such as seasonal spikes in traffic or sudden increases in order volumes. While distributed computing offers significant benefits for online shopping, retailers need to carefully consider the challenges and limitations of the system before implementing it. By addressing these challenges, retailers can ensure that they are providing a seamless and secure online shopping experience for their customers. Figure 15.1 shows the challenges and limitations of distributed computing in online shopping.

15.3.1 Technical Challenges

Implementing distributed computing in online shopping platforms is not without its technical challenges. One such challenge is the design of a distributed computing architecture that can handle the demands of online shopping platforms. Retailers need to consider factors such as load balancing, fault tolerance, and data consistency to ensure that the system is reliable and scalable. This involves careful planning and design of the architecture to ensure that the system can handle the large amounts of data that are processed and stored.

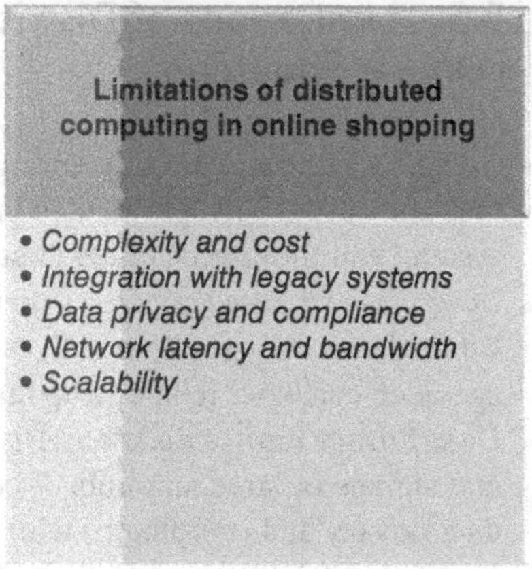

Figure 15.1 Challenges and limitations of distributed computing in online shopping.

As distributed computing involves the processing and storage of large amounts of data, retailers need to ensure that data is distributed across the system effectively and that data consistency is maintained. This requires careful management of data to ensure that it is available when needed and that it is accurate and up-to-date. Network latency is another challenge that retailers need to address when implementing distributed computing in online shopping platforms. As distributed computing relies on a network of servers, network latency can impact the performance of the system. Retailers need to ensure that the system is designed to minimize latency and that servers are located in geographically dispersed regions to reduce network latency. Security is also a significant concern when implementing distributed computing in online shopping platforms. Distributed computing introduces new security challenges, such as the need to secure data transmission across multiple servers and protect against cyberattacks that target the distributed system. Retailers need to implement robust security measures to protect customer data and ensure system integrity.

Interoperability is another technical challenge. Retailers may need to integrate their distributed computing system with other technologies, such as legacy systems or third-party services. Ensuring that these systems can work together effectively requires careful planning and implementation.

Finally, testing and debugging a distributed computing system can be challenging, as it involves multiple components and interactions between servers. Retailers need to implement effective testing and debugging strategies to ensure that the system performs as expected and that any issues are resolved quickly. Implementing this technology requires careful planning, design, and implementation to overcome the technical challenges associated with it. Retailers need to address these challenges to ensure that they are providing a seamless and engaging shopping experience for their customers [21–23].

15.3.2 Limitations of Distributed Computing in Improving All Aspects of Consumer Experience

While distributed computing offers many benefits for online shopping platforms, it is not a panacea and has its limitations in improving all aspects of consumer experience. Here are some limitations of distributed computing in this regard:

1) *User interface:* Distributed computing does not directly impact the user interface of an online shopping platform. The user interface is still designed and developed separately and needs to be optimized for an engaging shopping experience.
2) *Customer service:* Customer service is a critical component of consumer experience, and distributed computing cannot improve this aspect directly. Retailers still need to invest in customer service training, staffing, and technology to provide top-notch customer service.
3) *Pricing:* Pricing is a critical factor in consumer decision-making, and distributed computing does not impact pricing directly. Retailers need to focus on competitive pricing strategies to attract and retain customers.
4) *Product quality:* Distributed computing does not directly impact product quality, which is an important factor in consumer experience. Retailers need to ensure that they offer high-quality products to meet customer expectations.
5) *Shipping and delivery:* Shipping and delivery are critical aspects of consumer experience, and distributed computing does not directly impact this aspect. Retailers need to optimize their shipping and delivery processes to provide fast and reliable service to customers.

It is important to recognize its limitations in improving all aspects of consumer experience. Retailers need to address these limitations by investing in other areas, such as user interface design, customer service, pricing, product quality, and shipping and delivery.

15.3.3 Potential Drawbacks of Relying Heavily on Distributed Computing in Online Shopping

One of the potential drawbacks of relying heavily on distributed computing in online shopping is the increased dependency on technology. With a distributed computing system, the entire platform can be affected by a system failure or cyberattack, creating a single point of failure. This can be mitigated by investing in backup systems and disaster recovery plans. However, these measures can add to the cost of implementing and maintaining a distributed computing system, which can be a significant barrier for smaller retailers. The complexity of distributed computing can also pose a challenge for retailers. It requires specialized knowledge and expertise to implement and maintain the system effectively. Retailers may struggle to find qualified staff to manage the system, which can add to the cost and complexity of the technology. Cyberattacks that target the distributed system can be more challenging to detect and mitigate. Retailers need to implement robust security measures to protect customer data and ensure system integrity. Privacy is another concern when it comes to distributed computing, as it involves the processing and storage of large amounts of data. Retailers need to ensure that customer data is protected and that they comply with privacy regulations.

Compatibility issues between servers can also create performance issues with distributed computing. Retailers need to ensure that the system is designed to minimize compatibility issues and that servers are updated and maintained regularly. Network latency can also impact the performance of the system, and retailers need to ensure that the system is designed to minimize latency and that servers are located in geographically dispersed regions to reduce network latency. Retailers need to ensure that the system is updated and maintained regularly to prevent performance issues and security vulnerabilities. This can add to the cost and complexity of the technology.

Retailers need to address these potential drawbacks by investing in backup systems, disaster recovery plans, security measures, and privacy compliance. They also need to ensure that they have the resources and expertise to manage and maintain the system effectively. By doing so, retailers can leverage the benefits of distributed computing while mitigating its potential drawbacks [24–26].

15.4 Impact of Distributed Computing on Online Shopping Trends

In addition to the benefits and challenges of distributed computing in online shopping, this technology has also had a significant impact on online shopping trends. Here are some ways that distributed computing has influenced the online shopping landscape.

Real-time inventory management allows retailers to track inventory in real time across multiple locations. This enables them to offer products for sale online that may not be available in a physical store location, increasing the selection available to customers. Real-time inventory management also allows retailers to quickly restock popular items and avoid stockouts, which can lead to lost sales.

Faster order fulfillment to process orders quickly and efficiently. By using algorithms to determine the optimal location for order fulfillment, retailers can reduce shipping times and improve the speed of delivery. Improved personalization by leveraging data processing capabilities offers personalized recommendations to customers. This can improve the shopping experience by making it more relevant and tailored to individual customer needs and preferences.

Increased mobile shopping to optimize their platforms for mobile devices, which has led to an increase in mobile shopping. By using distributed computing to deliver content more efficiently and reduce page load times, retailers can provide a better mobile shopping experience, which has become increasingly important as more customers shop on their mobile devices.

Improved omnichannel integration: Distributed computing enables retailers to integrate their online and physical store channels more seamlessly. By using real-time inventory management and order fulfillment capabilities, retailers can offer in-store pickup and other omnichannel fulfillment options that provide greater convenience to customers. By enabling real-time inventory management, faster order fulfillment, improved personalization, increased mobile shopping, greater access to data, and improved omnichannel integration, distributed computing has transformed the way retailers operate and engage with their customers. As this technology continues to evolve and improve, we can expect to see further advancements in the online shopping landscape [27–29].

15.4.1 Distributed Computing in Improvising Consumer Expectations

In the past, consumers had limited options when it came to online shopping. They could only browse a limited selection of products and had to wait several days for their purchases to arrive. However, distributed computing has changed all that. One of the most significant changes that distributed computing has brought about is the ability to offer personalized recommendations to consumers. Retailers can now use ML algorithms to analyze consumer data and provide personalized product recommendations. This has led to an increase in consumer expectations, as they now expect retailers to offer personalized recommendations based on their browsing and purchasing history.

By enabling faster page load times, Online shoppers today expect web pages to load quickly and without any delays. Distributed computing allows retailers to distribute web content across multiple servers, reducing the load on any single server and improving page load times. This has become an important factor in providing a good user experience and meeting consumer expectations. Online shopping platforms can now offer an almost limitless selection of products, without the need to maintain large inventories. This has led to increased consumer expectations around product selection, with consumers now expecting to be able to find any product they are looking for online.

Real-time inventory management is another area where distributed computing has impacted consumer expectations. With real-time inventory management, retailers can provide accurate information about product availability, reducing the chances of customers being disappointed by out-of-stock items. This has raised consumer expectations around the accuracy of inventory information, with consumers now expecting retailers to provide up-to-date inventory information. With the advent of mobile computing and cloud-based services, consumers can now shop from anywhere, at any time. This has led to an increase in consumer expectations around the availability of online shopping platforms, with consumers expecting retailers to provide seamless experiences across multiple devices and platforms.

15.5 Ethical Implications of Distributed Computing in Online Shopping

Distributed computing in online shopping platforms has several ethical implications that need to be considered. Here are some of the key ethical considerations associated with this technology:

Privacy. They need to implement robust security measures, comply with privacy regulations, and be transparent about how they use and store customer data. Algorithmic bias personalized recommendations are a key benefit of distributed computing in online shopping platforms. However, these algorithms can be biased if they are trained on data that reflects existing social biases. Retailers need to ensure that their algorithms are designed to minimize bias and that they are transparent about how they make recommendations.

Worker exploitation distributed computing can be used to optimize supply chains and reduce costs, but this can come at the expense of workers' rights and well-being. Retailers need to ensure that they are not exploiting workers in their supply chains and that they are providing fair wages and safe working conditions. Environmental impact distributed computing relies on data centers, which consume significant amounts of energy and contribute to carbon emissions. Retailers have an ethical obligation to minimize their environmental impact by adopting sustainable practices, such as using renewable energy sources and optimizing data center efficiency.

Digital divide access to distributed computing technologies is not equal, and there is a risk that it could widen the digital divide between those who have access to technology and those who do not [11, 30]. Retailers need to ensure that their online shopping platforms are accessible to all customers, regardless of their technological proficiency or access to technology. Transparency distributed computing can be opaque, making it difficult for customers to understand how algorithms make recommendations and how their data is being used. Retailers have an ethical obligation to be transparent about how their systems work, how they use customer data, and how they make decisions. By addressing these ethical considerations, retailers can ensure that they are using distributed computing in a responsible and ethical way [31, 32].

15.6 Conclusion

In conclusion, the impact of distributed computing on online shopping and consumer experience has been significant. Distributed computing has revolutionized the way online shopping platforms operate, providing retailers with the ability to process and analyze large amounts of data, improve scalability, and enhance security measures. It has also changed the way consumers interact with online shopping platforms, providing them with a more personalized and streamlined shopping experience. The implementation of distributed computing has led to several benefits for both retailers and consumers. Retailers can now provide a more seamless and engaging shopping experience by offering personalized recommendations, targeted promotions, and optimized search results. Consumers can enjoy a more streamlined checkout process, faster load times, and improved product recommendations based on their preferences and past purchases. However, the implementation of distributed computing also presents challenges and potential drawbacks, including increased cost, complexity, and security concerns [33, 34]. Retailers must address these challenges to ensure that they are providing a reliable and secure shopping experience for their customers.

It has transformed the way online shopping platforms operate and has raised consumer expectations for a seamless and personalized shopping experience. As technology continues to evolve, it will be interesting to see how retailers leverage distributed computing to improve the online shopping experience even further.

References

1 Otterbring, T. and Lu, C. **(2018)**. Clothes, condoms, and customer satisfaction: the effect of employee mere presence on customer satisfaction depends on the shopping situation. *Psychol. Mark. 35*: 454–462.

2 Holmlund, M., Van Vaerenbergh, Y., Ciuchita, R. et al. **(2020)**. Customer experience management in the age of big data analytics: a strategic framework. *J. Bus. Res. 116*: 356–365.

3 Arijit, B. and Manjari, S. **(2020)**. A framework of online customer experience: an Indian perspective. *Glob. Bus. Rev. 21*: 800–817.

4 Xiao, L., Guo, F., Yu, F., and Liu, S. **(2019)**. The effects of online shopping context cues on consumers' purchase intention for cross-border e-commerce sustainability. *Sustainability 11*: 2777.

5 Otto, A.S., Szymanski, D.M., and Varadarajan, R. **(2020)**. Customer satisfaction and firm performance: Insights from over a quarter century of empirical research. *J. Acad. Mark. Sci. 48*: 543–564.

6 Soderlund, M. and Sagfossen, S. **(2017)**. The consumer experience: the impact of supplier effort and consumer effort on customer satisfaction. *J. Retail. Consum. Serv. 39*: 219–229.

7 Jain, N., Chaudhary, A., Sindhwani, N., and Rana, A. (2021). Applications of wearable devices in IoT. In: *2021 9th International Conference on Reliability, Infocom Technologies and Optimization (Trends and Future Directions) (ICRITO)*, 1–4. IEEE.

8 Sindhwani, N., Rana, A., and Chaudhary, A. (2021). Breast cancer detection using machine learning algorithms. In: *2021 9th International Conference on Reliability, Infocom Technologies and Optimization (Trends and Future Directions) (ICRITO)*, 1–5. IEEE.

9 Bruntha, P.M., Dhanasekar, S., Hepsiba, D. et al. (2023). Application of switching median filter with L 2 norm-based auto-tuning function for removing random valued impulse noise. *Aerosp. Syst. 6* (1): 53–59.

10 Kumar Pandey, B., Pandey, D., Nassa, V.K. et al. (2021). Encryption and steganography-based text extraction in IoT using the EWCTS optimizer. *Imaging Sci. J. 69* (1–4): 38–56.

11 Anand, R., Nirmal, V., Chauhan, Y., and Sharma, T. (2023). An image-based deep learning approach for personalized outfit selection. In: *2023 10th International Conference on Computing for Sustainable Global Development (INDIACom)*, 1050–1054. IEEE.

12 Govindaraj, V., Dhanasekar, S., Martinsagayam, K. et al. (2023). Low-power test pattern generator using modified LFSR. *Aerosp. Syst.* 1–8.

13 Levy, S. and Gvili, Y. **(2020)**. Online shopper engagement in price negotiation: the roles of culture, involvement and eWOM. *Int. J. Advert. 39*: 232–257.

14 Rahman, O., Fung, B., and Chen, Z. **(2020)**. Young Chinese consumers' choice between product-related and sustainable cues-The effects of gender differences and consumer innovativeness. *Sustainability 12*: 3818.

15 Hult, G.T.M., Sharma, P.N., Morgeson, F.V., and Zhang, Y. **(2019)**. Antecedents and consequences of customer satisfaction: do they differ across online and offline purchases? *J. Retail. 95*: 10–23.

16 Choi, Y. and Mai, D. **(2018)**. The sustainable role of the e-trust in the B2C e-commerce of Vietnam. *Sustainability 10*: 291.

17 Moslehpour, M., Pham, V., Wong, W.K., and Bilgiçli, İ. **(2018)**. E-purchase intention of Taiwanese consumers: sustainable mediation of perceived usefulness and perceived ease of use. *Sustainability 10*: 234.

18 Hoffman, D.L., Novak, T., and Peralta, M.A. **(1999)**. Information privacy in the marketplace: implications for the commercial uses of anonymity on the Web. *Inf. Soc. 15*: 129–139.

19 Jarvenpaa, S.L. and Todd, P.A. **(1997)**. Consumer reactions to electronic shopping on the World Wide Web. *Int. J. Electron. Commun 1*: 59–88.

20 Shankar, V., Urban, G.L., and Sultan, F. **(2002)**. Online trust: a stakeholder perspective, concepts, implications, and future directions. *J. Strategic Inf. Syst. 11*: 325–344.

21 Hennig-Thurau, T., Gwinner, K., and Gremler, D.D. **(2002)**. Understanding relationship marketing outcomes: an integration of relationship benefits and relationship quality. *J. Serv. Res. 4*: 230–247.

22 Leanne, H.Y.T., Souchon, A.L., and Thirkell, P.C. **(2001)**. Relationship marketing and customer loyalty in a retail setting: a dyadic exploration. *J. Mark. Manage. 17*: 287–319.

23 Gome, R., Mentzer, J.T., and Krafel, R.E. Jr. **(1989)**. Physical distribution service: a fundamental marketing concept. *J. Acad. Mark. Sci. 17*: 53–62.

24 Jang, H.-Y. **(2007)**. A comparative study on the structural interactions among customer satisfaction, trust, loyalty based on types of Internet shopping mall. *J. Glob. Sch. Mark. Sci. 17*: 23–49.

25 Wei, L. (2014). *A Study on Purchase Decision Factors of Fashion and Clothes Products of Chinese Twenties in On-Line Shopping Mall*. Daejeon, Korea: The Graduate School of International Commerce, Woosong University.

26 Niranjanamurthy, M., Kavyashree, N., Jagannath, S., and Chahar, D. **(2013)**. Analysis of e-commerce and m-commerce: advantages, limitations and security issues. *Int. J. Adv. Res. Comput. Commun. Eng. 2*: 2360–2370.

27 Park, E.O., Chae, B.K., Kwon, J., and Kim, W.H. **(2020)**. The effects of green restaurant attributes on customer satisfaction using the structural topic model on online customer reviews. *Sustainability 12*: 2843.

28 Krystallis, A. and Chrysochou, P. **(2014)**. The effects of service brand dimensions on brand loyalty. *J. Retail. Consum. Serv. 21*: 139–147.

29 Oliver, R.L., Rust, R.T., and Varki, S. **(1997)**. Customer delight: foundations, findings and managerial insight. *J. Retail. 73*: 311–336.

30 Singh, H., Pandey, B.K., George, S. et al. (2022). Effective overview of different ML models used for prediction of COVID-19 patients. In: *Artificial Intelligence on Medical Data: Proceedings of International Symposium, ISCMM 2021*, 185–192. Singapore: Springer Nature Singapore.

31 Zarantenello, L. and Schmitt, B.H. **(2000)**. Using the brand experience scale to profile consumers and predict consumer behavior. *J. Brand. Manag. 17*: 532–540.

32 Wu, T.J., Gao, J.Y., Wang, L.Y., and Yuan, K.S. **(2020)**. Exploring links between polychronicity and job performance from the person–environment fit perspective-the mediating role of well-being. *Int. J. Environ. Res. Public Health 17*: 3711.

33 Sindhwani, N., Anand, R., Vashisth, R. et al. (2022). Thingspeak-based environmental monitoring system using IoT. In: *2022 Seventh International Conference on Parallel, Distributed and Grid Computing (PDGC)*, 675–680. IEEE.

34 Pandey, B.K., Pandey, D., Anand, R. et al. (2022). The impact of digital change on student learning and mental anguish in the COVID era. In: *An Interdisciplinary Approach in the Post-COVID-19 Pandemic Era*, 197–206. Nova Science.

16

Wireless Sensor-based IoT System with Distributed Optimization for Healthcare

Rohit Anand[1], *Digvijay Pandey*[2], *Deena N. Gupta*[3], *M.K. Dharani*[4], *Nidhi Sindhwani*[5], *and J.V.N. Ramesh*[6]

[1]*Department of ECE, G.B. Pant DSEU Okhla-1 Campus (formerly GBPEC), New Delhi, India*
[2]*Department of Technical Education, IET, Dr. A.P.J. Abdul Kalam Technical University, Lucknow, Uttar Pradesh, India*
[3]*CDAC, Mumbai, Maharashtra, India*
[4]*Department of Artificial Intelligence, Kongu Engineering College, Erode, Tamil Nadu, India*
[5]*AIIT, Amity University, Noida, Uttar Pradesh, India*
[6]*Department of Computer Science and Engineering, Koneru Lakshmaiah Education Foundation, Vaddeswaram, Guntur, Andhra Pradesh, India*

16.1 Introduction

16.1.1 Wireless Sensor

To obtain sensory data and identify changes in local settings, you need a wireless sensor. Most wireless sensors are small, battery-operated devices that may be placed in a variety of locations and are programmed to take readings of a variety of environmental characteristics and send those readings as electrical impulses. Temperature, light, motion, and liquid leaks are just a few of the various stimuli that fall under this category [1–2].

16.1.2 Achieve Seamless Sensor-to-Cloud Solutions for a Range of Applications

As wireless sensors don't undertake any serious data processing on-board, they are very efficient with their energy usage and may function for years on a single

Meta-Heuristic Algorithms for Advanced Distributed Systems, First Edition. Edited by Rohit Anand, Abhinav Juneja, Digvijay Pandey, Sapna Juneja, and Nidhi Sindhwani.

battery, provided the right wireless technology is used. As a result of their modest data transmission rates, sensors may be readily maintained by slow networks.

Passive sensors are unpowered gadgets that gather data from their immediate environs. They don't actively probe, so they don't need any more power to function. A mercury-based thermometer, which exhibits bi-directional movement in response to changes in temperature but requires no external power, is an example of a passive sensor. Instead, active sensors need to be constantly powered by an external source in order to keep an eye on their immediate surroundings. Devices that employ radar or sonar to investigate their environment are examples of active sensors. The focus of this paper is on active sensors [3].

In order to keep tabs on the local environment, a network of wireless sensors may be set up. These wireless sensor networks (WSNs) consist of a large number of individually deployable sensors that are linked wirelessly. Nodes in a sensor network may collect data from other nodes and send it to a central hub, or individual sensors may connect to the hub directly if they have sufficient range. Gateways both a router and a wireless access point, mediate communications between local sensors and the wider internet.

16.1.3 Some Examples of Wireless Sensors

The sizes of WS may vary greatly. Several different things, from monitoring air quality to following people or animals, might benefit from them.

- Many sorts of things may be detected using **wireless proximity sensors**. Some examples of proximity sensors include inductive, ultrasonic, microwave, infrared, and radio frequency (RF) time-of-flight/doppler detectors. Hall effect sensors and reed switches are two of the most common types of proximity sensors used for sensing the presence of a magnet. As they just need a metal target to work, inductive proximity wireless sensors may be put to good use in tasks like process monitoring in factories and traffic optimization. Retractable-roof stadiums might benefit from using inductive sensors to track the status of different systems. As cars are waiting at a light for the signal to change, inductive sensors implanted in the road surface may detect their presence. A wide variety of materials, from liquids to rocks, may be detected with capacitive proximity sensors. Capacitive sensors' adaptability means they might be used for a variety of purposes, such as tracking rice and soybean stock in grain elevators or measuring powder in hoppers. In a similar vein to LDS, these devices may be used in the monitoring of tank levels [4].
- When used in noisy environments, ultrasonic proximity sensors employ high-frequency sound waves to calculate distances between objects. Besides their use in automated vehicle washes, ultrasonic sensors may also be used in garages to identify any impediments.

- Acceleration and tilt are only two of the forms of motion that may be detected by **wireless motion sensors**. For instance, owners may set up wireless motion sensor alarms to notify them whenever their expensive items or assets are in motion. Businesses may track asset movement and impact strength using acceleration sensors. Passive infrared (PIR) motion detectors work by reflecting back some of the infrared light that is reflected off of moving objects. Infrared (PIR) sensors have several uses in surveillance and police work. A machine's utilization or a pump's operation may be tracked with the use of vibration sensors. The vibration sensor's piezoelectric strip, for instance, may be fastened to a motor to monitor on/off states or to identify the onset of bearing failure [5].
- Glass breakage and window breakage may be immediately detected by installing these sensors in commercial buildings, which can be used by security companies to alert tenants.
- One kind of wireless sensor is a liquid sensor; it is sensitive enough to identify liquids like water and gasoline. A flow sensor will be able to tell whether water flow has stopped, allowing one to determine if pipes have frozen. Homeowners who have installed water sensors that send out wireless alerts may be notified in the event of floods or other types of overflows. Installing water leak sensors throughout a hotel is a quick and easy way for owners to locate and repair any leaks that may occur. These sensors may also be used to detect potentially lethal fuel leaks in manufacturing facilities. Ultrasonic liquid level sensors may be installed in reservoirs to notify enterprises or organizations of abnormally low or high levels.
- In times of medical or personal emergency, wireless push buttons' ability to send out messages upon being pressed is crucial. These wireless panic buttons are a component of a larger system called a PERS and may be pressed by the user in the event of an emergency. Wireless push-button sensors may also be utilized in service settings when customers need to seek assistance. Wireless push buttons in public bathrooms may double as service call buttons to notify cleaning staff of a cleaning emergency [6–10].
- Temperature, humidity, and the concentration of dangerous gases may all be determined with the use of wireless air sensors. Homeowners may monitor the humidity in their greenhouses or personal saunas, as well as identify any problems with their heating systems, by using wireless air temperature and humidity sensors. The use of wireless air sensors allows for accurate temperature management in art galleries and the early detection of refrigeration issues in restaurants. Air sensors may also be used to monitor the performance of heating, ventilation and air conditioning (HVAC) systems and identify any obstructions to airflow.
- In addition to monitoring ambient temperatures, wireless temperature sensors may also assess the heat of various substances. In the case of frozen pipes, for instance, probe-type temperature sensors may alert householders to the need

for preventative action. Temperature and humidity sensors will be installed in warehouses to monitor the heat index and safeguard the safety of workers [11–12].

- Water-proof temperature sensors are also available. Wireless water temperature sensors allow aquariums to constantly track the temperature of their inhabitants. It is also possible for amusement parks and leisure centers to monitor pool temperatures to ensure that visitors are not uncomfortable.
- Optical events, such as changes in light intensity or breaks in an optical beam, may be detected using wireless optical sensors. Greenhouses can monitor the day's solar and light levels with the use of light-detecting sensors. Light metering devices may be set up to alert museum staff when unsafe levels of ultraviolet radiation are present. Homeowners may use ambient light sensors to do things like check for fires or automate their lighting systems to save money on electricity. Infrared PIR motion detectors find widespread usage in surveillance and people counting systems [13–20].

16.1.4 The Different Types of Wireless Network Topologies

- There are many common topologies for WSNs. The star and mesh topologies are the most prevalent ones used to enable wireless sensor technologies. With a star topology, each individual node has a direct connection to the gateway. With this setup, nodes communicate with a central gateway, which forwards the data to the appropriate nodes. Since gateways may communicate with several nodes at once, expanding networks is a breeze. Less point-to-point connections are needed since nodes aren't transmitting data directly to one another. As new nodes only need to connect to a single hub, star topologies facilitate ease of deployment, setup, and management. In conclusion, star topologies offer an efficient and low-cost way to facilitate communication among a large number of wireless sensors. The problem with star topologies is their whole reliance on the wireless connection between sensors and the hub. In the absence of middle "hop" or repeater, range might be a concern. It's important to note that the gateway's ability to handle more nodes is crucial to any scaling efforts.
- With a mesh topology, each individual node in the network [21–22] is responsible for transferring data, rather than just one central hub. The nodes in a mesh topology act as routers that relay data to other nodes in the network. As there are several potential channels for data to take to reach the gateway, disruptions in connection at individual nodes represent less of a risk. Yet, there are a few major issues with mesh networks. There must be considerably more involved protocols in place to create a mesh network and relay data at runtime, and these protocols are typically too sophisticated. As certain nodes must always be on in order to transmit information, mesh networks have the additional drawback of

being substantially more power hungry than star topologies. Yet, the high initial cost of mesh networks makes it difficult to justify their adoption.

16.1.5 Traditional Wireless Sensor Protocols

Connectivity between sensors is made possible by a wide variety of wireless protocols (see Figure 16.1).

- **Wi-Fi** transmits data on two principal frequencies, 2.4 and 5 GHz, making it a very flexible and pervasive local area network technology. Wi-Fi networks allow for the transmission of big data packets at high rates across intermediate distances. Wi-key Fi's benefit is that it's already present in a large number of buildings, making it a very practical network to use. However, Wi-Fi signals can't go very far through walls, and due to the protocol's extra data overhead, linked devices require a lot more power than other wireless sensor protocols. A change in a key, which is managed by the local router, might easily render previously linked sensors useless. Furthermore, there is no easy way to refresh these keys. Most basic sensors lack an interface like those seen on televisions, computers, cellphones, etc., and instead need a provisioning procedure in order to update the key. Because of this, maintaining and ensuring the dependability of Wi-Fi sensors over time is challenging. In addition, the majority of internet of things (IoT) sensors don't need the enormous data transfer rates that can be achieved through Wi-Fi. As this is the case, it is not well suited for use in simple sensors.

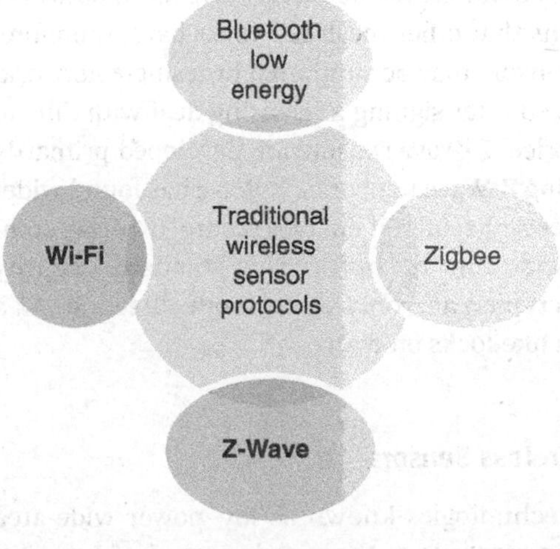

Figure 16.1 Traditional Wireless Sensor Protocols.

Third, there may be a lot [23–29] of interference from these high-bandwidth gadgets. As there are many devices competing for the same RF channels to stream music, video, and other complex data transfers over Wi-Fi, some of them may interfere with other devices that merely need to convey simple messages.

- **Bluetooth Low Energy** is a low-power protocol created to enable periodic low-data-rate wireless communication over short distances. To be more specific, regular Bluetooth is best suited for streaming music to speakers or headsets, whereas BLE is made for wireless sensors that deliver small packets of information. Technology is a low-cost alternative to Wi-Fi that consumes much less power. Nevertheless, BLE's limited range and inability to pass through walls are not its only disadvantages; it may also be disrupted by other 2.4 GHz devices.
- For low-bandwidth wireless sensors, Zigbee's existence as a low-power alternative to Bluetooth and Wi-Fi more than a decade ago has been invaluable. The invention in question is based on the IEEE 802.15.4 standard and transmits data through mesh networks. As a result, Zigbee is often used to enable smart homes with a plethora of low-power devices. As compared to Z-Wave, Zigbee can support an enormously greater number of nodes (65,000+). One limitation of Zigbee is that some nodes must be "on" in order to send data, as was discussed in the section on wireless topologies. Increasing range requires routers, which adds to the cost of setting up the required infrastructure. Mesh networks such as Zigbee, DigiMesh and others are often considered as costly "band-aids" for problems with poor RF performance, and transmission range.
- In the realm of home automation, Z-Wave is a radio standard that has been established. Zensys designed this technology to compete with Zigbee by using the "less noisy" 900 MHz frequency band. Nevertheless, Z-Wave mesh networks are limited by the same restrictions that other mesh networks have; therefore, only a finite number of wireless sensors may be supported by a single network. This technology can only be utilized after signing a licensing deal with Silicon Laboratories, which adds to the price. Z-Wave sensors are developed primarily to ensure compatibility with existing Z-Wave networks. Z-Wave has found widespread use in the home security sector because it enables secure, two-way communication between sensors and control hubs. The standard security mechanisms for homes are unencrypted and only work in one direction. As a result, they are not suited for uses like locks on doors.

16.1.6 LPWAN Standards for Wireless Sensors

Recently, a new class of wireless technologies known as low-power wide-area networks (LPWANs) has emerged in response to the growing trend of Internet-connecting basic devices like sensors and the envisioned internet connection of billions of ordinary things worldwide. LPWANs are a subset of wireless networking used to transmit modest quantities of data across great distances. Because of this, wireless sensors linked to LPWAN networks may save money and [30] energy. Users of LPWANs sacrifice some data transfer speed in exchange for greater wireless sensor deployment range. Companies may get greater returns on investment (ROI) from their IoT projects when they use LPWAN solutions. Nowadays, the industry offers a choice of numerous popular LPWAN protocols. LoRa, Sigfox, and NB-IoT are the most popular and efficient for supporting wireless sensors. LoRa® (long range) is an increasingly popular wireless protocol that can handle more data than Sigfox. Chirp spread spectrum, LoRa's patented modulation strategy, allows for high link margins and access to signals below the RF noise level. Hence, LoRa sensors are able to send bigger data packets across greater distances and in more challenging conditions. LoRaWAN®, a Media Access Control layer specification built atop LoRa modulation methods, is supported by the standard. Wireless sensors in less populated regions may greatly benefit from LoRa networks since they can utilize either public LoRaWAN base stations or private gateways. Companies like MultiTech provide LoRaWAN gateways. These gateways may then be linked to a LoRaWAN server hosted in the cloud. The information is then sent directly to the program. MachineQ, a Comcast subsidiary, offers fully managed gateways and network servers through gateway leasing and monthly fees for active gateway and network server maintenance. NB-IoT standard is the cellular industry's response to LPWAN. NB-IoT delivers low-power devices with low-cost, wide-area coverage. The standard is compatible with LTE base stations in the 200 kHz band and can function autonomously. Narrowband IoT is compatible with both 3G and 4G networks. Radio Bridge, a product line of MultiTech, offers wireless sensor solutions compatible with all of these new protocols and can advise clients on which one is best for their specific needs.

16.1.7 Wireless Sensor Technology Fits into the IoT

With no wires to tangle, the IoT can finally take off. Several large-scale IoT applications across various domains and contexts will be made possible by wireless sensors. With so many sensors to choose from, the IoT has practically limitless potential. WSNs will have a significant influence in many fields, including but not limited to "smart" homes, buildings, cities, agriculture, and supply chain management. Many concrete examples are provided below to highlight the future significance and adaptability of wireless sensors [31–34]. The wireless sensor technology with IoT is shown in Figure 16.2.

- **Connecting everyday objects in smart homes**
  Several wireless sensors may be used to monitor the environment and increase safety in a single dwelling. To keep tabs on when doors and windows are

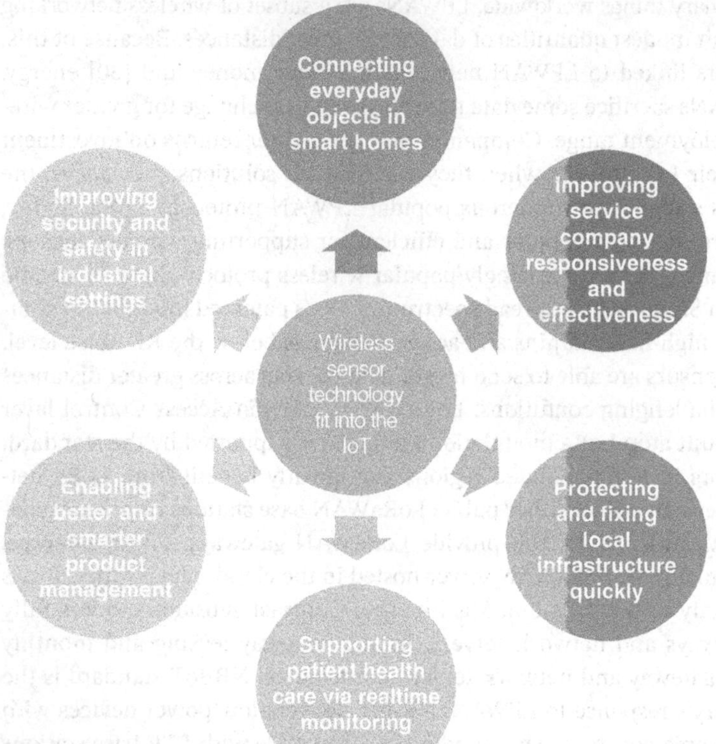

Figure 16.2 Wireless Sensor Technology Fit into the IoT.

opened and closed, a homeowner may choose to set up wireless sensors strategically placed around the property. Similar sensors may monitor the area surrounding safes and filing cabinets to record any intrusions. Wireless dry contact sensors may also be used in doorbells or other remote-control devices to notify homeowners when such buttons are pressed. With the help of wireless water sensors, plumbing problems like dripping faucets or burst pipes may be fixed before water damages valuables like carpets or furniture in the basement [35–37].

- **Improving service company responsiveness and effectiveness**
  Wireless water leak sensors are helpful for both plumbers and insurers. In apartment buildings and condominium communities, plumbers might have these sensors installed to be alerted instantly to any water damage. To reduce the cost of flood damage claims, insurance companies might install leak sensors in people's houses.

- **Supporting patient healthcare via real-time monitoring**
  Particularly useful in assisted living facilities, wireless call buttons may be programmed to alert personnel in the event of an emergency, much like PERS. In the same way that smart houses employ motion detectors to ensure no one leaves while they're away, assisted living facilities can do the same with wireless door or window sensors.
- **Enabling better and smarter product management**
  Security assets in supermarkets and shops may be monitored by a variety of wireless sensors placed strategically throughout the building. Facilities managers can monitor the temperature of refrigeration units and ensure the safety of perishables with the use of wireless air temperature sensors. They can create an efficient cold chain monitoring system by deploying wireless temperature sensors to track the temperature of perishable goods as they move through the supply chain. Wireless vibration sensors are very helpful for people who have big glass window displays, since they can immediately detect glass breakage and alert the proper authorities.
- **Improving security and safety in industrial settings**
  Wireless acceleration-based movement sensors may be installed in automobiles at dealerships, alerting fleet management to any suspicious nighttime motion. In order to keep their workers safe and comfortable in hot warehouses, facility managers might utilize wireless air sensors to determine the heat index. Tilt sensors might also be installed on loading dock doors to monitor their opening and shutting.
- **Preserving and maintaining fragile artwork**
  Wireless humidity sensors may be installed in museums and galleries and monitored by preservationists to provide the optimal environment for preserving antiques and artwork. It is feasible that optical sensors might be utilized to assess illumination levels and optimize the viewing experience for visitors.
- **Protecting and fixing local infrastructure quickly**
  Power providers may monitor transformer breakdowns using high-temperature sensors by mounting them on power poles. They might also set up tilt sensors to notify repair workers if a pole leans or has been hit by a car. These are just some of the many ways that wireless sensors will pave the way for IoT applications. Innovation across sectors and new, beneficial uses for the technology will continue to proliferate over time [38–41].

16.1.8 Healthcare Monitoring Devices

IoT devices provide several new methods for healthcare providers and patients to keep tabs on one another. As a result, the development of wearable IoT devices presents both possibilities and challenges for healthcare providers and their patients.

1. **Remote patient monitoring**
   Patient monitoring from afar (see Figure 16.3) is the primary application area for healthcare IoT devices. IoT devices can automatically gather health indicators like heart rate, BP, temperature, and more from patients who aren't physically present in a healthcare institution, eliminating the need for patients to either go to the doctors or collect the data on their own. When a medical IoT device collects data about a patient, it sends that data to a computer application that can be viewed by both physicians and patients. Algorithms designed for analyzing data might be used to recommend treatments or provide alerts. For instance, if a sensor connected to the internet determines that a patient's heart rate is dangerously low, an alarm may be sounded. Protecting the privacy of patients who rely on remote patient monitoring devices is a top priority [42–45].

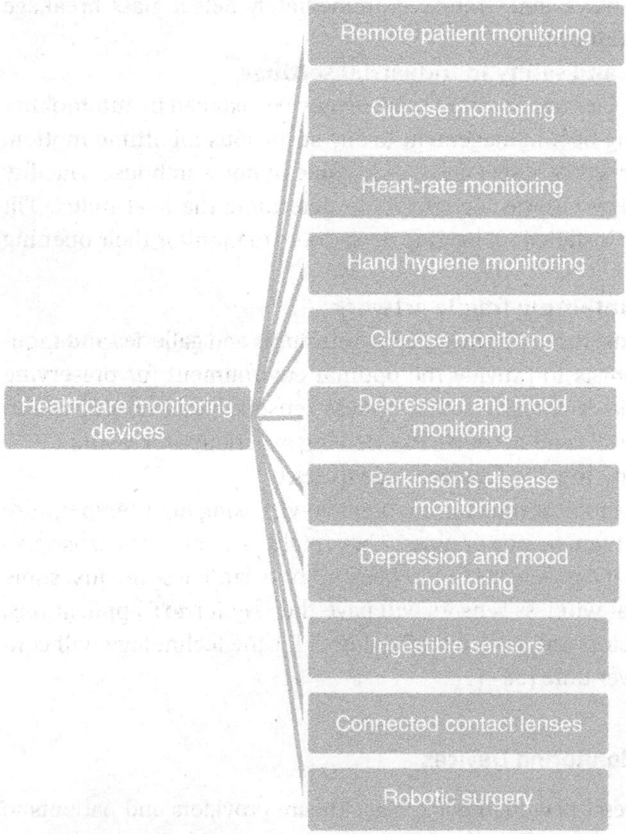

Figure 16.3 Remote patient monitoring.

2. **Glucose monitoring**
More than 30 million people have diabetes, and in the past, it has been difficult to monitor glucose levels. Manually measuring and documenting glucose levels is not only time consuming, but it also gives just a snapshot in time of the patient's glucose levels at the time of the test. Yet, if concentrations are prone to extreme fluctuations, even such frequent assessments may not always indicate an issue. Internet-connected gadgets might help with these problems by continuously and automatically monitoring patients' blood sugar levels. Glucose monitoring devices have the potential to alert patients when their glucose levels are unsafe and cut down on the requirement for constant monitoring and documentation.
3. **Heart-rate monitoring**
Monitoring heart rhythms may be as challenging as monitoring glucose levels, even for patients physically present at medical facilities [46–48]. Periodic heart rate checks cannot guard against sudden fluctuations in heart rates, and traditional methods for continuous cardiac monitoring in hospitals require patients to be attached to wire equipment at all times, restricting their mobility. Heart rates may now be monitored using tiny IoT sensors, giving patients greater mobility while still ensuring ongoing monitoring. While most state-of-the-art equipment can provide 90% accuracy or more, guaranteeing ultra-precise results is still a challenge.
4. **Hand hygiene monitoring**
If everyone at a hospital or other healthcare facility washed their hands often and thoroughly, it may help prevent the spread of illness. To ensure that visitors to patient rooms have washed their hands, the healthcare industry has adopted widespread usage of IoT devices. In addition, the devices might advise on the best ways to practice cleanliness to lessen the risk to a certain patient.

   Their limited effectiveness in encouraging regular hand washing is a major drawback. Yet research suggests that these methods might reduce hospital-acquired illnesses by as much as 60%.
5. **Depression and mood monitoring**
Other sorts of information, such as patient reports of depression and general well-being, have also proved difficult to gather chronically. Healthcare providers may periodically check in to see how their patients are doing, but they can't control their patients' mood changes. Another issue is that patients don't always provide accurate descriptions of their emotional states. The development of "mood-aware" IoT devices might be the solution to this kind of issue. By collecting and analyzing physiological data, such as heart rate and blood pressure, devices may make inferences about a person's mental state. High-tech IoT devices for tracking mental states may keep track of

things like eye movement. The primary issue is that these kinds of tests aren't very good at predicting when depression will come in or if there will be any other cause for concern. Yet, this cannot be accomplished by a regular, in-person mental assessment.

6. **Parkinson's disease monitoring**
It is important for doctors to be able to assess how much their patients' Parkinson's symptoms worsen from day to day. A significant amount of complexity might be removed from keeping track of a patient's Parkinson's disease symptoms with the help of connected sensors capable of doing so in real time. In addition, patients may stay at home and continue with their daily routines thanks to the gadgets, rather than being in the hospital for lengthy periods of time.
7. **Connected inhalers**
Attacks from conditions like asthma or chronic obstructive pulmonary disease (COPD) sometimes come on quickly and without warning. Connected inhalers from the IoT may aid patients by keeping track of how often they have attacks and by gathering environmental data that can be used by doctors to determine what precipitated an episode. Moreover, linked inhalers may notify patients when they use the inhaler incorrectly or forget to bring it with them to bed, without which they would be at danger for an assault.
8. **Ingestible sensors**
Getting readings from within a live thing is often a messy and inconvenient operation. Inserting a camera or probe, for example, into one's belly button is an uncomfortable experience for most people. Swallowable sensors make it possible to acquire data from the digestive system and other organs without causing any harm. They help find the source of internal bleeding, for example, or reveal the pH level of the stomach. The devices should be compact enough to be ingested. It's essential that they decompose, or at least move harmlessly through the body on their own [49, 50]. Numerous companies are now working on edible sensors that will meet these demands.
9. **Connected contact lenses**
The passive, non-invasive collection of healthcare data is aided by wearable technologies like smart contact lenses. Companies like Google have patented "connected" contact lenses, which might include microcameras that would allow wearers to take photos with their eyes. In the medical field and beyond, smart glasses might revolutionize digital interactions by turning the human eye into a powerful tool.
10. **Robotic surgery**
By placing small Internet-connected robots within a patient's body, surgeons are able to perform delicate procedures that would be too taxing for human hands. Using miniature IoT devices, robotic surgery may need fewer incisions, allowing patients to heal more quickly and with less discomfort. Such tools

need to be portable and trustworthy so that processes may be carried out with little disruption. To make the most informed decisions on surgical approach, they must also have the capacity to accurately examine inside body circumstances. Yet, the fact that IoT robots are already being used in surgical procedures shows that these issues can be resolved.

16.1.9 Security Matters for IoT in Healthcare

Critical security concerns must be solved before the healthcare industry can fully benefit from IoT. First and foremost, it is the responsibility of IoT device creators, managers, and healthcare providers to protect the confidentiality of patient data gathered by IoT devices. The majority of the information gathered by medical devices falls within the category of "protected health information" as defined by HIPAA and other laws. As a consequence, if they aren't adequately protected, IoT gadgets might serve as entry points for the theft of confidential information. In fact, 82% of healthcare institutions say that assaults on their IoT devices have occurred. One approach to solving this problem is to provide more secure hardware and software for the IoT. Yet, it is also essential to exercise adequate management over IoT devices in healthcare to prevent sensitive information from unmonitored devices from slipping into the wrong hands. Other potential entry points for attackers include patient monitoring devices running outdated software or firmware or devices that haven't been properly retired once they're no longer required. A healthcare provider's network may be protected against this threat if all IoT devices are discovered and classified correctly. When networks of IoT devices are correctly recognized, categorized, controlled, and protected, managers can monitor device activity to spot outliers, conduct risk assessments, and divide susceptible devices from mission-critical ones [51, 52].

16.1.10 Role of WSN in Healthcare

To transfer sensitive patient data to distant medical institutions for analysis, biosensors are implanted within the human body as part of a WMSN. To put it simply, a WSN is a network of wireless sensors that work together to monitor a certain area without relying on any central processing unit or other external data source [53]. A cooperative system is established to document and track the state of different regions. Healthcare WSNs are used to assess ADLs and collect data for long-term research. With this in mind, it's not hard to understand how WSNs of this kind might likewise provide risks of privacy invasion. Sensors measure patient's heart rate and blood pressure, and the ARDUINO UNO board is part of a high-tech health monitoring system that displays this information to the doctor.

16.1.11 Role of Distributed Optimization for Healthcare

A dispersed system with few tight couplings allows for interchange across healthcare systems and may be utilized to design adaptable infrastructure. The lack of standardized methods for exchanging health records is a major barrier to e-Health service adoption in third-world nations. Healthcare in most poor nations is being forced to adapt to the use of e-Health systems. The purpose of this research is to create a future-proof e-Health system for low-income nations. This study introduces a distributed-memory, heterogeneous-data-handling, loosely coupled e-Health framework. To improve communication across different health information systems (HISs), distributed e-Health was developed according to e-Health standards that are HL7-compliant. In order to ensure that all of a patient's medical records are safe, MPI has been deployed. Security incidents may be managed according to the HL7 specifications. A server-to-server data exchange between two e-Health systems has been carried out, with the findings of the experiments serving as the basis for the work. Using loosely connected technologies, the remote server now has access to the distributed database. It managed a large database in a decentralized fashion and offered e-Health data recovery capabilities as well. The research indicates that the designed system may successfully provide a low-cost service to the target group in a developing nation.

16.2 Literature Review

M. C. Selvi et al. introduced a cloud-based healthcare monitoring system based on wireless sensors. This research presents a collaborative technique for a wirelessly connected AHMS that measures vitals, including temperature, pulse, and movement. On the cloud, we will save information about the patient's health. Healthcare providers may monitor and retrieve patient data from anywhere in the world at any time thanks to the proposed system, which analyzes sensor data and provides real-time monitoring information on a patient's physiological status. It makes it possible to tailor care to each individual [2].

M. Rathika et al. provided work on IoT-based wireless body area networks for healthcare monitoring. Many support vector machine-equipped wearable sensor nodes are introduced in this research, paving the way for WBAN to be put into practice. Several sensor nodes were implanted at various anatomical sites to monitor vital signs, including temperature, BP, HR, ECG, glucose level, and heartbeat. In order to verify the aforementioned deviations, we have built Windows software to show the sensor data. Sensor lifespan and power consumption are both improved by the maximum power point tracking approach enabled by a flexible support vector machine. The suggested system with SVM shows it is feasible to provide round-the-clock healthcare monitoring based on WBAN [4].

V. D. A. Harshan et al. presented work on IoT enablement for WSN in smart healthcare. With the help of an Arduino UNO microcontroller, which can record the patient's heart rate and temperature, the paper proposes a system to construct so that even in the most remote areas without hospitals, patients can still receive first-rate medical care by connecting over the internet and grasping information through the devices included in the kit. In the event of a medical emergency, the system should notify the patient's loved ones and primary care physician of the patient's present condition and comprehensive medical history. Using data mining techniques on the collected information might help evaluate and predict chronic conditions like heart attacks at an early stage, which is important for making decisions [5].

R. Nivetha et al. did research on the state-of-the-art IoT-based health monitoring system. Designed to make daily life easier for the elderly with PHP, you can easily make a user-friendly version of this program. When a doctor isn't available in person, patients may still get help from him or her using this app; they can use the website to report any problems they're having. The doctor then receives the message from the patient and sends his prescription to the patient's cell phone. As a result, monitoring a patient's health entails not just making sure they're taking their medicine as prescribed but also checking in on them occasionally to make sure their ailments are improving. Patient health data may be captured via the use of healthcare IoT applications like mobile medical apps or wearable devices [6].

S. Ali et al. looked at the COVID-19 smart WMSN effect Analysis. This research seeks to analyze a subset of best practices gleaned from the current epidemic, with the overarching goal of using sensor networks to provide high-quality healthcare while reducing the risk of COVID-19 transmission to the general public during treatment [7].

K. Gulati et al. reviewed a complete assessment of the methods used by WSN in IoT. WSN was an integral part of the IoT, which has rapidly spread into many different real-time applications. Every aspect of modern life is touched in some way by the IoT and WSN. As a rule, the "nodes" in a WSN are very compact devices that run on batteries. Thus, the significance of EE data aggregation methods that lengthen the lifetime of the network is paramount. Data aggregation in IoT-WSN systems using low-power methods was discussed. In this study, they take a look back at the research on wireless networking with an emphasis on energy conservation and data pooling [12].

C. A. Subasini et al. reviewed a hybrid CNN to create a WSN-based threat detection platform for healthcare. Several methods were used to evaluate the efficacy of the proposed task, including FSO, PSO, an intelligent opportunistic routing algorithm, an independent component analysis based on Jensen-Shannon divergences, and a WSN that relies on RF identification. As compared to conventional methods, the suggested study may boost throughput by as much as 3.2 times while simultaneously doubling the lifespan of the underlying network [13].

R. K. Garg et al. focused on the mountaineers' health being monitored through low-power WSNs. The goal of this work was to provide a solution for mountaineers' healthcare problems both in a "regular" situation where Wi-Fi is available and in a "hidden" one where it is not. The electronic system suggested here makes use of low-power consumption chips that can operate at temperatures as low as −40 °C. Using innovations in WSN, LoRa, and satellite modems, this system collects data on vital signs and transmits it to a command center. The electrical system has a specific function that will activate Op-Mode-5 and transfer data at optimal power to the master node if victims are accidentally buried. Technology aids in the consistent evaluation of mountaineers' health, which is crucial for the timely execution of search and rescue operations and the saving of lives [14].

S. Anitha et al. introduced healthcare node replication attack detection with intelligence-based security monitoring approaches for WSNs. Intelligent healthcare monitoring systems were protected against replication attacks thanks to the new security measures. Potential applications of the presented approaches, such as the EMABRD, SACOP, and FZKA, were shown in a real-time setting. In a comparison of three algorithms, SACOP outperforms EMABRD and FZKA in terms of detecting malicious nodes, but at the cost of greater storage and communication overheads. In terms of detection probability, FZKA outperforms EMABRD, albeit at the expense of greater overheads. Thus, EMABRD has lower overheads, and SACOP has higher detection probabilities than the other two methods [15].

M. B. Mohamed et al. looked at safe and reliable machine learning-based illness detection in healthcare WSNs. In this research, they offer a method that is both secure and low-energy. Our studies provide light on the use of ECG, EMG, and BP for illness diagnosis, and they do it in a secure manner by using AES and SHA. Moreover, a classification approach based on supervised ML techniques was employed to reach a respectable range of reliability. Simulation results showed a 97% accuracy and 92% sensitivity for the system, resulting in a very secure system. To further confirm our proposal's viability in practice, they created a prototype for use by medical professionals [24].

A. Koren et al. focused on the privacy and data integrity of IoT-generated health data in 6G-Era EHRs. In this study, we'll examine the privacy and safety concerns associated with such a procedure. The report opens with a detailed inventory of the dangers inherent in centralized health information system's data gathering and storage processes, then moves on to discuss the difficulties in designing a secure system and concludes with suggestions for how to deal with the problems that have been identified both before and after the introduction of 6G networks [25].

Table 16.1 shows the overview of the literature review.

Table 16.1 Literature review.

Reference no.	Author/Year	Objective	Methodology	Limitation
[2]	M. Chengathir Selvi/2017	Using cloud computing and wireless sensors, a healthcare monitoring system	Healthcare, wireless sensor	Scope of this research is very less
[4]	M. Rathika/2017	Connected devices in healthcare monitoring using a wireless body area network	HealthCare, IoT	Lack of efficiency
[5]	V. Dini Aadhithya Harshan/2020	Facilitating IoT-based WSN for efficient medical care	WSN, Healthcare, IoT	Need to improve the performance and accuracy
[6]	R. Nivetha/2020	Smart health monitoring system based on the IoT for the elderly and the handicapped.	Healthcare, IoT	Need to consider optimization technique
[7]	S. Ali/2020	Covid-19: a literature study on the use of intelligent WMSN	Wireless medical sensor network	Research is limited to traffic flow
[12]	K. Gulati/2021	Using WSN in the IoT: A literature review	Internet of Things, WSN	There is less technical work
[13]	C. A. Subasini/2021	Convolutional neural network hybrids are being developed into a framework for detecting attacks on healthcare applications that rely on wireless sensor networks.	WSN, healthcare	Lack of security and accuracy
[14]	R. K. Garg/2021	Low-power WSN for mountaineers' health monitoring	Healthcare, WSN	This work is not long-lasting work

(Continued)

Table 16.1 (Continued)

Reference no.	Author/Year	Objective	Methodology	Limitation
[15]	S. Anitha/2021	Healthcare node replication attack detection using WSN using an intelligence-based monitoring approach	WSN, healthcare	Lack of technical work
[24]	M. B. Mohamed/ 2022	Safe and reliable ML-based illness diagnosis in WMSN	ML, WSN	Need to consider optimization technique
[25]	A. Koren/2022	Protecting personal information in the age of 6G for IoT health data in HER	IoT health data	Did not consider real-life solution

16.3 Challenges Faced by Existing Research

A considerable number of research have been conducted on the issue of wireless sensor-based IoT systems with distributed optimization for healthcare applications. The longevity of WSN has been the subject of investigation in a few research. Yet, there hasn't been a lot of research done in this area. While choosing cluster heads, one must prioritize methods that are both energy efficient and have a high throughput. The proportion of dropped calls and the associated delays are also crucial considerations. This may include using an optimization method.

16.4 Proposed Research Methodology

Consideration was given to previous research on IoT, WSN, optimization, healthcare systems, and related topics. The lifetime of the WSN and the current wireless sensor-based IoT mechanism are the primary areas of study at the moment. WSN resilience is improved by using the distributed optimization mechanism built into the IoT architecture. The ability to save energy is a must for any system that is both efficient and high throughput. When these factors are considered, the suggested model can be compared to an existing wireless sensor-based IoT procedure. This analysis incorporates prior work done on WSN, IoT, and the factors that determine the longevity of WSNs. Previous research concerns, such as latency and throughput, will be considered alongside problems like call drop % and energy

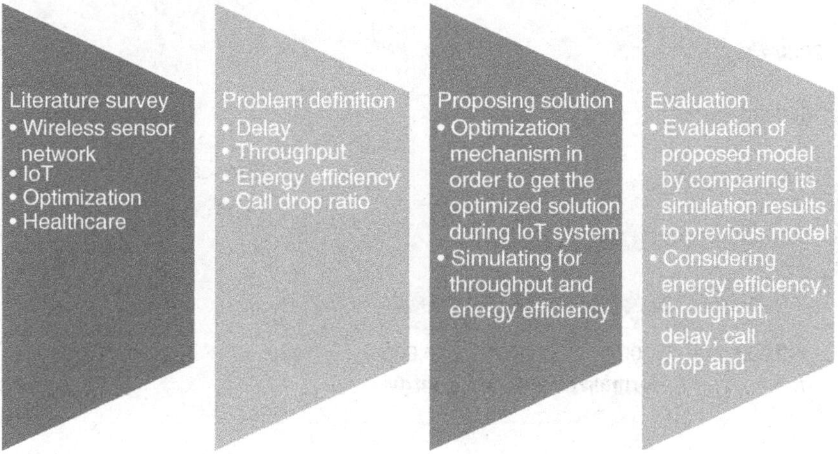

Figure 16.4 Process flow research methodology.

efficiency. In this endeavor, we would use algorithms that mimic those found in nature to get the best outcome possible. A deep learning model would also be used to train a WSN cluster head selection algorithm. Simulation outcomes would be compared if the conventional wireless sensor-based IoT system and healthcare models were used. The process flow of the research methodology is shown in Fig. 16.4.

16.5 Simulation of Research

The proposed methodology has been proven to be more energy-efficient than current techniques through simulations of cluster head selection.

16.5.1 Comparative Analysis of Energy Efficiency

Table 16.2 and Figure 16.5 display the results of a comparison between the proposed approach and the conventional one in terms of energy efficiency.

The graph (Figure 16.5) shows the normalized network energy with respect to the number of rounds.

16.5.2 Comparative Analysis of Delay

Table 16.3 and Figure 16.6 show that the new optimization technique has a shorter lag time than the previous one.

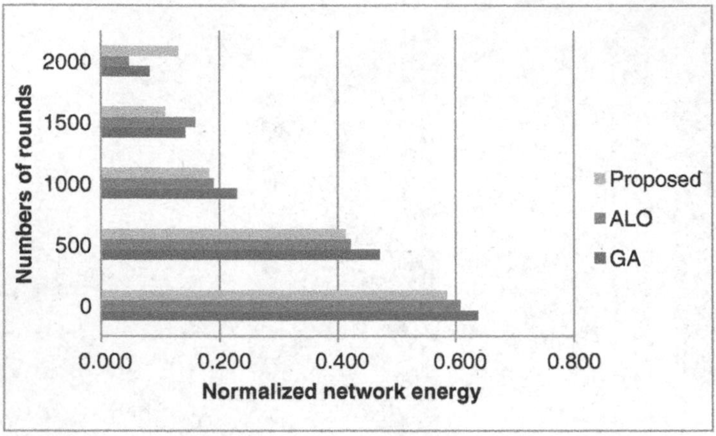

Figure 16.5 Comparison of normalized network energy.

Table 16.2 Comparison of energy efficiency.

Number of rounds	GA	ALO	Proposed
100	0.638	0.608	0.584
500	0.471	0.422	0.413
1000	0.229	0.190	0.183
1500	0.142	0.159	0.108
2000	0.083	0.048	0.131

Table 16.3 Comparison of delay.

Iteration	GA	ALO	Proposed
1	1.20076	0.736824	0.444515
2	2.282083	1.648078	1.054271
3	3.57766	2.804975	2.015148
4	4.821176	3.900637	3.450754
5	5.824493	5.070901	4.685391
6	6.788329	6.518903	5.632187
7	7.489426	7.050917	6.876205
8	9.186771	9.534296	8.490216
9	9.994942	9.757957	8.790192
10	10.84329	11.26117	10.1788

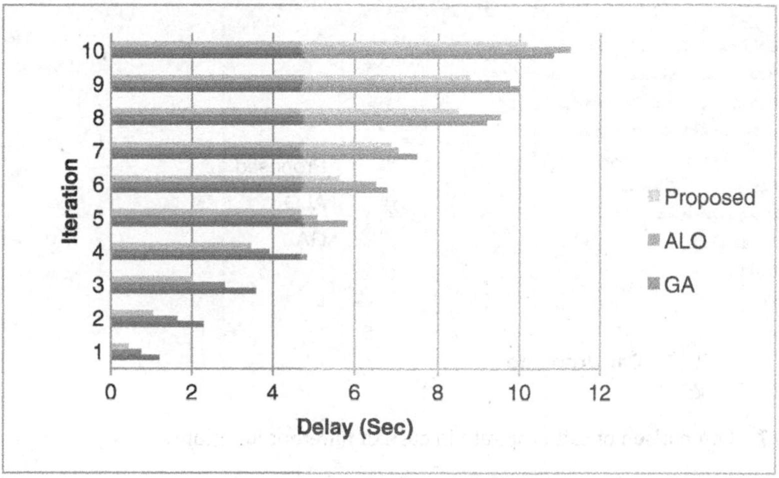

Figure 16.6 Comparison of delay in case of different iteration.

We provide the delay graph (Figure 16.6) for different iteration counts.

16.5.3 Comparative Analysis of Call Drop

The percentage of dropped calls between the old optimization process and the new one is shown in Table 16.4 and Figure 16.7.

A scatter plot depicting the call-drop percentage vs iteration count is shown in Figure 16.7.

Table 16.4 Comparison of call drop.

Iteration	GA	ALO	Proposed
1	0.383421	0.238194	0.097042
2	0.745196	0.618174	0.618908
3	1.118333	1.053265	1.039166
4	1.516095	1.469278	1.397629
5	1.947186	1.678192	1.601107
6	2.421427	2.197242	2.10632
7	2.768968	2.491272	2.490921
8	3.192165	3.010557	2.811987
9	3.51121	3.568368	3.429105
10	3.896592	3.94274	3.717517

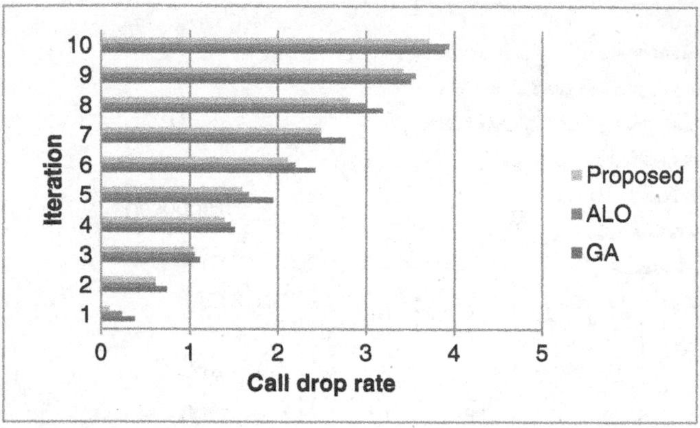

Figure 16.7 Comparison of call drop rate in case of different iterations.

16.5.4 Comparative Analysis of Throughput

Table 16.5 and Figure 16.8 demonstrate how the new method outperforms the current optimization procedure in terms of output.

Figure 16.8 shows a throughput graph for several iterations using data from Table 16.5.

Table 16.5 Comparison of throughput

Iteration	GA	ALO	Proposed
1	0.5960538	0.5994871	0.8203661
2	0.7368643	1.1474388	1.1076246
3	1.1374837	1.4581735	1.5350822
4	1.5647779	1.9181912	2.0441033
5	1.9877305	2.3216772	2.4930626
6	2.3269945	2.3978444	2.5456883
7	2.7958929	3.0398412	3.1721373
8	3.1887952	3.5700952	3.6239418
9	3.614217	3.6758767	3.680147
10	4.0237015	4.0501941	4.083073

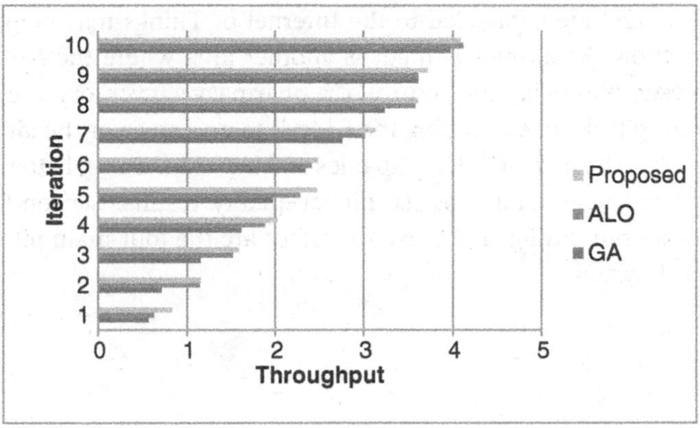

Figure 16.8 Comparison of throughput in case of different iterations.

16.6 Conclusion

An IoT WSN is a collection of sensors that are geographically dispersed and dedicated to monitoring and recording environmental conditions. These sensors then collectively transmit this information to an internet-based location via a wireless network. In addition to monitoring the health of patients, there are many other areas in which gadgets connected to the IoT may be extremely helpful in hospitals. The location of medical devices in real time may be tracked with the help of IoT devices that have been fitted with sensors. Wheelchairs, oxygen pumps, defibrillators, nebulizers, and other monitoring equipment fall into this category. Nonetheless, it has been noticed that the healthcare environment requires dispersed optimization [54, 55]. This requirement should not be ignored. It might be difficult to implement healthcare applications in IoT systems that are based on WSN. Hence, more traditional research in the fields of WSN-based IoT and healthcare is being investigated, utilizing a variety of study approaches.

16.7 Future Scope

With the use of IoT-enabled home monitoring devices and medical IoT wearables, doctors can keep closer tabs on their patients' well-being. The information collected by IoT healthcare devices may aid in the diagnosis and monitoring of patients. IoT use in the medical industry is skyrocketing. Medical gadgets that track a patient's hygiene and are connected to the Internet of Things may help reduce the risk of infection. Asset management is another area where the IoT comes in handy, with examples being the control of a pharmacy's inventory and environmental monitoring tasks like checking the fridge's temperature or the air conditioner's settings. With the help of IoT, companies and individuals may better interact with their environments and produce higher-quality results. Sensors/devices, connections, data processing, and a user interface are the four main pillars of an end-to-end IoT system.

References

1 Keserwani, H., Rastogi, H., Kurniullah, A.Z. et al. (2022). Security enhancement by identifying attacks using machine learning for 5G network. *Int. J. Commun. Networks and Info. Secur.* 14 (2): 124–141. https://doi.org/10.17762/ijcnis.v14i2.5494.

2 Chengathir Selvi, M., Rajeeve, T.D., Antony, A.J.P., and Prathiba, T. (2017). Wireless sensor based healthcare monitoring system using cloud. *Proc. Int. Conf. Inventive Syst. Control* 2017: 1–6. https://doi.org/10.1109/ICISC.2017.8068710.

3 Gupta, N., Janani, S., Dilip, R. et al. (2022). Wearable sensors for evaluation over smart home using sequential minimization optimization-based random forest. *Int. J. Commun. Networks Inf. Secur.* 14 (2): 179–188. https://doi.org/10.17762/ijcnis.v14i2.5499.

4 Rathika, M. (2017). A health care monitoring system with wireless body area network using IoT. *Int. J. Recent Trends Eng. Res.* 3 (11): 112–117. https://doi.org/10.23883/ijrter.2017.3499.edo9r.

5 Aadhithya, D., Harshan, V., Bala Subramanian, R. et al. (2020). Enabling wireless sensor networks for smart healthcare using IoT. *Int. J. Sci. Technol. Res.* 9 (3): 6647–6649.

6 Nivetha, R., Preethi, S., Priyadharshini, P. et al. (2020). Smart health monitoring system using iot for assisted living of senior and challenged people. *Int. J. Sci. Technol. Res.* 9 (2): 4285–4288.

7 Ali, S., Singh, R.P., Javaid, M. et al. (2020). A review of the role of smart wireless medical sensor network in covid-19. *J. Ind. Integr. Manage.* 5 (4): 413–425. https://doi.org/10.1142/S2424862220300069.

8 Kelly, J.T., Campbell, K.L., Gong, E., and Scuffham, P. (2020). The internet of things: impact and implications for health care delivery. *J. Med. Internet Res.* 22 (11): https://doi.org/10.2196/20135.

9 Hameed, K., Bajwa, I.S., Ramzan, S. et al. (2020). An intelligent IoT based healthcare system using fuzzy neural networks. *Sci. Program.* 2020: https://doi.org/10.1155/2020/8836927.

10 Shakeri, M., Sadeghi-Niaraki, A., Choi, S.M., and Riazul Islam, S.M. (2020). Performance analysis of iot-based health and environment wsn deployment. *Sensors (Switzerland)* 20 (20): 1–22. https://doi.org/10.3390/s20205923.

11 Gardašević, G., Katzis, K., Bajić, D., and Berbakov, L. (2020). Emerging wireless sensor networks and internet of things technologies—foundations of smart healthcare. *Sensors (Switzerland)* 20 (13): 1–30. https://doi.org/10.3390/s20133619.

12 Gulati, K., Kumar Boddu, R.S., Kapila, D. et al. (2021). A review paper on wireless sensor network techniques in Internet of Things (IoT). *Mater. Today Proc.* 51 (xxxx): 161–165. https://doi.org/10.1016/j.matpr.2021.05.067.

13 Subasini, C.A., Karuppiah, S.P., Sheeba, A., and Padmakala, S. (2021). Developing an attack detection framework for wireless sensor network-based healthcare applications using hybrid convolutional neural network. *Trans. Emerging Telecommun. Technol.* 32 (11): 1–17. https://doi.org/10.1002/ett.4336.

14 Garg, R.K., Bhola, J., and Soni, S.K. (2021). Healthcare monitoring of mountaineers by low power Wireless Sensor Networks. *Inf. Med. Unlocked* 27: 100775. https://doi.org/10.1016/j.imu.2021.100775.

15 Anitha, S., Jayanthi, P., and Chandrasekaran, V. (2021). An intelligent based healthcare security monitoring schemes for detection of node replication attack in wireless sensor networks. *Meas.: J. Int. Meas. Confederation* 167: 108272. https://doi.org/10.1016/j.measurement.2020.108272.

16 Baghezza, R., Bouchard, K., Bouzouane, A., and Gouin-Vallerand, C. (2021). From offline to real-time distributed activity recognition in wireless sensor networks for healthcare: a review. *Sensors* 21 (8): 1–34. https://doi.org/10.3390/s21082786.

17 Li, X. and Du, L. (2021). Review on the optimization of medical supplies distribution under major public health emergencies. *IOP Conf. Ser.: Earth Environ. Sci* 820 (1): https://doi.org/10.1088/1755-1315/820/1/012031.

18 Yang, Y., Dong, L., Rong, H., and Wu, J. (2021). Optimization on medical material distribution management system based on artificial intelligence robot. *J. Healthcare Eng.* 2021: https://doi.org/10.1155/2021/5511299.

19 Euchi, J., Zidi, S., and Laouamer, L. (2021). A new distributed optimization approach for home healthcare routing and scheduling problem. *Decis. Sci. Lett.* 10 (3): 217–230. https://doi.org/10.5267/j.dsl.2021.4.003.

20 Gope, P., Gheraibia, Y., Kabir, S., and Sikdar, B. (2021). A secure IoT-based modern healthcare system with fault-tolerant decision making process. *IEEE J. Biomed. Health. Inf.* 25 (3): 862–873. https://doi.org/10.1109/JBHI.2020.3007488.

21 Veeraiah, V., Gangavathi, P., Ahamad, S. et al. (2022). Enhancement of meta verse capabilities by IoT integration. In: *2022 2nd International Conference on Advance Computing and Innovative Technologies in Engineering (ICACITE)*, 1493–1498. https://doi.org/10.1109/ICACITE53722.2022.9823766.

22 Tiwari, D., Prasad, D., Guleria, K., and Ghosh, P. (2021). IoT based smart healthcare monitoring systems: a review. In: *Proceedings of IEEE International Conference on Signal Processing, Computing and Control, 2021-October(December)*, 465–469. https://doi.org/10.1109/ISPCC53510.2021.9609393.

23 Doshi, H. and Shankar, A. (2021). Wireless Sensor Network application for IoT-based healthcare system. In: *Data Driven Approach Towards Disruptive Technologies. Studies in Autonomic, Data-driven and Industrial Computing*, vol. 5(2), (ed. T.P. Singh, R. Tomar, T. Choudhury, et al.), 287–307. Singapore: Springer https://doi.org/10.1007/978-981-15-9873-9_24.

24 Mohamed, M.B., Meddeb-Makhlouf, A., Fakhfakh, A., and Kanoun, O. (2022). Secure and reliable ML-based disease detection for a medical wireless body sensor networks. *Int. J. Biol. Biomed. Eng.* 16: 196–206. https://doi.org/10.46300/91011.2022.16.26.

25 Koren, A. and Prasad, R. (2022). IoT Health data in electronic health records (EHR): security and privacy issues in Era of 6G. *J. ICT Stand.* 10 (1): 63–84. https://doi.org/10.13052/jicts2245-800X.1014.

26 Kaur, P., Saini, H.S., and Kaur, B. (2022). Modelling of IoT-WSN enabled ECG monitoring system for patient queue updation. *Int. J. Adv. Compu. Sci. Appl.* 13 (8): 298–304. https://doi.org/10.14569/IJACSA.2022.0130835.

27 Satyanarayana, T.V.V., Mohana Roopa, Y., Maheswari, M. et al. (2022). A secured IoT-based model for human health through sensor data. *Meas.: Sens.* 24 (August): 100516. https://doi.org/10.1016/j.measen.2022.100516.

28 Nourildean, S.W., Hassib, M.D., and Mohammed, Y.A. (2022). Internet of things based wireless sensor network: a review. *Indone. J. Electric. Eng. Comput. Sci.* 27 (1): 246, 246–261. https://doi.org/10.11591/ijeecs.v27.i1, 261.

29 Gupta, R., Singh, V., Nassa, K. et al. (2021). Investigating application and challenges of big data analytics with clustering. *Int. Conf. Adv. Electric. Electron. Commun. Comput. Autom.* 2021: 1–6. https://doi.org/10.1109/ICAECA52838.2021.9675483.

30 Veeraiah, V., Khan, H., Kumar, A. et al. (2022). Integration of PSO and deep learning for trend analysis of meta-verse. In: *2022 2nd International Conference on Advance Computing and Innovative Technologies in Engineering (ICACITE)*, 713–718. https://doi.org/10.1109/ICACITE53722.2022.9823883.

31 Anand, R., Shrivastava, G., Gupta, S. et al. (2018). Audio watermarking with reduced number of random samples. In: *Handbook of Research on Network Forensics and Analysis Techniques*, 372–394. IGI Global.

32 Meelu, R. and Anand, R. (2010)). Energy efficiency of cluster-based routing protocols used in wireless sensor networks. In: *AIP Conference Proceedings*, vol. 1324, No. 1, 109–113. American Institute of Physics.

33 Pandey, B.K. et al. (2023). Effective and secure transmission of health information using advanced morphological component analysis and image hiding. In: *Artificial Intelligence on Medical Data*, Lecture Notes in Computational Vision and Biomechanics, vol. 37 (ed. M. Gupta, S. Ghatak, A. Gupta, and A.L. Mukherjee). Singapore: Springer https://doi.org/10.1007/978-981-19-0151-5_19.

34 Veeraiah, V., Kumar, K.R., LalithaKumari, P. et al. (2022). Application of biometric system to enhance the security in virtual world. In: *2022 2nd International Conference on Advance Computing and Innovative Technologies in Engineering (ICACITE)*, 719–723. https://doi.org/10.1109/ICACITE53722.2022.9823850.

35 Bansal, R., Gupta, A., Singh, R., and Nassa, V.K. (2021). Role and impact of digital technologies in E-learning amidst COVID-19 pandemic. In: *2021 Fourth International Conference on Computational Intelligence and Communication Technologies (CCICT)*, 194–202. https://doi.org/10.1109/CCICT53244.2021.00046.

36 Shukla, A., Ahamad, S., Rao, G.N. et al. (2021). Artificial Intelligence Assisted IoT Data Intrusion Detection. In: *2021 4th International Conference on Computing and Communications Technologies (ICCCT)*, 330–335. https://doi.org/10.1109/ICCCT53315.2021.9711795.

37 Pathania, V. et al. (2023). A database application of monitoring COVID-19 in India. In: *Artificial Intelligence on Medical Data*, Lecture Notes in Computational Vision and Biomechanics, vol. 37 (ed. M. Gupta, S. Ghatak, A. Gupta, and A.L. Mukherjee). Singapore: Springer https://doi.org/10.1007/978-981-19-0151-5_23.

38 Dushyant, K., Muskan, G., Annu et al. (2022). Utilizing machine learning and deep learning in cybesecurity: an innovative approach. In: *Cyber Security and Digital Forensics: Challenges and Future Trends*, 271–293. Wiley https://doi.org/10.1002/9781119795667.ch12.

39 Babu, S.Z.D. et al. (2023). Analysation of big data in smart healthcare. In: *Artificial Intelligence on Medical Data*, Lecture Notes in Computational Vision and Biomechanics, vol. 37 (ed. M. Gupta, S. Ghatak, A. Gupta, and A.L. Mukherjee). Singapore: Springer https://doi.org/10.1007/978-981-19-0151-5_21.

40 Gupta, A., Anand, R., Pandey, D. et al. (2021). Prediction of breast cancer using extremely randomized clustering forests (ERCF) technique: prediction of breast cancer. *Int. J. Distrib. Syst. Technol.* 12 (4): 1–15.

41 Bansal, B., Jenipher, V.N., Jain, R. et al. (2022). Big data architecture for network security. In: *Cyber Security and Network Security*, 233–267. Wiley https://doi.org/10.1002/9781119812555.ch11.

42 Gupta, A., Kaushik, D., Garg, M., and Verma, A. (2020). Machine learning model for breast cancer prediction. In: *2020 Fourth International Conference on I-SMAC (IoT in Social, Mobile, Analytics and Cloud) (I-SMAC)*, 472–477. https://doi.org/10.1109/I-SMAC49090.2020.9243323.

43 Sreekanth, N., Rama Devi, J., Shukla, A. et al. (2022). Evaluation of estimation in software development using deep learning-modified neural network. *Appl. Nanosci.* https://doi.org/10.1007/s13204-021-02204-9.

44 Veeraiah, V., Rajaboina, N.B., Rao, G.N. et al. (2022). Securing Online Web Application for IoT Management. In: *2022 2nd International Conference on Advance Computing and Innovative Technologies in Engineering (ICACITE)*, 1499–1504. https://doi.org/10.1109/ICACITE53722.2022.9823733.

45 Anand, R., Singh, J., Pandey, D. et al. (2022). Modern technique for interactive communication in LEACH-based Ad Hoc wireless sensor network. In: *Software Defined Networking for Ad Hoc Networks*, 55–73. Cham: Springer.

46 Pandey, D., Pandey, B.K., Wariya, S. et al. (2020). Analysis of text detection, extraction and recognition from complex degraded images and videos. *J. Crit. Rev.* 7 (18): 427–433.

47 Sharma, G., Nehra, N., Dahiya, A. et al. (2022). Automatic heart-rate measurement using facial video. In: *Networking Technologies in Smart Healthcare*, 289–307. CRC Press.

48 Govindaraj, V., Dhanasekar, S., Martinsagayam, K. et al. (2023). Low-power test pattern generator using modified LFSR. *Aerosp. Syst.* 1–8.

49 Arora, S., Sharma, S., and Anand, R. (2022, July). A survey on UWB textile antenna for wireless body area network (WBAN) applications. In: *Artificial Intelligence on Medical Data: Proceedings of International Symposium, ISCMM 2021*, 173–183. Singapore: Springer Nature Singapore.

50 Gupta, A., Asad, A., Meena, L., and Anand, R. (2022). IoT and RFID-based smart card system integrated with health care, electricity, QR and banking sectors. In: *Artificial Intelligence on Medical Data: Proceedings of International Symposium, ISCMM 2021*, 253–265. Singapore: Springer Nature Singapore.

51 Sharma, R., Vashisth, R., and Sindhwani, N. (2023). Study and analysis of classification techniques for specific plant growths. In: *Advances in Signal Processing, Embedded Systems and IoT: Proceedings of Seventh ICMEET-2022*, 591–605. Singapore: Springer Nature Singapore.

52 Chaudhary, A., Bodala, D., Sindhwani, N., and Kumar, A. (2022)). Analysis of customer loyalty using artificial neural networks. In: *In 2022 International Mobile and Embedded Technology Conference (MECON)*, 181–183. IEEE.

53 Bommareddy, S., Khan, J.A., and Anand, R. (2022). A review on healthcare data privacy and security. *Networking Techno. Smart Healthcare* 165–187.

54 Anand, R. and Chawla, P. (2020). A novel dual-wideband inscribed hexagonal fractal slotted microstrip antenna for C-and X-band applications. *Int. J. RF Microwave Comput. Aided Eng.* 30 (9): e22277.

55 Anand, R. and Chawla, P. (2020). Optimization of inscribed hexagonal fractal slotted microstrip antenna using modified lightning attachment procedure optimization. *Int. J. Microwave Wireless Technolog.* 12 (6): 519–530.

17

Optimizing Financial Transactions and Processes Through the Power of Distributed Systems

K. Bhavana Raj[1], Kamakshi Mehta[2], Someshwar Siddi[3], M.K. Sharma[4], Dilip K. Sharma[5], Sunil Adhav[6], and José L.A. Gonzáles[7]

[1]*Department of Management Studies, Institute of Public Enterprise, Hyderabad, India*
[2]*TAPMI School of Business, Manipal University, Jaipur, Rajasthan, India*
[3]*St. Martin's Engineering College, Secunderabad, Telangana, India*
[4]*Department of Mathematics, Chaudhary Charan Singh University, Meerut, Uttar Pradesh, India*
[5]*Department of Mathematics, Jaypee University of Engineering and Technology, Guna, Madhya Pradesh, India*
[6]*Faculty of Management (PG), Dr. Vishwanath Karad, MIT World Peace University, Pune, Maharashtra, India*
[7]*Department of Business, Pontifical Catholic University of Peru, Lima, Peru*

17.1 Introduction

Multiple computers can work together as one system thanks to a type of computing architecture called distributed systems (DSs). The increased speed, efficiency, and security this offers financial transactions (FT) can be very advantageous. Traditional systems can't handle FT as quickly or as reliably as DSs can, which reduces the chance of fraud or mistakes. Blockchain technology (BT), which serves as the basis for digital currencies like Bitcoin and Ethereum, is among the most well-known instances of distributed networks in the world of finance. This has made it a seductive alternative for financial organizations looking to increase the security and transparency of their transactions. Blockchain, however, is only one type of DS used in finance. Peer-to-peer networks and cloud computing are two additional technologies that are used to streamline financial processes. Through the use of these technologies, FT can be made faster, more effective, and more secure, from risk management to payment processing. DSs can easily handle millions of transactions

Meta-Heuristic Algorithms for Advanced Distributed Systems, First Edition. Edited by Rohit Anand, Abhinav Juneja, Digvijay Pandey, Sapna Juneja, and Nidhi Sindhwani.

per second, whereas traditional financial systems are frequently constrained by their ability to handle small volumes of transactions. These characteristics make them perfect for high-volume applications like stock trading, where even a small delay can have significant financial repercussions. The ability of DSs to function in a decentralized fashion is another benefit. Commonly, a single organization centrally manages traditional financial systems. This may lead to flaws and inefficiencies because the system's security depends on the organization in charge of it. Contrarily, decentralized DSs work without a single entity in charge. They become more resistant to attacks and less prone to single points of failure as a result. The world of finance is changing as a result of DSs' improved speed, efficiency, and security in conducting FT. As these technologies advance and become more sophisticated, we might expect to see even more cutting-edge applications in the future [1, 2].

17.1.1 Importance of Distributed Systems

The DS is important in many ways [3–5]:

- *Increased Security*: DSs are designed to provide high levels of security by using encryption and cryptographic techniques to protect against fraud and cyberattacks, since an attacker would need to compromise multiple nodes to gain control of the system.
- *Improved Efficiency*: DSs can process FT and processes much more efficiently than traditional centralized systems. By leveraging the computing power of multiple nodes, DSs can handle large volumes of transactions and process them in near real-time, improving efficiency and reducing processing times.
- *Increased Resilience*: DSs are more resilient than centralized systems since they are designed to continue operating even if some of the nodes in the system fail. This means that the system can continue to operate even in the event of hardware or software failures, providing greater reliability and uptime.
- *Improved Transparency*: The use of DSs in finance can provide significant benefits in terms of security, efficiency, resilience, and transparency, making it an increasingly important area of focus for financial institutions.

17.2 Overview of Financial Transactions and Processes

The terms "FT and processes" refer to the actions taken in the management and exchange of money, such as loans, investments, and payments. The following types of FT and processes can be categorized:

Payment transactions, which involve the exchange of money between two or more parties, are a crucial component of contemporary commerce. Credit card payments, wire transfers, and online payments are just a few of the different ways that these transactions can be made. One of the most popular methods of payment is credit card transactions, which let customers buy things without carrying cash. For bigger payments, like those for business or real estate deals, wire transfers are a common choice. In recent years, online payments have grown in popularity. Many customers now use services like PayPal or Venmo to make purchases or send money to friends and family. Money is borrowed or lent in loan transactions like mortgages, personal loans, and business loans. A typical loan used to buy real estate is a mortgage. Large purchases, including cars and home renovations, are frequently financed by personal loans. Businesses can finance their operations, grow their facilities, or buy equipment with the help of business loans. The interest rate and terms of repayment are typically set by the lender, and loans are typically repaid with interest over a predetermined period. Important facets of contemporary finance include loan transactions, investment transactions, and payment transactions. Anyone wishing to successfully navigate the complicated world of finance must have a thorough understanding of these transactions and how they operate. The main problems with FT and its procedures are fraud, errors, delays, and excessive costs. Using traditional centralized systems can be difficult because they are frequently slow, expensive, and prone to fraud, making it difficult to ensure the security and integrity of FT and processes. These issues may be resolved and FT and procedures improved by modern technologies like DSs. These innovations can improve FT and process transparency, uphold security, cut costs, and foster effectiveness [6, 7].

17.2.1 Definition of Financial Transactions and Processes

The exchange, management, and handling of money are referred to as FT and processes. A wide range of activities, including payments, investments, loans, and financial reporting, can be included in them. FT typically entails the exchange of money between two or more parties, as well as the possible exchange of goods or services in exchange for cash. The different types of them include loan transactions, investment transactions, and payment transactions. The term "financial processes" describes the full range of actions taken in the management of finances [8].

17.2.2 Challenges Faced in Financial Transactions and Processes

FT and processes can be complex and involve many parties, which can lead to a number of challenges. Here are some of the main challenges faced in FT and processes [9, 10]:

1. *Fraud*: FT are susceptible to fraud, including phishing scams, identity theft, and counterfeiting. Fraud can cause financial loss for people and enterprises, as well as reputational harm.

2. *Errors*: Errors can occur during FT, such as mistakes in account numbers, incorrect amounts, or typos in personal information. These errors can lead to delays in processing, additional costs, and even financial loss.
3. *Delays*: FT can take time to process, especially when they involve multiple parties, such as in cross-border payments. Delays can result in additional costs, loss of business, and reduced customer satisfaction.
4. *High costs*: Traditional FT can be expensive, with high fees for services such as wire transfers and foreign currency exchange. These costs can be a barrier for individuals and businesses, especially those in developing countries.
5. *Lack of transparency*: In some FT and processes, there can be a lack of transparency, with limited visibility into the transaction details and the parties involved. This can make it difficult to identify fraudulent activities and ensure compliance with regulations.
6. *Security*: Security breaches can result in financial loss, identity theft, and damage to the reputation of individuals and businesses.

17.3 Distributed Systems in Finance

DS has an increasingly important role in finance, providing a range of benefits over traditional centralized systems. DSs are networks of computers that work together to achieve a common goal. They allow for decentralized decision making, fault tolerance, and increased security and transparency, which can be particularly beneficial for FT and processes. Here are some of the main ways in which DSs are being used in finance [11–13]:

- *Decentralization*: DSs are decentralized, meaning that there is no central point of control. Instead, the system is made up of multiple nodes that work together to process transactions and make decisions. Decentralization can also increase efficiency, as transactions can be processed faster and more securely without the need for intermediaries.
- *Cryptocurrencies*: To protect and verify transactions, cryptocurrencies, which are digital or virtual tokens, use cryptography. Cryptocurrencies have the potential to reduce transaction costs by enhancing security, transparency, and financial inclusion for both consumers and companies.
- *Financial Inclusion*: By granting access to financial services to people and companies that are underserved by conventional banking institutions, DSs have the potential to improve financial inclusion. DSs can increase access to financial services for people who would otherwise be shut out by removing intermediaries, lowering prices, and boosting transparency. DSs play a significant role in finance by enhancing FT and process efficiency, transparency, and security.

Table 17.1 Levels of facilities to move products from manufacturers to stores.

Level	Facility type	Facility name	Location	Capacity (sq. ft)	Lead time (days)	Service level (%)
Level 0	Store	Store A	City X	N/A	N/A	99
Level 1	Distribution Centre	DC 1	City Y	50,000	1–2	98
Level 2	Regional Hub	Hub 1	State Z	100,000	2–3	97
Level 3	National Hub	Hub N	Country W	500,000	4–5	95

The adoption of these systems faces difficulties with scale, interoperability, and regulatory compliance, yet there is great potential for gain.

Let's understand with a simple example.

In the below example, a retail company has a distribution network that includes several levels of facilities (see Table 17.1) to move products from manufacturers to stores, as shown in Figure 17.1. Each facility has different capacities, lead times, and service level requirements, which must be carefully managed to ensure the timely and efficient delivery of goods to customers. The distribution network is critical to the company's success, as it affects both customer satisfaction and the cost of goods sold, as shown in Figure 17.1. Proper management of the distribution network requires effective logistics and inventory management practices, as well as the use of advanced technologies such as supply chain (SC) management software and real-time tracking systems.

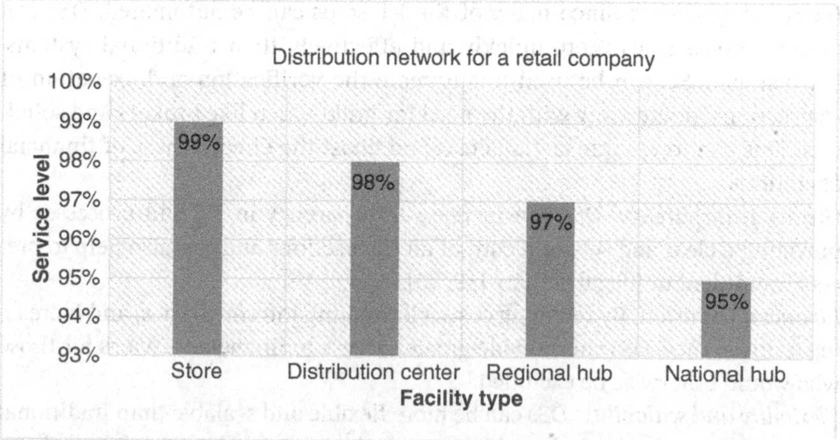

Figure 17.1 Distributed network for retail company.

The distribution network enables the retail company to:

1. *Serve customers in multiple locations*: By having distribution centers, regional hubs, and national hubs located in different geographic areas, the retail company can serve customers in different locations more efficiently. This results in faster delivery times, improved customer satisfaction, and higher sales.
2. *Optimize inventory management*: With a well-designed distribution network, the retail company can optimize its inventory levels to avoid stockouts and overstocking. This helps to reduce carrying costs, minimize waste, and improve profitability.
3. *Improve operational efficiency*: By using a combination of automation, real-time tracking, and data analytics, the retail company can improve its operational efficiency. This includes reducing lead times, improving order accuracy, and optimizing the use of resources.
4. *Reduce transportation costs*: The distribution network can help to reduce transportation costs by consolidating shipments and optimizing routes. It enables the company to deliver products to customers faster, at a lower cost, and with higher levels of quality and service.

17.3.1 Benefits

DSs offer several benefits for FT and processes compared to traditional centralized systems. Some of the key benefits include [14, 15]:

- *Decentralization*: The system consists of a network of nodes that work together to process transactions and make decisions. Decentralization helps to increase transparency, security, and resilience in FT and processes [16–18].
- *Increased efficiency*: Since many of the FT steps can be automated, DSs can process transactions more quickly and effectively than traditional systems. For instance, SC can be used to automate the verification and execution of transactions, doing away with the need for middlemen like brokers and solicitors. This can lower transaction costs and boost the effectiveness of financial operations.
- *Greater transparency*: DSs can increase transparency in FT and processes by providing a clear and secure record of all transactions and can also help to prevent fraudulent or illegal activity [19, 20].
- *Financial inclusion*: By reducing costs, eliminating intermediaries, and increasing transparency, DSs can provide greater access to financial services for those who would otherwise be excluded.
- *Flexibility and scalability*: DSs can be more flexible and scalable than traditional systems, as they can be designed to adapt to changing needs and to handle large volumes of transactions. This makes them well-suited to the dynamic and fast-paced nature of the financial industry.

The advantages of DSs for FT and processes are substantial and will probably lead to greater use of these technologies in the future [21–25]. Although scaling, interoperability, and regulatory compliance are issues that come with the implementation of DSs, the potential benefits are too great to ignore and are likely to cause a change in the financial landscape soon.

17.3.2 Types of Distributed Systems Used in Finance

There are several types of DSs used in finance, each with its own unique characteristics and use cases. Some of the most commonly used types of DSs in finance include [26–28]:

1. *BT*: BT is a type of DLT that is used to create a decentralized transaction. In finance, BT is often used to create digital currencies such as Bitcoin, as well as for SC, which can automate FT.
2. *Peer-to-peer networks*: P2P networks are used to connect users directly to each other. In finance, P2P networks can be used to facilitate peer-to-peer lending, payments, and other types of FT.
3. *Cloud computing*: Cloud computing is a type of distributed computing that allows users to access computing resources over the internet. In finance, cloud computing can be used to provide on-demand access to computing power, storage, and other resources, which can be useful for tasks such as risk modeling and algorithmic trading.
4. *Distributed databases*: The types of DSs used in finance are diverse and are often used in combination to create complex financial systems that are more efficient, transparent, and secure than traditional centralized systems.

17.4 Blockchain Technology and Finance

BT has been a significant disruptive force in the financial industry, providing new opportunities to transform the way FT are conducted. Figure 17.2 shows the ways in which BT is transforming the financial industry [29–32]:

1. *Digital currencies*: The most well-known application of BT in finance is digital currencies, such as Bitcoin and Ethereum. These currencies use BT to create a secure, decentralized payment system that operates without the need for intermediaries such as banks or payment processors.
2. *SC*: These contracts can be used to automate many aspects of FT, such as escrow services, insurance claims, and SC management.
3. *Improved security*: BT uses cryptographic techniques to secure and verify transactions, making it difficult to tamper with the data. This can reduce the risk of fraud and other types of financial crime.

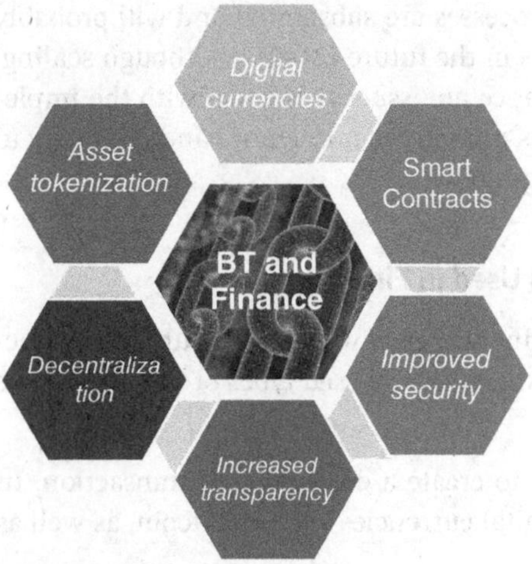

Figure 17.2 BT and Finance.

4. *Increased transparency*: BT provides a clear and secure record of all transactions, which can increase transparency and help to prevent fraudulent or illegal activity. This can help to build trust and confidence among participants in the financial system.
5. *Decentralization*: The decentralized nature of BT can eliminate the need for intermediaries or central authorities, making FT faster and more efficient. It can also reduce costs by eliminating the need for intermediaries, which can make financial services more affordable and accessible to a broader range of people.
6. *Asset tokenization:* There are also challenges that must be addressed, such as scalability, interoperability, and regulatory compliance. Despite these challenges, many financial institutions are investing in BT and exploring its potential applications, and it is likely that BT will continue to be an important part of the financial landscape for years to come.

17.4.1 Applications of Blockchain Technology in Finance

The creation of digital currencies like Bitcoin and Ethereum is one of the most well-known uses of BT in the financial sector, to name a few examples. More privacy, security, and financial control may be advantageous to users as a result of this. Another potential application for BT in the finance sector is cross-border payments. By doing away with middlemen and automating some steps of the process, BT can streamline cross-border payments, reducing costs and hastening the process. Trade finance is another area in which BT can be used. By digitizing and automating various trade finance processes, such as letters of credit and bills of lading, BT can cut down on the time and cost involved in these transactions as well as increase transparency and security. Asset tokenization is one more use case that BT might pursue in this space.

This might make it easier for investors to buy and sell these assets and increase market liquidity. For managing financial identity, BT is a good option. By creating a decentralized and secure identity management system, BT can lower the risk of fraud and identity theft. Since identity confirmation is a crucial part of many transactions, this can be especially helpful in the financial sector. Inside the insurance industry. This can increase the transparency and security of these processes while reducing their length and cost. Finally, BT can be used to create a more efficient and transparent stock market and other markets for securities. By simplifying the process, lowering costs, enhancing security, and increasing transparency, BT can make stock trading simpler [33–35].

17.4.2 Benefits of Blockchain Technology for Financial Transactions and Processes

- *Security*: One of BT's most important advantages is its security. It is very challenging for malicious actors to corrupt or alter the data on a BT since every transaction is recorded on a distributed ledger that cannot be tampered with. Furthermore, the use of sophisticated cryptography contributes to the security of data.
- *Decentralization*: FT no longer need middlemen like banks or payment processors thanks to blockchain. You could reduce transactional costs, time, and risk of fraud and error by doing this.
- *Efficiency*: In sectors like trade finance, where transactions can be complicated and time-consuming, BT can greatly boost the speed and efficiency of FT by removing intermediaries and streamlining processes.
- *Traceability*: All transactions are logged on a BT ledger, making it possible to track a transaction's history and confirm its validity. This is crucial in developing nations because a large portion of the population lacks access to banking services. The advantages of BT for FT and procedures are substantial. Even though scalability and regulatory compliance remain obstacles, the potential advantages of BT are spurring enormous investment and innovation in the financial sector.

17.5 Smart Contracts

Self-running programs (SC) are compatible with BT networks. When BT arrived, its potential was realized. Nick Szabo first proposed them in 1994. There are software applications called SC on a BT network. When specific requirements, such as the completion of a payment or the delivery of a product, are satisfied, they are carried out automatically. Additional transaction types can be automated thanks to SC, including payments, SC management, and digital identity verification. The absence of middlemen in transactions is one of SC's main advantages.

SC uses BT, so they also offer a high level of security. As a result, they are extremely resistant to fraud and hacking, which can be significant issues in conventional contracts. SC's openness is yet another significant advantage. This provides for high levels of openness, which may be helpful in sectors like SC management or real estate. A number of FT processes, such as payments, insurance claims, and asset management, can also be automated using SC. A smart contract could, for instance, automate the payment process for an insurance claim, cutting down on the time and expenses associated with processing the claim. Although there are still issues with scalability and regulatory compliance, the potential advantages of SC are spurring enormous investment and innovation in the creation of this technology. The revolutionary SC technology holds great promise for applications in a variety of industries, including finance, SC management, and real estate. SC offers many benefits to both businesses and consumers, including a high level of security and transparency. Despite the fact that there are still obstacles to be overcome, the potential advantages of SC are driving massive investment and creativity in the creation of this technology [36–38].

17.5.1 Role of Supply Chain in Financial Transactions and Processes

There are numerous ways in which SC has the potential to change FT and processes. SC plays a number of important roles in finance. The transaction automation offered by SC is one of its main benefits. SC can cut the time and expense associated with transactions while minimizing errors and delays by automating FT, such as payments and settlement processes. SC also reduces intermediaries, which is a benefit. In FT, SC can get rid of middlemen like banks or payment processors. SC can lower transaction costs, accelerate transaction times, and lower fraud risk by doing away with middlemen. As a result, FT might become quicker and more effective, in addition to being more reasonably priced and open to a wider audience. Additional security is provided by SC, which is extremely secure and fraud-resistant because it is stored on a decentralized network, like a BT. Through the use of SC, FT can become more secure and less vulnerable to hacking and other types of cybercrime. Within the monetary system. Another advantage of SC is transparency. A public BT network where SC is stored offers a high level of transparency. A clear and secure record of every transaction can be provided by SC, increasing transparency and assisting in the prevention of illegal or fraudulent activity. Last but not least, SCs are programmable, enabling them to be tailored to a variety of FT and processes. The ability to program can make it simpler for businesses to implement intricate financial procedures and guarantee that they are in compliance with pertinent laws. For FT, SC provides a variety of advantages, including automation, a reduction in intermediaries, improved security, transparency, and programmability [39].

17.5.2 Applicability of Supply Chain in Finance

SC has a wide range of applications in the financial industry. SC are digital protocols that automate processes and carry out predetermined conditions. SC has a variety of applications in the financial sector that have several benefits. One of SC's many advantages is its capacity to automate payments, which reduces the time and cost related to ft\.. For instance, SC can be used to execute payments automatically between parties. By automating insurance policies and claims, SC can reduce the time and cost associated with insurance transactions. SC can be set up to pay out claims automatically when specific conditions are met, like when a specific event occurs. Automation can speed up and reduce error-proneness in the claims process by streamlining it. Trade finance, which includes letters of credit and bills of lading, is another sector where SC can be used to automate processes. SC may also be used to confirm the legitimacy of individuals or groups taking part in ft\.. By confirming the identity of borrowers on peer-to-peer lending platforms, SC, for instance, can be used to reduce the risk of identity fraud. To automate processes like inventory control and product tracking, SC can also be used in SC management. In addition to increasing transparency and reducing the risk of fraud, SC can automate these processes to reduce the time and cost involved in asset management. SC's programmability makes it easier for businesses to implement complex financial procedures and ensure regulatory compliance [40].

17.6 Conclusion

The way FT and processes are carried out has undergone a paradigm shift recently, which has affected the finance industry. The emergence of DSs is one of the primary driving forces behind this shift. DSs have revolutionized the financial sector by enabling a decentralized method of carrying out FT and processes. The security, speed, and efficiency of this method have all improved. Financial processes and transactions, however, are not without difficulties. Security risks, complexity, and a lack of transparency are just a few of the difficulties the financial sector faces. By utilizing DSs like BT, these difficulties can be reduced. BT is regarded by the financial sector as a promising technology with enormous potential for lowering transaction costs and speeding up transaction times. Additionally, smart contracts, which are self-executing contracts in which the terms of the agreement between the buyer and seller are directly written into lines of code, are now possible thanks to BT. Contracts could be automated with the use of smart contracts, expediting transactions and lowering risks. To improve efficiency, security, and transparency, the financial sector will need to simplify financial operations and practices. DSs, in particular BT and smart contracts, will be crucial for this. As a result, in order for financial institutions to remain competitive and provide their clients with the best financial services possible, they must adopt these technologies and integrate them into their current systems.

References

1 Narayanan, A. and Viswanathan, S. (2017). Distributed ledger technology and BT. *J. Inf. Secur. Appl.* 38: 2–8. https://doi.org/10.1016/j.jisa.2017.06.008.

2 Crosby, M., Pattanayak, P., Verma, S., and Kalyanaraman, V. (2016). BT: beyond bitcoin. *Appl. Innovation* 2: 6–10. https://doi.org/10.1016/j.apin.2016.08.008.

3 De Filippi, P. and Wright, A. (2018). *BT and the Law: The Rule of Code*. Harvard University Press ISBN: 9780674988171.

4 Pop, C.S. and Pop, D.L. (2020). The impact of BT on financial services. In: *Advanced Studies in Emerging Technologies and Applications in a Global World*, 13–28. IGI Global https://doi.org/10.4018/978-1-7998-2624-8.ch002.

5 Swan, M. (2015). *BT: Blueprint for a New Economy*. O'Reilly Media, Inc. ISBN: 978-1491920497.

6 Tapscott, D. and Tapscott, A. (2016). *BT revolution: How the Technology Behind Bitcoin is Changing Money, Business, and the World*. Penguin ISBN: 978-0141986151.

7 Kshetri, N. (2018). BT's roles in meeting key supply chain management objectives. *Int. J. Inf. Manag.* 39: 80–89. https://doi.org/10.1016/j.ijinfomgt.2017.12.008.

8 Chen, Z., Zhu, Y., and Dong, Y. (2020). BT applications in finance: a systematic review. *J. Finance Data Sci.* 6: 3–20. https://doi.org/10.1016/j.jfds.2020.06.002.

9 Huckle, S., Bhattacharya, R., and White, M. (2016). Internet of things, BT and shared economy applications. *Procedia Comput. Sci.* 98: 461–466. https://doi.org/10.1016/j.procs.2016.09.136.

10 Zheng, Z., Xie, S., Dai, H. N., Chen, W., & Wang, H. (2017). An overview of BT: architecture, consensus, and future trends. *IEEE International Congress on Big Data*, Honolulu, HI, USA (25–30 June 2017). IEEE, 557-564. https://doi.org/10.1109/BigDataCongress.2017.85.

11 Phasinam, K., Kassanuk, T., Shinde, P.P., and Thakar, C.M. (2022). Application of IoT and cloud computing in automation of agriculture irrigation. *J. Food Qual.* 2022: 1–8. https://doi.org/10.1155/2022/8285969.

12 Shinde, P.P., Oza, K.S., Kamat, R.K., and Thakar, C.M. (2022). Big data analytics for mask prominence in COVID pandemic. *Mater. Today Proc.* 51 (Part 8): 2471–2475. https://doi.org/10.1016/j.matpr.2021.11.620.

13 Jagtap, S.T. and Thakar, C.M. (2021). A framework for secure healthcare system using blockchain and smart contracts. In: *2021 Second International Conference on Electronics and Sustainable Communication Systems (ICESC)*, 922–926. Coimbatore, India: https://doi.org/10.1109/ICESC51422.2021.9532644.

14 Parkhe, S.S. and Thakar, C.M. (2022). Implementation of IoT in production and manufacturing: an Industry 4.0 approach. *Mater. Today Proc.* 51 (Part 8): 2427–2430. https://doi.org/10.1016/j.matpr.2021.11.604.

15 Jagtap, S.T. and Thakar, C.M. (2022). Towards application of various machine learning techniques in agriculture. *Mater. Today Proc.* 51 (Part 1): 793–797. https://doi.org/10.1016/j.matpr.2021.06.236.

16 Jain, N., Chaudhary, A., Sindhwani, N., and Rana, A. (2021). Applications of wearable devices in IoT. In: *2021 9th International Conference on Reliability, Infocom Technologies and Optimization (Trends and Future Directions)(ICRITO)*, 1–4. IEEE.

17 Sindhwani, N., Rana, A., and Chaudhary, A. (2021). Breast cancer detection using machine learning algorithms. In: *2021 9th International Conference on Reliability, Infocom Technologies and Optimization (Trends and Future Directions)(ICRITO)*, 1–5. IEEE.

18 Bruntha, P.M., Dhanasekar, S., Hepsiba, D. et al. (2023). Application of switching median filter with L 2 norm-based auto-tuning function for removing random valued impulse noise. *Aerosp. Syst.* 6 (1): 53–59.

19 Kumar Pandey, B., Pandey, D., Nassa, V.K. et al. (2021). Encryption and steganography-based text extraction in IoT using the EWCTS optimizer. *Imaging Sci. J.* 69 (1–4): 38–56.

20 Govindaraj, V., Dhanasekar, S., Martinsagayam, K. et al. (2023). Low-power test pattern generator using modified LFSR. *Aerosp. Syst.* 1–8.

21 Anand, R., Nirmal, V., Chauhan, Y., and Sharma, T. (2023). An image-based deep learning approach for personalized outfit selection. In: *2023 10th International Conference on Computing for Sustainable Global Development (INDIACom)*, 1050–1054. IEEE.

22 Singh, H., Pandey, B.K., George, S. et al. (2022). Effective overview of different ML models used for prediction of COVID-19 patients. In: *Artificial Intelligence on Medical Data: Proceedings of International Symposium, ISCMM 2021*, 185–192. Singapore: Springer Nature Singapore.

23 Pandey, B.K., Pandey, D., Anand, R. et al. (2022). The impact of digital change on student learning and mental anguish in the COVID era. In: *An Interdisciplinary Approach in the Post-COVID-19 Pandemic Era*, 197–206.

24 Saxena, H., Joshi, D., Singh, H., and Anand, R. (2022). Comparison of classification algorithms for Alzheimer's disease prediction. In: *2022 Seventh International Conference on Parallel, Distributed and Grid Computing (PDGC)*, 687–692. IEEE.

25 Sindhwani, N., Anand, R., Vashisth, R. et al. (2022). Thingspeak-based environmental monitoring system using IoT. In: *2022 Seventh International Conference on Parallel, Distributed and Grid Computing (PDGC)*, 675–680. IEEE.

26 Thakar, C.M. and Phasinam, K. (2022). A review on role of artificial intelligence in food processing and manufacturing industry. *Mater. Today Proc.* 51 (Part 8): 2462–2465. https://doi.org/10.1016/j.matpr.2021.11.616.

27 Azaria, A., Ekblaw, A., Vieira, T., and Lippman, A. (2016). MedRec: using BT for medical data access and permission management. In: *Proceedings of the 2nd International Conference on Open and Big Data*, Vienna, Austria. https://doi.org/10.1145/3012029.3012041.

28 Böhme, R., Christin, N., Edelman, B., and Moore, T. (2015). Bitcoin: economics, technology, and governance. *J. Econ. Perspect.* 29 (2): 213–238. https://doi.org/10.1257/jep.29.2.213.

29 Crosby, M., Pattanayak, P., Verma, S., and Kalyanaraman, V. (2016). BT: beyond bitcoin. *Appl. Innovation* 2 (6-10): 71–81. https://doi.org/10.1016/j.apin.2016.10.008.

30 Elmaghraby, W. and Losavio, M. (2014). Cybersecurity challenges in smart cities: safety, security and privacy. *J. Adv. Res.* 5 (4): 491–497. https://doi.org/10.1016/j.jare.2014.03.008.

31 Fanning, K. and Centers, D.P. (2016). BT and its coming impact on financial services. *J. Corp. Acc. Financ.* 27 (5): 53–57. https://doi.org/10.1002/jcaf.22140.

32 Kshetri, N. (2018). BT's Roles in meeting key supply chain management objectives. *Int. J. Inf. Manag.* 39: 80–89. https://doi.org/10.1016/j.ijinfomgt.2017.12.002.

33 Yunitarini, R. and Santoso, P. (2018). A literature review of electronic data interchange as electronic business communication for manufacturing. *Manage. Prod. Eng. Rev.* 9: 117–128.

34 Zhao, B., Wang, R., Cai, Y., and Zhao, E. (2020). Block chain financial transaction using artificial neural network deep learning. In Proceedings of the IOP Conference Series: Materials Science and Engineering, Xi'an, China, 25–27 October 2019.

35 Jain, M., Kaswan, S., Pandey, D. et al. (2021). A blockchain-based fund management scheme for financial transactions in NGOS. *Recent Pat. Eng.* 16: 3–16.

36 Xue, B., Zhang, M., and Browne, W.N. (2013). Particle swarm optimization for feature selection in classification. A multi-objective approach. *IEEE Trans. Cybern.* 43: 1656–1671.

37 Liu, X., Wang, Q., Li, Y. et al. (2018). BT-based data integrity service framework for industrial internet of things. *IEEE Trans. Ind. Inf.* 14 (11): 5070–5080. https://doi.org/10.1109/TII.2018.2834438.

38 Nakamoto, S. (2008). Bitcoin: a peer-to-peer electronic cash system. https://bitcoin.org/bitcoin.pdf

39 Narayanan, A., Bonneau, J., Felten, E. et al. (2016). *Bitcoin and Cryptocurrency Technologies: A Comprehensive Introduction.* Princeton University Press.

40 Gupta, A., Srivastava, A., Anand, R., and Tomažič, T. (2020). Business application analytics and the internet of things: the connecting link. *New Age Anal.* 249–273.

18

Leveraging Distributed Systems for Improved Market Intelligence and Customer Segmentation

Luigi P.L. Cavaliere[1], K. Suresh Kumar[2], Dilip K. Sharma[3], Himanshu Sharma[4], Sujay M. Jayadeva[5], Makarand Upadhyaya[6], and Nadanakumar Vinayagam[7]

[1]Department of Economics, University of Foggia, Foggia, Italy
[2]MBA Department, Panimalar Engineering College, Chennai, Tamil Nadu, India
[3]Department of Mathematics, Jaypee University of Engineering and Technology, Guna, Madhya Pradesh, India
[4]United World School of Business, Karnavati University, Gandhinagar, Gujarat, India
[5]Department of Health System Management Studies, JSS Academy of Higher Education & Research, Mysuru, Karnataka, India
[6]University of Bahrain, College of Business, Bahrain
[7]Department of Automobile Engineering, Hindustan Institute of Technology and Science, Chennai, Tamil Nadu, India

18.1 Introduction

In the modern business world, market intelligence and customer segmentation play a vital role in helping businesses understand their target market and customers. Companies require this information to make informed decisions, which can affect their bottom line. With the rapid growth of technology, businesses can now use distributed systems (DSs) to enhance their market intelligence and customer segmentation capabilities. DS is made up of numerous nodes that cooperate to finish a task. These systems are capable of managing enormous volumes of data, processing it in real time, and offering insights into the market and customers. Businesses can strengthen their awareness of the industry and their customers by utilizing DSs, which will help them make better decisions, develop more successful marketing plans, and eventually generate more income. An in-depth

Meta-Heuristic Algorithms for Advanced Distributed Systems, First Edition. Edited by Rohit Anand, Abhinav Juneja, Digvijay Pandey, Sapna Juneja, and Nidhi Sindhwani.

examination of the advantages of using DS for better market information and client segmentation will be provided in this chapter. An outline of DS and its importance in the contemporary business environment will open the chapter. It will then discuss market intelligence and customer segmentation and the role they play in the success of a business. The chapter will explore the benefits of using DS for market intelligence, including how they can provide real-time insights, handle vast amounts of data, and process it more efficiently. It will provide examples of DS used for market intelligence, highlighting their advantages and disadvantages. The benefits of using DS for customer segmentation. It will provide insights into how DS can enhance the customer segmentation process by providing real-time data, enabling businesses to develop targeted marketing strategies and identify new customer segments. It will provide examples of DS used for customer segmentation and their advantages and disadvantages. It will highlight the challenges faced by businesses in implementing DS for market intelligence and customer segmentation, including the need for specialized skills, data privacy concerns, and infrastructure requirements. The chapter will also provide insight into the future of DS for market intelligence and customer segmentation, highlighting potential technological advancements and their impact on businesses. It will highlight their approach, the benefits they realized, and the challenges they faced. The review chapter will provide a comprehensive overview of the benefits of leveraging DS for improved market intelligence and customer segmentation. It will provide insights into the challenges and future directions for research and development in this area and highlight the real-world benefits of implementing DS for market intelligence and customer segmentation. The chapter will be of value to businesses looking to improve their market intelligence and customer segmentation capabilities and to researchers looking to explore the potential of DS in this area [1-3].

18.1.1 Overview of Distributed Systems

A DS is a group of independent computers working together through a network to accomplish a single objective. To give consumers a seamless and effective computing experience, the computers in a DS cooperate as a single system, pooling resources and planning their tasks. DS is used in a wide range of applications, including data processing systems, large-scale scientific simulations, and web-based platforms for social networks and e-commerce [4, 5]:

The main characteristics of DS include:

1. *Concurrency*: multiple processes or threads can execute concurrently on different computers.
2. *Transparency*: users and applications can access resources and services as if they were local, without knowledge of their physical location or configuration.

3. *Scalability*: DS can be scaled up or down by adding or removing computers from the network [6–8].
4. *Fault tolerance*: DS can continue to operate even if some of the computers in the network fail [9, 10].

Some of the key challenges of building DS include:

1. *Coordination and synchronization*: ensuring that multiple processes or threads work together correctly and efficiently.
2. *Consistency and replication*: ensuring that data is consistent and up-to-date across multiple copies of a dataset.
3. *Security*: ensuring that the system is secure against unauthorized access and attacks [11–13].
4. *Performance*: ensuring that the system can handle the required workload and respond quickly to user requests [14, 15].

However, they also pose significant technical and design challenges that must be carefully managed to build reliable, scalable, and secure systems.

18.1.2 Market Intelligence and Customer Segmentation

By segmenting customers, businesses can tailor their marketing efforts to specific groups, providing more personalized messaging and improving the likelihood of converting leads into customers. Market intelligence is critical for successful customer segmentation, as it provides the information necessary to identify the characteristics of different customer groups. For example, market intelligence might reveal that younger customers are more likely to buy eco-friendly products, while older customers are more price sensitive. Armed with this information, businesses can segment their customers based on age and develop marketing campaigns targeted at each group's specific preferences. Customer segmentation can be broken down into several different types. Demographic segmentation involves dividing a market based on age, gender, income, education, and other demographic factors. Psychographic segmentation considers customers' values, lifestyles, and personality traits. Behavioral segmentation focuses on customers' actions, such as their purchasing history or response to marketing efforts. Geographic segmentation considers customers' location and can be particularly useful for businesses that operate in specific regions or countries. Once a business has segmented its customers, it can develop targeted marketing strategies for each group. For example, a business might create social media campaigns aimed at younger customers or offer loyalty programs to frequent buyers. By tailoring marketing efforts to specific customer groups, businesses can improve customer engagement, increase sales, and ultimately grow their bottom line. By understanding the market and identifying customer groups with shared characteristics,

Figure 18.1 Market segmentation alternatives.

businesses can develop targeted marketing strategies that improve engagement, increase sales, and ultimately drive growth.

Market segmentation alternatives refer to the different methods or criteria used to divide a market into distinct groups. These options are based on a variety of variables, as indicated in Figure 18.1, including geography, behavior, psychographics, and demographics. Market segmentation alternatives include geographic segmentation, which divides a market according to factors like region or climate; demographic segmentation, which divides a market according to factors like age, gender, income, and education level; and psychographic segmentation, which divides a market according to personality traits, values, and way of life. Other options include usage segmentation, occasion segmentation, and benefit segmentation. Alternatives to market segmentation aid businesses in better comprehending their customers so they may target their marketing efforts toward meeting each one's unique needs and preferences [16–18].

18.1.3 Importance of Leveraging Desford to Improve Market Intelligence and Customer Segmentation

Leveraging DS can significantly improve market intelligence and customer segmentation by providing businesses with faster and more accurate data processing capabilities. DS involves breaking down large computational tasks into smaller, more manageable chunks that can be processed simultaneously across multiple nodes or computers. Businesses can grow their data processing capabilities to handle enormous volumes of data in real-time or near-real-time by using DSs, which can increase the precision and speed of market intelligence and consumer segmentation. Using DS for market intelligence and consumer segmentation has many advantages, one of which is its rapid processing and analysis of enormous amounts of data. The exponential development of data sources, including social media, online analytics, and customer behavior tracking, makes it difficult and time-consuming to analyze data using conventional methods. By spreading out the workload across several nodes, DS can analyze this data considerably more effectively, substantially reducing processing time and giving organizations insights faster than ever before. Another benefit of leveraging DS is the ability to provide near-real-time insights into market trends and customer behavior. In today's fast-paced business environment, businesses must be able to react quickly to market changes and customer preferences to stay competitive. SS can enhance the accuracy of market intelligence and customer segmentation by reducing errors and increasing data quality. Errors in traditional data processing methods, such as data loss, consistency issues, and accuracy issues, might occur. Businesses can use cloud-based DS that can offer scalability and cost savings in place of spending a fortune on high-end hardware. Businesses can only pay for the resources they really use using cloud-based systems, which can drastically lower maintenance expenses. Businesses can enhance their capacity to respond swiftly to market changes, keep ahead of the competition, and ultimately drive success by leveraging DS for market information and consumer segmentation [19–21].

18.2 Distributed Systems for Customer Segmentation

Market intelligence and customer segmentation are both critical components of successful marketing strategies. Market intelligence involves gathering and analyzing data about a particular market, including competition, customer preferences, and industry trends. Contrarily, customer segmentation entails breaking down a market into smaller groups based on shared traits like age, gender, wealth, or behavior. The effectiveness of market intelligence and consumer segmentation has substantially increased over the past several years, thanks to the usage of technology and data analytics. Big data and DS technologies, in particular, have made it possible for organizations to process and analyze enormous amounts of data quickly, giving them real-time insights into consumer and industry patterns. The use of DS for market intelligence and client segmentation has been examined in a number of research. An illustration would be the segmentation of customers using a distributed computing platform to evaluate extensive social media data. The use of machine learning algorithms and distributed computing platforms for customer segmentation. Moreover, the use of big data technologies, such as Hadoop and Spark, has significantly improved the efficiency and accuracy of market intelligence and customer segmentation. Previous research has highlighted the benefits of leveraging DS for market intelligence and customer segmentation. One study conducted by researchers at the University of Illinois at Urbana-Champaign explored the use of DS for customer segmentation in e-commerce. The study found that using DS enabled more accurate and efficient segmentation of customers, resulting in increased sales and customer satisfaction. Another study by researchers at the

University of Edinburgh examined the use of DS for market intelligence in the financial industry. The study found that using DS enabled faster and more accurate analysis of market trends, resulting in improved decision-making and increased profitability. A third study by researchers at the University of Cambridge explored the use of DS for market intelligence in the retail industry. The study found that using DS enabled more effective analysis of customer behavior and preferences, resulting in improved marketing strategies and increased customer engagement. Previous research has demonstrated the significant benefits of leveraging DS for market intelligence and customer segmentation, including increased accuracy, efficiency, and speed of data processing, improved decision-making, and increased profitability and customer satisfaction [22–25].

18.3 Distributed Systems for Market Intelligence

Due to the enormous amount of data that companies now have access to, Deshaye has grown more and more well-known for market intelligence. Businesses are now able to gather and analyze enormous volumes of data on customer behavior, industry trends, and rivalry thanks to the development of digital technology and the internet. Businesses may handle massive amounts of data more rapidly and accurately with this method, which helps them to gain useful insights more quickly. Moreover, DS can increase redundancy and fault tolerance, ensuring that data is not lost in the event of system problems or failures. The capacity to process data in close to real-time, allowing firms to react swiftly to shifting market conditions and client preferences, is one of the main advantages of using DS for market intelligence. Businesses may gain insightful knowledge into customer behavior and preferences by performing extensive real-time data analysis. This knowledge helps companies create more successful marketing campaigns, increase customer engagement, and eventually spur growth. Improved data quality is another advantage of adopting DS for market intelligence. DS can provide redundancy and fault tolerance by processing data across numerous nodes, lowering the possibility of mistakes and guaranteeing that data is correct and dependable. When working with sensitive or confidential data, this can be very crucial. Businesses can get a competitive edge by utilizing DS for market intelligence, which enables them to collect and analyze massive amounts of data quickly and correctly [26, 27].

18.3.1 Distributed Systems for Improvisation in Market Intelligence

1. *Increased processing power*: Businesses can spread out data processing duties among a number of nodes or computers using DSs, which boosts total processing capability. This makes it possible for companies to analyze massive amounts

of data more rapidly and effectively, leading to quicker insights and better decision-making.

2. *Real-time data analysis*: With DSs, businesses can analyze data in real-time, providing near-instantaneous insights into customer behavior and preferences. This enables businesses to respond quickly to changing market conditions, develop more effective marketing strategies, and improve customer engagement.
3. *Improved fault tolerance*: DS provides redundancy and fault tolerance, ensuring that data is not lost in case of system failures or errors. This reduces the risk of data loss and improves the accuracy and reliability of market intelligence.
4. *Scalability*: This ensures that businesses can continue to extract insights and improve their market intelligence as their data volumes increase.
5. *Cost-effectiveness*: DS can be more affordable than conventional data processing methods because it makes use of already-existing technology and infrastructure. Businesses may handle and analyze data more effectively as a result, reducing the need for them to invest in pricey hardware or software.

18.3.2 Advantages of Distribution System in Market Intelligence

1. *Scalability:* scale up or down to accommodate changes in data volume or processing requirements. This makes it easier to handle large amounts of market data as it grows over time.
2. *Fault tolerance:* DS can be designed to be fault-tolerant, meaning that if one component fails, the system can continue to function without interruption. This can help ensure that market intelligence is always available and up-to-date.
3. *Speed:* process large amounts of data quickly, which can be crucial for real-time market intelligence applications.

18.3.3 Disadvantages of Distribution System in Market Intelligence

1. *Complexity:* Building and maintaining DS can be complex and requires specialized knowledge, which may not be available in-house.
2. *Cost:* Building and maintaining DS can be expensive, both in terms of hardware and personnel costs.
3. *Security:* can be more vulnerable to security threats, such as hacking or data breaches, especially if they are not properly designed and maintained.

18.4 Distributed Systems for Customer Segmentation

For consumer segmentation, which is the process of grouping people who have similar characteristics from a client base. Businesses should employ this technique

Table 18.1 DS for customer segmentation.

Aspects to consider	Description	Examples
Data collection: DS may be used to collect a lot of consumer data from a variety of sources, such as transactional data, social media data, and customer reviews. After this data has been analyzed, certain client segments can be identified	Companies can use distributed data collection tools like Apache Flume, Apache NiFi, and Apache Kafka to collect customer data from various sources	Apache Flume, Apache NiFi, and Apache Kafka
Data processing: Faster analysis of customer segments is made possible by the parallel processing of massive amounts of client data using DS. This is crucial because huge and complicated customer data sets can be challenging to evaluate rapidly using conventional techniques	Distributed processing frameworks like Apache Spark and Apache Flink can be used to analyze consumer data in parallel, accelerating the analysis of large datasets	Apache Spark, Apache Flink
Real-time segmentation: Real-time client segmentation made possible by DS enables companies to react swiftly to shifting consumer demands and preferences. This is especially crucial for companies that have real-time decision-making requirements, such as e-commerce companies or customer care divisions	Real-time customer data streams may be analyzed using stream processing systems like Apache Kafka and Apache Storm, which enable companies to pinpoint specific client segments and quickly adapt to changes	Apache Kafka, Apache Storm

a useful tool for companies trying to divide up their clientele. Businesses can better understand their customers and target their marketing and sales activities by gathering and analyzing vast amounts of customer data concurrently. Real-time customer segmentation can also assist firms in reacting rapidly to shifting consumer wants and preferences, enhancing client loyalty and satisfaction.

because it enables them to focus their marketing and sales efforts on particular consumer segments, which can boost client satisfaction, brand loyalty, and profitability [28, 29]. Table 18.1 presents three factors to think about when utilizing DS for client segmentation.:

18.5 Challenges in Integrating Distribution System in Market Intelligence

Network latency and bandwidth: DS relies on network communication between nodes to share data and process information. The speed of the network and available bandwidth can affect the performance of the system. Network latency and bandwidth limitations can result in slower processing times and reduced system performance, affecting the ability to provide real-time insights. Businesses need to optimize their network infrastructure and consider bandwidth limitations when designing DS to ensure optimal performance.

1. *Data quality and relevance*: The quality and relevance of data are crucial to gain insights into customer behavior and enhance market intelligence. Data quality can be compromised due to inconsistencies, errors, or incomplete data. The relevance of data can be impacted by the selection of the wrong data sources, leading to inaccurate insights. Businesses need to establish data quality standards, ensure data accuracy, and select relevant data sources to gain actionable insights into customer behavior.
2. *Data privacy and ethics*: As businesses collect and process data from various sources, customers have a right to privacy, and businesses need to comply with data protection regulations while collecting, processing, and storing customer data. Ethical considerations should also be considered when using customer data to avoid negative impacts on customers or society as a whole.
3. *Interoperability and compatibility*: DS often comprises different technologies and systems that need to work together seamlessly. Ensuring interoperability and compatibility between different systems can be challenging, leading to integration problems and system failures. Businesses need to select compatible systems, use standardized protocols, and establish clear interfaces between different systems to ensure seamless interoperability.
4. *Expertise*: Leveraging DS requires specialized expertise, which can be challenging for businesses to acquire. The technology is complex and requires skilled professionals who can design, implement, and maintain the DS effectively. Businesses may need to invest in training and development programs to upskill their existing employees or hire new professionals with expertise in DSs. The shortage of skilled professionals in this area can make it challenging for businesses to implement and maintain DS effectively. This can result in increased costs, delays, and decreased productivity.

Network latency and bandwidth limitations, data quality and relevance, data privacy and ethics, and interoperability and compatibility are just a few of the challenges that need to be considered when designing, implementing, and maintaining DSs. Businesses need to address these challenges to effectively leverage DS, gain valuable insights into customer behavior, and enhance market intelligence [30, 31].

18.5.1 Future Directions for Research and Development in This Area

Artificial intelligence (AI) and machine learning (ML) have the power to completely change how companies gather and evaluate customer data. These tools can quickly evaluate enormous amounts of data, spot patterns and trends, and give precise insights into how customers behave. AI and ML can improve firms' capacity to precisely identify and target consumer categories in the context of DS for market data and customer segmentation. The availability of high-quality data is one of the major obstacles to employing AI and ML for market intelligence and customer segmentation. The caliber and variety of the data utilized to train AI and ML systems determine their efficacy and accuracy. Several AI and ML algorithms are referred to as "black box" models because their decision-making procedures are opaque or difficult for humans to comprehend. For firms that need to know why specific consumer segments are being targeted or specific market trends are being discovered, this can be troublesome. The development of methods to improve the interpretability of ML and AI algorithms, such as the use of explainable AI models, can therefore be the focus of future study. Companies must make sure that the way they utilize customer data is moral, open, and in accordance with data protection laws. The development of ethical and governance frameworks for the use of AI and ML in DS for market intelligence and consumer segmentation can be the subject of future studies. This might assist companies in gaining the consumer loyalty and trust that are crucial for sustained success. The main issues of data quality, algorithm interpretability, ethics, and governance can be the subject of future research. Businesses can then use AI and ML to enhance market intelligence, boost corporate performance, and acquire useful insights into client behavior. Blockchain technology is renowned for its capacity to offer transparent and secure data processing and storage. Blockchain technology can be applied to DS for market intelligence and consumer segmentation to guarantee data confidentiality and privacy.

This is particularly crucial in the data-driven business climate of today, when companies must safeguard client data from hacker assaults and data breaches. The potential of blockchain-based DSi to offer safe and private data storage is one of its main advantages. Blockchain-based systems store data over a network of nodes instead of traditional centralized databases, making it nearly impossible for hackers to infiltrate the system. This can improve the safety and privacy of client information, which is crucial for gaining the trust and loyalty of customers. Secure data processing and analysis are another advantage of blockchain technology. Smart contracts, which are self-executing contracts that uphold the terms of a contract between parties, are used by blockchain-based DS. This can improve data processing's effectiveness and accuracy, which is crucial for effective market intelligence and customer segmentation. However, there are drawbacks to employing blockchain-based DS for consumer segmentation and market analytics. The intricacy of deploying blockchain technology is one of the major difficulties. Because blockchain technology is still in its infancy, businesses might not have the knowledge or resources they need to adopt it successfully. Future research might therefore concentrate on creating accessible and user-friendly blockchain-based solutions that are simple to integrate into current business processes. When processing large amounts of data, blockchain-based solutions can be slow and ineffective, which can reduce their usefulness for market intelligence and customer segmentation. Future research can therefore concentrate on creating methods to improve the scalability of blockchain technology, such as creating sharding methods or improving consensus algorithms.

Future research can concentrate on addressing major implementation difficulty and scalability concerns, as well as developing user-friendly and accessible blockchain-based solutions that can help companies collect and process consumer data securely and effectively. Businesses can increase consumer loyalty and trust by doing this, which is crucial for long-term success in the cutthroat business world of today.

For businesses looking to extract insights from huge and complicated data sets, data visualization is a crucial tool. It enables companies to show data in a way that is easier to comprehend and interpret, like charts, graphs, and maps. Data visualization techniques can assist companies in identifying patterns, trends, and anomalies in consumer behavior that can guide marketing plans and boost company performance when used in the context of DS for market intelligence and customer segmentation. Data from many sources and platforms can be represented using data visualization techniques, making it simpler to spot trends and patterns that might not be apparent when reviewing data solely. For example, businesses can use data visualization techniques to analyze customer behavior across different channels, such as social media, e-commerce platforms, and physical stores. This can provide a holistic view of customer behavior, which can inform market intelligence and customer segmentation. Anomalies are data points that deviate significantly from the norm and may indicate a problem or opportunity that requires further investigation. Data visualization techniques can be used to highlight anomalies in customer behavior, such as a sudden increase or decrease in sales, or a change in customer preferences. However, there are also challenges in using data visualization techniques for market intelligence and customer segmentation. One of the key challenges is the need for expertise and resources to develop and implement effective data visualization techniques. Businesses may not have the necessary skills or resources to develop customized data visualization tools, which can limit their ability to gain insights from large and complex data sets. Therefore, future research can focus on developing user-friendly and accessible data visualization tools that can be easily integrated into existing business processes. Data visualization techniques rely on accurate and consistent data to provide meaningful insights. Therefore, businesses need to ensure that data from different sources and platforms is compatible and consistent, which can be a challenge in a DS environment. Future research can focus on developing data integration techniques that enable businesses to aggregate data from multiple sources and platforms in a consistent and accurate manner. Data visualization techniques are an essential tool for businesses seeking to gain insights from large and complex data sets. Future research can focus on developing user-friendly and accessible data visualization tools and data integration techniques that enable businesses to represent and interpret data in a meaningful and accurate manner. As businesses increasingly rely on customer data to inform their market intelligence and customer segmentation strategies, ethical and governance considerations become even more crucial. The use of DS to collect, process, and analyze customer data raises concerns around data privacy, security, and ownership.

Future research can focus on developing ethical and governance frameworks that address these concerns. For example, businesses can implement data anonymization techniques to protect the privacy of their customers. This involves removing personally identifiable information from customer data before it is collected and processed. In addition, governance frameworks can be developed to ensure that businesses are using customer data in a transparent and responsible manner. This involves establishing clear policies and procedures around data collection, processing, and analysis. It also involves ensuring that businesses are complying with relevant regulations around data privacy and security. Another important consideration is the ownership of customer data. Businesses must ensure that they are collecting customer data with their consent and that customers retain ownership of their data. Future research can explore ways to empower customers to control their data and to ensure that businesses are using customer data ethically and transparently. The development of ethical and governance frameworks is essential to ensure that businesses can leverage DS for market intelligence and customer segmentation while maintaining customer trust and loyalty. By addressing these concerns, businesses can build long-term relationships with their customers and enhance their business performance [32, 33].

18.6 Conclusion

In conclusion, using DS for consumer segmentation and market intelligence has grown in significance for organizations in the current data-driven environment. Businesses can acquire important insights into customer behavior and preferences by using DS to gain access to huge and complicated data sets. While employing DS for market intelligence and consumer segmentation has several benefits, there are a number of issues that must be resolved. The accuracy and dependability of insights produced by DSs can be impacted by several factors, which include data integration, scalability, and data consistency [34–36]. To overcome these challenges and improve the effectiveness of DS for market intelligence and customer segmentation, future research can focus on several areas. These include the use of artificial intelligence and machine learning algorithms to process data in real time, the development of blockchain-based DS to enhance data security and privacy, the use of data visualization techniques to simplify complex data sets, and the development of ethical and governance frameworks to ensure responsible use of customer data. By addressing these challenges and focusing on future research and development, businesses can leverage DS to gain a competitive advantage, improve customer satisfaction, and enhance their overall business performance.

References

1 Kunle, A.L.P., Akanbi, A.M., and Ismail, T.A. (2017). The influence of marketing intelligence on business competitive advantage (A study of Diamond Bank PLC). *J. Compet.* 9: 51–71.

2 Taherdoost, H. (2018). A review of technology acceptance and adoption models and theories. *Procedia Manuf.* 22: 960–967.

3 Snead, K.C., Magal, S.R., Christensen, L.F., and Ndede-Amadi, A.A. (2015). Attribution theory: a theoretical framework for understanding information systems success. *Syst. Pract. Action Res.* 28: 273–288.

4 McNamara, C.P. (1972). The present status of the marketing concept. *J. Mark.* 36: 50–57.

5 Narver, J.C. and Slater, S.F. (1990). The effect of a market orientation on business profitability. *J. Mark.* 54: 20–35.

6 Anand, R., Nirmal, V., Chauhan, Y., and Sharma, T. (2023). An image-based deep learning approach for personalized outfit selection. In: *2023 10th International Conference on Computing for Sustainable Global Development (INDIACom)*, 1050–1054. IEEE.

7 Govindaraj, V., Dhanasekar, S., Martinsagayam, K. et al. (2023). Low-power test pattern generator using modified LFSR. *Aerosp. Syst.* 1–8.

8 Bruntha, P.M., Dhanasekar, S., Hepsiba, D. et al. (2023). Application of switching median filter with L 2 norm-based auto-tuning function for removing random valued impulse noise. *Aerosp. Syst.* 6 (1): 53–59.

9 Deepa, R., Anand, R., Pandey, D. et al. (2022). Comprehensive performance analysis of classifiers in diagnosis of epilepsy. *Math. Probl. Eng.* 2022.

10 Pandey, D. and Pandey, B.K. (2022). An efficient deep neural network with adaptive galactic swarm optimization for complex image text extraction. In: *Process Mining Techniques for Pattern Recognition*, 121–137. CRC Press.

11 Khan, B., Hasan, A., Pandey, D. et al. (2021). Fusion of datamining and artificial intelligence in prediction of hazardous road accidents. In: *Machine Learning and IoT for Intelligent Systems and Smart Applications*, 201–223. CRC Press.

12 Sindhwani, N., Anand, R., Nageswara Rao, G. et al. (2023). Comparative analysis of optimization algorithms for antenna selection in MIMO systems. In: *Advances in Signal Processing, Embedded Systems and IoT: Proceedings of Seventh ICMEET-2022*, 607–617. Singapore: Springer Nature Singapore.

13 Juneja, S., Juneja, A., and Anand, R. (2019). Role of big data as a tool for improving sustainability for the betterment of quality of life in metro cities. *Int. J. Control. Autom.* 12: 553–557.

14 Saini, P. and Anand, M.R. (2014). Identification of defects in plastic gears using image processing and computer vision: a review. *Int. J. Eng. Res.* 3 (2): 94–99.

15 Meivel, S., Sindhwani, N., Valarmathi, S. et al. (2022). Design and method of 16.24 GHz microstrip network antenna using underwater wireless communication algorithm. In: *Cyber Technologies and Emerging Sciences: ICCTES 2021*, 363–371. Singapore: Springer Nature Singapore.

16 Walter, J., Lechner, C., and Kellermanns, F.W. (2016). Learning activities, exploration, and the performance of strategic initiatives. *J. Manag.* 42: 769–802.

17 Li, Q., Maggitti, P.G., Smith, K.G. et al. (2013). Top management attention to innovation: the role of search selection and intensity in new product introductions. *Acad. Manag. J.* 56: 893–916.

18 Helm, R., Krinner, S., and Schmalfuß, M. (2014). Conceptualization and integration of marketing intelligence: the case of an industrial manufacturer. *J. Bus. Bus. Mark.* 21: 237–255.

19 Egelhoff, W.G. (1991). Information-processing theory and the multinational enterprise. *J. Int. Bus. Stud.* 22: 341–368.

20 Rogers, P.R., Miller, A., and Judge, W.Q. (1999). Using information-processing theory to understand planning/performance relationships in the context of strategy. *Strateg. Manag. J.* 20: 567–577.

21 Isik, Ö. (2018). Big data capabilities: an organizational information processing perspective. In: *Analytics and Data Science*, 29–40. Cham, Switzerland: Springer.

22 Arbib, M.A. (1992). Schema theory. *Encycl. Artif. Intell.* 2: 1427–1443.

23 Corbacho, F.J. and Arbib, M.A. (1997). Schema-based learning: biologically inspired principles of dynamic organization. In: *International Work-Conference on Artificial Neural Networks*, 678–687. Berlin/Heidelberg, Germany: Springer.

24 Tsoukas, H. and Vladimirou, E. (2001). What is organizational knowledge? *J. Manag. Stud.* 38: 973–993.

25 Yoseph, F., Malim, N.H.A.H., and AlMalaily, M. (2019). New behavioral segmentation methods to understand consumers in retail industry. *Int. J. Comput. Sci. Inf. Technol.* 11: 43–61.

26 France, S.L. and Ghose, S. (2019). Marketing analytics: methods, practice, implementation, and links to other fields. *Expert Syst. Appl.* 119: 456–475.

27 Kotler, P.T. and Keller, K.L. (2015). *Marketing Management*, 15e. Pearson: Hoboken, NJ, USA.

28 Puranam, P. (2021). Human–AI collaborative decision-making as an organization design problem. *J. Organ. Des.* 10: 75–80.

29 Raisch, S. and Krakowski, S. (2021). Artificial intelligence and management: the automation–augmentation paradox. *Acad. Manag. Rev.* 46: 192–210.

30 Hung, P.D., Lien, N.T.T., and Ngoc, N.D. (2019). Customer segmentation using hierarchical agglomerative clustering. In: *Proceedings of the 2019 2nd International Conference on Information Science and Systems; Association for Computing Machinery: New York, NY, USA*, 33–37.

31 Wang, J.J., Qian, T.Y., Li, B., and Mastromartino, B. (2022). Reversing equity transfer in sponsorship for competitive advantage of emerging local events: quantitative evidence from an experimental study. *Int. J. Sports Mark. Spons.* 23: 748–766.

32 Gong, X., Zhang, K.Z., and Zhao, S.J. (2015). Halo effect on the adoption of mobile payment: a schema theory perspective. In: *International Conference on E-Technologies*, 153–165. Cham, Switzerland: Springer.

33 Umuhoza, E., Ntirushwamaboko, D., Awuah, J., and Birir, B. (2020). Using unsupervised machine learning techniques for behavioral-based credit card users segmentation in Africa. *SAIEE Afr. Res. J.* 111: 95–101.

34 Sharma, R., Vashisth, R., and Sindhwani, N. (2023). Study and analysis of classification techniques for specific plant growths. In: *Advances in Signal Processing, Embedded Systems and IoT: Proceedings of Seventh ICMEET-2022*, 591–605. Singapore: Springer Nature Singapore.

35 Sharma, G., Nehra, N., Dahiya, A. et al. (2022). Automatic heart-rate measurement using facial video. In: *Networking Technologies in Smart Healthcare*, 289–307. CRC Press.

36 Jain, S., Kumar, M., Sindhwani, N., and Singh, P. (2021). SARS-Cov-2 detection using deep learning techniques on the basis of clinical reports. In: *2021 9th International Conference on Reliability, Infocom Technologies and Optimization (Trends and Future Directions)(ICRITO)*, 1–5. IEEE.

19

The Future of Financial Crime Prevention and Cybersecurity with Distributed Systems and Computing Approaches

Veer B.P. Singh[1], *Pratibha Singh*[2], *Shouvik K. Guha*[3], *Asif I. Shah*[4], *Abdullah Samdani*[5], *M.Z.M. Nomani*[6], *and Mohit Tiwari*[7]

[1]*School of CSIT, Department of Cyber Security, Symbiosis Skills, and Professional University, Kiwale, Pune, India*
[2]*Department of CSE, Guru Ghasidas Vishwavidyalaya, Bilaspur, Chhattisgarh, India*
[3]*The West Bengal National University of Juridical Sciences, Kolkata, West Bengal, India*
[4]*Xavier Law School, St. Xavier's University, Kolkata, India*
[5]*School of Law, University of Petroleum & Energy Studies, Dehradun, India*
[6]*Faculty of Law, Aligarh Muslim University, Aligarh, India*
[7]*Department of Computer Science and Engineering, Bharati Vidyapeeth's College of Engineering, Delhi, India*

19.1 Introduction

The financial sector has undergone a revolution thanks to the growing use of technology and digitalization, which has improved the accessibility of financial services for consumers. New risks and threats have, however, also emerged as a result of this evolution, particularly in the fields of cybersecurity and financial crime prevention. We have seen a rise in cyberattack sophistication and frequency in recent years, which has caused financial institutions to suffer significant financial losses and reputational harm. Financial institutions must make an immediate investment in effective cybersecurity and financial crime prevention strategies. Artificial intelligence and machine learning technologies will probably be used more frequently in the future of cybersecurity and financial crime prevention. Financial institutions may be able to prevent and reduce financial crime in real time by using these technologies, which have the potential to

Meta-Heuristic Algorithms for Advanced Distributed Systems, First Edition. Edited by Rohit Anand, Abhinav Juneja, Digvijay Pandey, Sapna Juneja, and Nidhi Sindhwani.

increase the accuracy and speed of fraud detection. In order to find patterns and anomalies that might point to fraudulent behavior, machine learning algorithms can analyze huge volumes of data. The development of predictive models that can foresee and stop potentially fraudulent activities before they happen is another way that artificial intelligence can assist financial institutions. The adoption of blockchain technology is another significant trend that will probably influence future efforts to combat financial crime and improve cybersecurity. Financial crimes like money laundering and fraudulent transactions may be avoided thanks to blockchain technology's secure and transparent data storage and transfer capabilities. To improve transparency and traceability, financial institutions can use blockchain technology to build a tamper-proof ledger that records all transactions.

Technology advancements are not the only important factor in the future of financial crime prevention and cybersecurity; regulatory compliance is also likely to be a key element. In order to make sure that financial institutions have adequate safeguards in place to thwart financial crimes and protect customer data, governments and regulatory bodies are placing more and more onerous regulations on them. For instance, financial institutions are required to put protections in place to safeguard the personal information of their clients under the General Data Protection Regulation (GDPR) in Europe. Significant fines and reputational harm could be the result of breaking these rules. Finally, financial crime prevention and cybersecurity are likely to be impacted by the growing use of digital currencies like Bitcoin and other cryptocurrencies. Because they are decentralized and operate outside of the established banking system, digital currencies are difficult to regulate and keep track of. To stop money laundering and other financial crimes in the digital currency industry, financial institutions will need to create new technologies and strategies [1, 2].

19.1.1 Background on Financial Crime Prevention and Cybersecurity

In the financial industry, financial crime has long been a problem. It covers a broad range of illegal activities, such as money laundering, fraud, embezzlement, and bribery, that involve the use of financial resources to hide or facilitate criminal activity. These crimes have a significant negative effect on the world economy because they cause monetary losses, reputational harm, and a decline in public confidence in financial institutions. The financial industry has recently become extremely concerned about cybersecurity. Financial institutions are now more susceptible to cyberthreats like hacking, identity theft, and phishing due to the expansion of the internet and the rising use of digital technologies. Data breaches, financial losses, and reputational harm are just a few of the serious consequences that cyberattacks can have on financial institutions. The growing complexity of financial transactions and the expansion of the digital economy exacerbate the problems with financial crime prevention and cybersecurity. The risks of financial crime and cyber threats keep developing and getting more advanced as financial institutions use new technologies and broaden their global reach.

Financial institutions have put in place a number of measures to stop financial crime and safeguard against cyberthreats in response to these difficulties. These precautions include employing well-known security tools like firewalls, intrusion detection systems, and antivirus software. But in the face of fresh and sophisticated cyberthreats, these systems are becoming less and less effective.

Financial institutions are increasingly using distributed systems and computing techniques for financial crime prevention and cybersecurity to address these issues. While computing techniques like machine learning and artificial intelligence can identify and stop financial crime in real time, distributed systems like blockchain technology allow for the secure and transparent recording of financial transactions. Generally speaking, cybersecurity and financial crime prevention are major concerns for the financial sector, and distributed systems and computing approaches present promising solutions to these problems [3–5].

19.1.2 Overview of Distributed Systems and Computing Approaches

Distributed systems and computing approaches are emerging as promising solutions to the challenges of financial crime prevention and cybersecurity. Distributed systems are a type of computer network that allows multiple nodes to share processing power and data, making them ideal for handling large volumes of data and transactions [6–10]. Computing approaches, on the other hand, refer to the use of advanced computing technologies such as machine learning, artificial intelligence, and data analytics to detect and prevent financial crime. Distributed systems offer several advantages over traditional systems. They are more scalable, fault-tolerant, and efficient than traditional centralized systems, making them ideal for handling large volumes of data and transactions. In addition, distributed systems can offer greater security and privacy, as they allow for decentralized authentication and encryption. They can also be more accessible and flexible, as they can be deployed across multiple locations and devices [11–15].

Computing approaches, on the other hand, are revolutionizing the way financial crime prevention and cybersecurity are carried out. Machine learning and artificial intelligence, for example, can analyze vast amounts of data in real time, enabling financial institutions to detect and prevent financial crime before it occurs. Data analytics can also be used to identify patterns and anomalies in financial transactions, helping to detect fraud and money laundering. Despite the potential benefits of distributed systems and computing approaches, they also face several challenges and limitations. Interoperability and standardization are two key challenges, as different systems may use different protocols and standards [16–18]. The integration of new technologies with existing systems can also be a challenge, as legacy systems may not be compatible with new technologies. Finally, the ethical implications of using advanced technologies for financial crime prevention must also be considered, as the use of these technologies may raise privacy and data protection concerns [19, 20]. Distributed systems and computing approaches offer exciting possibilities for the future of financial crime prevention and cybersecurity. However, careful consideration must be given to their potential advantages and limitations, as well as their ethical implications, to ensure that they are used effectively and responsibly [21–24].

Distributed systems and computing approaches are a modern solution to the limitations of traditional systems, particularly in terms of performance, cost, security, accessibility, flexibility, regulatory compliance, adoption, maintenance, and innovation, as shown in Table 19.1.

In terms of performance, distributed systems can provide faster, more scalable, and reliable performance due to their ability to distribute processing power across multiple nodes. This means they can handle large volumes of data and transactions simultaneously, making them ideal for use cases that demand high performance. Traditional systems, on the other hand, are often limited by their hardware and processing power, resulting in slower performance, especially when dealing with large amounts of data or high levels of traffic.

When it comes to cost, distributed systems and computing approaches can be more cost-effective than traditional systems. This is because they can leverage cloud-based solutions and commodity hardware, which reduces hardware and maintenance costs. In contrast, traditional systems often require specialized hardware, maintenance, and staffing costs, which can be expensive.

In terms of security, distributed systems can provide better data encryption and user authentication, resulting in improved security. They can also leverage blockchain technology to create secure, decentralized ledgers that are resistant to tampering and hacking. Traditional systems, on the other hand, may be more vulnerable to cyberattacks and data breaches, which can compromise sensitive data.

Accessibility is another area where distributed systems and computing approaches can have an advantage over traditional systems. They can be more accessible through cloud-based solutions and easier user interfaces, making them ideal for remote work and collaborations. Traditional systems can be less accessible, with more complex user interfaces and limited compatibility with different devices.

Table 19.1 Comparison of distributed systems and computing approaches with traditional systems.

Comparison point	Distributed systems and computing approaches	Traditional systems
Performance	Can provide faster, more scalable, and reliable performance	Can be slower and less scalable or reliable
Cost	Can be more cost-effective due to lower hardware and maintenance costs	Can be more expensive due to hardware, maintenance, and staffing costs
Security	Can provide better data encryption and user authentication for improved security	Can be more vulnerable to cyberattacks and data breaches
Accessibility	Can be more accessible through cloud-based solutions and easier user interfaces	Can be less accessible, with more complex user interfaces and limited compatibility with different devices
Flexibility	Can be more flexible, with customization options and better integration with existing systems	Can be less flexible, with limited customization options and less adaptability to changing business needs
Regulatory compliance	Can be better suited for meeting regulatory compliance requirements, such as KYC and AML	Can be less suited for meeting regulatory compliance requirements
Adoption	Can be less widely adopted in some industries or regions but gain popularity in others	Can be more widely adopted due to their longer history and established market presence
Maintenance	Can require less maintenance and downtime, with frequent automatic updates and technical support	Can require more maintenance and downtime, with less frequent updates and less technical support
Innovation	Can offer more opportunities for innovation and new business models through emerging technologies and improved data analytics capabilities	Can be more limited in terms of innovation and adapting to emerging technologies

When it comes to flexibility, distributed systems and computing approaches can be more flexible due to their customization options and better integration with existing systems. They can also adapt to changing business needs more easily. In contrast, traditional systems may have limited customization options and be less adaptable to changes in the business environment. Regulatory compliance is another area where distributed systems and computing approaches can excel, particularly in meeting regulatory compliance requirements such as know-your-customer (KYC) and anti-money laundering (AML). They can provide transparency and traceability, ensuring compliance with regulations. Traditional systems may be less suited for meeting regulatory compliance requirements.

Adoption is an important consideration when choosing between distributed systems and traditional systems. Distributed systems may be less widely adopted in some industries or regions, but they are gaining popularity in others. Traditional systems, on the other hand, are more widely adopted due to their longer history and established market presence. Maintenance is another area where distributed systems and computing approaches can have an advantage over traditional systems. They can require less maintenance and downtime, with frequent automatic updates and technical support. In contrast, traditional systems may require more maintenance and downtime, with fewer frequent updates and less technical support.

Finally, innovation is an area where distributed systems and computing approaches can offer more opportunities for innovation and new business models through emerging technologies and improved data analytics capabilities. Traditional systems may be more limited in terms of innovation and adapting to emerging technologies. Overall, the choice between distributed systems, computing approaches, and traditional systems depends on the specific needs of the organization, including performance, cost, security, accessibility, flexibility, regulatory compliance, adoption, maintenance, and innovation. A thorough understanding of the advantages and disadvantages of each approach can help organizations make an informed decision that best meets their business requirements [25, 26].

19.2 Distributed Systems and Computing Approaches for Financial Crime Prevention and Cybersecurity

Innovative solutions are required to address these issues due to the increase in financial crime and cybersecurity threats. Two cutting-edge technologies that show great promise in overcoming these difficulties are distributed systems and computing paradigms. Rather than relying on a single central server, distributed systems share computing resources among numerous nodes or devices. For the prevention of financial crime and cybersecurity, this strategy offers several advantages. First off, distributed systems are better suited for processing and analyzing massive amounts of financial data because they can handle large volumes of data and transactions with greater efficiency. The risk of system failure and downtime can also be decreased by distributed systems' improved fault tolerance and redundancy. As data can be encrypted and authenticated at the node level, distributed systems can also increase security and privacy. This is because it is harder for hackers to access sensitive data when it is encrypted and authenticated at the node level. Additionally, cybersecurity and financial crime prevention are being transformed by computing techniques such as machine learning, artificial intelligence, and data analytics. Financial institutions can identify and stop financial crime before it happens, thanks to these technologies' ability to analyze huge amounts of data in real time. Financial institutions can be warned of potential fraud or money laundering by using machine learning algorithms, for instance, to spot patterns and anomalies in financial transactions. In order to gain insight into unauthorized financial activity, data analytics can also be used to track and analyze the movement of money among various accounts and institutions.

There are a number of obstacles to their implementation, despite the potential advantages of distributed systems and computing methods. In particular, when dealing with legacy systems that might not be compatible with new technologies, ensuring interoperability between various systems and protocols can be difficult. Furthermore, the use of cutting-edge technologies for financial crime prevention may give rise to moral questions about data protection and privacy. In conclusion, distributed systems and computing paradigms offer hopeful remedies for cybersecurity and financial crime prevention. The real-time analysis of enormous amounts of data is made possible by these technologies, which also provide advantages like improved efficiency, fault tolerance, security, and privacy. Financial institutions must take into account the potential benefits and constraints of distributed systems and computing approaches in order to develop efficient and responsible solutions to combat these issues as financial crime and cybersecurity threats continue to develop [27, 28].

19.2.1 Blockchain Technology and Its Applications in Financial Crime Prevention and Cybersecurity

Due to its potential applications in a variety of industries, including financial services, blockchain technology is an emerging technology that has recently attracted a lot of attention. The technology is based on a distributed ledger system, which records transactions across numerous network nodes while ensuring security.

In terms of cybersecurity and financial crime prevention, blockchain technology has a number of potential uses. The immutability and transparency of the ledger system are two of the most important advantages of blockchain technology. All transactions are documented and have a clear audit trail that can be used to track and look into financial crimes because they can be tracked back to their source. Additionally, because the blockchain is decentralized, there is no single point of failure, which makes it more challenging for hackers to access sensitive data without authorization. The use of smart contracts is yet another potential way that blockchain technology could be used to prevent financial crime. Self-executing contracts, or smart contracts, can be set up to take effect when specific criteria are met. This can be especially helpful in preventing money laundering because smart contracts can be set up to automatically identify and block suspicious transactions without human intervention. Blockchain technology can be used to strengthen the security of financial transactions, which will help cybersecurity. Hackers may find it more challenging to intercept and manipulate financial data when distributed ledger systems and encryption are used. Furthermore, because personal data is securely stored on the blockchain, the use of identity verification systems based on blockchain can aid in preventing fraud and identity theft.

The implementation of blockchain technology faces a number of difficulties, despite its potential advantages. As more transactions are added, blockchain networks may become crowded and slow, which is one of the major challenges for the technology. It may also be challenging to implement the technology in some financial institutions due to its complexity and difficulty for nontechnical users to understand it.

In summary, blockchain technology has a variety of potential uses in cybersecurity and financial crime prevention. One or two examples of the potential advantages of this new technology include the immutability and transparency of the ledger system, the use of smart contracts, and the increased security of financial transactions. Although there are obstacles in the way of its implementation, blockchain technology is expected to play a significant role in the future of financial services [29, 30].

19.2.2 Distributed Ledgers and Their Role in Preventing Financial Crimes

A type of distributed system called distributed ledger technology (DLT) makes it possible to securely and openly record transactions across numerous network nodes. DLTs are being used more frequently in financial services to stop financial crimes like money laundering and fraud.

The ability of DLTs to establish a transparent and unchangeable audit trail is one of their key advantages for preventing financial crime. Every transaction is documented on the ledger, which is distributed across several nodes, making it very difficult for any one party to manipulate or alter the records. As a result, it will be simpler to identify and look into financial crimes if DLTs are used to create a permanent and unchangeable record of financial transactions.

Trade finance is one area where a DLT is being used to prevent financial crime. Trade finance has historically involved a lot of paperwork and is prone to fraud and mistakes. To reduce the risk of fraud and mistakes, a DLT-based trade finance system allows all parties to a trade to securely and transparently exchange information. Financial crimes like trade-based money laundering may be avoided as a result of this. The use of DLT for identity verification is another instance of how financial crime can be prevented. The risk of identity theft and fraud can be decreased by using DLTs to store and share personal information in a secure and transparent manner. Financial institutions can decrease the risk of fraud and financial crimes by utilizing a DLT-based identity verification system to make sure that their customers are who they say they are.

With the aid of smart contracts, DLTs can also be used to stop financial crimes. Self-executing contracts, or "smart contracts," are those that can be set up to go into effect whenever a set of criteria is satisfied. For instance, if suspicious activity is discovered, a smart contract could be set up to automatically freeze an account. This can aid in the prevention of financial crimes like fraud and money laundering. DLTs may have advantages for preventing financial crime, but there are also obstacles to their implementation. Scalability is one of the main issues because DLT networks can get clogged and slow as more transactions are added. It can also be challenging to implement the technology in some financial institutions because it can be complicated and challenging for nontechnical users to understand [31, 32].

19.2.3 Distributed Computing Approaches for Cybersecurity

Distributed computing is a powerful tool for cybersecurity, allowing multiple computing devices to work together to solve complex security problems. By leveraging the processing power of multiple devices, distributed computing approaches can enable more robust and efficient cybersecurity systems.

One example of distributed computing for cybersecurity is in the area of malware detection. Malware is a persistent and ever-evolving threat to cybersecurity, and detecting and removing malware from a system can be a complex and time-consuming process. However, by using a distributed computing approach, multiple devices can work together to scan for and identify malware, greatly reducing the time and resources required for malware detection. Another example of distributed computing for cybersecurity is in the area of intrusion detection. Intrusion detection systems (IDS) are used to monitor networks for suspicious activity, such as unauthorized access attempts or data breaches. However, IDS can generate large volumes of data, making it difficult for a single device to analyze and process all of the information in real time. By using a distributed computing approach, multiple devices can work together to analyze the data and identify potential security threats.

Distributed computing approaches can also be used for distributed denial of service (DDoS) attack mitigation. DDoS attacks are a common type of cyberattack that floods a network with traffic, making it inaccessible to legitimate users. By using a distributed computing approach, a network can be designed to automatically detect and mitigate DDoS attacks, ensuring that the network remains available and accessible. In addition to these specific applications, distributed computing approaches can be used to provide more general cybersecurity protection. For example, by using a distributed computing approach to distribute the processing and storage of data, the risk of data breaches can be reduced. Similarly, by using a distributed computing approach to manage and secure access to systems, the risk of unauthorized access and data theft can be minimized.

However, as with any technology, there are challenges to the implementation of distributed computing approaches for cybersecurity. One of the main challenges is ensuring the security and integrity of the distributed system itself, as attacks on one device could potentially compromise the entire system. Additionally, ensuring that all devices are properly configured and updated can be a challenge, as can providing adequate security training to all users. Despite these challenges, the benefits of distributed computing for cybersecurity are significant, and the continued development and refinement of this technology is likely to have a significant impact on the future of cybersecurity. By leveraging the power of multiple devices, distributed computing approaches can provide a more efficient and effective way to protect against a wide range of cyberthreats [33–35].

19.3 Challenges and Opportunities in Implementing Distributed Systems and Computing Approaches

While distributed systems and computing approaches have the potential to greatly enhance financial crime prevention and cybersecurity, their implementation also presents a number of challenges.

One key challenge is the issue of interoperability. Distributed systems often involve multiple technologies and devices, and ensuring that these disparate components can work together seamlessly can be a significant challenge. This is particularly true in the case of legacy systems, which may not have been designed with distributed computing in mind. Ensuring that all components can communicate effectively with one another is essential to the success of a distributed system.

Another challenge is ensuring the security and privacy of data within a distributed system. Data may be stored and processed across multiple devices, and ensuring that this data remains secure and private can be a significant challenge. Proper encryption and access controls must be implemented to ensure that sensitive data is protected from unauthorized access.

Another challenge is ensuring the reliability and availability of the system. Distributed systems can be more complex than traditional centralized systems, and ensuring that all components are properly configured and functioning can be difficult. Proper monitoring and maintenance of the system is essential to ensuring that it remains operational and available.

In addition to these challenges, there are also a number of opportunities presented by distributed systems and computing approaches. These include:

- *Increased scalability*: Distributed systems can be designed to scale up or down depending on demand, allowing organizations to easily accommodate growth or changing needs.
- *Increased efficiency*: By distributing processing power and data storage across multiple devices, distributed systems can be more efficient than traditional centralized systems.
- *Improved resiliency*: Distributed systems can be designed to be more resilient to failures, as they can continue to function even if individual components fail.
- *Improved flexibility*: Distributed systems can be designed to be more flexible than traditional centralized systems, allowing organizations to adapt to changing needs and requirements.
- *Improved transparency*: Distributed systems can be designed to provide greater transparency, allowing stakeholders to easily track and monitor transactions and other activities.

In order to fully realize the potential of distributed systems and computing approaches, it will be essential to address the challenges and to capitalize on the opportunities presented by this technology. By doing so, financial institutions and organizations can greatly enhance their ability to prevent financial crimes and protect against cybersecurity threats.

19.3.1 Regulatory and Compliance Issues

Several regulatory and compliance issues must be resolved before distributed systems and computing methods can be implemented for cybersecurity and the prevention of financial crime. Financial institutions and other businesses handling sensitive data are subject to a number of laws and standards designed to protect that data. Compliance with laws governing data privacy, such as the California Consumer Privacy Act (CCPA) in the United States and the General Data Protection Regulation (GDPR) in the European Union, is a major problem. Organizations handling personal data, including information about financial transactions, are subject to stringent requirements under these regulations. Any distributed systems that organizations implement must comply with these laws, and this includes making sure that any data processed or stored on the system is properly secured and safeguarded.

Compliance with financial rules, such as those relating to KYC and AML, is another problem. The implementation of these controls and procedures by financial institutions is mandated by these regulations in order to stop money laundering and other financial crimes. These rules must be followed by any distributed system used by a financial institution, including making sure the system is capable of spotting and stopping any suspicious activity. Organizations must also abide by industry standards, such as the Payment Card Industry Data Security Standard (PCI DSS), which places obligations on businesses that handle credit card information, in addition to these laws. Organizations are required to take all necessary precautions, such as putting in place the right access controls and encryption, to make sure that any distributed system they implement complies with these standards.

Making sure that any third-party providers entrusted with carrying out the distributed system do so in accordance with all applicable laws and standards is a further concern. Organizations must make sure that any third-party vendors they work with have undergone thorough due diligence and that any contracts or service level agreements contain the proper compliance clauses.

Organizations must thoughtfully consider the design and implementation of any distributed system in order to address these legal and compliance concerns. This entails performing a thorough risk assessment and making sure that all pertinent laws and standards are taken into account during the design and implementation phases. To make sure that their distributed systems adhere to all relevant rules and standards, organizations may also need to interact with regulators and business associations. Organizations can make sure that their distributed systems are properly designed and implemented, capable of successfully preventing financial crimes, safeguarding against cybersecurity threats, and compliant with all applicable laws and standards by addressing these regulatory and compliance issues [36, 37].

19.3.2 Interoperability and Standardization Challenges

Interoperability and standardization are critical challenges that must be addressed when implementing distributed systems and computing approaches for financial crime prevention and cybersecurity.

Interoperability refers to the ability of different systems to work together seamlessly, and it is a critical requirement for distributed systems that are designed to operate across multiple organizations or platforms. In the context of financial crime prevention and cybersecurity, interoperability is essential for ensuring that different systems can communicate with one another and exchange critical data in real time. However, achieving interoperability is not always straightforward, particularly when different systems have been developed independently by different organizations or vendors. To ensure interoperability, standardization is critical. Standardization involves establishing common protocols, interfaces, and data structures that allow different systems to work together seamlessly.

One challenge in achieving standardization is the lack of clear industry standards and protocols for distributed systems and computing approaches. The field is still relatively new, and there are a wide variety of different platforms, protocols, and tools in use. Without clear standards, it can be difficult for different systems to communicate with one another effectively.

Another challenge is the need for coordination among different stakeholders in the financial industry. Different organizations may have different priorities, and they may be using different platforms and tools. Without coordination, it can be difficult to establish common standards and protocols that can be adopted across the industry. To address these challenges, there are a number of efforts underway to establish common standards and protocols for distributed systems and computing approaches in the financial industry. For example, the Financial Industry Business Ontology (FIBO) is a standardized vocabulary for describing financial concepts, and it is designed to improve interoperability between different financial systems. Additionally, organizations like the Enterprise Ethereum Alliance and the Hyperledger Foundation are working to establish common standards and protocols for blockchain-based distributed systems. In addition to these efforts, it is also important to ensure that different stakeholders in the financial industry are aligned with their priorities and goals. This requires effective communication and collaboration among different organizations, as well as a commitment to establishing common standards and protocols.

By addressing these interoperability and standardization challenges, the financial industry can ensure that distributed systems and computing approaches are able to operate effectively and securely. This will help to improve financial crime prevention and cybersecurity while also enabling greater innovation and efficiency in the industry.

19.3.3 Integration with Existing Systems and Infrastructure

Another challenge in implementing distributed systems and computing approaches for financial crime prevention and cybersecurity is the integration with existing systems and infrastructure. Many financial institutions have legacy systems that were developed over many years, and these systems can be difficult to modify or replace.

To achieve the benefits of distributed systems and computing approaches, it is essential that these new systems can be seamlessly integrated with existing infrastructure. This can be a significant challenge, particularly when legacy systems are not designed with interoperability in mind.

One approach to addressing this challenge is to use middleware or application programming interfaces (APIs) that enable different systems to communicate with one another. This approach can help to bridge the gap between different systems and enable the exchange of data and information.

Another approach is to adopt a phased implementation strategy, in which new systems are gradually integrated with existing infrastructure over time. This can help to minimize disruption and enable financial institutions to adopt new systems in a more controlled and manageable way.

In addition to these technical challenges, there may also be organizational challenges related to the integration of new systems with existing infrastructure. For example, there may be resistance from employees who are comfortable with existing systems, or there may be concerns about the impact on existing business processes. To address these challenges, it is important to engage stakeholders from across the organization in the implementation process. This includes IT personnel, business leaders, and end-users, among others. By involving stakeholders in the process, it is possible to identify and address concerns early on and ensure that everyone is aligned in their goals and priorities.

Ultimately, the integration of distributed systems and computing approaches with existing systems and infrastructure is critical for achieving the benefits of these new technologies. By addressing the technical and organizational challenges involved, financial institutions can ensure that they are able to operate more efficiently, securely, and effectively, while also enhancing their ability to prevent financial crimes and cybersecurity threats [38].

19.3.4 Opportunities for Innovation and Efficiency

Despite the difficulties associated with implementing distributed systems and computing methods for cybersecurity and financial crime prevention, these technologies offer significant opportunities for innovation and efficiency. Being able to automate and increase the efficiency of financial processes is one of the main benefits of distributed systems and computing paradigms. For instance, using blockchain technology can enable quicker and more secure transactions, as well as reduce the need for middlemen and boost transparency.

A greater level of innovation in financial services and products can also be made possible by distributed systems and computing paradigms. For instance, the use of smart contracts and other blockchain-based applications can facilitate the creation of brand-new financial instruments and investment opportunities while also enhancing the effectiveness and transparency of already-available financial products. Data analytics and artificial intelligence are two more fields where distributed systems and computing methods have room to grow. Financial institutions can better understand the risks and opportunities associated with financial crimes and cybersecurity threats by utilizing advanced analytics tools and distributed computing resources to gain deeper insights into their data.

Additionally, the use of distributed systems and computing techniques can aid in addressing some of the most urgent issues the financial sector is currently facing, like fraud and money laundering. These technologies can aid in lowering the frequency of financial crime and enhancing the efficiency and effectiveness of compliance and risk management by enabling more secure and transparent financial transactions. Distributed systems and computing methods present the financial sector with significant opportunities for innovation and efficiency. Financial institutions can increase the effectiveness and transparency of financial processes and products while also strengthening their capacity to combat cybersecurity threats and financial crimes by utilizing these technologies [39, 40].

19.4 Benefits of Distributed Systems in Financial Crime Prevention

1. *Increased security*: One of the key benefits of distributed systems and computing approaches is their ability to improve security. For example, the use of blockchain technology can provide greater transparency and reduce the risk of fraud and other financial crimes.
2. *Improved efficiency*: Another advantage of these technologies is that they can help to improve the efficiency of financial processes by reducing the need for intermediaries and automating certain functions.
3. *Greater transparency*: By enabling more secure and transparent financial transactions, distributed systems and computing approaches can help to enhance the transparency of financial processes, making it easier to detect and prevent financial crimes.
4. *Innovation*: The use of distributed systems and computing approaches can also enable greater innovation in the financial industry by providing new tools and platforms for the development of new financial products and services.

19.5 Limitations of Distributed Systems in Financial Crime Prevention

1. *Technical challenges*: One of the key limitations of distributed systems and computing approaches is the technical challenges involved in implementing

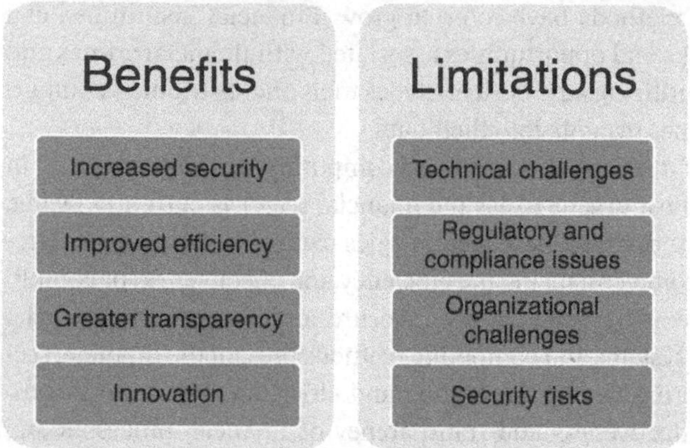

Figure 19.1 Analysis of benefits and limitations.

these technologies, such as the need for interoperability and the difficulty of integrating new systems with existing infrastructure.

2. *Regulatory and compliance issues*: Another limitation is the regulatory and compliance issues involved in the use of these technologies, such as the need to comply with existing financial regulations and the need to ensure data privacy and security.
3. *Organizational challenges*: In addition, there may be organizational challenges involved in the adoption of distributed systems and computing approaches, such as the need to overcome resistance from employees who are accustomed to existing systems and processes.
4. *Security risks*: Finally, the use of distributed systems and computing approaches can also pose certain security risks, such as the risk of cyberattacks or other types of data breaches.

Overall, while distributed systems and computing approaches offer a number of benefits for financial crime prevention and cybersecurity, there are also several limitations and challenges, as shown in Figure 19.1, that need to be addressed in order to fully realize their potential. By taking a holistic approach to implementing these technologies and addressing both the technical and organizational challenges involved, it is possible to leverage the benefits of these technologies while minimizing the risks and limitations.

19.6 Conclusion

In conclusion, distributed systems and computing approaches hold great promise for the future of financial crime prevention and cybersecurity, improving the security and effectiveness of financial transactions. Greater transparency, lower risk of fraud and other financial crimes, and increased innovation in the financial sector can all be achieved through the use of distributed ledgers, blockchain technology, and other distributed computing techniques. To fully utilize the potential of these technologies, however, a number of obstacles and constraints must be overcome. The successful implementation of distributed systems and computing approaches requires overcoming a number of technical obstacles, including interoperability and integration with existing systems, regulatory and compliance issues, and organizational obstacles, including employee resistance. Utilizing the advantages of these technologies while reducing the risks and limitations requires a comprehensive strategy for tackling these issues. The use of distributed systems and computing techniques will undoubtedly become more crucial as the financial sector develops and adopts new technologies, helping to ensure the efficiency and security of financial transactions.

References

1 DaCorte, A.M. (2022). The Effects of the Internet on Financial Institutions' Fraud Mitigation. PhD thesis, Utica University, Utica, NY, USA.

2 Li, Y. (2009). Credit risk prediction based on machine learning methods. In: *Proceedings of the 2019 14th International Conference on Computer Science & Education (ICCSE), Toronto, ON, Canada, 19–21 August 2019*, 1011–1013.

3 Zhu, L., Qiu, D., Ergu, D. et al. (2019). A study on predicting loan default based on the random forest algorithm. *Procedia Comput. Sci.* 162: 503–513.

4 Vojtek, M. and Koèenda, E. (2006). Credit-scoring methods. *Czech J. Econ. Financ.* 56: 152–167.

5 Arora, B. (2022). A review of credit card fraud detection techniques. *Recent Innov. Comput.* 832: 485–496.

6 Gupta, A., Asad, A., Meena, L., and Anand, R. (2022, July). IoT and RFID-based smart card system integrated with health care, electricity, QR and banking sectors. In: *Artificial Intelligence on Medical Data: Proceedings of International Symposium, ISCMM 2021*, 253–265. Singapore: Springer Nature Singapore.

7 Kumar Pandey, B., Pandey, D., Nassa, V.K. et al. (2021). Encryption and steganography-based text extraction in IoT using the EWCTS optimizer. *Imaging Sci. J.* 69 (1-4): 38–56.

8 Govindaraj, V., Dhanasekar, S., Martinsagayam, K. et al. (2023). Low-power test pattern generator using modified LFSR. *Aerosp. Syst.* 1–8.

9 Pandey, D., Pandey, B.K., Wariya, S. et al. (2020). Analysis of text detection, extraction and recognition from complex degraded images and videos. *J. Critic. Rev.* 7 (18): 427–433.

10 Pandey, D., Pandey, B.K., and Wariya, S. (2019). Study of various techniques used for video retrieval. *J. Emerg. Technol. Innov. Res.* 6 (6): 850–853.

11 Anand, R. and Chawla, P. (2020). Optimization of inscribed hexagonal fractal slotted microstrip antenna using modified lightning attachment procedure optimization. *Int. J. Microw. Wirel. Technol.* 12 (6): 519–530.

12 Anand, R. and Chawla, P. (2020). A novel dual-wideband inscribed hexagonal fractal slotted microstrip antenna for C-and X-band applications. *Int. J. RF Microwave Comput. Aided Eng.* 30 (9): e22277.

13 Meelu, R. and Anand, R. (2010). Energy efficiency of cluster-based routing protocols used in wireless sensor networks. In: *AIP Conference Proceedings*, vol. 1324, No. 1, , 109–113. American Institute of Physics.

14 Sansanwal, K., Shrivastava, G., Anand, R., and Sharma, K. (2019). Big data analysis and compression for indoor air quality. In: *Handbook of IoT and Big Data*, 1–21. CRC Press.

15 Anand, R., Singh, J., Pandey, D. et al. (2022). Modern technique for interactive communication in LEACH-based ad hoc wireless sensor network. In: *Software Defined Networking for Ad Hoc Networks*, 55–73. Cham: Springer International Publishing.

16 Nijhawan, M., Sindhwani, N., Tanwar, S., and Kumar, S. (2022). Role of augmented reality and internet of things in education sector. In: *IoT Based Smart Applications*, 245–259. Cham: Springer International Publishing.

17 Verma, S., Bajaj, T., Sindhwani, N., and Kumar, A. (2022). Design and development of a driving assistance and safety system using deep learning. In: *Advances in Data Science and Computing Technology*, 35–45. Apple Academic Press.

18 Sharma, G., Nehra, N., Dahiya, A. et al. (2022). Automatic heart-rate measurement using facial video. In: *Networking Technologies in Smart Healthcare*, 289–307. CRC Press.

19 Sharma, R., Vashisth, R., and Sindhwani, N. (2023). Study and analysis of classification techniques for specific plant growths. In: *Advances in Signal Processing, Embedded Systems and IoT: Proceedings of Seventh ICMEET-2022*, 591–605. Singapore: Springer Nature Singapore.

20 Chaudhary, A., Bodala, D., Sindhwani, N., and Kumar, A. (2022). Analysis of customer loyalty using artificial neural networks. In: *In 2022 International Mobile and Embedded Technology Conference (MECON)*, 181–183. IEEE.

21 Rehman, A.U., Jiang, A., Rehman, A., and Paul, A. (2019). Weighted based trustworthiness ranking in social internet of things by using soft set theory. In: *Proceedings of the 2019 IEEE 5th International Conference on Computer and Communications (ICCC), Chengdu, China, 6–9 December 2019*, 1644–1648.

22 Ghatasheh, N. (2014). Business analytics using random forest trees for credit risk prediction: a comparison study. *Int. J. Adv. Sci. Technol.* 72: 19–30.

23 Breeden, J.L. (2021). A survey of machine learning in credit risk. *J. Crédit. Risk* 17: 1–62.

24 Madaan, M., Kumar, A., Keshri, C. et al. (2021). Loan default prediction using decision trees and random forest: a comparative study. *IOP Conf. Series Mater. Sci. Eng.* 1022: 012042.

25 Pidikiti, S., Myneedi, P., Nagarapu, S. et al. (2019). Loan prediction by using machine learning models. *Int. J. Eng. Tech.* 5: 144–148.

26 Alhazmi, O.H. and Malaiya, Y.K. (2008). Application of vulnerability discovery models to major operating systems. *IEEE Trans. Reliab.* 57: 14–22.

27 Algarni, A.M. and Malaiya, Y.K. (2016). A consolidated approach for estimation of data security breach costs. In: *Proceedings of the 2016 2nd International Conference on Information Management (ICIM), London, UK, 7–8 May 2016.*

28 Layton, R. and Watters, P.A. (2014). A methodology for estimating the tangible cost of data breaches. *J. Inf. Secur. Appl.* 19: 321–330.

29 Thapa, C. and Camtepe, S. (2021). Precision health data: requirements, challenges and existing techniques for data security and privacy. *Comput. Biol. Med.* 129: 104130.

30 Westland, J.C. (2020). The information content of Sarbanes-Oxley in predicting security breaches. *Comput. Secur.* 90: 101687.

31 Da Veiga, A., Astakhova, L.V., Botha, A., and Herselman, M. (2020). Defining organizational information security culture—Perspectives from academia and industry. *Comput. Secur.* 92: 101713.

32 Diesch, R., Pfaff, M., and Krcmar, H. (2020). A comprehensive model of information security factors for decision-makers. *Comput. Secur.* 92: 101747.

33 Iannacone, M.D. and Bridges, R.A. (2020). Quantifiable & comparable evaluations of cyber defensive capabilities: a survey & novel, unified approach. *Comput. Secur.* 96: 101907.

34 Khalid, A., Zainal, A., Maarof, M.A., and Ghaleb, F.A. (2021). Advanced persistent threat detection: a survey. In: *In Proceedings of the 2021 3rd International Cyber Resilience Conference (CRC), Langkawi Island, Malaysia, 29–31 January 2021.*

35 Javed, S.H., Ahmad, M.B., Asif, M. et al. (2022). An intelligent system to detect advanced persistent threats in industrial internet of things (I-IoT). *Electronics* 11: 742.

36 Li, S., Zhang, Q., Wu, X. et al. (2021). Attribution classification method of APT malware in IoT using machine learning techniques. *Secur. Commun. Netw.* 2021: 9396141.

37 Bilge, L. and Dumitras, T. (2012). Before we knew it: an empirical study of zero-day attacks in the real world. In: *In Proceedings of the 2012 ACM conference on Computer and Communications Security, Raleigh, NC, USA, 16–18 October 2012*, 833–844.

38 Zhang, W., Guo, W., Liu, X. et al. (2018). LSTM-Based analysis of industrial IoT equipment. *IEEE Access* 6: 23551–23560.

39 Baracaldo, N., Chen, B., Ludwig, H. et al. (2018). Detecting poisoning attacks on machine learning in IoT environments. In: *Proceedings of the 2018 IEEE International Congress on Internet of Things (ICIOT), San Francisco, CA, USA, 2–7 July 2018.*

40 Papernot, N., McDaniel, P., Goodfellow, I. et al. (2017). Practical black-box attacks against machine learning. In: *Proceedings of the 2017 ACM on Asia Conference on Computer and Communications Security, Abu Dhabi, United Arab Emirates, 2–6 April 2017.*

20

Innovations in Distributed Computing for Enhanced Risk Management in Finance

Venkateswararao Podile[1], Syed M. Faisal[2], Gangu N. Mandala[3], Shaik Altaf[4], Nayana Harshitha[4], Cheedella A.S. Lakshmi[4], and Chunduru R. Chandan[4]

[1]*K. L. Business School, Koneru Lakshmaiah Education Foundation, Vaddeswaram, Andhra Pradesh, India*
[2]*Department of Management, Jazan University, Kabul, Saudi Arabia*
[3]*Department of Business Administration, Central Tribal University of Andhra Pradesh, Konda Karakam, Andhra Pradesh, India*
[4]*Koneru Lakshmaiah Education Foundation, Vaddeswaram, Andhra Pradesh, India*

20.1 Introduction

Risk management is a critical function in the financial industry, with the potential to minimize or eliminate losses arising from market volatility, credit, operational, or liquidity risks. As financial institutions process large amounts of data, the application of advanced technologies, such as distributed computing, has become essential to enable timely and accurate risk assessment. Analyze and manage large data volumes while simultaneously reducing the time and cost associated with risk management processes. The chapter highlights the theoretical frameworks that underpin distributed computing, the types of distributed computing technologies and applications, the challenges and limitations, as well as best practices for its implementation. The chapter concludes by identifying emerging trends and recommendations for future research on this topic. The ultimate goal is to provide insights that will help financial institutions optimize their risk management practices, thereby enhancing their competitiveness in the financial markets. Risk management in finance involves the identification, analysis, and evaluation of potential risks that may adversely affect a financial institution's

Meta-Heuristic Algorithms for Advanced Distributed Systems, First Edition. Edited by Rohit Anand, Abhinav Juneja, Digvijay Pandey, Sapna Juneja, and Nidhi Sindhwani.

assets, earnings, or reputation. Liquidity risks involve the inability to access sufficient funds to meet financial obligations. Reputational risks may occur when a financial institution's image is damaged due to negative public perception, poor performance, or unethical behavior [1–3]

20.1.1 Distributed Computing vs Traditional Risk Management

Table 20.1 compares two different computing systems for risk management in finance: a traditional system and a distributed computing system. It includes several criteria that are important for evaluating the performance of these systems. The first criterion is data processing speed, which is measured in transactions per second. The traditional system is capable of processing up to 10,000 transactions per second, while the distributed computing system can handle up to 100,000 transactions per second. This means that the distributed computing system is much faster at processing large volumes of data.

The traditional system can only handle up to 10 nodes, while the distributed computing system can scale up to 100 nodes. This means that the distributed computing system is much more flexible and can adapt to changing business needs. This means that the distributed computing system is more reliable and less prone to downtime. The traditional system has a centralized storage with 128-bit encryption, while the distributed computing system has a decentralized storage with 256-bit encryption. This means that the distributed computing system has stronger data security measures in place. Table 20.1 shows that the distributed computing system outperforms the traditional system on several important criteria, including data processing speed, scalability, fault tolerance, and cost. This illustrates the potential benefits of using innovative distributed computing approaches for enhanced risk management in finance.

Table 20.1 Traditional risk management vs distributed computing.

Criteria	Traditional system	Distributed computing system
Data processing speed (transactions/second)	10,000	1,00,000
Scalability (maximum nodes)	10	100
Fault tolerance (number of potential single points of failure)	1	0
Data security (encryption strength in bits)	128	256
Cost (USD per year)	10,00,000	5,00,000

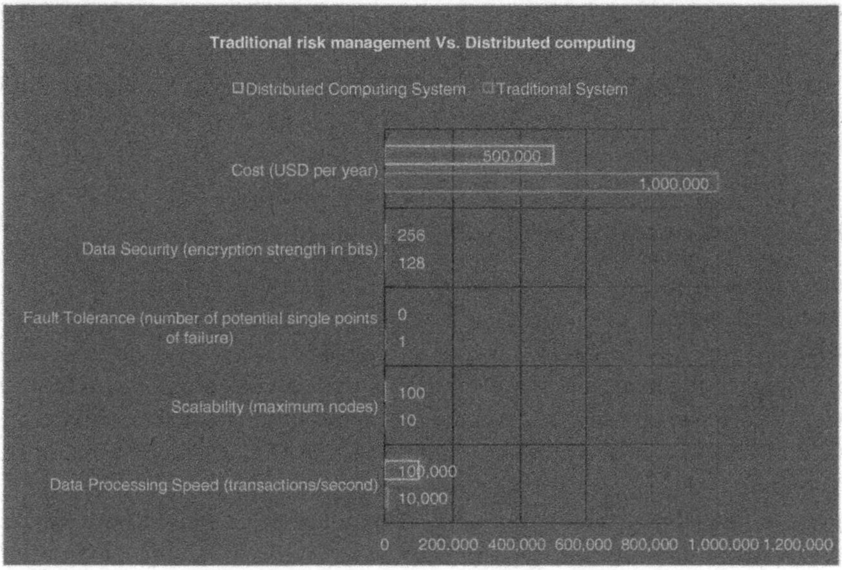

Figure 20.1 Traditional risk management vs distributed computing.

Figure 20.1 shows the differences between traditional risk management vs. distributed computing.

20.2 Theoretical Framework

The theoretical framework of distributed computing for finance risk management is based on several key concepts and principles. Firstly, distributed computing involves the processing of data across multiple computing devices, with each device performing a part of the computation. Secondly, distributed computing systems are designed to be fault-tolerant and scalable, enabling them to cope with failures in individual computing devices or sudden increases in data volumes. This is achieved through the use of redundancy and load-balancing techniques, which ensure that computing resources are distributed efficiently and effectively across the system.

Distributed storage systems use techniques such as sharing and replication to store data across multiple devices, providing greater resilience and scalability than traditional storage systems. Finally, distributed computing for finance risk management is underpinned by a range of regulatory frameworks that set out guidelines for the safe and secure processing of sensitive data. The theoretical framework of distributed computing for finance risk management is based on the principles of parallel processing, fault tolerance, scalability, distributed storage, advanced algorithms, and regulatory compliance. These principles provide a solid foundation for the effective use of distributed computing in finance risk management [4, 5].

20.2.1 Overview of Distributed Computing

Data processing on numerous computing units, frequently dispersed across various physical places, is the focus of the computer science discipline known as distributed computing. Parallel processing, which includes breaking down computational processes into smaller subtasks that can be done concurrently by several computing units, is the fundamental idea behind distributed computing. This is achieved through the use of redundancy and load-balancing techniques, which ensure that computing resources are distributed efficiently and effectively across the system. Distributed computing systems also rely on distributed storage systems, which allow for the efficient storage and retrieval of large amounts of data across multiple devices. Distributed storage systems use techniques such as sharding and replication to store data across multiple devices, providing greater resilience and scalability than traditional storage systems. In recent years, distributed computing has been increasingly used in finance risk management due to the large amounts of data involved in risk analysis and management [6–8].

20.2.2 Types of Distributed Computing Technologies for Finance Risk Management

There are various types of distributed computing technologies that can be used for finance risk management. Here are some examples [9, 10]:

1. *Spark*: Apache Spark is another open-source distributed computing framework that provides fast in-memory data processing capabilities. It is commonly used in finance risk management for processing and analyzing large datasets in real time, including credit card transactions and social media data.
2. *Blockchain*: It is increasingly being used in finance risk management for enabling secure and transparent recording of financial transactions and for detecting fraudulent activities.
3. *Cloud computing*: Cloud computing is widely used in finance risk management for processing and analyzing large datasets, enabling secure data storage, and providing flexibility in computing resources. The selection of a distributed computing technology for finance risk management will depend on the specific use case, the type of data being processed, the required speed of processing, and the level of security and scalability required.

20.3 Comparison of Distributed Computing Approaches for Finance Risk Management

There are various distributed computing approaches that can be used for finance risk management, each with its advantages and disadvantages. Here are some examples [11–13]:

1. *Edge computing*: Edge computing involves the processing of data at or near the edge of the network, rather than in a centralized data center [14–17]. Edge computing can be beneficial for finance risk management as it enables real-time processing of data and can help to reduce latency. However, edge computing can be more challenging to implement than other distributed computing approaches, as it requires the deployment of computing resources.
2. *Grid computing*: Grid computing involves the use of distributed computing resources across multiple organizations or locations [18–21]. Grid computing can be beneficial for finance risk management as it enables the sharing of computing resources and expertise and can help to reduce costs. However, grid computing can be more complex to implement than other distributed computing approaches, as it requires the coordination of resources across multiple organizations.
3. *Hybrid computing*: Hybrid computing involves the use of a combination of different distributed computing approaches, such as cloud-based and edge computing. Hybrid computing can be beneficial for finance risk management as it enables organizations to leverage the strengths of different computing approaches to meet their specific needs. However, hybrid computing can be more complex to implement than other distributed computing approaches, as it requires the integration of multiple technologies and architectures [22–26].

The organization's size and complexity, the type of financial data being examined, and the organization's particular risk management requirements will all influence the choice of distributed computing approach for finance risk management. Organizations must carefully consider their alternatives to determine which technique is best suited to their objectives because each approach has advantages and disadvantages.

20.4 Innovations in Distributed Computing for Enhanced Risk Management in Finance

Several distributed computing breakthroughs that have surfaced in recent years have the potential to enhance risk management in the financial sector. BT, a distributed ledger platform that offers safe, open, and decentralized transactions, is one such breakthrough. By offering a safe and transparent record of financial transactions and lowering the danger of fraud and other financial crimes, the usage of BT can improve risk management in finance. Moreover, BT can be used to develop self-executing contracts, which eliminate the requirement for middlemen by autonomously enforcing the terms of an agreement.

AI is a different distributed computing invention with the potential to improve risk management in finance. Large-scale financial data can be analyzed to find patterns and trends that could be signs of possible problems using AI technologies like machine learning and natural language processing. Aspects of risk management, like fraud detection and compliance monitoring, can also be automated using AI. Yet, enterprises must make sure that AI algorithms do not jeopardize the security, integrity, and accessibility of financial data. The application of AI in risk management can increase accuracy and efficiency.

Another distributed computing innovation that can improve risk management in finance is the Internet of Things [27, 28]. IoT devices like wearables and sensors can be used to gather real-time data on a variety of financial transaction-related factors like location, temperature, and pressure. Distributed computing technology can be used to evaluate this data in order to spot potential threats and facilitate quick decisions. IoT sensors, for instance, can be used to track the temperature in a server room in order to spot prospective equipment breakdowns that might result in financial losses. IoT technology adoption, however, is fraught with difficulties, including the requirement for new infrastructure and the susceptibility of IoT devices to cyberattacks.

The implementation of these distributed computing breakthroughs faces difficulties, even if they have the potential to enhance risk management in the financial sector. One of the difficulties is that new infrastructure is required in order to integrate these technologies with the current financial systems. Also, it takes specialized knowledge to implement and maintain these technologies in an organization, which can be difficult for people without a background in distributed computing. Strong privacy and security measures are required in order to safeguard sensitive financial data from online threats and breaches, which presents another difficulty.

Current advancements in distributed computing have the potential to significantly improve risk management in the financial sector. New and more efficient methods for gathering, processing, and analyzing financial data are made possible by BT, AI, and IoT. The implementation of these technologies is fraught with difficulties, including the requirement for new infrastructure, specialized knowledge, and stern privacy and security safeguards. Organizations that succeed in overcoming these obstacles, however, can gain from better risk management, enhanced productivity, and decreased financial losses [29–32].

20.4.1 New Distributed Computing Techniques for Finance Risk Management

There are several new and emerging distributed computing techniques that have the potential to enhance risk management in finance. Here are some examples [33, 34]:

- *Edge computing*: Edge computing is a distributed computing paradigm that involves processing data at the edge of the network, close to where the data is generated. This can be particularly useful in finance for real-time data processing and analytics, where the speed of data analysis is critical for effective risk management.
- *Homomorphic encryption*: Homomorphic encryption is a technique that allows data to be encrypted while still allowing computations to be performed on the encrypted data. This technique can be used in finance to protect sensitive financial data while still allowing for data analysis and processing.
- *Graph computing*: Graph computing is a distributed computing technique that is particularly suited to processing and analyzing large graphs, such as social networks or financial networks. This technique can be used in finance for applications such as fraud detection and credit risk analysis.
- *Swarm intelligence*: This technique can be used in finance for applications such as portfolio optimization and risk management. These emerging distributed computing techniques have the potential to significantly enhance risk management in finance by providing new and more effective ways to collect, process, and analyze financial data. However, these techniques are still in the early stages of development, and their effectiveness and suitability for risk management applications in finance are still being explored. It is important for organizations to carefully evaluate the potential benefits and challenges of these new techniques before implementing them in their risk management strategies.

20.4.2 Emerging Trends in Distributed Computing for Finance Risk Management

There are several emerging trends in distributed computing that have the potential to transform finance risk management. Here are some examples:

1. *Quantum computing*: Quantum computing is an emerging technology that uses quantum mechanics to perform computations that are impossible for classical computers. Quantum computing has the potential to significantly enhance risk management in finance by enabling more accurate and faster simulations of financial markets and scenarios.

2. *Serverless computing*: Serverless computing is a distributed computing model that involves running applications in cloud environments without having to manage servers or infrastructure. This can enable organizations to focus on developing risk management applications without worrying about the underlying infrastructure.
3. *Explainable AI*: Explainable AI is an emerging field of artificial intelligence that is focused on developing machine learning models that are more transparent and explainable. This can enable organizations to better understand and interpret the results of risk management models and to identify and address potential biases or errors.

These emerging trends in distributed computing have the potential to significantly enhance risk management in finance by enabling more accurate, faster, and transparent analysis and processing of financial data. However, these trends are still in the early stages of development, and their effectiveness and suitability for risk management applications in finance are still being explored [35–37].

20.5 Challenges and Limitations of Distributed Computing for Finance Risk Management

While distributed computing offers many benefits for finance risk management, there are also several challenges and limitations that need to be considered. Here are some examples:

1. *Latency and network congestion*: Distributed computing involves processing data across multiple nodes, which can introduce latency and network congestion. This can be particularly problematic for real-time risk management applications in finance, where timely and accurate data analysis is critical.
2. *Complexity*: Distributed computing systems can be complex and difficult to manage, particularly as the number of nodes and technologies involved increases. It is important for organizations to have the necessary expertise and resources to design, implement, and manage distributed computing systems effectively.
3. *Cost*: While distributed computing can be cost-effective in the long run, there can be significant upfront costs associated with designing and implementing distributed computing systems. It is important for organizations to carefully consider the costs and benefits of distributed computing before deciding to invest in this technology.
4. *Regulatory and compliance issues*: Financial organizations are subject to numerous regulatory and compliance requirements, which can make it challenging to

implement distributed computing solutions that meet these requirements. Distributed computing has many potential benefits for finance risk management, but there are also several challenges and limitations that need to be considered. It is important for organizations to carefully evaluate the risks and benefits of distributed computing before deciding to implement this technology in their risk management strategies [38].

20.5.1 Technical Challenges in Implementing Distributed Computing for Finance Risk Management

Implementing distributed computing for finance risk management can involve several technical challenges, including:

1. *Data integration*: Distributed computing involves processing and analyzing data from multiple sources, which can be challenging to integrate and manage. It is important to establish standardized data formats and protocols for data sharing to ensure efficient data integration across distributed systems.
2. *Fault tolerance*: Distributed computing involves multiple nodes and systems, which can increase the risk of system failures and errors. It is important to implement fault-tolerant mechanisms to ensure that system failures or errors do not compromise the accuracy or availability of financial risk management processes.
3. *Security*: Distributed computing involves processing and sharing data across multiple systems, which can introduce security vulnerabilities. It is important to implement strong security measures, such as encryption and access controls, to ensure the confidentiality and integrity of financial data.
4. *Network latency*: Distributed computing involves processing data across multiple systems, which can introduce network latency. It is important to minimize network latency to ensure real-time data processing and analysis for financial risk management applications.
5. *Data storage and retrieval*: Distributed computing involves processing and storing large volumes of data across multiple systems. It is important to design data storage and retrieval systems that can efficiently manage data storage, retrieval, and access across distributed systems.

Implementing distributed computing for finance risk management can involve several technical challenges that need to be carefully considered and addressed. It is important to design distributed systems that can effectively integrate and manage data, ensure fault tolerance and scalability, provide strong security measures, minimize network latency, and efficiently manage data storage and retrieval [39].

20.5.2 Limitations of Distributed Computing for Finance Risk Management

While distributed computing has many potential benefits for finance risk management, there are also several limitations that need to be considered. Here are some examples:

Infrastructure requirements: Implementing distributed computing requires significant infrastructure investments, including hardware, software, and networking equipment. These investments can be costly and may not be feasible for all organizations.

- *Technical expertise*: Implementing distributed computing requires technical expertise in areas such as systems architecture, software engineering, and networking. Organizations without this expertise may struggle to design, implement, and manage distributed computing systems effectively.
- *Integration with existing systems*: Distributed computing solutions must be integrated with existing systems, which can be challenging if the existing systems are not compatible with the distributed computing technology being used. This can result in additional costs and delays in implementation.
- *Regulatory compliance*: The use of distributed computing for finance risk management may be subject to regulatory compliance requirements that are difficult to meet. For example, some regulations require financial data to be stored within a specific jurisdiction, which can be challenging when data is being processed across multiple nodes.
- *Data privacy*: The use of distributed computing for finance risk management may raise concerns about data privacy. If sensitive financial data is being processed across multiple nodes, there is a risk that the data could be compromised or accessed by unauthorized parties.
- *Limited use cases*: The use of distributed computing for finance risk management may not be appropriate for all use cases. Some financial risk management processes may be better suited to centralized computing approaches, depending on the specific requirements of the process.

While distributed computing has many potential benefits for finance risk management, there are also several limitations that need to be considered. Organizations must carefully evaluate the costs and benefits of implementing distributed computing for their specific use cases and be aware of the technical, regulatory, and privacy challenges that may arise [40].

20.6 Future Directions

Here are some best practices and recommendations for implementing distributed computing in finance risk management. The first step is to define clear business objectives and ensure that the use of distributed computing aligns with these objectives. This helps to ensure that the solution meets the specific needs of the organization. A clear architecture is also essential for the successful implementation of distributed computing solutions. This architecture should define the role of each node and the communication channels between them, supporting the business objectives and being scalable for future needs. Leveraging existing infrastructure can help to minimize costs and reduce complexity. Using standard protocols for data transfer, communication, and security is important to ensure compatibility and interoperability. This can simplify integration and increase system dependability. To handle system failures and faults, fault tolerance methods like redundancy, failover, and error handling must also be put in place. For the management of financial risk, data security is also crucial in distributed computing. To guarantee the confidentiality, integrity, and accessibility of financial data, stringent data security controls must be in place. This entails putting in place monitoring systems, access limits, and encryption. Careful planning and the deployment of measures are needed to guarantee regulatory compliance. Distributed computing for risk management in finance must adhere to all applicable laws, rules, and standards, particularly those governing data security, privacy, and access. To make sure the solution is working as planned, it is crucial to monitor system performance. This involves monitoring network latency, system errors, and data transfer rates. Regular monitoring and maintenance can help to ensure that the distributed computing solution continues to meet the organization's needs. Implementing distributed computing in finance risk management requires careful planning, architecture design, and implementation. By following best practices and recommendations, organizations can realize the benefits of distributed computing while minimizing risks and ensuring compliance with regulations and standards [41].

20.6.1 Selection of Distributed Computing Approach

Selecting the right distributed computing approach for finance risk management requires a systematic approach. Here are some factors to consider when selecting a distributed computing approach: Before implementing a distributed computing solution for finance risk management, it is essential to identify the business requirements that the solution must meet. The first step is to understand the specific risk management functions that the solution must perform, such as risk analysis, stress testing, or portfolio optimization. This will ensure that the solution is tailored to the needs of the business and is effective in mitigating risks. Once the business requirements are identified, the next step is to identify the data requirements for the solution. This includes understanding the types of data that must be processed, the volume of data, and the frequency at which data is processed. Understanding the data requirements is essential for selecting the right distributed computing approach and ensuring that the solution can handle the volume of data. The third step is to identify the computational requirements for the solution. This includes understanding the types of algorithms that must be used, the complexity of the computations, and the computational resources required. Identifying the computational requirements will ensure that the solution is effective in performing the required risk management functions. Scalability requirements are also essential when implementing a distributed computing solution for finance risk management. It is important to identify the potential growth in data volume and computational requirements and ensure that the solution can be scaled to meet future needs. Data security is critical when dealing with sensitive financial data. The fifth step is to identify the security requirements for the solution. This includes understanding the data security and access control mechanisms required to ensure the confidentiality, integrity, and availability of financial data. The sixth step is to identify the regulatory requirements that the solution must comply with. This includes identifying the relevant regulations and standards, such as GDPR or HIPAA, and ensuring that the solution meets these requirements. Compliance is critical in finance, and organizations must ensure that their distributed computing solutions comply with all relevant regulations and standards. This includes considering the costs of hardware, software, and maintenance, as well as the potential cost savings associated with implementing a distributed computing solution. By considering all of these factors, organizations can select the right distributed computing approach and effectively mitigate risks in finance. Once these factors have been identified, it is possible to evaluate different distributed computing approaches and select the one that best meets the requirements. Some common approaches include cloud-based distributed computing, grid computing, and peer-to-peer computing. By carefully evaluating these approaches and selecting the one that best meets the requirements, organizations can implement an effective and efficient distributed computing solution for finance risk management [42].

20.6.2 Guidelines for Implementing Distributed Computing for Finance Risk Management

Implementing distributed computing for finance risk management can be complex and requires careful planning and execution. Here are some guidelines for implementing distributed computing for finance risk management: Implementing a successful distributed computing solution for finance risk management begins with clearly defining the problem that the solution is intended to solve. This involves identifying the specific risk management functions that the solution must perform, such as risk analysis, stress testing, or portfolio optimization [43].

Once the problem is defined, the next step is to evaluate available distributed computing technologies and determine which one is the best fit for the organization's needs. Factors such as cost, scalability, and ease of implementation should be considered. Choosing the right technology is crucial to the success of the solution, and it is important to conduct thorough research and analysis before making a decision. Establishing data governance policies is also important to ensure that the data used in the distributed computing solution is accurate, complete, and up-to-date. This includes establishing data quality standards, data retention policies, and data access controls. Ensuring the integrity of the data used in the solution is critical to the accuracy and effectiveness of the risk management functions.

Developing a project plan is necessary to outline the steps needed to implement the distributed computing solution. This should include timelines, resource requirements, and budget estimates. Choosing the right team with the necessary technical expertise and project management skills to implement the solution is also important. This may involve hiring additional staff or partnering with a vendor. Testing the distributed computing solution is necessary. This may involve testing for accuracy, reliability, and performance. This may involve monitoring performance, troubleshooting issues, and making updates as necessary. Ensuring compliance with relevant regulations and standards is also important. This includes data security, privacy, and access control regulations. Implementing a distributed computing solution for finance risk management requires careful planning, evaluation of available technologies, establishment of data governance policies, project management, testing, and monitoring. By following these best practices, organizations can effectively leverage distributed computing to mitigate risks and stay ahead in the rapidly evolving financial landscape. By following these guidelines, organizations can implement an effective and efficient distributed computing solution for finance risk management.

20.7 Conclusion

This chapter has explored the potential of distributed computing technology for enhancing risk management in finance. The chapter began with a comparison of traditional risk management systems and distributed computing-based risk management systems, highlighting the need for improved risk management strategies in the finance industry. The theoretical framework of distributed computing was discussed, including an overview of its types and technologies for finance risk management. This was followed by a comparison of various distributed computing approaches for finance risk management and the innovations in distributed computing that have enhanced risk management in finance. These include advancements in distributed computing architectures and frameworks, new techniques, and emerging trends in distributed computing for finance risk management. Challenges and limitations of using distributed computing for finance risk management were also discussed, including technical challenges in implementing distributed computing and the limitations of the technology. Finally, best practices and recommendations for implementing distributed computing in finance risk management were presented. This includes a framework for selecting the right distributed computing approach for finance risk management as well as guidelines for implementation. This chapter has provided a comprehensive overview of the use of distributed computing technology in finance risk management. It has highlighted the benefits, limitations, and best practices of using this technology for managing risk in the finance industry. The chapter concludes that while distributed computing offers significant potential for enhancing risk management in finance, careful consideration and planning are necessary to overcome the technical challenges and limitations of the technology.

References

1. Viriyasitavat, W., Xu, L.D., Bi, Z., and Pungpapong, V. (2019). Blockchain and internet of things for modern business process in digital economy-the state of the art. *IEEE Trans. Comput. Social Syst.* 6 (6): 1420–1432.
2. Li, B. and Li, Y. (2017). Internet of things drives supply chain innovation: a research framework. *Int. J. Organ. Innovation* 9 (3): 71–92.
3. Cockcroft, S. and Russell, M. (2018). Big data opportunities for accounting and finance practice and research. *Aust. Account. Rev.* 28 (3): 323–333.
4. Knezevic, D. (2018). Impact of blockchain technology platform in changing the financial sector and other industries. *Montenegrin J. Econ.* 14 (1): 109–120.
5. Nord, J.H., Koohang, A., and Paliszkiewicz, J. (2019). The internet of things: review and theoretical framework. *Expert Syst. Appl.* 133: 97–108.
6. Leong, K. and Sung, A. (2018). FinTech (financial technology): what is it and how to use technologies to create business value in fintech way? *Int. J. Innovation, Manage. Technol.* 9 (2): 74–78.
7. Papert, M. and Pflaum, A. (2017). Development of an ecosystem model for the realization of internet of things (IoT) services in supply chain management. *Electron. Mark.* 27 (2): 175–189.
8. Pavlou, P.A. (2018). Internet of things-will humans be replaced or augmented? *GfK Mark. Intell. Rev.* 10 (2): 42–47.
9. Wilner, A.S. (2018). Cybersecurity and its discontents: artificial intelligence, the internet of things, and digital misinformation. *Int. J.: Can. J. Global Policy Anal.* 73 (2): 308–316.

10 Kummitha, R.K.R. and Crutzen, N. (2019). Smart cities and the citizen-driven internet of things: a qualitative inquiry into an emerging smart city. *Technol. Forecast. Soc. Chang.* 140: 44–53.

11 Tang, T. and Ho, A.T.-K. (2019). A path-dependence perspective on the adoption of internet of things: evidence from early adopters of smart and connected sensors in the United States. *Gov. Inf. Q.* 36 (2): 321–332.

12 Phasinam, K., Kassanuk, T., Shinde, P.P., and Thakar, C.M. (2022, 2022). Application of IoT and cloud computing in automation of agriculture irrigation. *J. Food Qual.* 8285969. 8 pages. https://doi.org/10.1155/2022/8285969.

13 Shinde, P.P., Oza, K.S., Kamat, R.K., and Thakar, C.M. (2022). Big data analytics for mask prominence in COVID pandemic. *Mater. Today: Proc.* 51 (Part 8): 2471–2475. https://doi.org/10.1016/j.matpr.2021.11.620.

14 Gupta, A., Asad, A., Meena, L., and Anand, R. (2022, July). IoT and RFID-based smart card system integrated with health care, electricity, QR and banking sectors. In: *Artificial Intelligence on Medical Data: Proceedings of International Symposium, ISCMM 2021*, 253–265. Singapore: Springer Nature Singapore.

15 Kumar Pandey, B., Pandey, D., Nassa, V.K. et al. (2021). Encryption and steganography-based text extraction in IoT using the EWCTS optimizer. *Imaging Sci. J.* 69 (1-4): 38–56.

16 Govindaraj, V., Dhanasekar, S., Martinsagayam, K. et al. (2023). Low-power test pattern generator using modified LFSR. *Aerosp. Syst.* 1–8.

17 Pandey, D., Pandey, B.K., Wariya, S. et al. (2020). Analysis of text detection, extraction and recognition from complex degraded images and videos. *J. Critic. Rev.* 7 (18): 427–433.

18 Pandey, D., Pandey, B.K., and Wariya, S. (2019). Study of various techniques used for video retrieval. *J. Emerg. Technol. Innov. Res.* 6 (6): 850–853.

19 Meelu, R. and Anand, R. (2010). Energy efficiency of cluster-based routing protocols used in wireless sensor networks. In: *AIP Conference Proceedings*, vol. 1324 (1), 109–113. American Institute of Physics.

20 Sansanwal, K., Shrivastava, G., Anand, R., and Sharma, K. (2019). Big data analysis and compression for indoor air quality. In: *Handbook of IoT and Big Data*, 1–21. CRC Press.

21 Anand, R., Singh, J., Pandey, D. et al. (2022). Modern technique for interactive communication in LEACH-based ad hoc wireless sensor network. In: *Software Defined Networking for Ad Hoc Networks*, 55–73. Cham: Springer International Publishing.

22 Nijhawan, M., Sindhwani, N., Tanwar, S., and Kumar, S. (2022). Role of augmented reality and Internet of Things in education sector. In: *IoT Based Smart Applications*, 245–259. Cham: Springer International Publishing.

23 Verma, S., Bajaj, T., Sindhwani, N., and Kumar, A. (2022). Design and development of a driving assistance and safety system using deep learning. In: *Advances in Data Science and Computing Technology*, 35–45. Apple Academic Press.

24 Sharma, G., Nehra, N., Dahiya, A. et al. (2022). Automatic heart-rate measurement using facial video. In: *Networking Technologies in Smart Healthcare*, 289–307. CRC Press.

25 Sharma, R., Vashisth, R., and Sindhwani, N. (2023). Study and analysis of classification techniques for specific plant growths. In: *Advances in Signal Processing, Embedded Systems and IoT: Proceedings of Seventh ICMEET-2022*, 591–605. Singapore: Springer Nature Singapore.

26 Chaudhary, A., Bodala, D., Sindhwani, N., and Kumar, A. (2022). Analysis of customer loyalty using artificial neural networks. In: *2022 International Mobile and Embedded Technology Conference (MECON)*, 181–183. IEEE.

27 Anand, R. and Chawla, P. (2020). A novel dual-wideband inscribed hexagonal fractal slotted microstrip antenna for C-and X-band applications. *Int. J. RF Microwave Comput. Aided Eng.* 30 (9): e22277.

28 Anand, R. and Chawla, P. (2020). Optimization of inscribed hexagonal fractal slotted microstrip antenna using modified lightning attachment procedure optimization. *Int. J. Microw. Wirel. Technol.* 12 (6): 519–530.

29 Jagtap, S.T. and Thakar, C.M. (2021). A framework for secure healthcare system using blockchain and smart contracts. In: *2021 Second International Conference on Electronics and Sustainable Communication Systems (ICESC)*, 922–926. Coimbatore, India: https://doi.org/10.1109/ICESC51422.2021.9532644.

30 Parkhe, S.S. and Thakar, C.M. (2022). Implementation of IoT in production and manufacturing: an Industry 4.0 approach. *Mater. Today: Proc.* 51 (Part 8): 2427–2430. https://doi.org/10.1016/j.matpr.2021.11.604.

31 Jagtap, S.T. and Thakar, C.M. (2022). Towards application of various machine learning techniques in agriculture. *Mater. Today: Proc.* 51 (Part 1): 793–797. https://doi.org/10.1016/j.matpr.2021.06.236.

32 Thakar, C.M. and Phasinam, K. (2022). A review on role of artificial intelligence in food processing and manufacturing industry. *Mater. Today: Proc.* 51 (Part 8): 2462–2465. https://doi.org/10.1016/j.matpr.2021.11.616.

33 Lee, C.K.M., Zhang, S.Z., and Ng, K.K.H. (2017). Development of an industrial internet of things suite for smart factory towards re-industrialization. *Adv. Manuf.* 5 (4): 335–343.

34 Salami, I. (2018). Terrorism financing with virtual currencies: can regulatory technology solutions combat this? *Stud. Conflict Terrorism* 41 (12): 968–989.

35 Abualigah, L. and Diabat, A. (2020). A comprehensive survey of the Grasshopper optimization algorithm: results, variants, and applications. *Neural Comput. & Applic.* 32: 1–24.

36 Manavalan, E. and Jayakrishna, K. (2019). A review of internet of things (IoT) embedded sustainable supply chain for industry 4.0 requirements. *Comput. Ind. Eng.* 127: 925–953.

37 Wang, H., Guo, C., and Cheng, S. (2019). LoC-a new financial loan management system based on smart contracts. *Futur. Gener. Comput. Syst.* 100: 648–655.

38 Lim, S.H., Kim, D.J., Hur, Y., and Park, K. (2019). An empirical study of the impacts of perceived security and knowledge on continuous intention to use mobile Fintech payment services. *Int. J. Human Comput. Interact.* 35 (10): 886–898.

39 Ozili, P.K. (2018). Impact of digital finance on financial inclusion and stability. *Borsa Istanbul Rev.* 18 (4): 329–340.

40 Yao, M., Di, H., Zheng, X., and Xu, X. (2018). Impact of payment technology innovations on the traditional financial industry: a focus on China. *Technol. Forecast. Soc. Chang.* 135: 199–207.

41 Tan, Z., Tan, Q., and Rong, M. (2018). Analysis on the financing status of PV industry in China and the ways of improvement. *Renew. Sust. Energ. Rev.* 93: 409–420.

42 Mani, Z. and Chouk, I. (2018). Consumer resistance to innovation in services: challenges and barriers in the internet of things era. *J. Prod. Innov. Manag.* 35 (5): 780–807.

43 Abualigah, L. (2020). Group search optimizer: a nature-inspired meta-heuristic optimization algorithm with its results, variants, and applications. *Neural Comput. & Applic.* 33: 1–24.

21

Leveraging Blockchain and Distributed Systems for Improved Supply Chain Traceability and Transparency

Luigi P.L. Cavaliere[1], *S. Silas Sargunam*[2], *Dilip K. Sharma*[3], *Y. Venkata Ramana*[4], *K.K. Ramachandran*[5], *Umakant B. Gohatre*[6], *and Nadanakumar Vinayagam*[7]

[1]*Department of Economics, University of Foggia, Foggia, Italy*
[2]*Department of Management Studies, Anna University Regional Campus, Tirunelveli, Tamilnadu, India*
[3]*Department of Mathematics, Jaypee University of Engineering and Technology, Guna, Madhya Pradesh, India*
[4]*KL Business School, Koneru Lakshmaiah Education Foundation, Guntur, Andhra Pradesh, India*
[5]*Management/Commerce/International Business, DR. G R D College of Science, Coimbatore, Tamil Nadu, India*
[6]*Department of Electronics and Telecommunications Engineering, Smt. Indira Gandhi College of Engineering, Navi Mumbai, Maharashtra, India*
[7]*Department of Automobile Engineering, Hindustan Institute of Technology and Science, Chennai, Tamil Nadu, India*

21.1 Introduction

The movement of commodities, information, and financial transactions among several parties and geographical locations is a feature of complex systems or supply chains (SCs). The integrity, quality, and safety of products as they pass through the SC are dependent on SC traceability and transparency. Although transparency refers to the visibility and openness of actions, traceability refers to the capacity to track and trace the history and whereabouts of products, raw materials, and other SC elements. However, traditional SC systems often suffer from limitations in achieving traceability and transparency. These systems typically rely on centralized databases, chapter-based records, and manual processes that are prone to errors, fraud, and lack of visibility. Moreover, there are various risks and challenges, such as counterfeiting, fraud, and environmental and social issues, which can further undermine traceability

Meta-Heuristic Algorithms for Advanced Distributed Systems, First Edition. Edited by Rohit Anand, Abhinav Juneja, Digvijay Pandey, Sapna Juneja, and Nidhi Sindhwani.

and transparency. To address these challenges, there is a growing interest in leveraging blockchain and distributed systems (DSs) in SC. DS, on the other hand, are computing systems that are distributed across multiple nodes or devices and can provide increased resilience, scalability, and efficiency. By using blockchain and DS, SC can enhance traceability and transparency in several ways. DS, on the other hand, can enable the creation of a decentralized and resilient SC network that can withstand disruptions and failures. DS can also enable secure and efficient data sharing among SC participants, which can enhance collaboration and coordination and reduce the risk of errors and delays. Despite the potential advantages of DS and blockchain in SC, there are still issues and restrictions that must be resolved. For instance, DS and blockchain both demand large investments in technical infrastructure and know-how, and there may be problems with scalability, interoperability, and standardization. In order to improve SC traceability and transparency, this chapter will examine the existing level of knowledge and practice in this area. The chapter will give a review of blockchain technology and distributed ledger technology (DS), look at possible SC use cases and benefits, and assess their drawbacks [1, 2].

21.1.1 Supply Chain Traceability and Transparency

SC are complex networks that involve multiple stakeholders, including suppliers, manufacturers, distributors, retailers, and customers. The movement of goods and materials through the SC is often accompanied by various information flows and financial transactions, making it challenging to achieve full visibility and traceability. The ability to track and trace the movement of products and materials through the SC, from the point of origin to the point of consumption. This includes tracking the origin of raw materials, the production and assembly processes, the storage and transportation of products, and the disposal or recycling of waste. The openness and visibility of SC processes and activities, including information about suppliers, production practices, labor conditions, and environmental impact. Transparency is important for building trust and accountability among SC stakeholders, promoting social and environmental responsibility, and mitigating risks related to reputation and brand value. These systems often rely on centralized databases, chapter-based records, and manual processes that are prone to errors, fraud, and lack of visibility. This can lead to issues such as product recalls, counterfeiting, and SC disruptions, which can have serious consequences for businesses and consumers alike. The use of blockchain and DS can provide new opportunities for improving SC traceability and transparency. Blockchain is a decentralized digital ledger that allows secure and transparent transactions and information sharing among multiple parties without the need for intermediaries. DS are computing systems that are distributed across multiple nodes or devices and can provide increased resilience, scalability, and efficiency. By using blockchain and DS, SC can enhance traceability and transparency in several ways. The creation of a decentralized and resilient SC network that can withstand disruptions and failures can also enable secure and efficient data sharing among SC participants, which can enhance collaboration and coordination and reduce the risk of errors and delays. These technologies can improve SC efficiency, reduce costs, enhance customer trust, and promote social and environmental sustainability. However, there are also challenges and limitations that need to be addressed, such as the need for investment in technology infrastructure and expertise, issues related to standardization and interoperability, and regulatory and legal barriers [3, 4].

21.1.2 Challenges in Achieving Traceability and Transparency in Traditional Supply Chain Systems

1. *Fragmentation*: SC typically involves multiple stakeholders, including suppliers, manufacturers, distributors, and retailers, each with their own information systems and data standards. This fragmentation can make it challenging to track and trace products and materials as they move through the SC.
2. *Lack of data integration*: Many SC systems rely on manual data entry and chapter-based records, which can be time-consuming, error-prone, and difficult to integrate with other systems. This can result in incomplete or inconsistent data, making it challenging to achieve full visibility and traceability.
3. *Limited interoperability*: SC systems often use different data formats and standards, making it difficult to share data and communicate effectively between different systems. This can lead to silos of information and limited collaboration among SC stakeholders.
4. *Lack of transparency*: Traditional SC systems may not provide full transparency into the processes and activities of SC participants, such as suppliers, manufacturers, and distributors. This lack of transparency can make it challenging to identify and address issues related to social and environmental responsibility, labor conditions, and ethical practices.
5. *Limited accountability*: Traditional SC systems may lack the necessary mechanisms to hold SC participants accountable for their actions and practices. This can make it challenging to ensure compliance with regulations and standards, and it can also make it difficult to identify and address issues related to social and environmental responsibility. Blockchain and DS are among the technologies that can provide new opportunities for achieving these goals.

21.1.3 Potential Benefits of Leveraging Blockchain and Distributed Systems in Supply Chain

1. *Improved traceability and transparency*: the establishment of an auditable, tamper-proof record of all SC transactions and events that can give a complete picture of SC history. As a result, it may be simpler to track and trace goods as they pass through the SC, improving traceability and transparency.

2. *Enhanced efficiency and cost savings*: Blockchain and DS can assist in lowering costs, boosting efficiency, and boosting production by automating and streamlining SC procedures.
3. *Increased security and trust*: Blockchain and DS can provide increased security and trust in SC transactions and data sharing by using cryptography and decentralized networks. This can help to reduce the risk of fraud, counterfeiting, and cyberattacks, which can have serious consequences for businesses and consumers.
4. *Improved collaboration and coordination*: By enabling secure and efficient data sharing among SC participants, blockchain and DS can enhance collaboration and coordination, reducing the risk of errors and delays. This can help to improve SC performance and customer satisfaction.
5. *Promoting social and environmental responsibility*: By providing increased transparency into SC processes and activities, blockchain and DS can help to promote social and environmental responsibility. This can be achieved by enabling stakeholders to track and trace the origin of raw materials, monitor working conditions, and ensure compliance with ethical and sustainability standards.
6. *Resilience and scalability*: DS can provide increased resilience and scalability by creating a decentralized and resilient SC network that can withstand disruptions and failures. This can help to ensure the continuity of SC operations, even in the face of unexpected events such as natural disasters, pandemics, or geopolitical instability.

These technologies can improve SC efficiency, reduce costs, enhance customer trust, and promote social and environmental sustainability. There is a need for investment in technology infrastructure and expertise, issues related to standardization and interoperability, and regulatory and legal barriers.

21.2 Overview of Blockchain and Distributed Systems

These technologies may open up new possibilities for improved SC traceability, transparency, security, and effectiveness. This technology makes it challenging for malicious parties to corrupt or alter the data by using cryptography and a decentralized network of computers to validate and record transactions. A cryptographic hash of the previous block is included in each block of the blockchain, making the data transparent and impenetrable. In contrast, DS refers to a group of technologies that make it possible to share resources and data among many computers and networks. These systems use a decentralized architecture to enable more efficient and resilient data sharing, as well as increased security and privacy. In a DS, data is stored and processed across multiple nodes in the network, rather than in a central location, which can help to reduce the risk of single points of failure and increase network resilience. In the context of SC management, this can provide several potential benefits, including enhanced traceability and transparency, improved efficiency and cost savings, increased security and trust, improved collaboration and coordination, and promotion of social and environmental responsibility. By creating a tamper-proof and auditable record of all SC transactions and events, blockchain can enable more efficient tracking and tracing of products and materials as they move through the SC. Fraud and other forms of illicit activity, as well as improve product quality and safety. By automating and streamlining SC processes through the use of smart contracts, businesses can reduce the need for intermediaries and chapter work, which can lead to faster processing times and reduced costs. This can help to improve SC performance and customer satisfaction while also reducing operational expenses. Another important benefit of leveraging blockchain and DS in SC is increased security and trust. In SC transactions and data exchange, blockchain can boost security and privacy by utilizing cryptography and a decentralized network. The need for investment in technological infrastructure and skills, problems with standardization and interoperability, and regulatory and legal restrictions are only a few of the obstacles that need to be overcome. Businesses, governments, and other stakeholders must cooperate with one another to address these issues and create workable solutions [5–7].

21.2.1 Fundamental Concepts of Blockchain Technology

Table 21.1 outlines the fundamental concepts of blockchain technology, including decentralization, consensus mechanisms, cryptography, and smart contracts. Decentralization refers to the lack of a central authority or intermediary controlling the system, providing increased security and reduced transaction costs [8–12], but also leading to slower transaction speeds and difficulty in coordinating the network. Consensus techniques guarantee that all nodes on the network concur on the ledger's current state, enhancing security and efficiency but also raising the possibility of centralization and energy consumption problems. Cryptography is used to secure transactions and protect against fraud and tampering, providing increased security, privacy, and anonymity but also leading to complexity and vulnerability to quantum computing attacks [13–15]. Smart contracts automate and enforce contractual agreements between parties, providing increased efficiency, transparency, and accountability but also leading to difficulty in developing and testing, as well as limited applicability.

21.2.2 Characteristics and Benefits of Distributed Systems

1. *Parallel processing*: Systems can execute multiple tasks simultaneously, thereby improving processing speed and reducing latency. This is possible due to the ability to distribute tasks among multiple nodes.

Table 21.1 Fundamental concepts of blockchain technology.

Concept	Definition	Advantages	Challenges
Decentralization	A blockchain network is decentralized, which means that there isn't a single organization or middleman in charge of it. Instead, nodes that take part in the consensus process control the network.	Increased security Elimination of a single point of failure Reduced transaction costs	Slower transaction speed compared to centralized systems Difficulty in coordinating and governing the network
Consensus Mechanisms	To make sure that everyone on the network agrees on the ledger's current state, consensus procedures are employed.	Increased security and trust Elimination of the need for intermediaries Increased efficiency	Energy consumption and environmental impact Potential for centralization
Cryptography	Public and private keys, digital signatures, and hashing techniques are used to accomplish this.	Increased security and trust Protection against fraud and tampering Anonymity and privacy	Risk of losing private keys Complexity and difficulty of managing keys Vulnerability to quantum computing attacks

2. *Resource sharing*: Resources such as processing power, memory, and storage can be shared among multiple nodes. This allows for better resource utilization and reduces the cost of infrastructure.
3. *Flexibility*: Systems are more flexible than centralized systems as they allow for greater customization and adaptability [16–18]. Different nodes can be configured to perform specific tasks, and the system can be easily modified to meet changing business needs.
4. *Geographic distribution*: It can span across multiple geographical locations, allowing for better reach and accessibility. This is particularly useful for businesses that operate in different regions of the world.
5. *Improved fault tolerance*: There is less reliance on individual components. This reduces the risk of system failure due to a single point of failure.
6. *Improved security*: Less vulnerable to security breaches as they use multiple layers of security measures, including encryption, firewalls, and access controls [19, 20].

21.2.3 How Blockchain and Distributed Systems Can Enhance Supply Chain Traceability and Transparency

SC are complex networks of suppliers, manufacturers, distributors, and retailers, and they often lack visibility and transparency. This can result in inefficiencies, delays, and quality issues. This makes it possible to create an immutable and auditable record of all transactions in the SC, from raw materials to finished products. On the other hand, enable multiple parties to share data and collaborate in real time. This can enhance SC visibility and enable better coordination between different stakeholders. By leveraging DS, SC participants can have access to a shared ledger that contains a complete history of all transactions, enabling them to track products, monitor inventory levels, and optimize logistics.

With the use of these technologies, it becomes possible to track products throughout the SC, starting from the origin of raw materials and ending at the final destination of the product. This creates a comprehensive record of product movement, providing consumers with accurate and detailed information about the authenticity, quality, and environmental impact of products. In case of a foodborne illness outbreak, the movement of food products can be tracked using blockchain technology, which enables faster identification of the source of contamination. This can help prevent the spread of illness and improve food safety. It can also be used to prevent counterfeiting by creating a secure and tamper-proof record of product authenticity. The record of product authenticity can be accessed by anyone in the SC, making it easy to verify the authenticity of a product. Another significant benefit is improved efficiency in the SC. By providing real-time access to SC data, stakeholders can better coordinate their efforts, leading to improved efficiency and reduced costs. With blockchain technology, data can be easily shared between different stakeholders, making it easier to identify inefficiencies and optimize SC processes [21, 22]. The transparent and traceable nature of blockchain technology ensures that all stakeholders are accountable for their actions, which can help build trust between different parties in the SC. By tracking products throughout the SC, enhancing food safety, preventing counterfeiting, improving efficiency, and increasing transparency, these technologies can help build a more secure, reliable, and ethical SC [23–25].

21.3 Applications of Blockchain and Distributed Systems in Supply Chain

21.3.1 Tracking and Tracing Goods and Raw Materials

This can offer accountability and transparency across the industry, from the place where raw materials are sourced to where the finished product is shipped. An immutable and impenetrable record of all transactions in the SC can be made using blockchain technology, guaranteeing that the data cannot be changed or removed. This can assist in reducing the likelihood of fraud, preventing counterfeit goods, and guaranteeing that goods are created and sourced ethically. For instance, one of the biggest retailers in the world, Walmart, has introduced a blockchain-based system for food SC traceability. Walmart is able to follow the flow of food supplies from the farm to the store thanks to the technology, which offers real-time visibility into the source and caliber of products. This has helped Walmart increase customer trust, minimize waste, and improve the safety and quality of its products. Another example is the creation of a safe and impenetrable record of the diamond's origin and quality in the diamond industry. This can lower the possibility of fraud, stop the selling of conflict diamonds, and raise industry ethics standards [26, 27].

21.3.2 Ensuring Product Authenticity and Preventing Counterfeit

Counterfeit products pose a serious threat to the reputation and revenue of companies. To combat this issue, a unique digital identity can be assigned to each product, containing information about its origin and manufacturing process. This identity can be verified by customers and stakeholders to ensure product authenticity. To create a transparent and auditable trail of the product's journey, information about the product's location, ownership, and status can be recorded on the blockchain at each stage of the SC. With programming, smart contracts can automatically verify the authenticity of a product and alert stakeholders if any suspicious activity is detected. The use of systems can effectively ensure product authenticity and prevent the sale of counterfeit products. By providing real-time verification of product authenticity and creating a transparent and secure record of the product's journey through the SC, these technologies can enhance consumer trust and protect the brand's reputation [28, 29].

21.3.3 Enhancing Visibility and Accountability in Supply Chain

Visibility and accountability are crucial aspects of SC management. Companies need to be able to track and monitor their products as they move through the SC, while also ensuring that their suppliers and partners are following ethical and sustainable practices. However, achieving visibility and accountability can be a challenge, particularly in complex global SC. One approach to enhancing visibility and accountability in SC is to establish clear standards and requirements for suppliers and partners. This can include requirements around sustainability, social responsibility, and ethical practices. By setting these standards, companies can ensure that their suppliers and partners are aligned with their values and goals. Using technological solutions like Internet of Things (IoT) devices and sensors is another option to improve visibility and accountability. These gadgets provide real-time tracking and monitoring of products, giving businesses better SC visibility. IoT devices, for instance, can be used to monitor the temperature and humidity of perishable items during transportation to make sure they are maintained at the proper levels. Data analytics can also be utilized to understand SC operations and pinpoint opportunities for development. Companies can find opportunities to save costs, increase efficiency, and improve accountability by reviewing data on supplier performance, logistics costs, and product quality. In terms of accountability, companies can use third-party audits and certifications to ensure that their suppliers and partners are adhering to the established standards and requirements. These audits can be conducted by independent organizations to provide an unbiased assessment of suppliers' practices and performance. Collaboration and partnerships can also play a role in enhancing visibility and accountability in SC. By working closely with suppliers and partners, companies can establish a shared understanding of their goals and values. This can help foster a culture of transparency and accountability where all stakeholders are committed to achieving the same objectives. Enhancing visibility and accountability in SC is critical for companies looking to maintain their reputation, reduce risk, and improve performance. While technology solutions can play a role, it is important to establish clear standards, use data analytics, conduct third-party audits, and foster collaboration and partnerships to achieve these goals [30, 31].

21.3.4 Enabling Secure and Efficient Data Sharing Among Supply Chain Participants

The effectiveness of the process depends on the participants' ability to communicate effectively and share information. Yet, conventional data exchange techniques, like emails or electronic documents, can be sluggish, ineffective, and unsafe. New technologies are therefore required to provide for safe and effective data sharing among SC participants. Using safe data-sharing systems, which enable parties to communicate data in a managed and secure manner, is one solution. To make sure that only people with permission may access the data, these platforms employ sophisticated encryption and access control technologies. This reduces the risk of illegal access and data breaches while also preserving the confidentiality and integrity of the data. Another solution is the use of application programming interfaces (APIs) to enable seamless integration and data exchange between different SC systems. APIs provide a standardized way for systems to communicate with each other, making it easier for SC participants to share data and integrate their systems. Cloud-based solutions provide a centralized platform for participants to access and share data, reducing the need for complex and costly data-sharing infrastructures. In addition, data analytics and artificial intelligence can be used to analyze and make sense of the vast amounts of data generated in SC. By analyzing SC data, participants can identify areas for improvement, optimize their operations, and reduce costs. By using secure data-sharing platforms, APIs, cloud-based solutions, and data analytics, SC participants can improve their communication, collaboration, and decision-making, leading to a more efficient and cost-effective SC [32, 33].

21.4 Benefits and Limitations of Blockchain and Distributed Systems in Supply Chain

Benefits:

1. *Transparency*: By providing a transparent and auditable record of transactions, stakeholders would be able to follow the flow of materials and items throughout the SC.
2. *Security*: By using encryption and cryptographic techniques, blockchain and DS can secure SC data and protect against cyber threats and data breaches.
3. *Efficiency*: By providing real-time access to SC data, blockchain and DS can enable better coordination between different stakeholders, leading to improved efficiency and reduced costs.
4. *Accountability*: Systems can create an immutable record of all transactions in the SC, increasing transparency and accountability and helping to prevent fraud and unethical practices.

Limitations:

1. *Complexity*: Implementing blockchain and DS in SC can be complex and require significant resources and expertise.
2. *Cost*: The cost of implementing and maintaining blockchain and DS can be high, particularly for small and medium-sized enterprises (SMEs).
3. *Scalability*: As the size and complexity of the SC increase, blockchain and DS may face scalability issues, affecting their ability to handle large volumes of transactions.
4. *Interoperability*: Different blockchain platforms may not be interoperable, making it difficult for stakeholders to share data across different systems.

The benefits of transparency, security, efficiency, and accountability need to be weighed against the challenges of complexity, cost, scalability, and interoperability, these limitations are expected to be addressed, making blockchain and DS an even more powerful tool for enhancing SC traceability and transparency which are as shown in Figure 21.1.

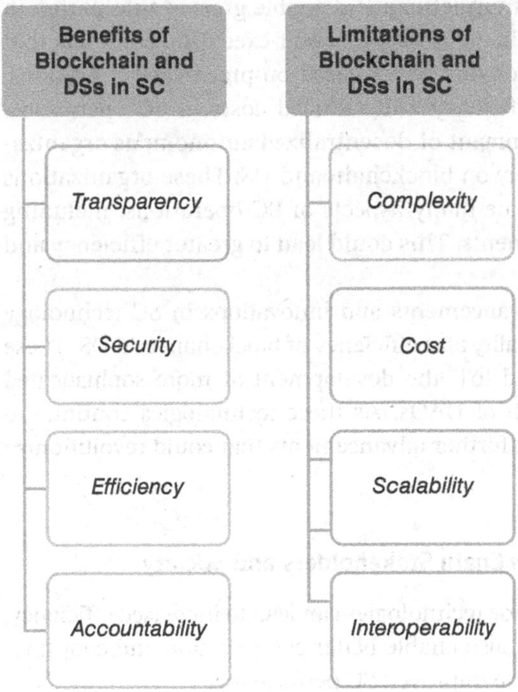

Figure 21.1 Benefits and Limitations Blockchain and DSs in SC.

21.4.1 Potential Advancements and Innovations in Blockchain and Distributed Systems for Supply Chain

Potential advancements and innovations in SC technology are constantly emerging, and blockchain and DS are no exception. As technology continues to evolve, there are several potential advancements that could transform SC operations. The use of ML to improve the functionality of blockchain and DS is one potential development. Participants in SCs could automate decision-making processes and get deeper insights into SC data by using AI and ML technologies. This might result in increased SC operations accuracy and efficiency. The DS and IoT integration, together with blockchain integration, is another potential development. With real-time tracking and monitoring of commodities across the SC made possible by this connection, participants would have a more accurate and current picture of their activities. This might result in more effective decision-making and increased SC operations efficiency. Furthermore, there is potential for the development of more sophisticated smart contracts that can execute more complex transactions and enable greater automation in SC operations. This could include the creation of self-executing contracts that automatically trigger payments or shipments based on predefined conditions. This could lead to improved efficiency and reduced costs in SC operations. There is potential for the development of decentralized autonomous organizations (DAOs) that operate entirely on blockchain and DS. These organizations could be programmed to automate many aspects of SC operations, including procurement, logistics, and payments. This could lead to greater efficiency and transparency in SC operations.

There are several potential advancements and innovations in SC technology that could transform the functionality and efficiency of blockchain and DS. These include the integration of AI and IoT, the development of more sophisticated smart contracts, and the creation of DAOs. As these technologies continue to evolve, it is likely that we will see further advancements that could revolutionize the way that SC operates [34].

21.4.2 Implications for Supply Chain Stakeholders and Society

For SC stakeholders, the use of these technologies can lead to increased efficiency, transparency, and security. It can also enable better collaboration and coordination among stakeholders, leading to improved SC performance.

Moreover, the use of blockchain and DS can help protect the reputation of brands and prevent the sale of counterfeit products, which can have a significant impact on customer trust and loyalty. It can also improve food safety and traceability, ensuring that consumers have access to accurate and reliable information about the products they purchase. On a broader level, the adoption of these technologies can lead to a more sustainable and ethical SC. By enabling better tracking and monitoring of products throughout the SC, it can help reduce waste, prevent the use of child labor and other unethical practices, and promote environmentally responsible practices. The implementation of DS and blockchain in SC is not without its difficulties, though. Lack of standardization and interoperability among various blockchain systems is one of the main issues, which might make it difficult for stakeholders to work together and share information. Furthermore, SMEs may find it difficult to compete with bigger companies in the market due to the significant expenses associated with integrating these technologies. Despite the inherent security of the blockchain, there is always a chance of data breaches or cyberattacks, which can do serious harm to organizations and their clients. Nonetheless, it is crucial for stakeholders to be aware of the potential hazards and issues connected to these technologies and take the necessary precautions to lessen them [35, 36].

21.5 Conclusion

By leveraging the decentralized and immutable nature of blockchain, SC stakeholders can create a secure and transparent record of the product's journey through the SC, providing real-time access to critical information and improving accountability. Also, the automation of many SC activities through the use of smart contracts and other cutting-edge technology can increase efficiency and save costs [37–39]. Despite the fact that blockchain and DS have many advantages, there are still some problems that need to be solved. The implementation will revolutionize the industry and address long-standing challenges related to traceability, transparency, and efficiency. The complexity of implementing these technologies, the need for standardized protocols, and the potential for regulatory issues are all areas that require further attention. Despite these challenges, the potential benefits of leveraging blockchain and DS for improved SC traceability and transparency are too significant to ignore [40–42]. By enabling real-time access to critical information, improving accountability, and preventing fraud and unethical practices, these technologies have the potential to create a more sustainable, ethical, and efficient SC industry. Therefore, it is essential for SC stakeholders to explore the potential of these technologies and work toward their implementation in the industry.

References

1 Liu, Z. and Li, Z. (2020). A blockchain-based framework of cross-border e-commerce supply chain. *Int. J. Inf. Manag.* 52: 102059.

2 He, Y., Qi, M., Zhou, F., and Su, J. (2020). An effective metaheuristic for the last mile delivery with roaming delivery locations and stochastic travel times. *Comput. Ind. Eng.* 145: 106513.

3 Zhou, F., He, Y., Chan, F.T. et al. (2022). Joint distribution promotion by interactive factor analysis using an interpretive structural modeling approach. *SAGE Open* 12: 21582440221079903.

4 Zhou, F., Wang, X., Lim, M.K. et al. (2018). Sustainable recycling partner selection using fuzzy DEMATEL-AEW-FVIKOR: a case study in small-and-medium enterprises (SMEs). *J. Clean. Prod.* 196: 489–504.

5 Marsal-Llacuna, M.-L. (2018). Future living framework: is blockchain the next enabling network? *Technol. Forecast. Soc. Change* 128: 226–234.

6 Zhou, F., Lim, M.K., He, Y. et al. (2019). End-of-life vehicle (ELV) recycling management: improving performance using an ISM approach. *J. Clean. Prod.* 228: 231–243.

7 Lotfi, R., Safavi, S., Gharehbaghi, A. et al. (2021). Viable supply chain network design by considering blockchain technology and cryptocurrency. *Math. Probl. Eng.* 2021: 7347389.

8 Chaudhary, A., Bodala, D., Sindhwani, N., and Kumar, A. (2022). Analysis of customer loyalty using artificial neural networks. In: *2022 International Mobile and Embedded Technology Conference (MECON)*, 181–183. IEEE.

9 Sharma, R., Vashisth, R., and Sindhwani, N. (2023). Study and analysis of classification techniques for specific plant growths. In: *Advances in Signal Processing, Embedded Systems and IoT: Proceedings of Seventh ICMEET-2022*, 591–605. Singapore: Springer Nature Singapore.

10 Sharma, G., Nehra, N., Dahiya, A. et al. (2022). Automatic heart-rate measurement using facial video. In: *Networking Technologies in Smart Healthcare*, 289–307. CRC Press.

11 Verma, S., Bajaj, T., Sindhwani, N., and Kumar, A. (2022). Design and development of a driving assistance and safety system using deep learning. In: *Advances in Data Science and Computing Technology*, 35–45. Apple Academic Press.

12 Nijhawan, M., Sindhwani, N., Tanwar, S., and Kumar, S. (2022). Role of augmented reality and internet of things in education sector. In: *IoT Based Smart Applications*, 245–259. Cham: Springer International Publishing.

13 Anand, R., Singh, J., Pandey, D. et al. (2022). Modern technique for interactive communication in LEACH-based ad hoc wireless sensor network. In: *Software Defined Networking for Ad Hoc Networks*, 55–73. Cham: Springer International Publishing.

14 Sansanwal, K., Shrivastava, G., Anand, R., and Sharma, K. (2019). Big data analysis and compression for indoor air quality. In: *Handbook of IoT and Big Data*, 1–21. CRC Press.

15 Meelu, R. and Anand, R. (2010). Energy efficiency of cluster-based routing protocols used in wireless sensor networks. In: *AIP Conference Proceedings*, vol. 1324, No. 1, , 109–113. American Institute of Physics.

16 Pandey, D., Pandey, B.K., and Wariya, S. (2019). Study of various techniques used for video retrieval. *J. Emerg. Technol. Innov. Res.* 6 (6): 850–853.

17 Pandey, D., Pandey, B.K., Wariya, S. et al. (2020). Analysis of text detection, extraction and recognition from complex degraded images and videos. *J. Critic. Rev.* 7 (18): 427–433.

18 Govindaraj, V., Dhanasekar, S., Martinsagayam, K. et al. (2023). Low-power test pattern generator using modified LFSR. *Aerosp. Syst.* 1–8.

19 Kumar Pandey, B., Pandey, D., Nassa, V.K. et al. (2021). Encryption and steganography-based text extraction in IoT using the EWCTS optimizer. *Imaging Sci. J.* 69 (1-4): 38–56.

20 Gupta, A., Asad, A., Meena, L., and Anand, R. (2022). IoT and RFID-based smart card system integrated with health care, electricity, QR and banking sectors. In: *Artificial Intelligence on Medical Data: Proceedings of International Symposium, ISCMM 2021*, 253–265. Singapore: Springer Nature Singapore.

21 Anand, R. and Chawla, P. (2020). A novel dual-wideband inscribed hexagonal fractal slotted microstrip antenna for C-and X-band applications. *Int. J. RF Microwave Comput. Aided Eng.* 30 (9): e22277.

22 Anand, R. and Chawla, P. (2020). Optimization of inscribed hexagonal fractal slotted microstrip antenna using modified lightning attachment procedure optimization. *Int. J. Microw. Wirel. Technol.* 12 (6): 519–530.

23 Wu, K.-J., Liao, C.-J., Tseng, M.-L. et al. (2017). Toward sustainability: using big data to explore the decisive attributes of supply chain risks and uncertainties. *J. Clean. Prod.* 142: 663–676.

24 Tseng, M.-L., Chiu, A.S.F., Liu, G., and Jantaralolica, T. (2020). Circular economy enables sustainable consumption and production in multi-level supply chain system. *Resour. Conserv. Recycl.* 154: 104601.

25 Frei, R., Jack, L., and Krzyzaniak, S.-A. (2020). Sustainable reverse supply chains and circular economy in multichannel retail returns. *Bus. Strateg. Environ.* 29: 1925–1940.

26 Chatras, C., Giard, V., and Sali, M. (2015). High variety impacts on bill of materials structure: carmakers case study. *IFAC-PapersOnLine* 48: 1067–1072.

27 Baah, C., Agyeman, D.O., Acquah, I.S.K. et al. (2021). Effect of information sharing in supply chains: understanding the roles of supply chain visibility, agility, collaboration on supply chain performance. *Benchmarking Int. J.* 29: 434–455.

28 Uddin, M., Salah, K., Jayaraman, R. et al. (2021). Blockchain for drug traceability: Architectures and open challenges. *Health Inform. J.* 27: 14604582211011228.

29 Duan, J., Zhang, C., Gong, Y. et al. (2020). A content-analysis based literature review in blockchain adoption within food supply chain. *Int. J. Environ. Res. Public Health* 17: 1784.

30 Calvão, F. and Archer, M. (2021). Digital extraction: blockchain traceability in mineral supply chains. *Polit. Geogr.* 87: 102381.

31 Ahimbisibwe, A., Ssebulime, R., Tumuhairwe, R., and Tusiime, W. (2016). Supply chain visibility, supply chain velocity, supply chain alignment and humanitarian supply chain relief agility. *Eur. J. Logist. Purch. Supply Chain. Manage* 4: 34–64.

32 Chang, A., El-Rayes, N., and Shi, J. (2022). Blockchain technology for supply chain management: a comprehensive review. *FinTech* 1: 191–205.

33 Francis, V. (2008). Supply chain visibility: lost in translation? *Supply Chain. Manag. Int. J.* 13: 180–184.

34 Barrat, M. and Oke, A. (2007). Antecedents of supply chain visibility in retail supply chain: a resource—based theory perspective. *J. Oper. Manag.* 25: 1217–1233.

35 Lechaptois, L. (2020). Framing supply chain visibility through a multifield approach. *Proc. Hambg. Int. Conf. Logist.* 29: 487–519.

36 Pournader, M., Shi, Y., Seuring, S., and Koh, S.C.L. (2020). Blockchain applications in supply chains, transport and logistics: a systematic review of the literature. *Int. J. Prod. Res.* 58: 2063–2081.

37 Saberi, S.M., Kouhizadeh, Sarkis, J., and Shen, L. (2019). Blockchain technology and its relationships to sustainable supply chain management. *Int. J. Prod. Res.* 57: 2117–2135.

38 Wang, S., Zhang, X., Yu, W. et al. (2020). Smart contract microservitization. In: *Proceedings of the 2020 IEEE 44th Annual Computers, Software, and Applications Conference (COMPSAC), Madrid, Spain, 13–17 July 2020*, 1569–1574.

39 Makowski, L. and Sawicki, B. (2011). The feasibility study for application of distributed hashing tables into WSN. *Prz. Elektrotechniczny* 87: 220–223.

40 Kim, S.-I. and Kim, S.-H. (2020). E-commerce payment model using blockchain. *J. Ambient. Intell. Humaniz. Comput.* 13: 1673–1685.

41 Moosavi, J., Naeni, L.M., Fathollahi-Fard, A.M., and Fiore, U. (2021). Blockchain in supply chain management: a review, bibliometric, and network analysis. *Environ. Sci. Pollut. Res.*ahead-of-print.

42 Pandey, D. and Pandey, B.K. (2022). An efficient deep neural network with adaptive galactic swarm optimization for complex image text extraction. In: *Process Mining Techniques for Pattern Recognition*, 121–137. CRC Press.

22

Advances in Resource Management Through the Integration of Distributed Computing Approaches

K. Jayalakshmamma[1] *Veena P. Vemuri*[2], *Elena Y. Zegarra*[3], *Jitendra Gowrabhathini*[4], *Fred Torres-Cruz*[5], *Julio C.L. Huanca*[6], *and José L.A. Gonzáles*[7]

[1]*Government RC College of Commerce and Management, Bengaluru, Karnataka, India*
[2]*NKES College of Arts, Commerce, and Science, Mumbai, India*
[3]*Academic Department of Accounting Sciences, Universidad Nacional del Altiplano de Puno, Puno, Peru*
[4]*K L Business School, Koneru Lakshmaiah Education Foundation, K L University, Vijayawada, Andhra Pradesh, India*
[5]*Academic Department of Statistics and Computer Engineering, Universidad Nacional del Altiplano de Puno, Puno, Peru*
[6]*Academic Department of Basic Sciences, Universidad Nacional de Juliaca, Puno, Peru*
[7]*Department of Business, Pontifical Catholic University of Peru, Lima, Peru*

22.1 Introduction

Resource management is a critical function for organizations that rely on computing resources to support their operations. In today's complex and dynamic computing environments, traditional approaches to resource management are no longer sufficient. Distributed computing approaches, such as grid computing, cloud computing, and EC, are increasingly being used to manage computing resources across different locations, networks, and systems. These approaches offer significant benefits, including improved scalability, flexibility, and efficiency. However, integrating these approaches for resource management can also present several challenges, including complexity, data management, security, governance, and cost. To address these challenges, organizations need to carefully plan and implement an integrated approach to resource management that leverages the strengths

Meta-Heuristic Algorithms for Advanced Distributed Systems, First Edition. Edited by Rohit Anand, Abhinav Juneja, Digvijay Pandey, Sapna Juneja, and Nidhi Sindhwani.

of different distributed computing approaches. This chapter will explore the advances in resource management through the integration of distributed computing approaches. The chapter will begin by defining resource management and providing an overview of the challenges that organizations face in managing computing resources. The chapter will then provide an overview of the different distributed computing approaches, including grid computing, cloud computing, and EC, and their applications in resource management. The chapter will then focus on the advantages of integrating distributed computing approaches for resource management, including improved scalability, flexibility, and efficiency. A discussion of the future directions of research in the field of resource management through the integration of distributed computing approaches. The chapter will argue that advances in technologies such as artificial intelligence (AI), machine learning (ML), and blockchain will continue to reshape the landscape of resource management. Organizations that can effectively leverage these technologies to integrate different distributed computing approaches will be well-positioned to achieve their resource management goals in the future. This chapter will provide a comprehensive review of the advances in resource management through the integration of distributed computing approaches and provide insights into the future directions of research in this field [1–3].

22.1.1 Definition of Resource Management

Resource management refers to the process of efficiently and effectively allocating and utilizing various resources, such as computing power, storage, network bandwidth, and human resources, to meet the requirements of different applications or projects. Resource management involves monitoring, controlling, and optimizing the use of resources to achieve the desired performance, quality, and cost objectives. It is an essential task in various fields, including distributed computing, project management, supply chain management, and business operations [4, 5].

22.1.2 Overview of Distributed Computing Approaches

Distributed computing approaches are becoming increasingly popular due to their scalability, flexibility, and cost-effectiveness. Grid computing, for example, allows organizations to share resources that might otherwise be underutilized, resulting in cost savings and increased efficiency. Cloud computing provides a convenient way for businesses to access computing resources on demand, without having to invest in expensive hardware or software. EC, on the other hand, is designed to address the challenges of latency and network bandwidth constraints by enabling data processing. For example, cloud computing providers can quickly provision additional resources to meet increased demand, while grid computing resources can be dynamically allocated and shared among users. Integration of distributed computing approaches can help to address some of these challenges by providing a more robust and flexible computing infrastructure that leverages the strengths of each approach. Distributed computing approaches are playing an increasingly important role in modern computing environments, and integration of these approaches is likely to become an increasingly important area of research and development in the coming years [6–10].

22.1.3 Significance

Integrating distributed computing approaches for resource management is significant for several reasons. First, resource management by combining the strengths of different computing approaches. For example, cloud computing can provide on-demand access to computing resources, while grid computing can enable resource sharing and collaboration among organizations. EC can facilitate real-time data processing and analysis, enabling faster decision-making.

Secondly, integrating distributed computing approaches can help to overcome the limitations and challenges of individual approaches [11–12]. For example, cloud computing is known to have issues with latency and network bandwidth, which can be addressed by integrating EC to enable data processing closer to the source. Additionally, integrating grid computing with cloud computing can help to address security and privacy concerns associated with public cloud environments.

Finally, it is possible to build a more reliable and scalable computer infrastructure that can serve a variety of applications, from scientific research to smart city initiatives, by fusing the advantages of several methodologies. The future of computing will be significantly impacted by the use of distributed computing techniques for resource management. As data volumes continue to grow and applications become more complex, it is essential to find innovative and effective ways to manage computing resources [13–16].

22.2 Distributed Computing Approaches for Resource Management

Distributed computing approaches, such as grid computing, cloud computing, and EC, have become popular for managing resources efficiently and cost-effectively. Each of these approaches has its strengths and limitations, but by integrating them, it is possible to create a more robust and flexible computing infrastructure that can meet the demands of various applications. By integrating these approaches, organizations can create a more flexible and scalable resource management infrastructure. For example, by combining grid computing with cloud computing, it is possible to

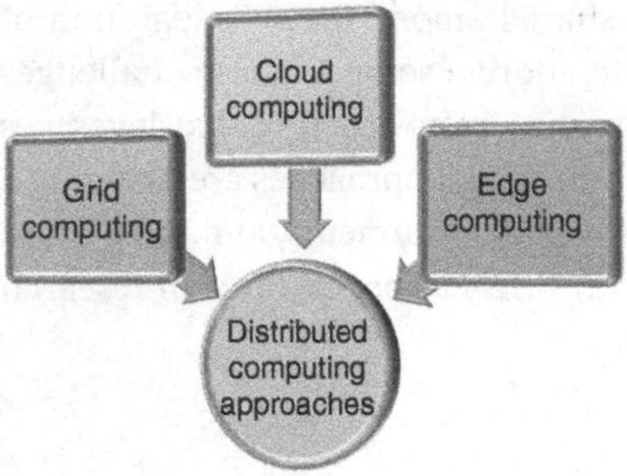

Figure 22.1 Distributed Computing Approaches.

achieve resource sharing and collaboration among multiple organizations while addressing security and privacy concerns associated with public cloud environments. By integrating EC with cloud computing, it is possible to enable real-time data processing and analysis while minimizing latency and network bandwidth issues. The integration of distributed computing approaches for resource management has significant implications for various fields, including scientific research, business operations, and smart city initiatives. By leveraging the strengths of each approach, it is possible to create a more efficient, secure, and cost-effective computing infrastructure that can support applications. As the volume of data continues to grow, it is likely that the integration of distributed computing approaches will become increasingly important for effective resource management [17–20].

Figure 22.1 shows the distributed computing approaches.

22.2.1 Grid Computing

Distributed computing in the form of "grid computing" enables businesses to pool computing resources across numerous sites and networks. Applications like scientific research, data analysis, and simulations that demand a lot of processing power, storage, and network bandwidth benefit the most from this system. By enabling users to access and share resources that might otherwise be underutilized, grid computing can improve efficiency, reduce costs, and accelerate time to completion for these applications. Systems typically consist of a set of nodes, which can be either computing resources or users. These nodes are interconnected through a network, which may be private or public. The software that manages the allocation of resources in a grid computing system is called a resource management system or a middleware. Computing resources across multiple locations and networks, enabling collaboration and resource sharing among multiple organizations. Organizations can avoid the expense and complexity of creating and maintaining their own computing infrastructure by combining their resources. Its capacity to provide dynamic resource allocation is another advantage. Systems have the ability to instantly assign computing resources, allowing users to easily and quickly scale their computing resources up or down in response to shifting needs. Despite this, grid computing has become a valuable tool for many businesses and academic institutions, and it is anticipated that it will continue to play a vital part in the development of distributed computing [21, 22].

22.2.2 Applications in Resource Management

- Applications in resource management refer to the use of various approaches and technologies to manage resources effectively and efficiently. Resource management can refer to a variety of resources, such as computing resources, energy, water, or natural resources, and the applications for managing these resources in a specific context.
- In the context of computing, applications in resource management typically involve the use of distributed computing approaches such as grid computing, cloud computing, and EC to manage computing resources effectively. For example, resource management in cloud computing involves the use of virtualization technologies and resource allocation algorithms to ensure that computing resources are allocated optimally, with a focus on maximizing performance, minimizing costs, and ensuring high availability [23–25].
- In the context of energy management, applications in resource management might involve the use of smart grids and energy storage technologies to manage energy consumption and reduce waste. Similarly, in the context of water management, applications in resource management might involve the use of sensor technologies and data analytics to optimize water usage and reduce waste.
- In the context of natural resource management, applications in resource management might involve the use of remote sensing technologies and geographic information systems to monitor and manage natural resources such as forests, oceans, and wildlife. For example, satellite imagery can be used to monitor changes in land cover and deforestation, while acoustic sensors can be used to monitor marine life and ocean ecosystems.
- The development and implementation of applications in resource management are becoming increasingly important as the world faces challenges related to climate change, population growth, and resource scarcity. By using approaches and technologies to manage resources more effectively, organizations can reduce waste, improve efficiency, and minimize the impact on the environment.

22.2.3 Cloud Computing

This distributed computing approach has made it possible for users to access computing resources over the internet. Instead of relying on local servers and hardware, users can access computing resources like storage, processing power, and software over a network of remote servers operated by third parties. Cloud computing has become more well-liked recently due to its scalability, flexibility, and cost. The approach is based on the principles of distributed computing, which is a method of dividing work among several computers or nodes to achieve faster processing and better resource utilization. With cloud computing, users have access to resources that are spread over several servers and data centers via a web browser or application programming interface (API) [26, 27].

With this strategy, users can scale their processing capacity up or down as necessary without spending money on expensive hardware upgrades or upkeep. Users can benefit from cloud computing in a number of ways, such as lower prices, more flexibility, and better scalability. Users can lower their operating costs for maintenance and updates, as well as their capital expenditures on hardware and software, by outsourcing their computing requirements to cloud providers. Additionally, cloud computing gives users the flexibility to access computing resources from any location with an internet connection, increasing the potential for remote work and collaboration. Greater scalability is a benefit of cloud computing as well. Depending on consumer demand, cloud providers can easily and quickly increase or decrease the quantity of computing resources made accessible to them. Users can handle demand spikes as a result without purchasing new gear or software. Cloud computing, however, also comes with some difficulties. The problem of security is one of them. Users must put their trust in cloud service providers to keep and maintain their data securely, which can be problematic for private or sensitive data. To safeguard consumer data from online threats and breaches, cloud service providers must deploy strong security measures [28, 29].

22.2.4 Edge Computing

A method of computing known as edge computing (EC) includes processing data locally rather than sending it to a centralized data center for processing. It is a type of computing that takes place at or close to the network's edge rather than in a single location. Because of the development of Internet of Things (IoT) devices, which produce enormous amounts of data that must be handled rapidly and effectively, this strategy is growing in popularity. EC helps businesses to process data more quickly and with less latency by being so near the source of the data. This is due to the fact that the processing of the data does not require the transmission of the data over large distances to a centralized data center. As an alternative, it can be handled locally at the network's edge, which could speed up the response time. The increased reliability of EC is another advantage. Organizations can lessen their reliance on a centralized data center, which is prone to outages and other problems, by processing data locally.

Moreover, EC might aid businesses in improving data management. Organizations can filter and analyze data at the network's edge by processing it locally, which can lessen the quantity of information that needs to be sent to a centralized data center. Organizations may benefit from greater data management and data analysis skills as a result. EC, however, also comes with some difficulties. The problem of security is one of them. Due to their frequent unsecured or remote locations, edge devices are susceptible to cyber assaults. To safeguard their edge devices and the data they process, organizations must put strong security measures in place. The issue of scalability is another one. The processing capacity and memory of edge devices are frequently constrained, which can hinder their capacity to handle massive amounts of data. Businesses must make sure their EC infrastructure is scalable and capable of handling growth in data volume and processing demands.

22.3 Integration of Distributed Computing Approaches for Resource Management

The integration of distributed computing approaches, such as grid computing, cloud computing, and EC, can lead to significant advances in resource management. By combining these different approaches, organizations can optimize the use of their computing resources, reduce costs, and improve performance. Using hybrid cloud architectures is one method by which distributed computing techniques can be incorporated for resource management. Private clouds, which are run and owned by businesses, are combined with public clouds, which are run and owned by service providers. Organizations can benefit from the protection and control of private clouds as well as the flexibility and scalability of public clouds by integrating these various types of clouds.

Another way that distributed computing approaches can be integrated is through the use of EC for resource management. This can be particularly useful in applications such as the IoT, where real-time processing is critical. Grid computing can also be integrated with other distributed computing approaches for resource management. Grid computing can also be used to manage resources across different types of hardware and software, allowing organizations to take advantage of a variety of computing resources and platforms. The integration of distributed computing approaches can lead to significant advances in resource management, allowing organizations to optimize the use of their computing resources, reduce costs, and improve performance. By combining different approaches we can create a more flexible and efficient computing environment [30, 31].

22.3.1 Advantages Distributed Computing Approaches for Resource Management

1. *Flexibility*: Integrating distributed computing approaches can provide greater flexibility in the types of computing resources available to an organization. For example, by integrating cloud and EC.
2. *Improved performance*: The source of data or processing, organizations can reduce latency and improve performance. This is particularly important in applications where real-time processing is critical, such as the IoT.
3. *Improved resource utilization*: Integrating distributed computing approaches can help organizations to optimize the use of their computing resources [32, 33]. For example, grid computing can be used to manage resources across different clouds, allowing organizations to use the most appropriate resources for each workload.
4. *Enhanced security*: By integrating different distributed computing approaches, organizations can achieve a more secure computing environment. For example, they can use private clouds for sensitive workloads, which can provide greater security, and public clouds for less sensitive workloads, which can be less secure.

Integrating distributed computing approaches for resource management can provide several advantages, such as cost savings, flexibility, improved performance, improved resource utilization, and enhanced security. These advantages can help organizations to achieve a more efficient, flexible, and secure computing environment.

22.3.2 Challenges of Distributed Computing Approaches for Resource Management

Integrating distributed computing approaches for resource management can also present several challenges, including:

1. *Complexity*: Integrating different distributed computing approaches can be complex, as each approach has its own architecture, protocols, and standards. This can require significant effort and expertise to ensure that the different approaches can work together effectively.
2. *Security*: Integrating different distributed computing approaches can introduce security risks, as data may need to be transferred across different networks and systems.
3. *Governance*: Integrating different distributed computing approaches can make it more difficult to manage and govern computing resources. This can include issues such as ensuring compliance with regulations and standards, managing service level agreements (SLAs), and allocating resources effectively.

4. *Cost*: Integrating different distributed computing approaches can require significant investment in infrastructure, hardware, software, and expertise. This can require careful planning and budgeting to ensure that the benefits of integration outweigh the costs.

Integrating distributed computing approaches for resource management can present several challenges, such as complexity, data management, security, governance, and cost. Organizations need to carefully consider these challenges when planning and implementing an integrated approach to resource management.

22.3.3 Techniques for Integrating Distributed Computing

Some techniques that can be used to address these challenges include:

1. *Standardization*: Using standardized protocols and interfaces can help to reduce the complexity of integrating different distributed computing approaches. This can enable organizations to more easily integrate different clouds, edge devices, and data centers.
2. *Data integration*: Integrating data across different distributed computing approaches requires careful planning and management. This can involve techniques such as data federation, data virtualization, and data warehousing to ensure that data can be accessed and analyzed effectively.
3. *Security measures*: Integrating different distributed computing approaches can increase the risk of security breaches. Appropriate security measures, such as encryption, access control, and identity management, should be implemented to protect data and computing resources.
4. *Governance frameworks*: Governance frameworks, such as ITIL, COBIT, and ISO 20000, can help organizations to manage and govern distributed computing resources effectively. This can include managing SLAs, ensuring compliance with regulations and standards, and allocating resources appropriately.
5. *Cost optimization*: Integrating distributed computing approaches can be expensive, but there are techniques that can be used to optimize costs. This can include using automated resource provisioning and hybrid clouds to reduce costs.
6. *Monitoring and analytics*: Monitoring and analytics tools can be used to monitor the performance and availability of distributed computing resources and to identify potential issues before they become problems. This can help to ensure that resources are used effectively and efficiently.

Addressing the challenges of integrating distributed computing approaches for resource management requires careful planning and the use of appropriate techniques. By using these techniques, organizations can achieve the benefits of integration while minimizing the risks and costs.

22.4 Future Directions and Research Challenges

As the field of resource management through the integration of distributed computing approaches continues to evolve, new research challenges and opportunities will emerge. In this section, we will discuss some of the key research directions and challenges that are likely to shape the future of this field. One of the most significant research directions is the development of new technologies and standards that enable seamless integration of distributed computing approaches. For example, the use of containerization and microservices architectures can facilitate the integration of different computing resources and platforms, making it easier to deploy and manage applications across different environments. Another key research direction is the development of new techniques for data management, security, and governance in distributed computing environments. As more organizations adopt distributed computing approaches, they will need to find new ways to manage and secure their data while also ensuring compliance with regulatory requirements.

Figure 22.2 shows the addressing challenges in distributed resource management.

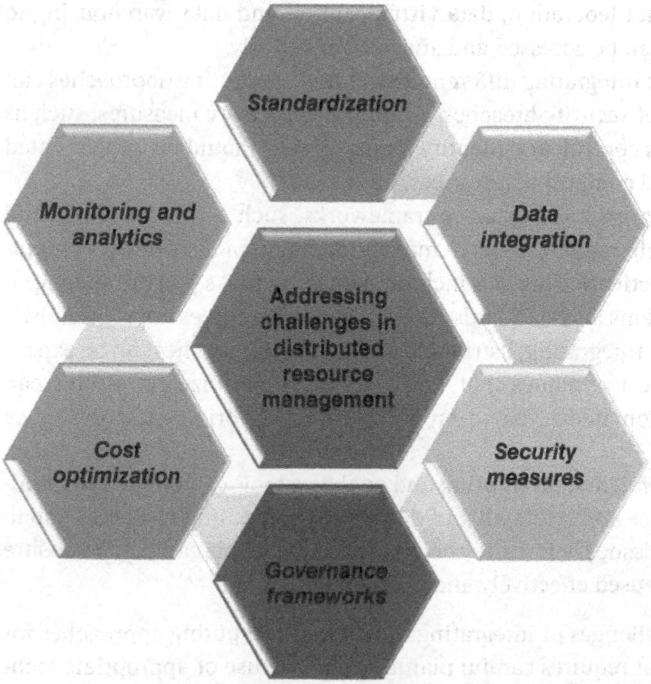

Figure 22.2 Addressing challenges in distributed resource management.

Additionally, the use of AI and ML is likely to play an increasingly important role in resource management. For example, AI and ML can be used to automate resource allocation, optimize performance, and identify potential security threats or vulnerabilities.

The adoption of blockchain technology is also likely to have a significant impact on resource management in distributed computing environments. Blockchain can be used to provide a secure and decentralized framework for managing and tracking computing resources, and can help ensure the integrity of data and transactions in complex distributed systems.

However, there are also several significant research challenges that must be addressed in order to realize the full potential of resource management through the integration of distributed computing approaches. One of the key challenges is the need for more robust and scalable governance frameworks that can help manage the complexities of distributed systems.

Another challenge is the need for more effective methods for monitoring and analyzing performance data in distributed computing environments. As systems become more complex and dynamic, it can be challenging to identify and address performance issues in a timely manner.

Finally, there is a need for more research on the social and organizational factors that influence the adoption and implementation of distributed computing approaches for resource management. This includes issues such as organizational culture, stakeholder engagement, and change management.

The integration of distributed computing approaches has the potential to revolutionize resource management by providing greater scalability, flexibility, and efficiency. However, to realize this potential, significant research is needed to address the challenges of integration and to develop new techniques and technologies that can help organizations manage and secure their computing resources. By addressing these challenges, we can unlock the full potential of distributed computing for resource management and support the needs of organizations in an increasingly complex and dynamic computing environment.

22.4.1 Emerging Trends

With new trends and technologies constantly developing, the field of resource management through the integration of distributed computing systems is fast evolving. We'll talk about some of the most significant new trends in this area and how they might affect resource management in this part. The growing use of hybrid cloud environments, which mix resources from both public and private clouds into a single system, is one of the most important trends. Hybrid cloud solutions have a number of benefits, such as increased scalability and flexibility as well as the capacity to better control expenses. They do, however, also pose considerable difficulties, particularly in terms of data management and security. The usage of EC, which entails placing computing resources closer to the network's edge rather than merely relying on centralized data centers, is another rising trend. EC is well suited for applications like real-time data processing and analytics since it can help to lower latency and enhance reaction times. In resource management, containerization is also becoming increasingly prevalent, especially with the development of microservice architectures. Application management and scalability across dispersed systems are made simpler by containerization, which enables applications to be easily packaged and deployed across various computer environments.

The adoption of serverless computing is also on the rise, particularly in the context of event-driven architectures. Serverless computing allows applications to be executed without the need for dedicated infrastructure, which can help to reduce costs and improve scalability.

AI and ML are also playing an increasingly important role in resource management, particularly with regard to automation and optimization. For example, AI and ML can be used to automate resource allocation, identify performance bottlenecks, and detect potential security threats.

Finally, the adoption of blockchain technology is also on the rise in the context of distributed computing approaches for resource management. Blockchain can be used to provide a secure and decentralized framework for managing and tracking computing resources, which can help to improve the security and integrity of distributed systems. However, along with these emerging trends come significant challenges that must be addressed in order to realize their full potential. For example, hybrid cloud environments require new approaches to security and data management, particularly with regard to managing and securing data across different environments.

The use of EC also presents challenges with regard to managing and securing distributed resources, as well as ensuring the interoperability of different systems and protocols.

Similarly, containerization and microservices architectures require new approaches to monitoring, management, and orchestration, particularly as systems become more complex and distributed.

AI and ML also present challenges with regard to data governance, transparency, and accountability, particularly as these technologies become more widely adopted and integrated into resource management processes.

Finally, the adoption of blockchain technology presents challenges with regard to scalability and interoperability, particularly as systems become more complex and dynamic.

The integration of distributed computing approaches for resource management is a rapidly evolving field with many emerging trends and technologies. While these trends offer significant benefits in terms of scalability, efficiency, and flexibility, they also present significant challenges that must be addressed in order to realize their full potential. By addressing these challenges, we can unlock the full potential of distributed computing for resource management and support the needs of organizations in an increasingly complex and dynamic computing environment [34–37].

22.4.2 Limitations in Integration of Distributed Computing Approaches for Resource Management

While the integration of distributed computing approaches for resource management offers many benefits, it also presents significant challenges that must be addressed in order to realize their full potential. In this section, we will discuss some of the key research challenges that must be addressed in order to advance the field of resource management through the integration of distributed computing approaches. One of the key research challenges is the development of effective resource allocation and scheduling algorithms. In distributed computing environments, resources are often limited and shared among multiple users and applications, which can lead to contention and competition for resources. To address this challenge, researchers must develop algorithms that can allocate resources effectively and fairly, taking into account the needs and priorities of different users and applications.

Another important challenge is the development of effective monitoring and management tools for distributed systems. As distributed systems become more complex and dynamic, it becomes increasingly difficult to monitor and manage these systems effectively. Researchers must develop tools and techniques that can provide real-time monitoring and analysis of distributed systems, enabling administrators to quickly identify and resolve issues before they become critical. Data management is also a critical challenge in the integration of distributed computing approaches for resource management. In distributed computing environments, data is often stored and processed across multiple nodes and systems, which can lead to data consistency and synchronization issues. Researchers must develop techniques for managing data effectively across distributed systems, ensuring data consistency and integrity while minimizing the impact on system performance.

Security is another critical challenge in the integration of distributed computing approaches for resource management. In distributed systems, data is often transmitted across untrusted networks and systems, which can make it vulnerable to interception and tampering. Researchers must develop effective security techniques and protocols that can protect data and systems from unauthorized access while still maintaining the flexibility and efficiency of distributed computing environments. Interoperability is also a critical challenge in the integration of distributed computing approaches for resource management. As distributed systems become more complex and diverse, it becomes increasingly difficult to ensure that different systems and protocols can communicate and work together effectively. Researchers must develop techniques and standards for interoperability that can enable different systems and protocols to communicate and work together seamlessly. Finally, there is a need for more research into the social and ethical implications of the integration of distributed computing approaches for resource management. As these technologies become more widespread and integrated into our daily lives, they can have significant social and ethical implications, particularly with regard to privacy, fairness, and accountability. Researchers must conduct more research in these areas, developing techniques and frameworks that can ensure that these technologies are used ethically and responsibly.

The integration of distributed computing approaches for resource management presents many research challenges that must be addressed in order to realize its full potential. These challenges include the development of effective resource allocation and scheduling algorithms, the development of effective monitoring and management tools, effective data management techniques, the development of effective security protocols, the development of techniques for ensuring interoperability, and the exploration of the social and ethical implications of these technologies. By addressing these challenges, researchers can help to unlock the full potential of distributed computing for resource management and support the needs of organizations in an increasingly complex and dynamic computing environment [38–42].

22.5 Discussion

The integration of distributed computing approaches for resource management is a promising area of research that offers many benefits for organizations in an increasingly complex and dynamic computing environment. This chapter has provided an overview of the key distributed computing approaches for resource management, including grid computing, cloud computing, and EC. It has also discussed the advantages and challenges of integrating these approaches and the techniques that can be used to address these challenges. One of the key advantages of integrating distributed computing approaches for resource management is improved scalability and flexibility. By leveraging the resources of multiple systems and networks, organizations can more easily scale their computing infrastructure to meet changing demands and requirements. This can also lead to increased efficiency and cost savings, as organizations can make more efficient use of their existing resources.

Another advantage of integrating distributed computing approaches is improved data processing and analysis capabilities. By distributing data processing and analysis tasks across multiple systems and networks, organizations can more quickly and accurately analyze large volumes of data, enabling faster and more informed decision-making. However, integrating distributed computing approaches for resource management also presents significant challenges. These include the need to develop effective resource allocation and scheduling algorithms, the need to develop effective monitoring and management tools for distributed systems, and the need to address security and data management issues in distributed computing environments. To address these challenges, researchers must develop new algorithms and techniques that can effectively manage and allocate resources across distributed computing environments. They must also develop new monitoring and management tools that can provide real-time insight into distributed systems, enabling administrators to quickly identify and resolve issues. Additionally, they must develop new security and data management techniques that can protect data and systems from unauthorized access and ensure data consistency and integrity across distributed environments. The integration of distributed computing approaches for resource management is an exciting area of research that has the potential to transform the way organizations manage their computing infrastructure. While there are many challenges that must be addressed, researchers are making significant progress in developing new techniques and tools that can help to unlock the full potential of these technologies. As organizations continue to face increasingly complex and dynamic computing environments, the integration of distributed computing approaches for resource management will likely become an increasingly important area of research and development.

22.6 Conclusion

An area of research that is quickly developing and has many advantages for organizations is the integration of distributed computing technologies for resource management. Three major distributed computing paradigms Grid, cloud, and EC can be combined to increase scalability, flexibility, and data processing and analysis capabilities. While combining these approaches has many benefits, there are also considerable obstacles that must be overcome. To successfully integrate distributed computing systems for resource management, it is imperative to have efficient resource allocation and scheduling algorithms, monitoring and management tools, and security and data management procedures. Despite these challenges, researchers are making significant progress in developing new techniques and tools to address these issues. As organizations continue to face increasingly complex and dynamic computing environments, the integration of distributed computing approaches for resource management is becoming an increasingly important area of research and development. Future research in this area will need to focus on addressing these challenges and further developing techniques for effectively managing and allocating resources across distributed computing environments. As this research progresses, the benefits of integrating distributed computing approaches for resource management will become increasingly apparent, enabling organizations to manage their computing infrastructure more effectively and efficiently [43]. The way organizations approach computers may change as a result of the incorporation of distributed computing techniques for resource management. Organizations can more readily scale their computer infrastructure, enhance data processing and analytical capabilities, and increase overall efficiency and cost savings by utilizing the resources of many systems and networks [44, 45]. Although there are numerous obstacles to overcome, the advantages of these technologies make them a crucial field for future research and development.

References

1 De Rafael, G.H. and Fernández-Prados, J.S. (2018). Intensive agriculture, marketing, and social structure: the case of South-eastern Spain. *Agric. Econ.* 64: 367–377.

2 Cazcarro, I., Duarte, R., Martín-Retortillo, M. et al. (2015). Water scarcity and agricultural growth in Spain: From curse to blessing. In: *Natural Resources and Economic Growth: Learning from History; Routledge*, 339–361. London, UK.

3 Aznar-Sánchez, J.A., Belmonte-Ureña, L.J., Velasco-Muñoz, J.F., and Valera, D.L. (2019). Aquifer sustainability and the use of desalinated seawater for greenhouse irrigation in the campo de Níjar, southeast Spain. *Int. J. Environ. Res. Public Health* 16: 898.

4 Garcia-Caparros, P., Contreras, J.I., Baeza, R. et al. (2017). Integral management of irrigation water in intensive horticultural systems of Almería. *Sustainability* 9: 2271.

5 Ocampo-Martinez, C., Puig, V., Cembrano, G., and Quevedo, J. (2013). Application of predictive control strategies to the management of complex networks in the urban water cycle. *IEEE Control. Syst. Mag.* 33: 15–41.

6 Verma, S., Bajaj, T., Sindhwani, N., and Kumar, A. (2022). Design and development of a driving assistance and safety system using deep learning. In: *Advances in Data Science and Computing Technology*, 35–45. Apple Academic Press.

7 Nijhawan, M., Sindhwani, N., Tanwar, S., and Kumar, S. (2022). Role of augmented reality and Internet of Things in education sector. In: *IoT Based Smart Applications*, 245–259. Cham: Springer International Publishing.

8 Sharma, G., Nehra, N., Dahiya, A. et al. (2022). Automatic heart-rate measurement using facial video. In: *Networking Technologies in Smart Healthcare*, 289–307. CRC Press.

9 Sharma, R., Vashisth, R., and Sindhwani, N. (2023). Study and analysis of classification techniques for specific plant growths. In: *Advances in Signal Processing, Embedded Systems and IoT: Proceedings of Seventh ICMEET-2022*, 591–605. Singapore: Springer Nature Singapore.

10 Chaudhary, A., Bodala, D., Sindhwani, N., and Kumar, A. (2022). Analysis of customer loyalty using artificial neural networks. In: *In 2022 International Mobile and Embedded Technology Conference (MECON)*, 181–183. IEEE.

11 Anand, R., Singh, J., Pandey, D. et al. (2022). Modern technique for interactive communication in LEACH-based ad hoc wireless sensor network. In: *Software Defined Networking for Ad Hoc Networks*, 55–73. Cham: Springer International Publishing.

12 Sansanwal, K., Shrivastava, G., Anand, R., and Sharma, K. (2019). Big data analysis and compression for indoor air quality. In: *Handbook of IoT and Big Data*, 1–21. CRC Press.

13 Pascual, J., Romera, J., Puig, V. et al. (2013). Operational predictive optimal control of Barcelona water transport network. *Control. Eng. Pract.* 21: 1020–1034.

14 Lopez Farias, R., Puig, V., Rodriguez Rangel, H., and Flores, J. (2018). Multi-model prediction for demand forecast in water distribution networks. *Energies* 11: 660.

15 Bhojwani, S., Topolski, K., Mukherjee, R. et al. (2019). Technology review and data analysis for cost assessment of water treatment systems. *Sci. Total Environ.* 651: 2749–2761.

16 Roca, L., Sánchez-Molina, J.A., Rodríguez, F. et al. (2016). Predictive control applied to a solar desalination plant connected to a greenhouse with daily variation of irrigation water demand. *Energies* 9: 194.

17 Gil, J.D., Álvarez, J., Roca, L. et al. (2019). Optimal thermal energy management of a distributed energy system comprising a solar membrane distillation plant and a greenhouse. *Energy Convers. Manag.* 198: 111791.

18 Lee, S.W., Sarp, S., Jeon, D.J., and Kim, J.H. (2015). Smart water grid: The future water management platform. *Desalin. Water Treat.* 55: 339–346.

19 Meelu, R. and Anand, R. (2010). Energy efficiency of cluster-based routing protocols used in wireless sensor networks. In: *AIP Conference Proceedings*, vol. 1324 (1), 109–113. American Institute of Physics.

20 Pandey, D., Pandey, B.K., and Wariya, S. (2019). Study of various techniques used for video retrieval. *J. Emerg. Technol. Innov. Res.* 6 (6): 850–853.

21 Bibri, S.E. (2018). The IoT for smart sustainable cities of the future: an analytical framework for sensor based big data applications for environmental sustainability. *Sustain. Cities Soc.* 38: 230–253.

22 Sodhro, A.H., Pirbhulal, S., Luo, Z., and de Albuquerque, V.H.C. (2019). Towards an optimal resource management for IoT based green and sustainable smart cities. *J. Clean. Prod.* 220: 1167–1179.

23 Pandey, D., Pandey, B.K., Wariya, S. et al. (2020). Analysis of text detection, extraction and recognition from complex degraded images and videos. *J. Critic. Rev.* 7 (18): 427–433.

24 Kumar Pandey, B., Pandey, D., Nassa, V.K. et al. (2021). Encryption and steganography-based text extraction in IoT using the EWCTS optimizer. *Imaging Sci. J.* 69 (1-4): 38–56.

25 Govindaraj, V., Dhanasekar, S., Martinsagayam, K. et al. (2023). Low-power test pattern generator using modified LFSR. *Aerosp. Syst.* 1–8.

26 Dijkman, R., Sprenkels, B., Peeters, T., and Janssen, A. (2015). Business models for the Internet of Things. *Int. J. Inf. Manag.* 35: 672–678.

27 Pham, X. and Stack, M. (2018). How data analytics is transforming agriculture. *Bus. Horizons* 61: 125–133.

28 Thou, A.D.M. (2014). Community and social responses to land use transformations in the Nairobi Rural-Urban Fringe, Kenya. http://factsreports.revues.org/435 ().

29 Fulazzaky, M.A. and Gany, A.H.A. (2009). Challenges of soil erosion and sludge management for sustainable development in Indonesian. *J. Environ. Manag.* 90: 2387–2392.

30 Gupta, A., Asad, A., Meena, L., and Anand, R. (2022, July). IoT and RFID-based smart card system integrated with health care, electricity, QR and banking sectors. In: *Artificial Intelligence on Medical Data: Proceedings of International Symposium, ISCMM 2021*, 253–265. Singapore: Springer Nature Singapore.

31 Pandey, D. and Pandey, B.K. (2022). An efficient deep neural network with adaptive galactic swarm optimization for complex image text extraction. In: *Process Mining Techniques for Pattern Recognition*, 121–137. CRC Press.

32 Anand, R. and Chawla, P. (2020). A novel dual-wideband inscribed hexagonal fractal slotted microstrip antenna for C-and X-band applications. *Int. J. RF Microwave Comput. Aided Eng.* 30 (9): e22277.

33 Anand, R. and Chawla, P. (2020). Optimization of inscribed hexagonal fractal slotted microstrip antenna using modified lightning attachment procedure optimization. *Int. J. Microw. Wirel. Technol.* 12 (6): 519–530.

34 Ranjan, R. (2008). Environmental restoration of invaded ecosystems: how much versus how often? *J. Environ. Manag.* 86: 616–626.

35 Noël, C. (2009). *Organization of Water Management in France: Capacity Building for Better Water Management*. International Office for Water: Paris, France.

36 Bearden, B.L. (2010). The legal regime of the Mekong River: a look back and some proposals for the way ahead. *Water Policy* 12: 798–821.

37 Brils, J. (2008). Sediment monitoring and the European Water Framework Directive. *Ann. Ist. Super. Sanita* 44: 218–223.

38 Zerol, G. and Newig, J. (2008). Evaluating the success of public participation in water resources management: five key constituents. *Water Policy* 10: 639–655.

39 World Health Organization (WHO) (2003). *Climate Change and Human Health: Risks and Responses* (ed. A.J. McMichael, D.H. Campbell-Lendrum, C.F. Corvalán, et al.). Geneva, Switzerland: WHO.

40 Fulazzaky, M.A. and Akil, H. (2009). Development of data and information system to improve water resources management in Indonesia. *Water Resour. Manag.* 23: 1055–1066.

41 Fulazzaky, M.A. and Sutardi, S. (2008). *Integrated Water Resources Management in View of Environmental Sustainability Aspects*. Penerbit UTHM: Batu Pahat, Malaysia.

42 Government of Indonesia (GOI) (2004). *Indonesian Law No. 7/2004 on Water Resources; Indonesian Law and Regulation Document*. Jakarta, Indonesia: GOI.

43 Gupta, A., Srivastava, A., and Anand, R. (2022). Internet protocols: transition, security issues and the world of IoT. In: *Recent Developments in Artificial Intelligence and Communication Technologies*, 18–41. Bentham Science.

44 David, S., Duraipandian, K., Chandrasekaran, D. et al. (2023). Impact of blockchain in healthcare system. In: *Unleashing the Potentials of Blockchain Technology for Healthcare Industries*, 37–57. Academic Press.

45 Kohli, L., Saurabh, M., Bhatia, I. et al. (2021). Design and development of modular and multifunctional UAV with amphibious landing, processing and surround sense module. In: *Unmanned Aerial Vehicles for Internet of Things (IoT) Concepts, Techniques, and Applications*, 207–230. Wiley.

Index

Note: Page numbers in *italic* and **bold** refers to figures and tables, respectively.

Meta-Heuristic Algorithms for Advanced Distributed Systems, First Edition. Edited by Rohit Anand, Abhinav Juneja, Digvijay Pandey, Sapna Juneja, and Nidhi Sindhwani.

m

n